Biology of Plant-Microbe Interactions Volume 3

Edited by
Sally A. Leong, Caitilyn Allen, and Eric W. Triplett

Proceedings of the 10th International Congress on Molecular Plant-Microbe Interactions
Madison, Wisconsin, U.S.A., July 10-14, 2001

Published by the
International Society for Molecular Plant-Microbe Interactions
St. Paul, Minnesota, U.S.A.

This book has been reproduced directly from edited, computer-generated copy submitted by the authors to the editors of this volume. The editors have verified text formatting, references, and quality of text and figures and identified keywords to include in the index. No editing or proofreading has been done by the publisher.

Reference in this publication to a trademark, proprietary product, or company name by personnel of the U.S. Department of Agriculture or anyone else is intended for explicit description only and does not imply approval or recommendation to the exclusion of others that may be suitable.

Library of Congress Control Number: 2002105617
International Standard Book Number: 0-9654625-2-8

Printed in the United States of America on acid-free paper

International Society for Molecular Plant-Microbe Interactions
3340 Pilot Knob Road
St. Paul, Minnesota 55121-2097, U.S.A.

Editors

Sally A. Leong
USDA/ARS Plant Disease Resistance Research Unit
Department of Plant Pathology
University of Wisconsin
1630 Linden Dr.
Madison, WI 53706
U.S.A.

Caitilyn Allen
Department of Plant Pathology
University of Wisconsin
1630 Linden Dr.
Madison, WI 53706
U.S.A.

Eric W. Triplett
Department of Agronomy
University of Wisconsin
1575 Linden Dr.
Madison, WI 53706
U.S.A.

Preface

The 10th Congress explored current, major aspects of the new biology related to the study of plant-microbe interactions. Major themes of the 10th Congress included: 1)Recognition of pathogens by plants, 2)Defense signal transduction, 3)Local and systemic resistance, 4)Plant-fungus interactions, 5)Plant-virus interactions, 6)Plant-nematode interactions, 7)Secretion of Avr and Vir factors; 8)Ecology and population biology of plant-associated microbes, 9)Cell biology of plant-microbe interactions, 10)Plant-Rhizobium interactions, and 11)Functional genomics and biotechnology.

Sixty-nine speakers presented their latest findings, which are summarized here in their contributions to the Proceedings of the Congress. Over 1000 participants were in attendance from 41 countries. They contributed over 700 poster presentations, highlighting the increasing role of posters in our Congress.

The 10th Congress emphasized new research on the molecular basis of disease resistance. David Baulcombe presented the keynote address. His work demonstrating the practical application of virally-induced gene (RNA) silencing (VIGS) as a tool to "knock out" gene expression at will in several plants has far reaching implications beyond the fundamental understanding of virus biology. Stunning progress on the molecular dissection of disease resistance was illustrated in his presentation and the many posters from his laboratory, which point to the use of VIGS in high through-put screens of all known genes in a plant for functional studies. In the pilot studies using VIGS on a large scale Baulcombe discovered novel genes not previously described in forward genetic screens including a gene for chaperonin homologue. Most exciting was the finding that genes required for the hypersensitive response could be separated out from those required for specific pathogen resistance, supporting earlier work on the *dnd* (defense no death) mutants of Arabidopsis by Andrew Bent.

The emerging field of genomics involving large scale, genome-wide analysis of plant-microbe interactions was presented. Comparative analysis of whole genome sequences of pathogenic bacteria has revealed unexpected aspects of the evolution of bacterial genomes. Comparative analysis of fungal genomes is providing insights on candidate pathogenicity genes. High through put analysis of pathogenicity genes is taking place both in the public and private sectors. John Ryals from Paradigm Genetics closed the Congress with a stimulating discussion of systems biology as applied to plant-microbe interactions in the private sector where speed matters. Key to the success of this systems approach to science is the use of refined, analytical tools that can discriminate phenotypic variation while minimizing the biological variation that is inherent in the study of life processes, and the use of flexible informatic tools for management, integration and analysis of phenomenal amounts of data.

A teaching workshop organized by Caitilyn Allen was included for the first time to add a new dimension to professional development to the ISMPMI Congresses. Most graduate biology teachers are eager to teach well, but lack the opportunity to discuss teaching or learn about alternative approaches to traditional methods. Because biology faculty often receive no formal instruction in teaching beyond acting as laboratory teaching assistants, many would benefit enormously from some exposure to modern teaching ideas about assessment, collaborative learning, writing across the curriculum, new technologies for distance learning, etc. Seventy participants from different countries attended this workshop and many contributed their syllabi and openly discussed their teaching experiences. A summary of this workshop is included in this volume.

The Local and International Organizing Committees provided important insights on programmatic issues which led to the selection of topic areas for sessions, candidate speakers, session chairs, as well as guidance on how to run poster sessions and the number of poster speakers. Andrew Bent as the Congress Associate Chair provided invaluable daily feedback on organizational and logistical issues. Jan Leach also provided considerable guidance on these matters. Acknowledgement is due to Carol Grabins and her staff who work on special events in the University of Wisconsin Memorial Union and who coordinated the abstract submission service, and to Maureen Sundell and her staff at the University of Wisconsin Extension Conference Planning Service for coordinating all the activities of the conference including booking facilities and tours, registration, and accounting. Glenn Heckard at the Printing House organized the abstract book and Irene Golembiewski created the graphical designs for brochures, signs, t shirts, the abstract book and the Proceedings using the background image kindly provided by Andrew Bent. Judith Kozminski solved technical problems that were encountered with the graphics and text format of the book chapters. Wendy Beckman deserves special acknowledgement for developing a user friendly, well-designed conference web site. We owe thanks to all the local farmers who provided such wonderful ingredients for the meals we ate at the Memorial Union, Julie Etheridge and her staff at Union Catering for their willingness to prepare this food, and Janet Parker for serving as a liaison between the farmers and Julie. Finally, we thank Frederick Blattner and his jazz ensemble for a delightful performance at the banquet reception on the rooftop of Monona Terrace and Gary Stacey for organizing a successful poster competition.

The 10th Congress would not have been possible without the generous support of public and private donors. The USDA National Research Initiative provided grant support for the 10th Congress, Teaching Workshop and the Medicago Satellite Workshop. Additional sponsors include: the International Society for Plant-Microbe Interactions, the USDA

Agricultural Research Service, Wisconsin Alumni Research Foundation, the Department of Plant Pathology-University of Wisconsin, Dow AgroSciences, DNASTAR, Epicentre Technologies, PanVera, Promega, Monsanto, Paradigm Genetics, and Syngenta.

Sally A. Leong, Chair of the Congress, Coeditor
Caitilyn Allen, Coeditor
Eric W. Triplett, Coeditor
University of Wisconsin, Madison

Table of Contents

Teaching Molecular Plant-Microbe Interactions

Sense and Susceptibility: Dissecting Disease Resistance Using Viruses and Silencing

David C. Baulcombe, Andrew Hamilton, Olivier Voinnet, Rui Lu, Jack R. Peart, Isabelle Malcuit and Peter Moffett

The Sainsbury Laboratory, Norwich UK NR4 7UH

RNA silencing is an immune system in plants and animals for detection and elimination of foreign RNA. It plays an important role in defense against mobile DNA and viruses. Here we describe how RNA silencing was discovered and summarize recent progress towards understanding its role and mechanism. We also describe a virus-induced system of silencing that has been used in the dissection of disease resistance in plants.

Cosuppression and Other Silencing Phenomena

Towards the end of the 1980s the first hints of RNA silencing came from the finding that sense orientation transgenes interfered with the expression of similar endogenous genes (Napoli et al. 1990; van der Krol et al. 1990). These 'gene silencing' phenomena, called sense- or co-suppression because there is coordinate suppression of both transgenes and endogenous genes, are due to a posttranscriptional process that involves targeted mRNA degradation (Van Blokland et al. 1994).

Some of the first clues to the mechanism of silencing were from virus resistance in plants carrying viral transgenes. The posttranscriptional mechanism resembled cosuppression (Lindbo et al. 1993; English et al. 1996) and was effective against viruses that replicate in the cytoplasm. From these results it was concluded that silencing is cytoplasmic rather than nuclear.

Further clues from *Neurospora*, worms, flies and Arabidopsis showed that silencing in these different organisms involves homologous EIF2C/Argonaut-like proteins, putative RNA dependent RNA polymerases and RNAse D-like proteins (reviewed in Hammond et al. 2001). The involvement of double stranded (ds) RNA is also common feature of RNA silencing in both animals and plants.

Nucleotide sequence-specificity is a hallmark of silencing in these different systems. For example, the silencing-mediated virus resistance in transgenic plants is specific for strains of the virus that are very similar to the viral transgene (Mueller et al. 1995). Similarly, in worms, the specificity of silencing was determined by the ds RNA that was injected into the animals (Fire et al. 1998).

The simplest way to account for this specificity involves antisense RNA produced directly or indirectly from sense transgenes or dsRNA. However, despite many efforts, it had never been possible to correlate silencing with antisense RNA. The reason, we now know, is because the antisense RNA is only 21-25 nucleotides long (Hamilton and Baulcombe 1999). It had been missed previously because the methods used were not adapted to such small molecules. These small interfering (si)RNA molecules, determine the specificity of RNA silencing (Elbashir et al. 2001a; Elbashir et al. 2001b). It is thought that the siRNA guides an RNAse, through a base pairing interaction, to the target RNA of silencing. The siRNA-RNase complex is known as the RNA induced silencing complex (RISC) (Hammond et al. 2000).

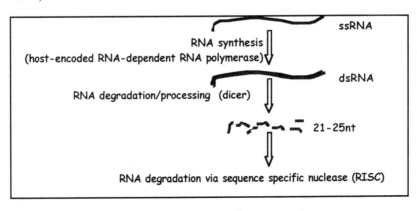

Fig. 1 A general model of RNA silencing

The siRNA exists as both sense and antisense of the silencing target (Hamilton and Baulcombe 1999) and is processed from long dsRNA by an RNAseIII with dsRNA binding motifs (Dicer) (Bernstein et al. 2001). Combined biochemical, genetic and molecular analyses suggest that the core silencing mechanism, as shown in Figure 1, involves RNA synthesis and two RNAse steps. The RNA synthesis step produces dsRNA but can be bypassed if dsRNA is introduced directly (Dalmay et al. 2000). Since the process operates entirely at the RNA rather than DNA level I use the term 'RNA silencing' instead of the previously used 'gene silencing' and 'cosuppression'.

Eventually the understanding of RNA silencing will be more detailed than the scheme shown in Figure 1. There will be other, as yet unknown, proteins to accommodate. In addition it will be necessary to account for systemic signaling that was discovered in grafting experiments (Palauqui et al. 1997) and when silencing was initiated in localized parts of transgenic plants carrying a GFP transgene (Voinnet and Baulcombe 1997; Voinnet et al. 1998). The signaling process, like the intracellular phase of the silencing mechanism molecule is highly nucleotide sequence specific. It is likely therefore that the signal specificity determinant will be RNA. However, as yet, the identity of the signal is unknown.

RNA Silencing and Protection Against Viruses

It was striking that RNA silencing produces exceptionally strong virus resistance in transgenic plants (Mueller et al. 1995). Often there is no detectable accumulation of virus in the inoculated leaf and the resistance cannot be overcome even by high titre inocula. These observations prompted speculation that the transgenic resistance is based on a natural resistance mechanism. Consistent with that idea an RNA silencing-like mechanism is active in non transgenic virus-infected plants (Ratcliff et al. 1997)(Ratcliff et al. 1999). Presumably a dsRNA intermediate of viral replication participates in the core RNA silencing mechanism, as shown in Figure 1 and targets the RISC against viral RNA. In a virus-infected cell this targeted RISC would eventually cause viral RNA accumulation to slow down and stop.

Silencing Suppressors

The discovery of viral suppressors of RNA silencing further supports an antiviral role (Anandalakshmi et al. 1998; Brigneti et al. 1998; Kasschau and Carrington 1998). These suppressors of silencing are structurally diverse (Voinnet et al. 1999) and it seems likely that they evolved several times to counteract the antiviral effects of RNA silencing. If the virus encodes a strong suppressor of RNA silencing it would become abundant in the infected cell. Conversely if the suppressor is weak in a particular host, the virus would accumulate and spread slowly or not at all.

The 25kDa movement protein (p25) of PVX is one of these viral suppressors of silencing (Voinnet et al. 2000). It was originally thought that p25 facilitates viral movement by opening the plasmodesmatal channels between cells (Angell et al. 1996). However it now seems that the situation is more complex because, as well as opening plasmodesmata, p25 interferes with either production or movement of the silencing signal (Voinnet et al. 2000). From these results it appears that viral movement requires both opening of movement channels and blocking of a defense molecule, the suppressor of silencing. Perhaps other viral pathogenicity or virulence factors that are currently thought of as activators of replication or movement will also turn out to suppress silencing.

Virus-Induced Silencing

RNA silencing in virus vector-infected cells is targeted against all sequences in the viral genome. Consequently, if the insert corresponds to an endogenous sequence, the corresponding host RNA is targeted by the silencing mechanism and the symptoms on the infected plant resemble the phenotype of a reduced or loss of function mutant (Baulcombe 1999).

We have tested virus-induced gene silencing (VIGS) with tobacco rattle virus (Ratcliff et al. 2001) and PVX (Ruiz et al. 1998) vectors on a range of plants including various *Solanaceae* and *Arabidopsis thaliana*. On many of these species there is some evidence for VIGS but it is normally transient and restricted to regions around the veins. Only on *Nicotiana benthamiana* and *N. clevelandii* is the VIGS phenotype extensive although, even on those plants, it is strongest on lower leaves of the plant.

RNA and DNA viruses have been used to target VIGS against mRNAs of various enzymes (Kjemtrup et al. 1998; Ruiz et al. 1998; Ratcliff et al. 2001). VIGS with a TRV vector has also been targeted against a homologue of a *leafy*, a gene required for development of floral meristems. The infected *N. benthamiana* plants have the appearance of a *leafy* mutant (Ratcliff et al. 2001). We have also used VIGS to suppress *Prf* (Salmeron et al. 1996), a gene required for *Pto*-mediated resistance against *Pseudomonas syringae* pv *tabaci* (hereafter *Ps. tabaci*).

From these results we inferred that VIGS would be useful as a general tool for gene identification (Baulcombe 1999) and we planned a reverse approach in which candidate cofactors of disease resistance could be targeted by VIGS. In addition, because the use of the virus vector is amenable to high throughput applications, we devised a forward screen with a library of PVX vectors carrying *N.benthamiana* RNA inserts. Each PVX clone carried a single insert and 5000 independent clones were tested. Because the RNA inserts were from a normalized cDNA library it is likely that these 5000 clones represent more than 4000 independent genes.

The procedure for these experiments involved first cloning 200 or more nucleotides of a host gene into a TRV or PVX vector. The vector was then inoculated to the host plant and after two or three weeks a second challenge inoculum was applied to test for disease resistance. Our aim was to identify genes required for *Rx*-mediated resistance against PVX, *Pto*-mediated resistance against *Ps. tabaci*, *N*-mediated resistance against tobacco mosaic virus (TMV) and for resistance against *Phytophthora infestans*. The *Rx* (Bendahmane et al. 1999), *Pto* (Rommens et al. 1995) and *N* genes were introduced into *N. benthamiana* as a transgene while the Inf1 elicitin-induced resistance against *P. infestans* is a natural property of *N. benthamiana* (Kamoun et al. 1998).

In the first round of tests we exploited the association of the disease resistance with hypersensitive cell death. In *N. benthamiana* the hypersensitive response (HR) can be activated in an *Agrobacterium* transient expression assay by simultaneous expression of the resistance gene and the

4

corresponding elicitor protein. We reasoned that there would be loss of the HR in this assay if VIGS targeted a gene required for the resistance.

Table 1 summarizes the results with the forward screen of approximately 5000 genes. According to these data more than 1% of the genome would be devoted to certain types of disease resistance. This number was surprisingly high and we were concerned that many of these genes would be specific to an HR and not necessarily required for disease resistance. To address this possibility we carried out direct tests for growth of the pathogen. We reasoned that the pathogen would grow more rapidly after VIGS if the target RNA encodes a protein required for disease resistance. The results of these resistance tests, summarized in Table 1, implicate fewer genes than in the HR assay.

Table 1 Summary results of a VIGS screen for disease resistance

	Number of VIGS targets	
	HR test	Pathogen test
Rx	19	0
Pto	>60	1
Infl	>80	9

The sequence of the insert in the VIGS vectors is an indicator of the target gene identity. However if there is a multigene family or, if conserved domains are present in different genes, the loss of resistance may be due to suppression of genes that are similar to, but not the same as the vector insert. At present there are no precise rules about mismatch in the viral insert and VIGS target. With transgenes the RNA silencing phenotype breaks down if there is more than 20% mismatch over several hundred nucleotides (Mueller et al. 1995). However since it is possible to initiate VIGS with only 28 nucleotides of similarity between a virus vector and the target gene (Thomas et al. 2001) the overall measure of nucleotide similarity may not necessarily indicate which genes are the potential targets of VIGS.

When the target of VIGS is a multigene family it it is sometimes helpful to target different regions of genes in a family. Conserved coding regions may help identify function when different members of the protein family carry out the same function. The 3' untranslated region or other variable regions is informative when different members of the family carry out different roles. Ideally biochemical and genetic approaches will be used to confirm that genes identified by VIGS are required for disease resistance.

The VIGS targets identified in our survey fall into two groups. They are either required for an HR and not resistance or they are required for both an HR and for suppression of the pathogen. It seems that suppression of the pathogen does not require the HR. At present we do not understand why VIGS of so many targets affects the HR. One possible explanation is that the HR is particularly sensitive to perturbation of normal cellular functions by VIGS.

So far none of the VIGS targets from the forward screen had been previously identified in mutant screens of genes required for disease resistance. In part this may be because the VIGS screen was relatively small – the 5000 targets most likely correspond to less than 20% of the potential total. It may also be because the cDNA library was prepared from non-infected leaves – many genes involved in signaling of disease resistance, for example *EDS1*, show an increase of mRNA following pathogen induction (Falk et al. 1999). These pathogen-induced genes would be under represented in our VIGS library.

The lack of overlap in the output of mutant and VIGS screens may also reflect fundamental differences in these two approaches. Mutant screens can give complete loss of function whereas VIGS produces only a partial reduction in targets mRNA (Ruiz et al. 1998). In addition mutant screens are only informative about single copy genes whereas VIGS, which acts in a nucleotide sequence-specific manner, can target multi-gene families with functional redundancy. A third reason for the lack of overlap is the potential of VIGS to be informative about essential genes. Such genes may have a lethal mutant phenotype and be difficult to identify in genetic screens.

What could be the role of the proteins identified by VIGS? In principle they could be novel signaling components. However they could also include proteins required for assembly of multimeric structures involved for recognition or signaling in disease resistance. Candidates for these structural components include a chaperonin homologue and a nucleotide binding site-leucine rich repeat proteins that are implicated in disease resistance by our recent VIGS results.

Rx Redux...Eventually

It is now seven years since the IS-MPMI symposium in Edinburgh at which we first heard about the molecular characterization of the *RPS2*, *Cf9* and *N* resistance genes. In the previous year, Greg Martin, had described *Pto*, which was the first R gene to be cloned (Martin 1993). Since then many other R genes have been cloned including the *Rx* PVX resistance gene (Bendahmane et al. 1999).

Originally our interest in *Rx* was because the resistance is extreme. There is no detectable accumulation of PVX in the inoculated leaf of genotype potato and no HR (Kohm et al. 1993). In contrast, with many examples of disease resistance there is some accumulation of the pathogen at the site of inoculation and an HR. We expected that *Rx* would differ fundamentally from most of the other R genes under investigation. However, the more we found out about *Rx* the more we suspected that it would be similar to other R genes. Eventually the cloning of *Rx* revealed that like many other R genes it encodes a nucleotide binding site-leucine rich repeat protein (NB-LRR) with a coiled coil (CC) motif at the amino terminus.

The elicitor of *Rx* is the coat protein of PVX (Bendahmane et al. 1995). Genetic analysis, as with other R genes, leads to the prediction that there is a direct physical interaction of the elicitor and the protein encoded by the R gene. However, as with other NBS-LRR R proteins, it is impossible to detect the interaction *in vitro*. In part this may be because the elicitor-R protein interaction requires additional factors. If so, perhaps one or more of the proteins identified in the VIGS screen are these additional factors.

Postscript

In his keynote talk at the Amsterdam IS-MPMI Jeff Dangl pointed to the issues in plant disease resistance that were unresolved in 1999. Since then there has been enormous progress. However the elicitor-receptor interaction, as discussed above, is still not understood. The lack of information about integration of signaling pathways in disease resistance also exposes enormous gaps in our understanding.

Jeff stressed the need for new tools and technologies and we hope that we have convinced you that VIGS fulfills part of that need. In future I expect that new virus vectors will be developed for VIGS in Arabidopsis. In addition, with the better understanding of the mechanism of RNA silencing, it should be possible to develop high throughput transgenic approaches that avoid the complications of virus infection that are an inevitable with VIGS. It should be possible, for example, to develop a set of about 25000 transgenic lines in which each of the mRNAs or mRNA families of Arabidopsis have been silenced individually. If the silencing transgenes in these lines are coupled to inducible promoters we will then have a resource that will allow us to investigate the role of any gene in disease resistance. The resource will be useful irrespective of whether there is redundancy due to a multigene family or whether the target is essential for growth and development. It will also be useful for investigation of biological processes other than disease resistance.

Literature Cited

Anandalakshmi, R., Pruss, G. J., Ge, X., Marathe, R., Smith, T. H., and Vance, V. B. 1998. A viral suppressor of gene silencing in plants Proc. Natl. Acad. Sci. USA 95:13079-13084.

Angell, S. M., Davies, C., and Baulcombe, D. C. 1996. Cell-to-cell movement of potato virus X is associated with a change in the size exclusion limit of plasmodesmata in trichome cells of *Nicotiana clevelandii* Virology 215:197-201.

Baulcombe, D. C. 1999. Fast forward genetics based on virus-induced gene silencing Curr. Opin. Plant. Biol. 2:109-113.

Bendahmane, A., Kanyuka, K., and Baulcombe, D. C. 1999. The *Rx* gene from potato controls separate virus resistance and cell death responses. Plant Cell 11:781-791.

Bendahmane, A., Köhm, B. A., Dedi, C., and Baulcombe, D. C. 1995. The coat protein of potato virus X is a strain-specific elicitor of *Rx*1-mediated virus resistance in potato Plant J. 8:933-941.

Bernstein, E., Caudy, A. A., Hammond, S. M., and Hannon, G. J. 2001. Role for a bidentate ribonuclease in the initiation step of RNA interference Nature 409:363-366.

Brigneti, G., Voinnet, O., Li, W. X., Ji, L. H., Ding, S. W., and Baulcombe, D. C. 1998. Viral pathogenicity determinants are suppressors of transgene silencing in *Nicotiana benthamiana* EMBO J. 17:6739-6746.

Dalmay, T., Hamilton, A. J., Rudd, S., Angell, S., and Baulcombe, D. C. 2000. An RNA-dependent RNA polymerase gene in Arabidopsis is required for posttranscriptional gene silencing mediated by a transgene but not by a virus Cell 101:543-553.

Elbashir, S. M., Harborth, J., Lendeckel, W., Yalcin, A., Weber, K., and Tuschl, T. 2001a. Duplexes of 21-nucleotide RNAs mediate RNA interference in cultured mammalian cells Nature 411:494-498.

Elbashir, S. M., Lendeckel, W., and Tuschl, T. 2001b. RNA interference is mediated by 21-and 22-nucleotide RNAs Genes & Development 15:188-200.

English, J. J., Mueller, E., and Baulcombe, D. C. 1996. Suppression of virus accumulation in transgenic plants exhibiting silencing of nuclear genes. Plant Cell 8:179-188.

Falk, A., Feys, B. J., Frost, L. N., Jones, J. D. G., Daniels, M. J., and Parker, J. E. 1999. EDS1, an essential component of R gene-mediated reistance in Arabidopsis has homology to eukariotic lipases Proc. Natl. Acad. Sci. USA 96:3292-3297.

Fire, A., Xu, S., Montgomery, M. K., Kostas, S. A., Driver, S. E., and Mello, C. C. 1998. Potent and specific genetic interference by double-stranded RNA in *Caenorhabditis elegans* Nature 391:806-811.

Hamilton, A. J., and Baulcombe, D. C. 1999. A novel species of small antisense RNA in post-transcriptional gene silencing Science 286:950-952.

Hammond, S. M., Bernstein, E., Beach, D., and Hannon, G. 2000. An RNA-directed nuclease mediates post-transcriptional gene silencing in *Drosophila* cell extracts Nature 404:293-296.

Hammond, S. M., Caudy, A. A., and Hannon, G. J. 2001. Post-transcriptional gene silencing by double-stranded RNA Nature Reviews Genetics 2:110-119.

Kamoun, S., vanWest, P., Vleeshouwers, V., deGroot, K. E., and Govers, F. 1998. Resistance of Nicotiana benthamiana to Phytophthora infestans is mediated by the recognition of the elicitor protein INF1 Plant Cell 10:1413-1425.

Kasschau, K. D., and Carrington, J. C. 1998. A counterdefensive strategy of plant viruses: suppression of post-transcriptional gene silencing Cell 95:461-470.

Kjemtrup, S., Sampson, K. S., Peele, C. G., Nguyen, L. V., Conkling, M. A., Thompson, W. F., and Robertson, D. 1998. Gene silencing from plant DNA carried by a geminivirus Plant J. 14:91-100.

Kohm, B. A., Goulden, M. G., Gilbert, J. E., Kavanagh, T. A., and Baulcombe, D. C. 1993. A Potato Virus-X Resistance Gene Mediates an Induced, Nonspecific Resistance In Protoplasts Plant Cell 5:913-920.

Lindbo, J. A., Silva-Rosales, L., Proebsting, W. M., and Dougherty, W. G. 1993. Induction of a highly specific antiviral state in transgenic plants: implications for regulation of gene expression and virus resistance. Plant Cell 5:1749-1759.

Martin, G. B., Brommonschenkel, S.H., Chunwongse, J., Frary, A., Ganal, M.W., Spivey, R., Wu, T., Earle, E.D. and Tanksley,S.D. 1993. Map-based cloning of protein kinase gene conferring disease resistance in tomato. Science 262:1432-1436.

Mueller, E., Gilbert, J. E., Davenport, G., Brigneti, G., and Baulcombe, D. C. 1995. Homology-dependent resistance: transgenic virus resistance in plants related to homology-dependent gene silencing. Plant J. 7:1001-1013.

Napoli, C., Lemieux, C., and Jorgensen, R. A. 1990. Introduction of a chimeric chalcone synthase gene into Petunia results in reversible co-suppression of homologous genes *in trans*. Plant Cell 2:279-289.

Palauqui, J.-C., Elmayan, T., Pollien, J.-M., and Vaucheret, H. 1997. Systemic acquired silencing: transgene-specific post-transcriptional silencing is transmitted by grafting from silenced stocks to non-silenced scions EMBO J. 16:4738-4745.

Ratcliff, F., Harrison, B. D., and Baulcombe, D. C. 1997. A similarity between viral defense and gene silencing in plants. Science 276:1558-1560.

Ratcliff, F., MacFarlane, S., and Baulcombe, D. C. 1999. Gene silencing without DNA: RNA-mediated cross protection between viruses. Plant Cell 11:1207-1215.

Ratcliff, F., Martin-Hernandez, A. M., and Baulcombe, D. C. 2001. Tobacco rattle virus as a vector for analysis of gene function by silencing Plant J. 25:237-245.

Rommens, C. M. T., Salmeron, J. M., Oldroyd, G. E. D., and Staskawicz, B. J. 1995. Intergeneric transfer and functional expression of the tomato disease resistance gene *Pto*. Plant Cell 7:1537-1544.

Ruiz, M. T., Voinnet, O., and Baulcombe, D. C. 1998. Initiation and maintenance of virus-induced gene silencing Plant Cell 10:937-946.

Salmeron, J. M., Oldroyd, G. E. D., Rommens, C. M. T., Scofield, S. R., Kim, H.-S., Lavelle, D. T., Dahlbeck, D., and Staskawicz, B. J. 1996. Tomato *Prf* is a member of the leucine-rich repeat class of plant disease resistance genes and lies embedded within the *Pto* kinase gene cluster Cell 86:123-133.

Thomas, C. L., Jones, L., Baulcombe, D. C., and Maule, A. J. 2001. Size constraints for targeting post-transcriptional gene silencing and for RNA-directed methylation in *Nicotiana benthamiana* using a potato virus X vector Plant J. 25:1-11.

Van Blokland, R., Van der Geest, N., Mol, J. N. M., and Kooter, J. M. 1994. Transgene-mediated suppression of chalcone synthase expression in *Petunia hybrida* results from an increase in RNA turnover. Plant J. 6:861-877.

van der Krol, A. R., Mur, L. A., Beld, M., Mol, J. N. M., and Stuitji, A. R. 1990. Flavonoid genes in petunia: Addition of a limited number of gene copies may lead to a suppression of gene expression. Plant Cell 2:291-299.

Voinnet, O., and Baulcombe, D. C. 1997. Systemic signalling in gene silencing Nature 389:553.

Voinnet, O., Lederer, C., and Baulcombe, D. C. 2000. A viral movement protein prevents systemic spread of the gene silencing signal in *Nicotiana benthamiana* Cell 103:157-167.

Voinnet, O., Pinto, Y. M., and Baulcombe, D. C. 1999. Suppression of gene silencing: a general strategy used by diverse DNA and RNA viruses Proc. Natl. Acad. Sci. USA 96:14147-14152.

Voinnet, O., Vain, P., Angell, S., and Baulcombe, D. C. 1998. Systemic spread of sequence-specific transgene RNA degradation is initiated by localised introduction of ectopic promoterless DNA. Cell 95:177-187.

Cladosporium fulvum Infection of Tomato: a "Gene-for-Gene" Model for Extracellular Elicitor Perception

Jonathan D G Jones, T Romeis, C Thomas, O Rowland, J Krueger, S Rivas, B Wulff, M Smoker, C Golstein, M Dixon, A Ludwig

The Sainsbury Laboratory, Norwich UK

Plant disease resistance genes confer race-specific recognition of and reaction to plant pathogens. For the most part, how they do this is still a complete mystery. Some of the moving parts have been identified, but the whole mechanism is still obscure. Our laboratory, like many others, is trying to understand R protein function.

R Gene Systems

We study the tomato *Cf-* genes that confer resistance to different races *of Cladosporium fulvum*, and have isolated the *Cf-2, Cf-4, Cf-5* and *Cf-9* genes and carried out a comparative analysis of *Cf-9* homologues. *Cf-* genes encode C- terminally membrane anchored leucine rich repeat (LRR) proteins that confer recognition of the corresponding Avr2, Avr4, Avr5 and Avr9 peptides. Using epitope tagged Cf-9, we have shown that Cf-9 is likely to be a plasma membrane protein (Piedras et al. 2000). Recent domain swap and gene shuffling experiments have identified the central LRRs of Cf-4 and Cf-9 as most responsible for race- specific recognition of Avr4 and Avr9 peptides (Wulff et al. 2001).

We have also isolated the Arabidopsis *RPP5* and *RPP1* genes that confer resistance to different races of the downy mildew pathogen *Peronsopora parasitica*. *RPP1* and *RPP5*, like the *Cf-* genes, are members of clustered multigene families. Unlike the *Cf-* genes, *RPP1* and *RPP5* encode TIR:nucleotide binding/ LRR (NB:LRR) *R* genes, resembling the *N* gene of tobacco that confers resistance to mosaic virus. TIR indicates homology with the cytoplasmic domain of the Drosophila Toll receptor and the mammalian interleukin 1 receptor. We are studying the mechanism of RPP1A and RPP1C protein function, using epitope tagged alleles.

11

The Arabidopsis TIR:NB:LRR gene RPS4 confers recognition of *Pseudomonas syringae* carrying AvrRPS4. In cooperation with Walter Gassmann and Brian Staskawicz, we are also currently studying the interaction between epitope tagged RPS4 and AvrRPS4 in Arabidopsis cells, in various mutant backgrounds, so that we can investigate a TIR:NB:LRR gene with a defined ligand. A central goal will be test whether direct interactions between RPS4 and AvrRPS4 can be detected in planta.

Mutational Analysis Identifies *Rcr3*, a Gene Required for *Cf-2* Function

Mutational analysis is a powerful tool to dissect signalling pathways, and has been used to reveal genes required for *R* gene function. We used mutagenesis to identify genes required for *Cf-2* function. Mutagenesis of the tomato Cf2 line led to the recovery of 4 mutations from 3,200 Cf2 M_2 families. Progeny from mutant intercrosses were sensitive to infection by *C. fulvum* race 4 marked with GUS, so these mutations are allelic. This locus was designated *Rcr3* (required for *C. fulvum* resistance locus 3) (Dixon et al. 2000).

Inoculation with *C. fulvum* race 5 revealed that rcr3-2 (the line carrying rcr3-2) and rcr3-3 allowed as much fungal growth as Cf0 whereas rcr3-1 appeared significantly less susceptible. Fungal development was barely detectable on rcr3-1 at seven days post inoculation while hyphae had already invaded the mesophyll layers and were proliferating around the vascular tissue of rcr3-2, rcr3-3 and Cf0 cotyledons. Further analysis confirmed that this was not due to other mutations in the genetic background. In summary, *rcr3-2* and *rcr3-3* are strong suppressors of *Cf-2* function, and *rcr3-1* is weak.

To generate a mapping population where *rcr3* and molecular markers were segregating, rcr3-1 was crossed to *Lycopersicon pennellii*. F_1 progeny from this cross were resistant to infection with *C. fulvum* race 4 GUS demonstrating that the *L. pennellii Rcr3* allele can complement the *rcr3* mutation. A single F_1 plant was back-crossed to rcr3-1 to give back-cross (BC_1) individuals that segregated 1:1 for resistance or susceptibility to infection by *C. fulvum* race 4 marked with GUS. DNA gel blot analysis was used to screen resistant BC_1 plants for *Cf-2* homozygotes and one was used as male parent in a back-cross to rcr3-1. In the resulting BC_2 population all plants were homozygous for *Cf-2* and, as expected, segregated 1:1 for resistance or susceptibility to *C. fulvum* race 4 GUS infection.

The chromosomal location of *Rcr3* was determined by AFLP analysis of bulked segregant pools. DNA was extracted from pools of 24 resistant and 34 susceptible plants, and subjected to AFLP analysis. Several AFLP markers linked to the *L. pennellii Rcr3* allele were identified. AFLP analysis of *L. esculentum* x *L. pennellii* introgression lines showed these markers were located on tomato chromosome 2.

Rcr3 is Required Specifically for Cf-2 Function

To determine whether *Rcr3* is required for the function of other *Cf* genes, rcr3 mutants were crossed to Cf5 and Cf9 NILs. *Rcr3* will segregate independently of *Cf-5* and *Cf-9* since they map to different chromosomes. In a cross between Cf9 and rcr3 lines, F_2 progeny should segregate 3 resistant to 1 susceptible when inoculated with *C. fulvum* race 2,4 if *Rcr3* is not required for *Cf-9* function. (*C. fulvum* race 2,4 lacks *Avr2* and *Avr4* and is virulent on tomato lines carrying either *Cf-2* or *Cf-4*, so in a cross between Cf9 and rcr3, *Cf-2* confers no effective resistance to *C. fulvum* race 2,4). If *Rcr3* is required for *Cf-9* function the progeny should segregate 9 resistant to 7 susceptible when inoculated with *C. fulvum* race 2,4. Progeny from this cross segregated 3 resistant to 1 susceptible demonstrating *rcr3* is not required for *Cf-9*-mediated resistance. Further confirmation of this result was obtained from analysis of back cross progeny. DNA gel blot analysis confirmed that none of the susceptible progeny contained *Cf-9*.

A similar analysis was used to determine whether *Rcr3* is required for *Cf-5*-mediated resistance. *Cf-5* and *Cf-2* are allelic and their products are more than 90% identical. F_2 progeny from a cross between rcr3-2 and Cf5 were screened by inoculation with *C. fulvum* race 2,4 and segregated at a ratio of 3 resistant to 1 susceptible demonstrating *Rcr3* is not required for *Cf-5*-mediated resistance. DNA from all *C. fulvum* race 2,4 susceptible plants were analysed by PCR for the presence of *Cf-5* (data not shown). None of the susceptible progeny carried *Cf-5* whereas one third would have contained it if Rcr3 is required for its function.

This is a truly remarkable observation. Since Cf-5 and Cf-2 are nearly identical, how could Cf-2 need a gene that is not required by Cf-5? We have interpreted this in terms of the 'guard hypothesis", which holds that R genes monitor the state of targets for pathogenicity factors made by the attacking microbe. Rcr3 may be guarded by Cf-2, which detects a conformational change contingent upon "attack" from Avr2, whereas Cf-5 protects a different host factor and does not need Rcr3 (Dixon et al. 2000).

Map based cloning of Rcr3 has revealed that it encodes a homologue of secreted cysteine proteases. The biological mechanism by which such a protein might play a role in *Cf-2-* dependent activation of the defence response is currently under investigation.

Models for Initiation of *Cf-* Dependent Signalling

The mechanism by which Cf- gene products initiate defence mechanisms upon detection of Avr gene products is unknown, and is an active area of research in the lab. We have engineered functional *Cf-9* alleles that encode a myc tag at either the N- or C terminus of the protein. These alleles still confer activation of defence responses upon exposure to Avr9 peptide. Cf-9 is predominantly localized in the plasma membrane, despite the presence of KKRY as the last 4 amino acids, which would be expected to mark Cf-9 for retrieval into the ER (Piedras et al. 2000). Mutations of this KKRY sequence do not compromise Cf-9 function, suggesting ER retrieval is not required (Van der Hoorn et al. 2001).

Does Cf-9 directly bind Avr9? The work of Pierre de Wit and colleagues has shown that even in the absence of a functional *Cf-9* gene, Avr9 binds with high affinity to a plasma membrane localized receptor in both tomato and tobacco. Work in our lab and the de Wit lab using various approaches has failed to reveal any direct binding between Avr9 and immunoprecipitated Cf-9 protein. Thus, we now consider it unlikely that direct recognition of Avr9 by Cf-9 is responsible for initiating signal transduction. Conceivably, Avr9 binds to its high-affinity binding site, and Cf-9 recognizes the complex of Avr9 and its receptor prior to somehow initiating signal transduction.

The Earliest Resistance Responses as a Clue to Signalling; Shared Aspects of Responses to Many Elicitors

We have conducted a series of analyses to try and establish the earliest events that ensue upon Avr product recognition. An important general conclusion is that there is considerable similarity between the Cf-9/Avr9 response, and the responses of plant cells to many other elicitors, such as flagellin, systemin, PEP13 and other elicitins.

A burst of active oxygen species (AOS) was identified as the most rapidly detected response in Cf9 tomato leaves into which Avr9 elicitor had been infiltrated. We have established transgenic tobacco plants and cell cultures (Piedras et al. 1998) that carry the *Cf-9* gene and that activate defence responses upon exposure to Avr9. In guard cells of Cf0 tobacco leaves, we detected rapid, protein kinase dependent activation of K+ channel efflux and inhibition of K+ channel influx (Blatt et al. 1999). A major advantage of cell cultures is that they can be synchronously exposed to elicitor and then biochemically assayed and pharmacologically modified. Using these approaches, we could show that AOS production in cell cultures in response to Avr9 could be blocked by applying protein kinase inhibitors and calcium channel blockers (Piedras et al. 1998). Two mitogen activated protein (MAP) kinases of tobacco, SIPK and WIPK are activated in tobacco cell cultures within 5 minutes of elicitation (Romeis et al. 1999). SIPK and WIPK are also associated with the response to salicylate, to various non-specific elicitors, wounding and the *N*-dependent resistance response to tobacco mosaic virus. We detected activation of a calcium dependent protein kinase (CDPK), initially observed as a shift in mobility of a CDPK rapidly upon elicitation (Romeis et al. 2000). Furthermore, using AFLP-cDNA, we have identified ~260 gene fragments that are induced within 30' of Avr9 elicitation in an AOS-independent manner (Durrant et al. 2000). These have been termed Avr9, Cf-9, Rapidly Elicited (ACRE) genes. Approximately 1% of the genes in cells 30' after elicitation are ACRE genes. Remarkably, ACRE genes are also induced by mechanical stress.

Conceivably, some ACRE genes encode signalling components that are used up during the Avr9-dependent activation of defence mechanisms, and need to be replaced. This would suggest that at least some ACRE genes might be required for Avr9, Cf-9- dependent signalling. We have identified many of the genes corresponding to these AFLP fragments, and subjected them to functional analysis using the Baulcombe lab technology for virus-induced gene silencing (VIGS). Most ACRE genes when silenced have no effect on the Cf-9/Avr9 HR; however, several do, including a novel protein kinase and some components of the ubiquitin-dependent proteolysis pathway. This approach has thus created some new leads to identify genes that are required for Cf- dependent signalling.

Concluding Remarks

We still have a great deal to learn about many aspects of Cf-9. Facile reverse genetics using VIGS, and more sophisticated protein chemistry, in combination with standard forward genetic approaches, is starting to advance our understanding. The fog is still thick, but it is beginning to clear.

Literature Cited

Blatt, M. R., Grabov, A., Brearley, J., Hammond-Kosack, K. E., and Jones, J. D. G. 1999. K+ channels of Cf-9 transgenic tobacco guard cells as targets for Cladosporium fulvum Avr9 elicitor-dependent signal transduction Plant Journal 19:453-462.

Dixon, M. S., Golstein, C., Thomas, C. M., van der Biezen, E. A., and Jones, J. D. G. 2000. Genetic complexity of pathogen perception by plants: The example of Rcr3, a tomato gene required specifically by Cf-2. Proc National Acad Sci USA 97:8807-8812.

Durrant, W. E., Rowland, O., Piedras, P., Hammond-Kosack, K. E., and Jones, J. D. G. 2000. cDNA-AFLP reveals a striking overlap in race-specific resistance and wound response gene expression profiles. Plant Cell 12:963-977.

Piedras, P., Hammond-Kosack, K. E., Harrison, K., and Jones, J. D. G. 1998. Rapid, Cf-9- and Avr9-dependent production of active oxygen species in tobacco suspension cultures. Molecular Plant-Microbe Interactions 11:1155-1166.

Piedras, P., Rivas, S., Droge, S., Hillmer, S., and Jones, J. D. G. 2000. Functional, c-myc-tagged Cf-9 resistance gene products are plasma-membrane localized and glycosylated. Plant Journal 21:529-536.

Romeis, T., Piedras, P., and Jones, J. D. G. 2000. Resistance gene-dependent activation of a calcium-dependent protein kinase in the plant defense response. Plant Cell 12:803-815.

Romeis, T., Piedras, P., Zhang, S. Q., Klessig, D. F., Hirt, H., and Jones, J. D. G. 1999. Rapid Avr9- and Cf-9-dependent activation of MAP kinases in tobacco cell cultures and leaves: Convergence of resistance gene, elicitor, wound, and salicylate responses. Plant Cell 11:273-287.

Van der Hoorn, R. A. L., Van der Ploeg, A., de Wit, P., and Joosten, M. 2001. The C-terminal dilysine motif for targeting to the endoplasmic reticulum is not required for Cf-9 function. Molecular Plant-Microbe Interactions 14:412-415.

Wulff, B. B. H., Thomas, C. M., Smoker, M., Grant, M., and Jones, J. D. G. 2001. Domain swapping and gene shuffling identify sequences required for induction of an Avr-dependent hypersensitive response by the tomato Cf-4 and Cf-9 proteins. Plant Cell 13:255-272.

Molecular Mechanisms in Disease Resistance
to Powdery Mildew Fungi

Paul Schulze-Lefert[1], Ken Shirasu[2], Christina Azevedo[2], Pietro Piffanelli[2],
Candace Elliott[2], Fasong Zhou[2], Ralph Panstruga[1], Min-Chul Kim[3,1],
Moo-Je Cho[3]

[1]Max-Planck-Institut für Züchtungsforschung, Germany; [2]The Sainsbury
Laboratory, United Kingdom; [3] Gyeongsang National University, Korea

Powdery mildews (*Erysiphe* and *Blumeria*) are economically significant
obligate biotrophic fungal pathogens of dicot and monocot plants, and plant
resistance genes have been employed to combat the disease. One of our
interests is to understand the molecular basis of disease resistance in barley
to barley powdery mildew, *Blumeria graminis* f. sp. *hordei* (*Bgh*).
Characterized resistance genes to barley powdery mildew can be placed into
two categories, comprising (*i*) mutant alleles of the *Mlo* gene which confer
broad-spectrum resistance against all tested isolates of the fungus, and (*ii*)
genes that confer race-specific resistance against subsets of fungal isolates.
Mutation and gene interaction studies have shown that the broad-spectrum
and race-specific resistance (*R*) genes act through at least two distinct
signaling pathways, requiring the *Ror1* and *Ror2* genes, and the *Rar1* and
Rar2 genes, respectively (reviewed in Schulze-Lefert and Vogel 2000). A
map-based cloning strategy has been used to isolate the barley genes *Mlo*,
Rar1, and the race-specific resistance genes *Mla1*, *Mla6*, and *Mla12*
(Büschges et al. 1997; Shirasu et al. 1999a; Zhou et al. 2001; Halterman et
al. 2001; Zhou et al. unpublished). The availability of the cloned genes is
providing the opportunity to explore the mechanisms underlying powdery
mildew resistance using powerful molecular tools.

Powdery Mildew *R* genes at the Complex *Mla* Locus

The *Mla* locus encodes an exceptionally large number of characterized
resistance specificities, each recognizing unique powdery mildew

determinants that are encoded by cognate fungal avirulence (*Avr*) genes. Curiously, although many tested *Mla* resistance genes require *Rar1* and *Rar2* for their function, some appear to have different signaling requirements. The *Mla* locus is also of interest because of the diversity of resistant phenotypes that are conferred by different *Mla* resistance specificities. These phenotypes can range from near immunity, associated with a rapid single-cell epidermal HR and early growth arrest of the fungus, to a late and spatially extended hypersensitive cell death consuming mesophyll cells, allowing the development of some fungal mycelium.

The *Mla* locus was mapped physically to a 240-kb region on barley chromosome 1HS that exhibits suppressed recombination (Wei et al. 1999). Sequencing of bacterial artificial chromosome DNA clones from a cultivar lacking a known *Mla* resistance specificity indicated the presence of eight genes with products similar to those of nucleotide binding, leucine-rich repeat (NB-LRR)–type *R* genes, the predominant class of known plant *R* genes. On the basis of sequence similarity, the *R* gene homologs (*RGH*) at *Mla* were classified into three families, *RGH1*, *RGH2*, and *RGH3*.

Molecular isolation of *Mla1*, *Mla6*, and *Mla12* has shown that each of these genes encodes approximately 110-kD proteins containing an N-terminal coiled-coil structure, a central nucleotide binding domain, and a C-terminal leucine-rich repeat region. A comparison between the MLA proteins revealed 97-98% sequence identity in the coiled-coil and nucleotide binding domain, and 86-88% identity in the LRR region (Fig. 1). The unusual sequence conservation of *Mla* powdery mildew *R* genes is not restricted to coding sequences. Both positions and intron sequences of *Mla1*, *Mla6*, and *Mla12* are also highly conserved. We identified a $(TA)_n$.

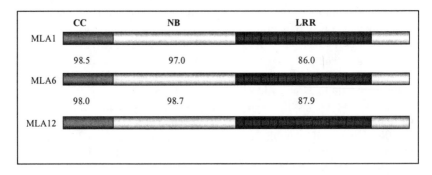

Fig. 1. Schematic diagram of MLA proteins. Numbers indicate % sequence identity in the subdomains of MLA1, MLA6, and MLA12. CC, coiled-coil domain; NB, nucleotide binding domain; LRR, Leucine rich repeat.

simple sequence repeat in the third intron of *Mla1*, *Mla6*, and *Mla12* that appears to be absent in other NB-LRR homologues at *Mla*, suggesting that powdery mildew resistance specificities at this complex locus may be encoded by an allelic series of genes.

We have begun to analyze structure/function relationships of MLA proteins by domain swap experiments. Constructs encoding MLA chimeras were tested for their potential to trigger race-specific resistance using a system for biolistic delivery of DNA constructs into barley leaf epidermal cells (Shirasu et al. 1999b). We concentrated our work on chimeras of MLA1 and MLA6 because these proteins differ in their requirement for the signaling gene *Rar1* (MLA1 functions independently of and MLA6 function is dependent on *Rar1*). Out of eight chimeras tested, each containing swaps in the LRR domain, six were found to be nonfunctional. Two chimeras, containing reciprocal swaps of the entire LRR domain, mediated race-specific resistance that was dictated by the LRR domains. Analysis of the MLA chimeras in *Rar1* wild type and *rar1* mutant plants revealed that the LRR also determined signaling requirements. The chimera containing the coiled-coil and nucleotide binding domain of MLA1 and the LRR from MLA6 exhibited *Rar1*-dependent resistance whilst the reciprocal chimera containing the LRR of MLA1 conferred *Rar1*-independent resistance. These data indicate that the LRR of MLA resistance proteins determines both recognition specificity and signaling requirements.

RAR1 and SGT1 Link *R* Gene-mediated Resistance to the Plant Ubiquitination Machinery

The 25.5 kD RAR1 protein is sequence-conserved in plants, protozoa, and metazoa (Shirasu et al. 1999a). RAR1 is required for the function of many but not all *Mla*-specified resistance reactions to the powdery mildew fungus. Susceptible *rar1* mutants loose the ability to mount a whole-cell H_2O_2 burst of attacked leaf epidermal cells and are defective in executing host cell suicide at sites of attempted invasion, two rapid host responses tightly linked to *Mla*-specified resistance. A characteristic of the deduced cytoplasmic RAR1 proteins is a tandem array of 60 amino acid domains, designated CHORD-I and CHORD-II, which were each shown to bind specifically Zn^{2+} ions (Shirasu et al. 1999a). Yeast two-hybrid experiments revealed that RAR1 interacts with SGT1, another conserved protein present in plants, protozoa, and metazoa. In yeast, SGT1 is known to be required for the activation of the ubiquitination machinery and substrate-specific protein degradation.

To find out whether *Sgt1* is required for *Mla*-specified resistance, we developed a single-cell gene silencing technique that is based on the biolistic delivery of double stranded RNA interference (dsRNAi) constructs into barley leaf epidermal cells. We constructed a dsRNAi plasmid containing an inverted repeat of barley SGT1 cDNA, separated by an approximately 1 kb intron stuffer fragment, behind the strong constitutive maize ubiquitin promoter. To monitor the efficiency of *Sgt1* single-cell silencing, we employed a reporter plasmid driving expression of *GFP* and a fusion protein of barley SGT1 and red fluorescence protein (RFP), SGT1::RFP, behind two separate ubiquitin promoters. Delivery of the reporter construct alone resulted in more than 90% of transformed epidermal cells co-expressing GFP and the fusion protein SGT1::RFP. Co-bombardment of the reporter and the SGT1 dsRNAi construct resulted in selective loss of red fluorescence in more than 80% of transformed epidermal cells, indicating efficient single-cell silencing of *Sgt1*.

We tested the effect of single-cell *Sgt1* silencing in *Mla6*-specified resistance, which is known to be dependent on *Rar1*. Delivery of a DNA construct driving expression of *Mla6* resulted in *AVRMla6*-dependent powdery mildew resistance in all transformed epidermal cells. Co-bombardment of *Mla6* together with the SGT1 dsRNAi construct compromised resistance in about half of transformed epidermal cells. Co-bombardment of *Mla6* together with dsRNAi constructs of *Sgt1* and *Rar1* resulted in growth of fungal colonies on almost all transformed epidermal cells. The results strongly suggest that *Sgt1* is required for *Mla6*-specified resistance.

To find out whether *Sgt1* function is conserved in yeast and plants, we expressed Arabidopsis *Sgt1* in wild type and temperature-sensitive yeast *sgt1* mutants. Growth of yeast *sgt1* temperature-sensitive mutants is arrested at non-permissive temperatures (35 °C). Expression of Arabidopsis *Sgt1* restored the growth defect, indicating a common function of yeast and plant *Sgt1*. Our findings suggest that MLA proteins may activate the plant ubiquitination machinery *via* RAR1 and SGT1. Whether this leads to substrate-specific protein degradation of host components (e.g. of negative regulators of cell death) to initiate cellular suicide at sites of attempted infection, remains to be examined in future experiments.

The MLO Defence Modulator is Regulated by Calmodulin

Screens of chemically and radiation mutagenized barley populations have yielded recessively inherited mutations at the *Mlo* locus that confer broad-spectrum resistance to powdery mildew. A current working hypothesis is that the wild-type MLO protein acts as a negative regulator of a defense response, such that its loss leads to a more rapid and/or greater response that is more effective at stopping the fungal pathogen. The wild type MLO protein resides in the plasma membrane, has 7-transmembrane domains (7-TM), and is the prototype of a sequence-diversified family of MLO homologues unique to plants (Büschges et al. 1997). The high within-species sequence diversity of MLO family members, a common 7-TM scaffold topology that accommodates hypervariable domains, and the location in the plasma membrane are characteristics reminiscent of the 7-

TM receptors in fungi and animals (Devoto et al. 1999). The latter, commonly referred to as G-protein coupled receptors (GPCRs) because of their requirement for heterotrimeric G-proteins in signal transmission, exist in three main families lacking sequence similarity, and are thought to represent an example of molecular convergence.

We identified a Calmodulin binding domain (CaMBD) in the C-terminal cytoplasmic tail of barley MLO. Wild type MLO was found to form a Ca^{2+}-dependent interaction with calmodulin (CaM) *in vitro*. Site-directed mutagenesis of the MLO CaMBD either disrupted or enhanced *in vitro* complex formation with CaM. *In vivo* analysis of MLO CaMBD derivatives using the single-cell transient expression assay indicates that loss of CaM binding halves the ability of MLO to negative regulate powdery mildew defence. CaM facilitates Ca^{2+} dependent responses by undergoing a $[Ca^{2+}]$ dependent coordination of four Ca^{2+}-ions which alters the affinity of CaM for its targets proteins. A rapid rise in cytoplasmic free Ca^{2+} levels ($[Ca^{2+}]_{cyt}$) has been shown to be a common response of plant cells to pathogen challenge in a number of plant/pathogen systems. If a rapid increase of $[Ca^{2+}]_{cyt}$ is also a response of barley epidermal cells to barley mildew, as preliminary Fluo-4 based Ca^{2+} indicator dye experiments suggest, the resistance suppressing activity of MLO might become boosted soon after pathogen challenge, *via* Ca^{2+} dependent CaM binding.

Literature Cited

Büschges, R., et al. 1997. The barley *Mlo* gene: A novel control element of plant pathogen resistance. Cell 88:695-705.

Devoto, A., et al. 1999. Topology, subcellular localization, and sequence diversity of the Mlo family in plants, *Journal of Biological Chemistry* 274, 34993-35004.

Halterman, D., et al. 2001. The *Mla6* coiled-coil, NBS-LRR prtoein functions in barley and wheat to confer resistance specificity to *Blumeria graminis* f sp *hordei*. Plant J. 25(3):335-348.

Schulze-Lefert, P., and Vogel, J. 2000. Closing the ranks to attack by powdery mildew. Trends Plant Sci. 5:343-348.

Shirasu, K., et al. 1999a. A novel class of eukaryotic zinc-binding proteins is required for disease resistance signaling in barley and development in *C. elegans*. Cell 99:355-366.

Shirasu, K., et al. 1999b. Cell-autonomous complementation of *mlo* resistance using a biolistic transient expression system. Plant J. 17:293-299.

Wei, F., et al. 1999. The *Mla* (powdery mildew) resistance cluster is associated with three NBS-LRR gene families and suppressed recombination within a 240-kb DNA interval on chromosome 5S (1HS) of barley. Genetics 153:1929-1948.

Zhou, F., et al. 2001. Cell-autonomous expression of barley *Mla1* confers race-specific resistance to the barley powdery mildew fungus *via* a *Rar1* independent signaling pathway. Plant Cell 13:337-350.

Natural and Artificial Evolution of Disease Resistance Genes

Richard Michelmore

Department of Vegetable Crops, and the Center for Engineering Plants for Resistance Against Pathogens (CEPRAP), University of California, Davis, CA 95616, USA.

Over the past 20 years our research has focused on the characterization and manipulation of disease resistance genes in plants. This can be viewed as various forms of natural and artificial evolution of these genes. The studies of natural evolution include characterizing resistance genes within individual genomes and within populations as well as determining the genetic basis for spontaneous mutations in resistance genes. The artificial evolution of resistance genes includes our breeding programs to introgress resistance from wild species, irradiation and chemically induced mutations, site-directed mutagenesis, and most recently *in vitro* DNA shuffling.

We have studied three plant species. The breeding and the majority of the genetic work have involved the lettuce-*Bremia lactucae* (downy mildew) interaction due to the importance of the disease and the extensive genetic material that we have available. The more structure-function oriented studies have involved the interaction between tomato-*Pseudomonas syringae* pv *syringae* (bacterial speck) because of the number of molecular components that have been identified and the convenient size of the *Pto* gene and protein compared to NBS-LRR encoding genes. The global genomic studies have focused on *Arabidopsis* due to the availability of the genomic sequence and numerous other tools available in this species.

This article describes our recent work on the evolution of resistance genes in *Arabidopsis*, lettuce and tomato and how it relates to the practical goal of increasing disease resistance in crop plants. Due to space constraints, it could not comprehensively review work by others in the field (e.g. reviewed in Ellis et al. 2000; Stahl & Bishop 2000; Holub 2001; Hulbert et al. 2001).

The Evolution of Models for Resistance Gene Evolution

Based on little data, mainly relating to the spontaneous instability of rust resistance genes in corn and the observation that resistance genes were often clustered in the genomes of many plant species, the hypothesis developed that clusters of resistance genes were rapidly evolving, dynamic arrays of genes and that unequal crossing over between paralogs within clusters was of major importance in the generation of new specificities (Pryor 1987; Michelmore et al. 1987). However, sequence comparisons of a limited number of haplotypes indicated that orthologs at the *Pto* locus in tomato and the *Dm3* locus in lettuce were more similar than paralogs (Michelmore 1999; D. Lavelle unpublished; S.-S. Woo unpublished). This suggested that resistance genes are ancient and not evolving rapidly and led to the proposal of a birth-and-death model for the evolution of resistance genes (Michelmore and Meyers 1998). As described below, additional sequence analysis of multiple haplotypes has revealed a more complex situation. Although some resistance genes are ancient, some resistance genes are evolving more rapidly. Our understanding is still incomplete. However, we are now at a point where we can both investigate the genetic events and evolutionary forces that have shaped the spectrum of resistance genes currently in plants as well as drive the evolution of new resistance specificities *in vitro*.

Comparative and Functional Genomics in *Arabidopsis*

The availability of the complete sequence of the *Arabidopsis* genome provides the opportunity for a detailed characterization of all resistance genes within a genotype. We have focused on NBS-LRR encoding genes. Extensive information can be accessed at www.niblrrs.ucdavis.edu.

A search of the genome with previously identified sequences (Meyers et al. 1999) detected a non-redundant set of 165 sequences. These were used to train an HMM model that was utilized to rescreen the genome (A. Kozik et al. unpublished). This resulted in the detection of a further 14 more distantly related sequences. These 179 sequences represent ~0.7% of all *Arabidopsis* ORFs. Approximately a third are currently misannotated; this is being corrected by a combination of computer and wetlab analyses (B. Meyers, X. Tan, et al. unpublished). The majority encode complete open reading frames and are therefore potentially functional genes.
Approximately 2/3 of the NBS-LRR encoding genes contain a TIR domain rather than a coiled-coil (CC) motif N-terminal to the NBS domain. NBS-LRR encoding genes have an uneven distribution within and between chromosomes. There are 51, 4, 19, 32, and 59 sequences on chromosomes 1, 2, 3, 4, and 5 respectively. These occur in clusters as well as singlets: over 23 are singlets, ~22 are in pairs, 22 are within 3 Mb on chr.1, 10 within

1 Mb on chr. 4, and 39 within 5 Mb on chr. 5. There are mixtures of TIR and non-TIR (CC) types within clusters and there is sometimes greater sequence similarity between clusters than within clusters indicating fairly recent sequence exchange or duplication. There is no correlation between the type of resistance gene and the pathogen detected.

Our current studies are directed at the functional analysis of NBS-LRR encoding genes, particularly their expression patterns and whether they all encode resistance genes or whether they are involved in other aspects of plant biology. In collaboration with A. Bent et al. (University of Wisconsin), we are analyzing the spectrum of genes induced downstream using ligand-independent assays (www.niblrrs.ucdavis.edu). 'Anonymous' NBS-LRR encoding genes of unknown function are being expressed from a chemically induced promoter in the absence of a ligand and the downstream induced expression signature (IES) determined using microarrays. These will be compared to the IES resulting from the interactions between known resistance genes and their cognate ligands to provide an indication as to the function of the anonymous genes.

Evolution of the Major Cluster of Disease Resistance Genes in Lettuce

The major cluster of resistance genes in lettuce is a complex and highly duplicated array of ~ 10 to 35 NBS-LRR encoding paralogs (*RGC2* homologs; Meyers et al. 1998a). The copy number depends on the genotype (Sicard et al. 1999; H. Kuang et al. unpublished). *RGC2* ORFs are 70 to 98% identical (H. Kuang et al. unpublished). The majority of *RGC2* paralogs are expressed. Analysis of EMS-induced mutations and transgenic complementation have demonstrated that a single NBS-LRR encoding *RGC2* homolog, *Dm3*, is necessary and sufficient to confer specificity to all isolates of *B. lactucae* tested that expressed *Avr3* (K. Shen, D. Chin et al. unpublished). *Dm3* is a large gene, encoding ~1800 aa with ~41 LRR motifs. The function of the other *RGC2* paralogs is unknown.

A variety of genetic events have influenced the composition of the *RGC2* cluster. Clearly, gene conversion and unequal crossovers have occurred (Meyers et al. 1998b; Chin et al. 2001; H. Kuang et al. unpublished). However, at least in some cases, these seem to have been ancient events because some orthologs are more similar than paralogs. Analysis of synonymous and non-synonymous nucleotide substitution rates indicated significant divergent selection on putative exposed residues of the LRR (Meyers et al. 1998b). Analysis of the genetic events underlying spontaneous losses of resistance indicated that the majority were due to unequal crossing-over (Chin et al. 2001). One spontaneous mutant was due to gene conversion. Although the number of *RGC2* homologs changed, no novel chimeric genes were detected as the result of the unequal crossing-over. In half the families in which it could be measured, the spontaneous deletions resulted in elevated levels of subsequent recombination in the region.

Detailed sequence analysis of *RGC2* homologs from multiple genotypes revealed unequal rates of evolution within the cluster (H. Kuang et al. unpublished). One group of homologs appears to be evolving relatively rapidly with extensive sequence exchange between paralogs in the 3' region of the gene. Their introns are more conserved than the coding regions in this region. Sequence exchange seems to be more prevalent than point mutations. Obvious orthologous relationships are rare. A second group appears to be evolving more slowly. These homologs have prevalent and obvious orthologs; point mutations and recombination are more frequent than sequence exchange between paralogs. Their introns are at least as divergent as their coding regions. The differences in intron divergence between the two groups suggest that the degree of intron similarity influences and is a consequence of the frequency of sequence exchange between paralogs. The data is consistent with a birth-and-death model for the evolution of resistance genes with trans-specific polymorphisms maintained by density-dependent, balancing selection.

The existence of these two patterns of evolution suggests that there may be different patterns of selection favoring each mode of evolution. This may be a consequence of the mutability of the ligands detected by each group. The slow evolving group may detect pathogen-derived ligands that are prevalent in nature and/or incur a fitness penalty when not expressed. In contrast, the fast evolving group may encode an evolutionarily-flexible detection component that reacts to ligands that are readily lost by the pathogen population. The testing of this hypothesis requires the characterization of multiple avirulence gene products detected by each group of genes.

Evolution of New Resistance Specificities *In Vitro*

DNA shuffling is a powerful approach for generating chimeric molecules *in vitro* and provides the opportunity for molecular breeding (Stemmer 1994). However, most studies published to date have focused on generating proteins with enhanced performance (Lassner and Bedbrook 2001) rather than utilizing shuffling as an experimental tool for dissecting protein function. The *Pto* gene and encoded protein are ideally suited to DNA shuffling experiments. Both the gene and the protein are small (Martin et al. 1993). There are no introns within the gene. There is significant natural variation in related genes, numerous orthologs and paralogs have been sequenced and several have been functionally characterized from Solanaceous species (Vleeshouwers et al. 2001; Reily et al. 2001, D. Lavelle, L. Rose et al. unpublished). The Pto sequence can be threaded onto known crystal structures of protein kinases. Biochemical characterization of Pto is consistent with the functions of various domains and individual residues that have been characterized for multiple kinases (e.g. Rathjen et al. 1999).

We are using DNA shuffling to dissect the function of Pto further. In the longer term we will generate sequences that have new specificities and/or function in non-Solanaceous species. We have so far conducted a single round of shuffling using *Pto* and four paralogs as templates (A. Bernal, Q. Pan, J. Pollock, L. Rose et al. unpublished). A library of progeny sequences was screened in the yeast two-hybrid system for interaction with AvrPto. Approximately 100 potential interactors and ~100 non-interactors have been sequenced and are being tested in transient *in planta* assays for their ability to elicit AvrPto-dependent HR. The majority of progeny clones were full-length chimeras of six to eight segments. A variety of combinations of phenotypes have been observed. These are currently being correlated to the amino acid residues to identify the determinant sequences. Inferences will be validated by additional generations of shuffling and site-directed mutagenesis.

Consequences of the Birth-and-Death
Model to Breeding for Resistance

The birth-and death model has several implications for breeding for disease resistance. All genotypes have large numbers of resistance genes. There are hundreds and maybe thousands of resistance genes in crop plants. No genotype lacks resistance genes; although some may not have resistance genes that are detected using pathogen screens. Backcross programs introgress clusters of resistance genes not just single genes; recombination during introgression may result in the loss of one or more resistance specificities. Also, introgression will replace resistance genes initially present in recurrent parent. Consequently, backcrossing may inadvertently introduce susceptibility to a different pathogen.

A large number and wide variety of recognition specificities are possible. However, there may be only a finite number of specificities against a particular pathogen present in the gene pool and some resistance specificities may be widespread. There is, therefore, the possibility of repeated introgression of the same resistance specificity from very different wild germplasm. There is evidence of this having occurred in lettuce (Witsenboer et al. 1995). Some resistance specificities may be cryptic but could possibly be expressed following recombination events that generate new combinations of promoter and open reading frame.

It should be possible to pyramid orthologous genes by unequal crossing-over, if suitable combinations of isolates are available to detect the desired recombinant products. Some forms of non-host resistance may be pyramids of specific resistance genes.

There are opportunities for transferring resistance specificities across sexual compatibility barriers. However, attempts to transfer NBS-LRR encoded resistance between species in different families has so far failed for reasons that are not understood. DNA shuffling approaches may help to address this question as well as to generate new resistance specificities.

Acknowledgements

I gratefully acknowledge the numerous people in my lab for their hard work and intellectual input to the studies described above. I also thank the USDA National Research Initiative & Initiative for Future Agriculture and Food Systems programs, the NSF Plant Genome and Science & Technology Centers programs as well as the California Lettuce Research Board for financial support.

Literature Cited

Chin, D.B., Arroyo-Garcia, R., Ochoa, O., Kesseli, R.V., Lavelle, D.O., and Michelmore, R.W. 2001. Recombination and spontaneous mutation at the major cluster of resistance genes in lettuce (*Lactuca sativa*). Genetics 157:831-849.

Ellis, J., Dodds, P., and Pryor, T. 2000. Structure, function and evolution of plant disease resistance genes. Curr. Opin. Plant Biol. 3:278-284.

Holub, EB. 2001. The arms race is ancient history in *Arabidopsis*, the wildflower. Nat. Rev. Genet. 2:516-527.

Hulbert, S.H., Webb, C.A., Smith, S.M., and Sun, Q. 2001. Resistance gene complexes: evolution and utilization. Annu. Rev. Phytopathol. 39:285-312.

Lassner, M., and Bedbrook, J. 2001. Directed molecular evolution in plant improvement. Curr. Opin. Plant Biol. 4:152-156.

Martin, G.B., Brommonschenkel, S.H., Chunwongse, J., Frary, A., Ganal, M.W., Spivey, R., Wu, T., Earle, E.D., and Tanksley, S.D. 1993. Map-based cloning of a protein kinase gene conferring disease resistance in tomato. Science 262:1432-1436.

Meyers, B.C., Chin, D.B., Shen, K.A., Sivaramakrishnan, S., Lavelle, D.O., Zhang, Z., and Michelmore, R.W. 1998. The major resistance gene cluster in lettuce is highly duplicated and spans several megabases. Plant Cell 10:1817-1832.

Meyers, B.C., Dickerman, A.W., Michelmore, R.W., Sivaramakrishnan, S., Sobral, B.W., and Young, N.D. 1999. Plant disease resistance genes encode members of an ancient and diverse protein family within the nucleotide-binding superfamily. Plant J. 20:317-332.

Meyers, B.C., Shen, K.A., Rohani, P., Gaut, B.S., and Michelmore, R.W. 1998. Receptor-like genes in the major resistance locus of lettuce are subject to divergent selection. Plant Cell 10:1833-1846.

Michelmore, R. W., Hulbert, S. H., Landry B. S., and Leung, H. 1987. Towards a molecular understanding of lettuce downy mildew. Pages 221-231 in: Genetics and Plant Pathogenesis, P. R. Day and G. J. Jellis, eds. Blackwell Scientific Publications, Oxford.

Michelmore R.W. 1999. Structure, function and evolution of resistance gene clusters in plants, particularly the *Pto* and *Dm3* loci. Proc. 9th Int. Congr. Mol. Plant Microbe Interact. pp 232-237.

Michelmore, R.W., and Meyers, B.C. 1998. Clusters of resistance genes in plants evolve by divergent selection and a birth-and-death process. Genome Research 8:1113-1130.

Pryor, T. 1987. Origin and structure of disease resistance genes in plants. Trends in Genetics 3:157-161.

Rathjen, J.P., Chang, J.H., Staskawicz, B.J., and Michelmore, R.W. 1999. Constitutively active Pto induces a Prf-dependent hypersensitive response in the absence of avrPto. EMBO J. 18:3232-3240.

Reily, B.K., and Martin, G.B. 2001. Ancient origin of pathogen recognition specificity conferred by the tomato disease resistance gene *Pto*. Proc. Natl. Acad. Sci. U.S.A. 98:2059-2064.

Sicard, D., Woo, S.-S., Arroyo-Garcia, R., Ochoa. O., Nguyen, D., Korol, A., Nevo, E., and Michelmore, R.W. 1999. Molecular diversity at the major cluster of disease resistance genes in cultivated and wild *Lactuca* spp. Theor. Appl. Genet. 99:405-418.

Stahl, E.A., and Bishop, J.G. 2000. Plant-pathogen arms races at the molecular level. Curr. Opin. Plant Biol. 3:299-304.

Stemmer, W.P.C. 1994. Rapid evolution of a protein *in vitro* by DNA shuffling. Nature 370:389-391.

Vleeshouwers, V.G., Martens, A.A., van Dooijeweert, W., Colon, L.T., Govers, F., and Kamoun, S. 2001. Ancient diversification of the Pto kinase family preceded speciation in Solanum. Mol. Plant-Microbe Interact 14:996-1005.

Witsenboer, H., Kesseli, R.V., Fortin, M., Stangellini, M., and Michelmore, R.W. 1995. Sources and genetic structure of a cluster of genes for resistance to three pathogens in lettuce. Theor. Appl. Genet. 91:178-188.

Characterization of *RPW8*-Mediated Mildew Resistance in *Arabidopsis* and Tobacco

Shunyuan Xiao, Ozer Calis, Samantha Brown, Piyavadee Charoenwattana, Kumrop Ratanasut, Elaine Patrick, Lucy Holcombe, Mark Coleman, Dan Jaggard and John G. Turner

School of Biological Sciences, University of East Anglia, Norwich NR4 7TJ, England

Plant disease resistance (*R*) genes control the recognition of specific pathogens and activate subsequent defense responses. The *Arabidopsis* locus *RPW8* contains two naturally polymorphic, dominant *R* genes, *RPW8.1* and *RPW8.2*, which individually control resistance to a broad range of powdery mildew pathogens (Xiao et al. 2001). The predicted RPW8 proteins are small (~20 kDa) and basic (pI>9) and differ from previously characterised R-proteins. However, *RPW8.1* and *RPW8.2* (referred to hereafter as *RPW8.1/2*) induce salicylic-acid-dependent defense responses similar to those regulated by other types of *R*-gene. Here we report the signalling components required by *RPW8.1/2*; the regulation of *RPW8.1* expression; and we describe spontaneous cell death conferred by *RPW8.1/2*-overexpression. We also characterize *RPW8* homologues from *Brassica* species and report that the *Arabidopsis RPW8.1/2* confers resistance to a powdery mildew disease of *Nicotiana tabacum*.

Signalling Components Required by *RPW8.1/2*

Previously we showed that a mutation in *EDS1* (*eds1-2*), or SA-depletion by the *nahG* transgene, compromised *RPW8*-mediated resistance, but that a mutation in *NDR1* (*ndr1-1*) had no effect (Xiao et al. 2001). To extend our analysis of *RPW8*-mediated signalling, we introduced *RPW8* by genetic crossing into a number of other characterised mutant backgrounds. These mutants included *pad4-1, eds5-1, npr1-1 pbs3,* and *coi1-1*. We report that mutations in *EDS5* and *PAD4* completely, and in *NPR1* partially,

30

compromise *RPW8.1/2*-mediated resistance to the 4 *Erysiphe* species tested. However, mutations in *PBS3*, and *COI1* do not affect resistance.

Table 1. Signalling requirements of *RPW8*-mediated resistance.

RPW8 genotype	phenotype*	mutant background							
		nahG	eds1-2	pad4-1	eds 5-1	npr1-1	ndr1-1	pbs3	coi1-1
-/-	H_2O_2 2dpi	-	-	-	-	-	-	-	-
	disease, 8 dpi	ES	ES	ES	ES	S	S	S	S
RPW8/ RPW8	H_2O_2 2dpi	-	-	-	-	+/-	+	+	+
	disease, 8 dpi	S	S	S	S	I	R	R	R

* "ES", enhanced susceptibility; "S", Susceptible; "I", Intermediate or partially susceptible; "R", Resistant; "- ", No H_2O_2 accumulation detected by diaminobenzidine staining; "+", H_2O_2 accumulation detected; "+/-", little H_2O_2 accumulation detected.

These conclusions are based on observations that plants containing *RPW8.1/2* in *eds1-2*, *nahG* transgene, *pad4-1* and *eds5-1* backgrounds lacked a hypersensitive response (HR) which can normally be revealed at cellular level as a brown stain from the reaction of applied diaminobenzidine (DAB) with H_2O_2 formed at the sites of fungal penetration (Table 1), and they were susceptible to the powdery mildew pathogens. By contrast plants containing *RPW8.1/2* in *ndr1-1*, *pbs3*, and *coi1-1* had localised H_2O_2 accumulation in response to fungal penetration and they were resistant to the pathogens. Thus, we envisage that *RPW8.1/2* functions through a SA-dependent signaling pathway involving *EDS1*, *PAD4*, *EDS5* and *NPR1*, which is also used by the TIR-NB- LRR *R* genes *RPP5* and *RPS4* (Aarts et al. 1998). The partial resistance when *RPW8.1/2* is in the *npr1-1* background implies that *RPW8* may also recruit an *NPR1*-independent but SA-dependent pathway for cell death and resistance.

Regulation of *RPW8* Expression

Northern analysis showed that *RPW8.2* is expressed at a higher level in leaves inoculated with *E. cichoracearum* than in controls (Xiao et al. 2001). We analysed the transcriptional regulation of *RPW8* expression by fusing the *RPW8.1* and *RPW8*.2 promoters to the *E. coli uidA* (*GUS*) gene. Interestingly, wounding induced GUS expression in transgenic Col-0 plants containing either *RPW8.1p::GUS* or *RPW8.2p::GUS*. GUS expression was also induced when the transgenic seedling were treated with exogenous SA (100 μM for 2 days), but not JA (50 μM for 2 days). These results reveal that *RPW8.1/2* are transcriptionally regulated by wounding and add weight to the growing evidence for inter-connection or convergence of the wound-responsive and pathogen-responsive signal pathways (Romeis et al. 1999). Transcriptional regulation of *RPW8.1/2* is presumably downstream of pathogen perception and wounding. SA-induction of *RPW8*p::*GUS* expression indicates not only that *RPW8* signals through SA accumulation (Xiao et al. 2001), but also that the signal is amplified by SA, possibly through a feedback loop.

Overexpression of *RPW8*

SPONTANEOUS CELL DEATH (SCD)

Approximately one third of Col-0 lines (32 of 97 independent *T1* lines tested) containing a 14 kb genomic fragment with both *RPW8*.1 and *RPW8*.2 controlled by their native promoters had necrotic lesions and reduced stature when germinated on soil. Southern analysis showed a correlation between the number of insertions of the *RPW8* transgene and SCD. *T5* progenies of two lines, S5 carrying a single insertion, and S24 harbouring multiple copies of the insert, were used for further characterisation. S5 plants grown in soil normally did not develop necrotic lesions unless inoculated with the *Erysiphe* isolates, whereas S24 uninoculated plants growing in soil developed extensive SCD in the leaves and failed to survive to maturity. Northern analysis showed *RPW8.1* and *RPW8.2* transcripts were respectively ~12- and ~8- fold greater in S24 than in S5. A detailed comparison of these two lines, cultivated under different growth conditions showed that *RPW8*-mediated SCD was spontaneous, and was attenuated or enhanced by external conditions. The results are summarized in Table 2. The conditions under which S24 plants develop SCD are close to the natural environment of Arabidopsis, whereas the conditions under which the SCD is suppressed or attenuated, are atypical for normal growth of *Arabidopsis*. The mechanisms by which the SCD of S24 is permitted or suppressed are not known.

ENHANCED RESISTANCE TO PERONOSPORA AND CAMV

To determine if S24 has enhanced resistance to pathogens other than powdery mildews, we inoculated S5, S24 and Col-0 plants with *Peronospora parasitica* NOCO2, cauliflower mosaic virus (CaMV) and *Pseudomonas syringae* pv *maculicola* ES4326, all of which are virulent on Col-0. S24 plants grown under SCD-non-permissive conditions were

Table 2. The effect of environmental conditions on spontaneous cell death of S24 line.

Growth Conditions [1]		SCD of S24 plants
medium	MS agar	suppressed
	soil or perlite	permitted
light	normal intensity or higher	permitted or promoted
	dark or low intensity [2]	suppressed or delayed
temperature	22 ˚C	permitted
	30 ˚C	suppressed
humidity	85% or lower	permitted
	96% or higher	attenuated

[1] S24 seeds were sown on MS agar plates to germinate where seedlings were grown for 2 weeks before transfer to fresh MS agar plates and grow for another 2 weeks. The seedlings were then transferred to different conditions. The basic conditions were short day (8 hour day and 16 hour dark), 22 ˚C, with a light intensity of ~85 $\mu MOLm^{-2}s^{-1}$ in autoclaved perlite wetted with MS liquid media without sucrose. Plants were grown in Magenta Vessels (Sigma) under aseptic condition all times.
[2] Low light intensity: 1/6 of normal light intensity (i.e. ~14 $\mu Mm^{-2}s^{-1}$).

susceptible to all pathogens. However, S24 plants grown under SCD-permissive conditions developed necrotic lesions at the site of infection and had enhanced resistance to the *Peronospora.* Under SCD permissive conditions, S24 also exhibited enhanced resistance to CaMV. We did not, however, observe enhanced resistance of S24 to *P. syringae* ES4326 (under SCD permissive conditions, in three independent experiments in which S24, S5 and Col-0 leaves were infiltrated with a bacterial suspension of OD_{600}=0.0002, S24 exhibited the same typical disease symptoms as S5 and Col-0).

Homologues in *Brassica*

We identified three tandemly clustered *RPW8* homologues from both *Brassica oleracea,* and *B. rapa* by screening two *Brassica* BAC libraries using *RPW8* genomic DNA as probe. These *Brassica* homologues (named *BrHR1/BoHR1, BrHR2/BoHR2,* and *BrHR3/BoHR3*) are highly homologous to each other (>88% identity at nucleotide level when the predicted whole genes are compared) and show considerable homology (56-72% identity) to *RPW8.1, RPW8.2, HR1-3 and Col-HR4.* Phylogenetic analysis indicates that the *Arabidopsis RPW8* homologues are more divergent than the *Brassica* homologues. Initial mapping with *BrHR*

33

homologues placed this *RPW8*-like locus in a 2 cM interval flanked by marker pW207E3N and pW104E2, on chromosome 8 of *B. rapa*. We are testing whether these *Brassica* homologues also function as *R* genes.

Transfer of *RPW8* to Tobacco

We transferred a 7.5 kb genomic fragment containing *RPW8*.1 and *RPW8*.2 under control of their native promoters into *Nicotiana tabacum* through stable transformation. The transgenic *T1* lines were tested with *Erysiphe orontii* MGH. Wild type *N. tabacum* plants were fully susceptible to this isolate (disease rating 2-3 or 3). In contrast, all the 4 *T1* line tested were resistant (no visible fungus; disease rating 0). Microscopic examination after $DiOC_6$ staining and DAB /trypan blue staining showed that the *RPW8* transgene triggered a hypersensitive response manifested by rapid H_2O_2 accumulation at fungal penetration sites, and localised cell death. A test of the *T2* progenies derived from the 4 *T1* lines further confirmed that *RPW8* confers resistance in in tobacco. Transient expression of *RPW8.1* and *RPW8.2* in *N. benthamiana* by agroinfiltration caused cell death. We believe this represents the first example of an *R* gene that confers specific resistance in a host from a different plant family. Evidently, the *RPW8* signalling pathway(s) for disease resistance is conserved in *Arabidopsis* and tobacco.

Acknowledgement

The authors thank Fred M. Ausubel, Jane Glazebrook, Xinnian Dong, Roger Innes, and Jane Parker for mutant seeds, and Ian Bancroft, Carmel O'Neill and Elisabeth Bent for BAC filters. This work was supported by grants from the BBSRC to JGT.

Literature Cited

Aarts N., Metz M., Holub E., Staskawicz B. J., Daniels M. J., aned Parker J. E. 1998. Different requirements for *EDS1* and *N D R 1* by disease resistance genes define at least two *R* gene-mediated signaling pathways in *Arabidopsis*. Proc Natl Acad Sci USA 95:10306-10311.

Romeis T., Piedras P., Zhang S., Klessig D. F., Hirt H., and Jones J. J. G. 1999. Rapid *Avr 9*- and *Cf-9* –dependent activation of MAP kinases in tobacco cell cultures and leaves: convergence of resistance gene, elicitor, wound, and salicylate responses. Plant Cell 11: 273-288.

Xiao S., Ellwood S., Calis O., Patrick E., Li T., Coleman M., and Turner J. G. 2001. Broad-spectrum mildew resistance in *Arabidopsis thaliana*. Science 291:118-120.

Recognition of the *Pseudomonas* Avirulence Protein AvrPphB by Arabidopsis

Roger W. Innes, Michal R. Swiderski, and Jules Ade

Department of Biology, Indiana University, Bloomington, IN 47405-3700

Recognition of pathogens by resistant plants is often governed by disease resistance (*R*) genes in the plant and avirulence (*avr*) genes in the pathogen. Although many *avr* and *R* genes have now been cloned, the mechanisms by which *R* gene proteins enable pathogen recognition are not understood. To provide molecular insights into this process, we have been studying how the avirulence protein AvrPphB from *Pseudomonas syringae* is detected by Arabidopsis.

The *avrPphB* gene was originally identified as an avirulence gene from *P. syringae* pv. *phaseolicola* races 3 and 4 that confers avirulence on bean cultivar Tendergreen (Jenner et al. 1991). It was subsequently shown to confer avirulence on Arabidopsis variety Col-0, but not on variety Ler (Simonich and Innes 1995). Using recombinant inbred lines derived from a cross between Col-0 and Ler, we identified a single dominant resistance gene in variety Col-0 that conferred the ability to recognize AvrPphB (Simonich and Innes 1995). We named this gene *RPS5*, and cloned it using a positional cloning strategy (Warren et al. 1998). *RPS5* encodes a standard R gene protein of the NBS-LRR class.

To identify additional proteins that are involved in AvrPphB recognition, we screened for mutants of variety Col-O that became susceptible to *P. syringae* strain DC3000(*avrPphB*). This screen led to the identification of three genes, *PBS1, PBS2,* and *PBS3*, all of which are required for full resistance to this strain (Warren et al. 1999). Significantly, we found that *PBS1* is not required for resistance to DC3000 strains carrying *avrB, avrRpt2,* or *avrRps4*, indicating that PBS1 may function specifically in the recognition of AvrPphB (Warren et al. 1999). In contrast, mutations in *PBS2* and *PBS3*affected recognition of multiple Avr proteins, indicating that the PBS2 and PBS3 proteins function in some aspect of resistance shared by multiple *R* genes.

The AvrPphB protein appears to be recognized inside the plant cell as expression of AvrPphB in transgenic Arabidopsis plants induces a hypersensitive response that is dependent on *PBS1* (Swiderski and Innes 2001). It is not yet known whether this recognition event is direct, via protein:protein interactions, or if AvrPphB functions as an enzyme, with the enzymatic product serving as the ligand. We have tested for direct interactions between PBS1 and AvrPphB and between RPS5 and AvrPphB by yeast two-hybrid analyses, but have obtained only negative results to date. It is thus unclear whether PBS1, RPS5, both, or neither function as a receptor for the AvrPphB protein.

We have recently cloned the *PBS1* gene and shown it to encode a functional protein kinase (Swiderski and Innes 2001). Unpublished work from our laboratory has shown that PBS1 is a relatively promiscuous kinase *in vitro* and can phosphorylate itself, RPS5, RPS2, and AvrPphB. It does not phosphorylate maltose binding protein or bovine serum albumin, however. It is thus a formal possibility that PBS1 functions to modify RPS5 and/or AvrPphB *in vivo* and that this modification is required for recognition of AvrPphB.

The PBS1 kinase represents the second example in plants in which both a kinase and an NBS-LRR protein are required for specific recognition of a *P. syringae* Avr protein; recognition of the AvrPto protein by tomato plants requires the Pto kinase and the Prf NBS-LRR protein. These similarities might suggest that Pto and PBS1 fulfill similar functions in Avr protein recognition. A phylogenetic analysis of plant protein kinases indicates that this is probably not true, however. In Arabidopsis, the most closely related protein kinases to Pto belong the transmembrane receptor-like protein kinase family, with the most similar kinase domain being 65% identical to Pto. PBS1 is only 42% identical to Pto, thus is quite distantly related to Pto (Swiderski and Innes 2001).

PBS1 appears to be well conserved among plants, as potato, soybean and maize all contain kinases that are over 90% identical to PBS1, which is significantly more similar than the most closely related *Arabidopsis* kinase. These data indicate that PBS1 is performing a function that is common between monocots and dicots, and is evolving very slowly. In addition, *Arabidopsis* lines that lack RPS5 contain a functional *PBS1* gene. Together, these observations suggest that the primary role of PBS1 may be something other than the recognition of *AvrPphB*. Surprisingly, however, *pbs1* mutants display no visible phenotypes other than susceptibility to strain DC3000(*avrPphB*).

The PBS1, RPS5 and AvrPphB proteins all contain potential myristylation motifs. We have recently determined that PBS1 and RPS5 are membrane localized in Arabidopsis (data not shown). Thus these three proteins may co-localize in the plant cell, which would suggest that they may physically interact with each other. From the above data it is difficult to predict the precise roles of PBS1 and RPS5 in the recognition of AvrPphB. Below we discuss the pros and cons of five potential models.

In Model 1, RPS5 functions as a receptor for the AvrPphB-derived ligand, while the PBS1 kinase functions as a downstream signal transduction component. We do not favor this model because it implies that the sole function of PBS1 is to transmit the RPS5 signal. If this were the case, it would not be conserved in *Arabidopsis* varieties that lack RPS5, and would not be conserved in distantly related species. Although one could argue that PBS1 is conserved because it serves a similar role for other *R* gene signal transduction pathways, we have found no evidence that PBS1 is required in any other *R* gene pathway (Swiderski and Innes 2001; Warren et al. 1999). This model is also inconsistent with data from John Rathjen and colleagues, who have shown that the Pto kinase functions upstream, or at the same level as Prf (Rathjen et al. 1999).

In Model 2, the relative positions of the kinase and NB-LRR proteins are simply reversed, with the kinase functioning as a receptor. We view this model as unlikely because the kinase would then be expected to be the more rapidly evolving gene relative to the NB-LRR protein. This is clearly not the case for PBS1. In addition, there would be no reason to maintain PBS1 function in the absence of RPS5.

In Model 3, the role of PBS1 is to phosphorylate AvrPphB, which then enables recognition by RPS5. We view this model as unlikely for the essentially the same reasons as given for Model 2. PBS1 would not be expected to be conserved in plants that do not contain RPS5, or that are not exposed to AvrPphB. Furthermore, it is unclear what the selective advantage would be of this mechanism, as it introduces the requirement of a second protein for Avr recognition with no apparent benefit over accomplishing the same task with just the NB-LRR protein.

In Model 4, the role of PBS1 is to phosphorylate RPS5 (as well as other unknown *R* gene proteins), which modifies the specificity of the R protein. This model would explain how a single R protein can mediate recognition of multiple Avr proteins (Bisgrove et al. 1994). It also raises the possibility of combinatorial interactions, increasing the number of potential ligands that NB-LRR proteins can recognize. However, this model also predicts that the kinase should function in multiple *R* gene pathways, as it would otherwise not be conserved. As mentioned above, we have no evidence that PBS1 functions in any pathway other than the RPS5 pathway.

In Model 5, PBS1 is not a receptor for AvrPphB, but a "target". By this, we mean that AvrPphB plays a role in virulence and in fact targets PBS1 in order to enhance the virulence of *P. syringae*. RPS5 then functions to "guard" the PBS1 protein, activating resistance when it senses that PBS1 has been attacked by AvrPphB. This model is essentially the same as that proposed by van der Biezen and Jones to explain the Pto/Prf data (van der Biezen and Jones 1998). This model is attractive for several reasons. First, the targets of pathogen virulence factors would be expected to be quite diverse, depending on what aspect of cell physiology is being modified. This is consistent with the large dissimilarity between PBS1 and Pto. Second, the target would be expected to function "upstream" of the NB-LRR protein, as shown for Pto. Third, the target need not be a rapidly evolving gene, especially if it regulates a fundamental cellular process. Fourth, a single NB-LRR protein could mediate recognition of many different Avr proteins if these pathogen virulence factors all target the same plant protein.

There are a couple inconsistencies to the guard model, however. The first is that elimination of either PBS1 or Pto does not affect the virulence function AvrPphB or AvrPto, respectively (Chang et al. 2000; Shan et al. 2000). Thus, if PBS1 and Pto are targets, they cannot be the only targets. The second is that one would not expect a rapid evolution of NB-LRR proteins under the guard model, as once the subset of potential targets have been identified in a plant cell, there should not be rapid changes in these targets. In particular, one would not expect large differences in the repertoire of NB-LRR genes from one variety to another within a plant species, but in fact that is exactly what is seen.

One way to get around the latter criticism is to require the NB-LRR protein to recognize BOTH the Avr protein and the target as a complex. This mechanism would force the NB-LRR gene to co-evolve with the pathogen Avr protein. It would also prevent activation of defense responses by "free-floating" antigens that may be harmless (akin to antigen presentation in vertebrate T-cells), and would eliminate the activation of defenses by accidental misfolding of the target protein. However, such a recognition mechanism reduces the ability of a single NB-LRR protein to recognize multiple Avr proteins.

Given the highly speculative nature of the above discussion, it is obvious that we need solid data to distinguish among these models. One prediction of the guard model is that PBS1 and AvrPphB (or an AvrPphB-derived molecule) should interact. Similarly, RPS5 would be expected to interact with a complex of PBS1 and AvrPphB. Thus far we have been unable to detect such interactions by yeast two-hybrid analyses, while *in vitro* assays have been compromised by a loss of specificity in the interactions observed (e.g. RPS2 also interacts with PBS1 *in vitro*). We are therefore turning our attention to assaying protein:protein interactions inside plant cells. If successful, these assays should shed new light on the molecular mechanisms underlying pathogen recognition.

Acknowledgements

Work in our laboratory was supported by grant number R01 GM46451 from the National Institutes of Health.

Literature Cited

Bisgrove, S.R., M.T. Simonich, N.M. Smith, A. Sattler, and R.W. Innes. 1994. A disease resistance gene in Arabidopsis with specificity for two different pathogen avirulence genes. Plant Cell 6:927-933.

Chang, J. H., J. P. Rathjen, A. J. Bernal, B. J. Staskawicz, and R. W. Michelmore. 2000. avrPto enhances growth and necrosis caused by *Pseudomonas syringae* pv.*tomato* in tomato lines lacking either Pto or Prf. Mol. Plant Microbe Interact. 13:568-571.

Jenner, C., E. Hitchin, J. Mansfield, K. Walters, P. Betteridge, D. Teverson, and J. Taylor. 1991. Gene-for-gene interactions between *Pseudomonas syringae* pv. *phaseolicola* and Phaseolus. Mol. Plant-Microbe Interact. 4:553-562.

McNellis, T. W., M. B. Mudgett, K. Li, T. Aoyama, D. Horvath, N. H. Chua, and B. J. Staskawicz. 1998. Glucocorticoid-inducible expression of a bacterial avirulence gene in transgenic Arabidopsis induces hypersensitive cell death. Plant J 14:247-257.

Rathjen, J. P., J. H. Chang, B. J. Staskawicz, and R. W. Michelmore. 1999. Constitutively active Pto induces a Prf-dependent hypersensitive response in the absence of avrPto. EMBO J 18:3232-3240.

Shan, L., P. He, J. M. Zhou, and X. Tang. 2000. A cluster of mutations disrupt the avirulence but not the virulence function of AvrPto. Mol. Plant-Microbe Interact. 13:592-598.

Simonich, M. T., and R. W. Innes. 1995. A disease resistance gene in Arabidopsis with specificity for the avrPph3 gene of *Pseudomonas syringae* pv. *phaseolicola*. Mol. Plant-Microbe Interact. 8:637-640.

Swiderski, M. R., and R. W. Innes. 2001. The *Arabidopsis PBS1* resistance gene encodes a member of a novel protein kinase subfamily. Plant J 26:101-112.

van der Biezen, E.A., and J.D.G. Jones. 1998. Plant disease-resistance proteins and the gene-for-gene concept. Trends Biochem. Sci. 23:454-456.

Warren, R. F., P. M. Merritt, E. Holub, and R. W. Innes. 1999. Identification of three putative signal transduction genes involved in R gene-specified disease resistance in Arabidopsis. Genetics 152:401-412.

Warren, R. F., A. Henk, P. Mowery, E. Holub, and R. W. Innes. 1998. A mutation within the leucine-rich repeat domain of the Arabidopsis disease resistance gene RPS5 partially suppresses multiple bacterial and downy mildew resistance genes. Plant Cell 10:1439-1452.

Target Specificity in Leucine-Rich Repeat (LRR) Proteins

Partho Ghosh and Tara Chapman

Department of Chemistry and Biochemistry, University of California at San Diego, La Jolla, California, USA

Proteins containing leucine-rich repeats (LRR), which form ligand-binding surfaces, are evolutionarily widespread and functionally diverse. They are especially prevalent in certain plant genomes. For example, LRR proteins compose about 1% of the *Arabidopsis* genome. The majority of plant disease resistance genes (R) contain LRR domains, which are thought to confer recognition of specific pathogen-derived macromolecules. This role has a parallel in LRR proteins belonging to the large family of toll-like receptors of the mammalian innate immune response. LRR proteins are also found in bacterial pathogens of animals and plants. *Listeria monocytogenes*, a facultative intracellular pathogen of humans, encodes a large family of LRR proteins called internalins. The X-ray crystal structure of the LRR domain of one of the internalins, InlB, has been determined and provides an understanding of how these domains generate target specificity (Marino et al. 1999).

InlB is a *L. monocytogenes* surface-attached protein that promotes bacterial invasion of a number of mammalian cell types, including hepatocyte, epithelial, endothelial, and fibroblast-like cell lines. The LRR domain of InlB (24 kDa), which is located at its N-terminus as in other internalins, is necessary and sufficient to trigger bacterial entry into host cells. It binds to and activates a host cell receptor tyrosine kinase, the hepatocyte growth factor receptor (HGFR, also call Met) (Shen et al. 2000). Through action on HGFR, InlB causes downstream activation of a number of signaling pathways including the phosphoinositide (PI) 3-kinase pathway. Production of phosphosinositide second messengers by PI 3-kinase (Ireton et al. 1996) is thought to bring about changes in the actin cytoskeleton and subsequent engulfment of the bacterium through a zippering action of the membrane.

LRR Sequence Motifs

The InlB LRR domain contains seven and one-half tandem repeats, which are each 22 residues in length, as in other internalins (Marino et al. 2000). LRR lengths vary from 20 to 29 residues in other proteins, and unlike the internalins, some proteins have repeats of differing lengths. The number of repeats may be as few as two or as many as 30. The LRR forms a coil-like structure, which is composed of a β-strand and (almost always) a helical segment (Fig. 1). The β-strand and helix run anti-parallel to each other and are connected by loops. The β-strand is invariably short (three residues) and in precise register (Fig. 1, residues 4-6), presumably because it is constrained by having to form hydrogen bonds with β-strands of adjacent repeats. In contrast, the helical segment varies in length and register. Indeed, this segment need not be α-helical, and is a β-strand in a few repeats of other proteins. In InlB, 3_{10}- rather than α-helices are found. The 3_{10}-helix, which is an overwound version of an α-helix, accommodates the short 22 residue repeat length, and is expected to be found in other LRR proteins with short repeats. The helical segment does not form hydrogen bonds with other repeats, and is therefore not constrained in the same way that the β-strand is.

The half of the coil containing the β-strand is the most conserved segment among LRR proteins (Fig. 1, bold-face). Positions 2, 5, 7, and 12 contribute leucines, valines, isoleucines, and more rarely methionines and phenylalanines that form the hydrophobic core of the domain. Position 10 usually contributes an asparagine to the hydrophobic core; this residue forms hydrogen bonds to main chain atoms. Cysteines, serines, and

Fig. 1. Structure of a single InlB LRR. The sequence motif of positions 1-12 (bottom, 'x' is any amino acid) is highly conserved among LRR proteins.

threonines are also observed to occupy position 10. The remaining seven positions in this half of the coil are surface-exposed and not constrained by structural roles. They are free to vary through evolution without structural consequence to create ligand-binding sites (Marino et al. 2000). Among these, positions 3, 4, 6, 8, and 9 are likely to play dominant functional roles because of their location on the concave surface of the molecule. The packing of adjacent coils in an LRR domain leads to a curved, tube-like structure, with the β-strand side forming a concave surface and the helical side forming a convex surface. The concave side presents a topographically ideal surface for protein-protein interactions, and indeed has been observed to form most of the binding surface in structures of complexes of LRR-proteins with their cognate targets.

Target Specificity of InlB LRR

HGFR, the mammalian cell surface receptor for InlB, is a receptor tyrosine kinase that is expressed on a wide range of cell types including hepatocytes, epithelial and endothelial cells. In contrast to intracellular invasion evoked by InlB, activation of HGFR by its endogenous ligand, hepatocyte growth factor/scatter factor (HGF/SF), induces cellular proliferation, differentiation and motility. Despite binding the same receptor, HGF/SF and InlB are structurally dissimilar. HGF/SF, a disulfide-linked αβ heterodimer (69 kDa and 34 kDa, respectively), is not an LRR protein. Rather, it contains a unique structural domain termed an 'N-terminal hairpin' and four kringle domains in the α subunit, and a serine protease-like domain in the β subunit. Kringles are ~80 residue domains that contain loops connected in a canonical disulfide bonded pattern, and are thought to mediate protein-protein interactions. A fragment of HGF/SF called NK1, which contains the N-terminal hairpin and initial kringle domain, is sufficient to bind HGFR, and in the presence of glycosaminoglycans to cause activation. Glycosaminoglycans are thought to play a substantial role in HGFR activation through dimerization of monomeric HGF/SF, similar to the effect of these molecules on fibroblast growth factor and vascular endothelial growth factor activation of their cognate receptors. HGFR activation proceeds through receptor dimerization induced by dimeric ligand, and subsequent receptor autophosphorylation. In the absence of glycosaminoglycans, NK1 acts as an antagonist of HGF/SF-induced activation of HGFR. The structure of the NK1 domain reveals a patch of lysines and arginines that is likely to be a glycosaminoglycan binding site (Fig 2a) (Ultsch et al. 1998; Chirgadze et al. 1999).

Like HGF/SF, InlB LRR is a monomer, even at the high protein concentrations used for crystallization. Its ability to induce HGFR

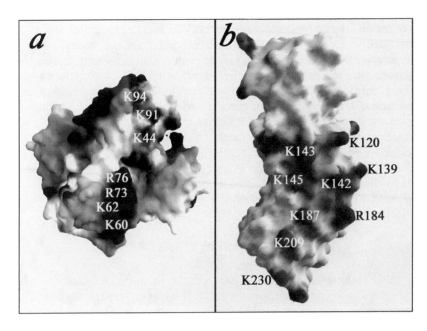

Fig. 2. Positively charged patches (black) on (a) HGF/SF NK1 and (b) InlB LRR.

activation suggests that either it may contain two receptor binding sites which can induce receptor dimerization in a 1:2 (ligand:receptor) complex, or that some other agent induces dimerization. A potential glycosaminoglycan binding site similar to the one in NK1 is observed in the InlB LRR domain. This region (K120, K139, K142, K143, K145, R184, K187, K209, K230) is located on an edge between the concave and convex faces of the LRR domain, in a lengthwise arrangement that is spatially suitable for binding an extended glycosaminoglycan polymer (Fig 2b). A second but smaller patch of positively charged residues (K89, K109, K131, K133, K175) is observed on the edge opposite to the first patch.

HGF/SF residues involved in receptor binding have been identified by mutagenesis studies (Lokker et al. 1994). Several of these residues (E159, F162, E195, and Y198) localize to a region in or near a pocket in the NK1 kringle domain that is similar to ligand-binding sites of other kringle domains (Fig. 3a). Intriguingly, the InlB LRR has a potentially analogous binding pocket on its concave surface (Fig. 3b). The pocket is formed by residues belonging to LRR positions 4 (W124), 6 (F104 and Y170), 8 (E194), and 9 (E129). The similarities in potential glycosaminoglycan and receptor binding sites between the structurally disparate molecules HGF/SF and InlB LRR are striking. The spatial analogy among these residues suggests that InlB may use molecular mimicry to bind and activate HGFR.

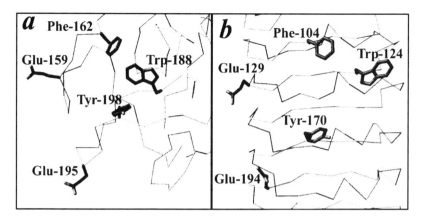

Fig. 3. Potential HGFR-binding sites in HGF/SF and InlB. (a) HGF/SF residues E159, F162, E195, and Y198 are required for wild type binding of HGFR. (b) Potential HGFR-binding site of the InlB LRR domain.

Literature Cited

Chirgadze, D. Y., Hepple, J. P., Zhou, H., Byrd, R. A., Blundell, T. L., and Gherardi, E. 1999. Crystal structure of the NK1 fragment of HGF/SF suggests a novel mode for growth factor dimerization and receptor binding. Nature Structural Biology 6:72-79.

Ireton, K., Payrastre, B., Chap, H., Ogawa, W., Sakaue, H., Kasuga, M., and Cossart, P. 1996. A role for phosphoinositide 3-kinase in bacterial invasion. Science 274:780-782.

Lokker, N. A., Presta, L. G., and Godowski, P. J. 1994. Mutational analysis and molecular modeling of the N-terminal kringle-containing domain of hepatocyte growth factor identifies amino acid side chains important for interaction with the c-Met receptor. Protein Engineering 7:895-903.

Marino, M., Braun, L., Cossart, P., and Ghosh, P. 1999. Structure of the InlB leucine-rich repeats, a domain that triggers host cell invasion by the bacterial pathogen *L. monocytogenes*. Molecular Cell 4:1063-1072.

Marino, M., Braun, L., Cossart, P., and Ghosh, P. 2000. A framework for interpreting the leucine-rich repeats of the *Listeria* internalins. Proc. Nat. Acad. Sci. USA 97:8784-8788.

Shen, Y., Naujokas, M., Park, M., and Ireton, K. 2000. InlB-dependent internalization of *Listeria* is mediated by the Met receptor tyrosine kinase. Cell 103:501-510.

Ultsch, M., Lokker, N. A., Godowski, P. J., and de Vos, A. M. 1998. Crystal structure of the NK1 fragment of human hepatocyte growth factor at 2.0 A resolution. Structure 6:1383-1393.

Structure-Function and Molecular Studies on Fungal Polygalacturonases and their Inhibitor PGIPs

G. De Lorenzo, C. Capodicasa, C. Caprari, L. Federici*, S. Ferrari, B. Mattei, A. Raiola, F. Sicilia, D. Vairo, A. Devoto, F. Cervone

Department of Plant Biology and *Department of Biochemical Sciences, University of Roma "La Sapienza", Roma, Italy

Polygalacturonase-inhibiting proteins (PGIPs) are extracellular plant proteins capable of inhibiting fungal endopolygalacturonases (PGs), which cause wall degradation and plant tissue maceration. PGs also release from the plant cell walls oligogalacturonides (OG), which are elicitors of a variety of defense responses. Elicitor-active OGs are produced by the action of PGs if the enzyme activity is controlled by PGIPs. As parasitic fungi tend to maintain PGs, recognition of these enzymes by PGIPs is an effective defense strategy devised for plant self-defense. Against the many PGs produced by fungi, plants have evolved different PGIPs with specific recognition abilities. PGIPs occur in a variety of dicotyledonous plants, as well as in the pectin-rich monocotyledonous plants onion and leek (De Lorenzo et al. 2001, and references therein).

PGIPs are typically effective against fungal PGs and ineffective against other pectic enzymes either from microbial or plant origin. Not only do PGIPs from different plant sources differ in their inhibitory activities, but also PGIPs from a single plant source inhibit, with different strength, PGs from different fungi or different PGs from the same fungus. Several observations indicate that total PGIP activity in some plants is a composite of different inhibitory activities (Desiderio et al. 1997).

The Genes Encoding PGIPs in *Phaseolus vulgaris* and Arabidopsis

Pgip genes have been cloned from many plants, where they usually exist as gene families (De Lorenzo et al. 2001, and references therein). Typically, *pgip* genes code for protein products comprising a signal peptide for secretion and a mature polypeptide of 300-315 amino acids with several potential glycosylation sites. The mature PGIP is characterized by the presence of 10 leucine-rich repeat (LRR) elements matching the extracytoplasmic consensus GxIPxxLxxLxxLxxLxLxxNxLx also found in several *R* genes, which participate in gene-for-gene resistance (De Lorenzo et al. 1994; Jones and Jones 1997).

In the genome of *P. vulgaris*, four *pgip* genes are clustered, as indicated by the isolation of two overlapping BAC clones which exhibit, in a Southern blot analysis, hybridization fragments corresponding to all the signals observed with total genomic DNA. The characterization of *Pvpgip1* and *Pvpgip2* provides a striking example of the structural diversification within a *pgip* gene family and its functional significance. The coding sequence of *Pvpgip1* and *Pvpgip2* differ by 26 nucleotides (Toubart et al. 1992; Leckie et al. 1999). The 11 nonsynonymous nucleotide substitutions show a nonrandom distribution as they occur within or very close to the regions encoding the xxLxLxx motifs predicted to form solvent-exposed β-sheet/β-turn structures important for ligand binding. The crucial role that nonsynonymous variations play in determining the recognition specificity of PGIP is discussed later. The genes *Pvpgip3* and *Pvpgip4* are closely related to each other (93.4% identity), but share only 79% identity with *Pvpgip1/Pvpgip2*.

Two Arabidopsis genes, *Atpgip1* and *Atpgip2,* which share 80% identity, are located 400 bp apart on chromosome 5.

Functional Characteristics of Homogeneous PGIPs

To date, only plants have been successfully used to express functional PGIPs. We have expressed all the isolated *pgip* genes of bean and Arabidopsis either stably through genetic transformation or transiently through infection of *Nicotiana benthamiana* with a modified potato virus X (PVX) (Desiderio et al. 1997; Leckie et al. 1999). The products of *Pvpgip1* and *Pvpgip2,* expressed either in transgenic tomato and tobacco plants or in PVX-infected *N. benthamiana* plants, exhibit identical inhibitory activity and specificity irrespective of the plant used for expression. PvPGIP2 is the most efficient inhibitor, with the broadest recognition specificity, whereas PvPGIP3 inhibits PG from *Colletotrichum* sp. and *Stenocarpella maydis* but does not inhibit PG of *F. moniliforme*. AtPGIP1 and AtPGIP2 separately expressed in transgenic Arabidopsis have been purified and shown to inhibit PG from *Colletotrichum* sp. and *B. cinerea* but not PGs from *A. niger* or *F. moniliforme*.

Pgip Genes are Differentially Regulated

The genes encoding PGIPs not only encode proteins with different specificity, but are also differentially regulated. Previous studies on the pattern of expression of the bean *pgip*s showed that several stress stimuli induce PGIP expression. Transcripts accumulate in suspension-cultured bean cells following addition of elicitors such as OGs and fungal glucan, and in *P. vulgaris* hypocotyls in response to wounding or treatment with salicylic acid (Bergmann et al. 1994). In the interaction between *C. lindemuthianum* and *P. vulgaris*, rapid accumulation of mRNA at the infection site correlates with the appearance of the hypersensitive response in incompatible interactions (Devoto et al. 1997; Nuss et al. 1996). RT-PCR analysis shows that *Pvpgip1, Pvpgip2* and *Pvpgip3* are regulated in a different manner. *Pvpgip2* transcripts are induced by wounding, salicylic acid, OGs and glucan, whereas *Pvpgip3* transcripts are induced by glucan and OGs, but not by wounding or salicylic acid; *Pvpgip1* responds to wounding only.

Northern blot analyses and functional studies of promoter::GUS fusions have been carried out to elucidate the regulation of the Arabidopsis *pgip* genes. Local transcript accumulation in response to wounding and pathogen infection has been observed for both *Atpgip1* and *Atpgip2*. The expression of both genes is induced upon infection with *B. cinerea*, or with avirulent *Pseudomonas syringae* pv *maculicola* carrying the *AvrRpt2* gene; induction by virulent bacteria occurs to a much lesser extent. Defense-related signals such as ethylene, salicylic acid, and methyl jasmonate do not activate *Atpgip1* expression; however, methyl jasmonate induces *Atpgip2*.

The Structural Basis of PG-PGIP Interaction

Modeling studies based on the known structure of the porcine RNAse inhibitor (PRI) (Kobe and Deisenhofer 1995) suggest that PGIP exhibits a parallel stacking of β-strand/β-turns, forming a solvent-exposed surface; the protein assumes an arch-shaped protein fold resembling that of the β-helical structure (Leckie et al. 1999). A detailed analysis of the secondary structure of PvPGIP2 by far-UV CD and infrared spectroscopies coupled to constrained prediction methods indicates the presence of 12 α and 12 β secondary structure segments. The protein consists of three domains, namely the central LRR region and two cysteine-rich flaking domains. Two N-linked oligosaccharides with a structure resembling the typical complex plant N-glycan are located on Asn 64 and Asn 141 (Mattei et al. 2001).

The mature proteins encoded by *Pvpgip1* and *Pvpgip2* of *P. vulgaris* differ by only 8 amino acid residues located preferentially within or contiguous to the motif xxLxLxx. The two proteins exhibit distinct specificities: PvPGIP1 is not able to interact with PG of *F. moniliforme* and interacts with PG of *A. niger*; PvPGIP2 interacts with both. The single mutation of a lysine at position 253 of PvPGIP1 into the corresponding amino acid of PvPGIP2, a glutamine, is sufficient to confer to the protein the capacity of interacting with *F. moniliforme* PG (Leckie et al. 1999).

These data provide evidence that variations in the solvent-exposed β-sheet/β-turn structure of PGIP have a functional significance and determine the discriminatory ability for a specific recognition of PG.

The residues of PG involved in the interaction with PGIP are also under investigation (Caprari et al. 1996). Recently, the 3-D structures of *F. moniliforme* PG has been elucidated. The enzyme exhibits, like other characterized pectic enzymes, an β-helix structure (Herron et al. 2000). The enzyme has a substrate binding cleft characterized by a highly positive electrostatic potential for the polyanionic polygalacturonic acid. Several amino acids of *F. moniliforme* PG, located inside or in proximity of the cleft, have been mutated and their contribution to the formation of the complex with PvPGIP2 has been investigated. The enzyme forms multiple contacts with the inhibitor; Lys269 and Arg 267, located inside the active side cleft, and His 188, at the edge of the active site cleft, are among the residues directly involved in the formation of the complex. Since Lys 269 and Arg 267 putatively bind the substrate at subsites +1 and −1, they cannot easily mutate without affecting the enzyme activity, and therefore their involvement in the interaction with PGIP minimizes the possibility for the fungal PGs to escape recognition.

Conclusions

PGIP, a widespread, if not ubiquitous, cell wall protein, exhibits features typical of the defence and pathogenesis-related proteins, and also belongs to the super-family of LRR proteins, which includes the LRR-based resistance gene products. The interaction between PGIPs and their ligand PGs is a unique model system to gain knowledge on the recognition specificity of LRR proteins in plants. Knowledge of the structural requirements that confer on PGIPs the ability of interacting specifically with their ligands can be exploited to devise in vitro mutagenesis-based strategies to obtain more efficient inhibitors, or inhibitors with novel recognition abilities. Improvement of resistance may therefore be obtained by transforming crop plants either with a set of different *pgip* genes with complementary recognition abilities, or with single genes with multiple specificities. Moreover, the information gained may pave the way to a "directed" manipulation of the LRR receptor proteins structurally related to PGIPs, for example to create new resistance traits in plants.

Acknowledgements

We thank the Armenise-Harvard Foundation and the Institute Pasteur-Fondazione Cenci Bolognetti for supporting our research.

Literature Cited

Bergmann, C., Y. Ito, D. Singer, P. Albersheim, A. G. Darvill, N. Benhamou, L. Nuss, G. Salvi, F. Cervone, and G. De Lorenzo. 1994. Polygalacturonase-inhibiting protein accumulates in *Phaseolus vulgaris* L. in response to wounding, elicitors, and fungal infection. Plant J. 5:625-634.

Caprari, C., B. Mattei, M. L. Basile, G. Salvi, V. Crescenzi, G. De Lorenzo, and F. Cervone. 1996. Mutagenesis of endopolygalacturonase from *Fusarium moniliforme*: Histidine residue 234 is critical for enzymatic and macerating activities and not for binding to polygalacturonase-inhibiting protein (PGIP). Mol.Plant-Microbe Interact. 9:617-624.

De Lorenzo, G., F. Cervone, D. Bellincampi, C. Caprari, A. J. Clark, A. Desiderio, A. Devoto, R. Forrest, F. Leckie, L. Nuss, and G. Salvi. 1994. Polygalacturonase, PGIP and oligogalacturonides in cell-cell communication. Biochem.Soc.Trans. 22:396-399.

De Lorenzo, G., R. D'Ovidio, and F. Cervone. 2001. The role of polygacturonase-inhibiting proteins (PGIPs) in defense against pathogenic fungi. Annu.Rev.Phytopathol. 39:313-335.

Desiderio, A., B. Aracri, F. Leckie, B. Mattei, G. Salvi, H. Tigelaar, J. S. C. Van Roekel, D. C. Baulcombe, L. S. Melchers, G. De Lorenzo, and F. Cervone. 1997. Polygalacturonase-inhibiting proteins (PGIPs) with different specificities are expressed in *Phaseolus vulgaris*. Mol.Plant-Microbe Interact. 10:852-860.

Devoto, A., A. J. Clark, L. Nuss, F. Cervone, and G. De Lorenzo. 1997. Developmental and pathogen-induced accumulation of transcripts of poly-galacturonase-inhibiting protein in *Phaseolus vulgaris* L. Planta. 202:284-292.

Herron, S. R., J. A. Benen, R. D. Scavetta, J. Visser, and F. Jurnak. 2000. Structure and function of pectic enzymes: virulence factors of plant pathogens. Proc.Natl.Acad.Sci.USA 97:8762-8769.

Jones, D. A. and J. D. G. Jones. 1997. The role of leucine-rich repeat proteins in plant defence. Adv.Bot.Res. 24:89-166.

Kobe, B. and J. Deisenhofer. 1995. A structural basis of the interactions between leucine-rich repeats and protein ligands. Nature 374:183-186.

Leckie, F., B. Mattei, C. Capodicasa, A. Hemmings, L. Nuss, B. Aracri, G. De Lorenzo, and F. Cervone. 1999. The specificity of polygalacturonase-inhibiting protein (PGIP): a single amino acid substitution in the solvent-exposed β- strand/β-turn region of the leucine-rich repeats (LRRs) confers a new recognition capability. EMBO J. 18:2352-2363.

Mattei, B., M. S. Bernalda, L. Federici, P. Roepstorff, F. Cervone, and A. Boffi. 2001. Secondary structure and post-translational modifications of the leucine-rich repeat protein PGIP (polygalacturonase-inhibiting protein) from *Phaseolus vulgaris*. Biochem. 40:569-576.

Nuss, L., A. Mahé, A. J. Clark, J. Grisvard, M. Dron, F. Cervone, and G. De Lorenzo. 1996. Differential accumulation of polygalacturonase-inhibiting protein (PGIP) mRNA in two near-isogenic lines of *Phaseolus vulgaris* L. upon infection with *Colletotrichum lindemuthianum*. Physiol.Mol.Plant Pathol. 48:83-89.

Toubart, P., A. Desiderio, G. Salvi, F. Cervone, L. Daroda, G. De Lorenzo, C. Bergmann, A. G. Darvill, and P. Albersheim. 1992. Cloning and characterization of the gene encoding the endopolygalacturonase-inhibiting protein (PGIP) of *Phaseolus vulgaris* L. Plant J. 2:367-373.

NBS-LRR R Gene Products: Functional Domains and Divergent Downstream Transcript Profiles

Andrew Bent[1,2], Jinrong Wan[1], Diya Banerjee[1,2], Eric Baima[2], Mark Dunning[1], Blake Meyers[3], Richard Michelmore[3], Christine Pfund[1], Gracia Zabala[2] and Xiaochun Zhang[2]

[1]University of Wisconsin – Madison, Madison, WI
[2]Formerly University of Illinois at Urbana-Champaign, Urbana, IL
[3]University of California - Davis, Davis, CA

Plant disease resistance genes (*R* genes) control recognition of pathogens and subsequent activation of a strong multi-factorial defense response (Ellis et al. 2000). Individual *R* genes are effective against pathogen strains that express an avirulence (*avr*) gene of matched specificity. *R* genes often encode NBS-LRR proteins that include a nucleotide binding site and a leucine-rich repeat domain. This chapter discusses our use of the *R* gene *RPS2* of Arabidopsis to study the function of the NBS and LRR domains. We also discuss both technical and biological findings from our use of oligonucleotide microarray expression profiling to compare the host responses mediated by four different *R/avr* interactions.

Studies of the NBS Domain

Putative nucleotide binding sites have been identified in a wide variety of proteins (Traut 1994), but their role in *R* gene function is not understood. Paradigms for the function of NBS domains in the regulation of signal transduction are suggested by the very well-studied mammalian oncogene Ras and related small monomeric GTP-binding proteins (Coleman and Sprang 1996). Signaling is active when Ras is in the GTP-bound state and inactive in the GDP-bound state. Accessory proteins associate with Ras and, in response to external stimuli, foster a GDP-GTP exchange reaction that activates signaling, or a GTP hydrolysis activity that inactivates signaling.

To initiate functional investigation of the NBS of NBS-LRR *R* gene products, we have pursued two projects: *in vivo* function tests of *RPS2* NBS mutants and *in vitro* biochemical studies of nucleotide binding using recombinant RPS2 protein. Our site-directed mutagenesis has focused on the P-loop domain of the NBS0. A set of eleven new *RPS2* alleles were generated and then moved back into Arabidopsis *rps2/rps2* mutant plant lines to test the disease resistance function of these new alleles (unpublished data). Plants were stably transformed with the new *RPS2* alleles expressed under control of the native *RPS2* promoter. We found that mutation of functionally conserved P-loop residues such as K_{188} or T_{189} disrupted function (induction of the hypersensitive response and ability to restrict growth of *P. syringae* pv. *tomato* strain DC3000 expressing *avrRpt2*). Although we have not confirmed expression of RPS2 protein in plants carrying the novel *RPS2* alleles, similar mutations are known to cause only subtle structural shifts in other NBS proteins for which x-ray crystal structure data are available (e.g., ref. (Muegge et al. 1996)), and other *RPS2* alleles studied in this set of experiments retained function in plants. These results provide evidence that the NBS domain is critical for the disease resistance function of NBS-LRR gene products. The Baker and Katagiri labs have reached similar conclusions (Dinesh-Kumar et al. 2000; Tao et al. 2000).

In addition to NBS amino acid changes that disrupt function, we also identified more subtle changes that are allowable. For example, within the canonical P-loop sequence GxxxxGK(T/S), a serine-threonine substitution ($T_{189}S$) allele of *RPS2* apparently retained full function.

In vitro study of NBS-LRR proteins has been hindered by the difficulties many laboratories have experienced in expressing and purifying full-length protein for these *R* gene products. We have used an *E. coli* expression system to express GST-RPS2. The photo-crosslinkable 8-azido ^{32}P-nucleotide analogs were then used to study nucleotide binding by RPS2 (unpublished data). These reagents are noted for their low cross-reactivity at non-specific binding sites (Haley 1991). We have observed nucleotide binding activity of RPS2 that is Mg^{2+} dependent. While yields of recombinant RPS2 protein are modest and are not 100% pure, we can use the size-shift following thrombin cleavage of the GST segment to track RPS2 in SDS-PAGE gels and confirm that nucleotide binding activity is not due to a co-migrating contaminant. Hence the putative nucleotide binding sites observed in *R* gene derived amino acid sequences do, at least in the case of RPS2, appear to function as a true nucleotide binding sites. Both ATP and GTP will bind, and we are now working to determine the relative preference of RPS2 for binding of different nucleotides.

Studies of the LRR Domain

The LRR-encoding domain is known to determine pathogen recognition specificity in a number of *R* genes (Ellis et al. 2000). We have recently observed that the LRR can also determine effective interaction with other host factors. Our studies of the LRR domain were initiated when we observed allele-specific interaction between *RPS2* and other loci in

Arabidopsis ecotypes Po-1 and Col-0. *RPS2* from Col-0 functions in both ecotypes, but *RPS2* from Po-1 functions only in Col-0 and not in Po-1. We performed domain-swap experiments between the promoter, amino-terminal and LRR-encoding domains of *RPS2* from Po-1 and Col-0 to discover that the LRR domain determines effective interaction with other host proteins. An *RPS2* allele carrying the Col-0 *RPS2* LRR domain fused with the Po-1 *RPS2* promoter and amino-terminus functions in either ecotype, while the Po-1 LRR domain fused to Col-0 *RPS2* promoter and amino-terminus only functions in Col-0 and not in Po-1. Six amino acids differentiate the LRR domains encoded by the Po-1 and Col-0 alleles. One or more of these amino acids apparently accounts for the differential functionality. More generally, these results demonstrate that the LRR of NBS-LRR *R* gene products not only can control pathogen recognition specificity, but can also control effective interaction with other host factors. These studies were recently published (Banerjee et al. 2001).

Expression Profiling of Plant Responses Mediated by Different *R* genes

We are interested to learn about differences as well as similarities in the defense activation processes mediated by different *R* genes. We hope to relate the structures of different *R* gene products to the downstream signaling pathways that they activate. Some differences between different *R* gene pathways are already known (Glazebrook 2001).

As part of this work, we have been studying the mRNA expression profiles in plants carrying out different *R/avr* responses (unpublished data). We adopted a highly isogenic experimental system for this work, using Arabidopsis ecotype Col-0 (contains *RPS2, RPM1, RPS5*, and *RPS4*) and *P. syringae* strains that differ only by the presence of a single cloned avr gene (*avrRpt2, avrRpm1, avrPphB,* or *avrRps4*). Changes in mRNA level were monitored using Affymetrix GeneChip Arabidopsis Genome Arrays, which interrogate approximately 8,200 Arabidopsis genes with 16 different oligonucleotide probe-pairs per gene (Zhu and Wang 2000). Two different vehicles were used for Avr signal delivery: *P. syringae* pv. *tomato* strain DC3000 (virulent on Arabidopsis), and *P. syringae* pv. *glycinea* strain R4 (virulent on soybean, non-virulent on Arabidopsis, but still delivers *avr* gene signals to Arabidopsis to elicit *R/avr*-dependent host responses).

TECHNICAL CONSIDERATIONS

Technical issues merit close attention at this stage in the adoption of expression profiling technologies. Our experiments involved six treatments (*P. syringae* + one of four *avr* genes, *P. syringae* carrying plasmid vector with no *avr* gene, or mock-inoculation with buffer only). Treatments and RNA processing within an experiment were done in parallel to maximize equivalent handling of all six treatments. For each chip, RNA was pooled on an equal-mass basis from three sets of plants grown under similar environmental settings but at separate locations. All experiments were done at the same time in the diurnal cycle.

Reproducibility of the experimental system was examined by doing each experiment on two separate dates. Perhaps not surprisingly, we observed that such replication is essential to avoid erroneous findings. Affymetrix arrays give extremely reproducible results when the same RNA sample is tested on two separate arrays. In addition, we found that levels of any given transcript correlated very well between two entirely separate replicate treatments (r typically >0.9). However, when fold-induction is calculated ([transcript level in treatment] / [transcript level in control]), reproducibility was poor between biological replications (example: r = 0.55).

Expression profile data analysis methods typically seek to identify differentially regulated transcripts, but many commonly available methods lack statistical validity. For example, an "average fold-change" of 2.5 might be called significant, but may result from a poorly reproducible result in which the fold-changes in two replicates were 4.1 and 0.9. Removal of data for which treatment and control both give low transcript levels (near the signal:noise limit) is essential, but only partially corrects this problem. Affymetrix "Difference Calls," while lacking statistical support, do represent an improvement over "average fold-change" in that they take into account other signal-to-noise issues of the technology. However, we found that the recently developed "dChip" program provides many benefits (Li and Wong 2001). This program performs statistical tests across multiple chips from related experiments. Raw data for each oligonucleotide are compared across chips, and data are removed from further analysis for oligonucleotides that did not follow the trend of most of the 16 oligonucleotide probe-pairs for a given gene (due for example to small contaminating particles or scratches in the array image, or more importantly, due to cross-hybridization of a given oligonucleotide to other transcripts). Equally important, the dChip program establishes statistical confidence intervals for each transcript level determination. The "lower bound of the confidence interval for fold-change" appears to be a more reliable indicator as one seeks to identify transcripts that show differential abundance between biological treatments.

We also find that quantitative data can be difficult for researchers to view and interpret. Evaluation of results is expedited by assignment of quantitative fold-change data to one of a few qualitative categories ("no-change" "moderate increase" "strong increase") prior to clustering of transcripts into groups of similarly regulated genes

BIOLOGICAL FINDINGS

Initial analyses of our data revealed approximately 300 genes that showed differential transcript abundance between different treatments. The data are being used to start defining "fingerprints" - sets of genes that are commonly regulated by most or all *R/avr* interactions, or only by particular subsets of *R/avr* interactions.

We were intrigued to observe substantially different expression profiles depending on whether the same Avr signal was delivered by the virulent Pst strain DC3000 or the non-virulent Psg strain R4. Many phenomena other than *R/avr* signaling are underway during every gene-for-gene interaction, and these other levels of host-pathogen interaction can influence not only the "background" expression profile, but also the *R/avr*-dependent signaling events. Comparison of the profiles obtained for the Pst and Psg strains in the absence of a cloned *avr* gene is of substantial interest.

We note (again not surprisingly) that very different gene sets are identified depending on the control or "denominator" that is used for fold-change calculations. This control can for example be the transcript level for untreated plants, or for mock-inoculated plants, or for plants inoculated with the pathogen strain not carrying the cloned *avr* gene.

Some of the ~300 differentially regulated genes are the chitinases, glucanases and other PR proteins that have previously been associated with plant defense responses. A small number of apparent *R* genes show differential expression. However, most of the differentially regulated genes were previously characterized only in a generic sense (similar to cytochrome P450, or protein kinase, or lipase, or myb transcription factor, etc.), or encode totally unknown proteins. Further study of these genes, for example using gene-knockout or gene-silenced plants, is clearly of interest.

Literature Cited

Banerjee, D., Zhang, Z., and Bent, A. F. 2001. The LRR domain can determine effective interaction between *RPS2* and other host factors in Arabidopsis *RPS2*-mediated disease resistance. Genetics 158:439-450.

Coleman, D. E., and Sprang, S. R. 1996. How G proteins work: a continuing story. Trends Biochem. Sci. 21:41-44.

Dinesh-Kumar, S. P., Tham, W. H., and Baker, B. J. 2000. Structure-function analysis of the tobacco mosaic virus resistance gene *N*. Proc. Natl. Acad. Sci. U S A 97:14789-94.

Ellis, J., Dodds, P., and Pryor, T. 2000. Structure, function and evolution of plant disease resistance genes. Curr. Opin. Plant Biol. 3:278-84.

Glazebrook, J. 2001. Genes controlling expression of defense responses in Arabidopsis--2001 status. Curr. Opin. Plant Biol. 4:301-8.

Haley, B. E. 1991. Nucleotide photoaffinity labeling of protein kinase subunits. Meth.. Enzymol.. 200:477-487.

Li, C., and Wong, W. H. 2001. Model-based analysis of oligonucleotide arrays: model validation, design issues and standard error application. Genome Biol. 2:http://genomebiology.com/2001/2/8/research/0032.1.

Muegge, I., Schweins, T., Langen, R., and Warshel, A. 1996. Electrostatic control of GTP and GDP binding in the oncoprotein p21ras. Structure 4:475-489.

Tao, Y., Yuan, F., Leister, R. T., Ausubel, F. M., and Katagiri, F. 2000. Mutational Analysis of the Arabidopsis Nucleotide Binding Site-Leucine-Rich Repeat Resistance Gene *RPS2*. Plant Cell 12:2541-2554.

Traut, T. W. 1994. The functions and consensus motifs of nine types of peptide segments that form different types of nucleotide-binding sites. Eur. J. Biochem. 222:9-19.

Zhu, T., and Wang, X. 2000. Large-scale profiling of the Arabidopsis transcriptome. Plant Physiol. 124:1472-6.

Recognition of *Pseudomonas* Effector Proteins by Tomato and Profiling of Plant Gene Expression Changes that Occur During Plant-Pathogen Interactions

Timothy P. Devarenne, Brendan K. Riely, Nai-Chun Lin, Young-Jin Kim, Jonathan Cohn, Kirankumar Mysore, Suma Charkravarthy, Adam J. Bogdanove, Mark D'Ascenzo, Paul Debbie, Bob Tuori and Gregory B. Martin

Boyce Thompson Institute for Plant Research and Cornell University Ithaca, NY 14853-1801

Bacterial Speck Disease Resistance in Tomato

The molecular basis of "gene-for-gene" resistance in *Pseudomonas syringae* pv *tomato* infection of tomato lies in the interaction of Pto (a host R protein) and AvrPto (a bacterial Avr protein)(Scofield et al. 1996). Disease occurs when either the *Pto* or *avrPto* genes are lacking from the corresponding organism. The *Pto* gene encodes a serine/threonine protein kinase that is likely to be localized in the plant cell cytoplasm (Martin et al. 1993). The *avrPto* gene encodes a small hydrophilic protein that likely enters the plant cell through a type III secretion system (Ronald et al. 1992; van Dijk et al. 1999). The recognition of AvrPto by Pto is determined by a single threonine residue in Pto and leads to changes in gene expression (Frederick et al., 1998; Zhou et al. 1998). Additional defense responses such as the oxidative burst, nitric oxide production, and the hypersensitive response (HR) ultimately leads to disease resistance.

The recent characterization of several other genes involved in Pto-mediated resistance further enhances the potential of this system for understanding host recognition of a bacterial effector proteins. We have isolated the *Pti1* (Pto-interactor 1) gene, which encodes a protein kinase that is phosphorylated by Pto, and three genes, Pti4, Pti5, and Pti6, that encode defense related transcription factors (Zhou et al. 1995; 1997). By using a yeast three-hybrid system five AvrPto-Pto dependent interactor (Adi) proteins have been identified that interact specifically with the AvrPto-Pto complex and may play a role in resistance to pathogens (Bogdanove and Martin 2000).

Recognition and Signaling Events Involving the Pto Kinase and *Pseudomonas* Effector Proteins

LOCALIZATION OF PTO AND AVRPTO PROTEINS IN THE PLANT CELL

AvrPto contains a myristylation motif (MGNICV) at its N terminus which is required for localization of the protein to the plasma membrane of the plant cell (Shan et al. 2000a). Substitution of the potentially myristylated glycine residue with alanine (G2A) abolishes the avirulence activity of AvrPto in the plant cell as well as its localization to the plasma membrane. However, this G2A mutation in AvrPto does not affect its interaction with Pto (Shan et al. 2000a). These data suggest a model in which the localization of AvrPto to the plant cell membrane recruits Pto to the cell membrane as an initial event in the recognition process. In order to study this process *in vivo* we have generated expression constructs to produce AvrPto:GFP and Pto:GFP chimeric proteins. Analysis of the transiently expressed GFP chimeric proteins in *Nicotiana benthamiana* by confocal microscopy for GFP expression indicates that the AvrPto:GFP protein is localized to the plasma membrane while the AvrPto:GFP (G2A) myristylation mutant is not. While Pto contains a putative myristylation motif, Pto:GFP does not appear to be localized to the plasma membrane. Experiments to analyze Pto:GFP cell localization when co-transiently expressed with AvrPto:GFP are underway.

DISCOVERY AND CHARACTERIZATION OF A SECOND *PSEUDOMONAS* EFFECTOR PROTEIN THAT INTERACTS WITH PTO

We have recently identified another *Pseudomonas* effector gene, *avrPto2*, from *P. syringae* pv. *tomato* strain DC3000 that encodes a protein which interacts with the Pto kinase in a yeast two-hybrid system. AvrPto2 protein is about 40% similar to VirPphA from *P. s. phaseolicola* (Jackson et al. 1999). Southern hybridization analysis revealed that almost all *P. syringae* pathovars contain *avrPto2* homologs and alignment of the predicted amino acid sequences of these *avrPto2* genes indicates conservation at the N- and C- terminus with high variability in the center portion of the proteins. Like AvrPto, AvrPto2 is predicted to be secreted into the plant cell by the type III secretion system and it elicits resistance in tomato plants containing *Pto*. However, AvrPto2 does not contain a myristylation motif. Transient expression of an AvrPto2::GFP construct in *N. benthamiana* and analysis of GFP expression by confocal microscopy indicates that AvrPto2 is not localized to the plant cell periphery.

Alignment of AvrPto and AvrPto2 indicates that overall the proteins do not share a high degree of similarity. However, several small regions appear to be conserved and may indicate the region by which they interact with Pto.

We are also investigating signal transduction steps that lie downstream of the Pto kinase. By using a yeast two-hybrid screen for Pto interacting proteins three transcription factors, Pti4, Pti5, and Pti6 were identified and later found to bind the GCC-box cis element present in the promoters of many pathogenesis-related (*PR*) genes (Zhou et al. 1997). Pti4 and Pti5 are similar to ethylene-responsive element binding proteins (Thara et al. 1999). Thus, they potentially define a key link between pathogen recognition and activation of defense response genes. We have found that the Pti4 protein is specifically phosphorylated by the Pto kinase, and that this phosphorylation enhances binding of Pti4 to the GCC-box. Pti4 is also induced by salicylic acid (SA) and ethylene which is consistent with SA and ethylene being implicated as mediators of defense responses (Gu et al. 2000). In addition, we have found that overexpression of Pti4 in Arabidopsis leads to overexpression of a variety of defense-related genes and to a decrease in symptoms after bacterial or fungal infection of leaves.

AVRPTO PROMOTES DISEASE PROGRESSION WHEN PTO IS ABSENT FROM THE PLANT HOST

It has always seemed counterintuitive that a pathogen would deliver a protein to a host cell that allows it to be recognized. Although the original work with *avrPto* gene focused on its Avr activity it has recently been shown that expression of *avrPto* in the pathogen when *Pto* is absent from the plant host leads to increased pathogen growth (Chang et al. 2000; Shan et al. 2000b). Interestingly, three mutations in AvrPto that abolished interaction with Pto and eliminated AvrPto avirulence activity had no effect on virulence activity of this protein (Shan et al. 2000b). Other possible manifestations of virulence activity are observable when *avrPto* is expressed directly in leaves of tomato and tobacco using a transient expression system. In tobacco, expression of *avrPto* in leaf cells causes chlorosis within 2-3 days while expression in tomato produces cell death within the same time frame. Possible host targets of susceptibility have been identified by using AvrPto in a yeast two-hybrid system with a tomato cDNA library as the prey (Bogdanove and Martin 2000). Four such AvrPto-interacting (Api) proteins were identified: 1) Api1, similar to a stress-related protein from field bean (*Phaseolus vulgaris*); 2) Api2, a Rab8-like GTP binding protein; 3) Api3, another Rab-like protein; and 4) Api4, a myristyl-CoA protein N-myristyltransferase. The possible involvement of the Api proteins in promoting AvrPto virulence is currently being investigated.

A Model for the Compatible and Incompatible Interactions of *Pseudomonas syringae* pv *tomato* and Tomato

Based on the findings discussed above, a model has been proposed for AvrPto avirulence activity (incompatible interaction) in which AvrPto is secreted into the plant cell and localized to the cell membrane. This recruits Pto to the cell membrane and the physical interaction of Pto and AvrPto (possibly involving the Adi proteins and/or the Prf protein) activates the Pto kinase. Activated Pto then phosphorylates and activates diverse downstream target proteins, each with a unique role in the resistance response (Fig. 1, right; Cohn and Martin 2001). The Pti1 kinase is one such target and is involved in the HR leading to localized cell death. The Pti4/5/6 transcription factors are involved in a separate pathway leading to activation of certain PR genes. In the absence of Pto, AvrPto exhibits virulence activity (compatible interaction) and Api1/2/3/4 are host proteins that may be targets of AvrPto. Inhibition of these proteins may inhibit plant defense responses and lead to disease development (Fig. 1, left).

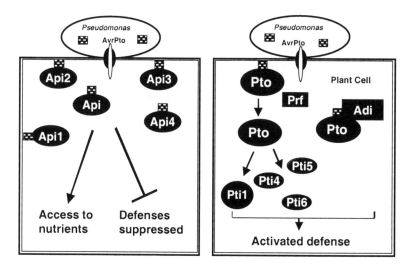

Fig. 1. A model for AvrPto virulence activity (left) and avirulence activity (right) during infection of tomato leaves by *Pseudomonas syringae* pv. *tomato*.

Profiling Plant Gene Expression Changes that Occur in Response to Pto Recognition of AvrPto

We have utilized three methods to identify genes that are differentially expressed in the incompatible Pto/AvrPto interaction in order to array these genes on microscope slides for a detailed analysis of gene expression during the Pto/AvrPto interaction. The first two methods are cDNA and computer based subtraction methods to identify differentially expressed genes between *Pseudomonas syringae* pv *tomato* (*avrPto*) infected Pto overexpressing plants and plants lacking Pto. The third method is a gel based, mRNA-profiling technique termed GeneCalling (done in association with CuraGen Corporation) that was utilized to identify differentially expressed genes from both a compatible and incompatible *Pseudomonas*-tomato interaction. All together over 700 EST clones and controls were arrayed, in triplicate, on microarray slides and probed with fluorescently labeled RNA from resistant and susceptible tomato plants challenged with an avirulent strain of *P. syringae* pv *tomato*. Analysis of the microarrays indicated that over 100 genes were differentially expressed in response to the pathogen. Genes whose expression was induced in response to the pathogen include genes from the ubiquitination pathway, PR genes, the phenylpropanoid pathway, transcription factors, genes related to the oxidative burst and programmed cell death, and the jasmonic acid pathway. Genes whose expression was suppressed include those associated with cell wall degradation and photosynthesis. This method is allowing us to analyze alterations in total gene expression and to build an overall picture of the cell processes affected in response to pathogen attack on tomato.

Literature Cited

Bogdanove, A.J., Martin, G.B. 2000. AvrPto-dependent Pto-interacting proteins and AvrPto-interacting proteins in tomato. Proc. Natl. Acad. Sci. US*A* 97:8836-8840.

Chang, J.H., et al. 2000. *avrPto* enhances growth and necrosis caused by Pseudomonas syringae pv tomato in tomato lines lacking either *Pto* or *Prf*. Mol. Plant-Microbe Interac. 13:568-571.

Cohn, J., Martin, G.B. 2001. Pathogen recognition and signal transduction in plant immunity. in: Infectious Diseases, in press.

van Dijk, K., et al. 1999. The Avr (effector) proteins HrmA(HopPsyA) and AvrPto are secreted in culture from *Pseudomonas syringae* pathovars via the Hrp (Type III) protein secretion system in a temperature- and pH-sensitive manner. J. Bacteriol. 181:4790-4797.

Frederick, R.D., et al. 1998. Recognition specificity for the bacterial avirulence protein AvrPto is determined by Thr-204 in the activation loop of the tomato Pto kinase. Mol. Cell 2:241-5.

Gu, Y-Q., et al. 2000. Pti4 is induced by ehtylene and salicylic acid, and its product is phosphorylated by the Pto kinase. Plant Cell 12:771-785.

Jackson et al. 1999. Identification of a pathogenicity island, which contains genes for virulence and avirulence, on a large native plasmid in the bean pathogen *Pseudomonas syringae* pathovar *phaseolicola*. Proc. Natl. Acad. Sci. USA 96:10875-10880.

Martin, G.B., et al. 1993. Map-based cloning of a protein kinase gene conferring disease resistance in tomato. Science 262:1432-1436.

Ronald, P.C., et al. 1992 The cloned avirulence gene *avrPto* induces disease resistance in tomato cultivars containing the *Pto* resistance gene. J. Bacteriol. 174:1604-1611.

Scofield, S.R., et al. 1996. Molecular basis of gene-for-gene specificity in bacterial speck disease of tomato. Science 274:2063-2065.

Shan, L., et al. 2000a. The *Pseudomonas* AvrPto protein is differentially recognized by tomato and tobacco and is localized to the plant plasma membrane. Plant Cell 12:2323-2337.

Shan, L., et al. 2000b. A cluster of mutations disrupt the avirulence but not the virulence function of AvrPto. Mol. Plant-Microbe Interac. 13:592-598.

Thara, V.K., et al. 1999. Pseudomonas syringae pv tomato induces the expression of tomato EREBP-like genes Pti4 and Pti5 independent of ethylene salicylate, and jasmonate. Plant J. 20:475-483.

Zhou, J., et al. 1997. The Pto kinase conferring resistance to tomato bacterial speck disease interacts with proteins that bind a cis-element of pathogenesis-related genes. EMBO J. 16:3207-3218.

Zhou, J., et al. 1998. Pathogen recognition and signal transduction by the Pto kinase. J. Plant Sci Res. 111:353-356.

Towards the Elucidation of the Pathway
Leading to Salicylic Acid Biosynthesis

Christiane Nawrath and Jean-Pierre Métraux

University of Fribourg, Department of Biology, 1700 Fribourg, Switzerland.

Salicylic acid (SA) plays an important physiological role in the induction of plant defense responses against several types of pathogens, including viruses, bacteria, fungi and oomycetes. Resistance to pathogens is often correlated with programmed cell death also referred to as the hypersensitive response (HR). An intricate relationship between SA and cell death has been discovered indicating that SA is both required for and induced by cell death. Necrosis appears to be an important component for the induction and maintenance of systemic acquired resistance (SAR), a long-lasting broad-spectrum resistance to different pathogens. Whether or not SA acts as the primary systemic signal for SAR is still under debate. SA also plays an important role in decreasing the damage caused by virulent pathogens. Recent advances in the understanding of the role of SA in cell death and plant disease resistance have been described in a detailed review (Alvarez 2000).

NahG Plants as a Model for SA-Deficient Plants

Most of our knowledge on the biological role of SA in plant disease resistance comes from transgenic NahG plants expressing a SA hydroxylase that potently degrades SA. In Arabidopsis, NahG plants are hypersusceptible to virulent and avirulent pathogens and cannot establish SAR (Delaney et al. 1994). In these interactions, NahG plants do not express the pathogenesis-related proteins PR-1, PR-2 and PR-5. In addition, they accumulate only small amounts of the phytoalexin camalexin in comparison to wild-type plants (Zhao and Last 1996). NahG plants have been extensively used to evaluate the importance of SA for different plant-pathogen interactions and have played a central role for the dissection of the signal transduction pathway resulting in plant resistance in Arabidopsis (reviewed in Glazebrook 1999). Several indications have also accumulated indicating that NahG plants might have more defects than only an inability to accumulate SA (Cameron 2000).

Induction of the SA-Biosynthesis Pathway

Plants have developed a large network of defense pathways in which SA represents one of several key players besides JA and ethylene (Dong, 1998; Feys and Parker 2000). Arabidopsis mutants, such as *eds1, ndr1 and pad4* are impaired in the activation of the SA-dependent signaling pathway after attack with certain strains of *Pseudomonas syringae* and *Peronospora parasitica* (Feys and Parker 2000; Glazebrook 1999). These mutants led to the identification of genes and proteins acting upstream of SA. EDS1 is required for the activation of defense after pathogen recognition via the TIR-NBS-LRR class of R-genes. In contrast, NDR1 is involved in the activation of the pathway after pathogen recognition via R-genes of the LZ-NBS-LRR structure (Aarts et al. 1999). PAD4 can restrict damage after attack by virulent as well as by certain avirulent pathogens (Glazebrook et al. 1997). After inoculation with virulent *P. syringae, pad4* is impaired in the accumulation of SA, the expression of PR-1 as well as the accumulation of camalexin (Zhou et al. 1998). Similarly as in NahG plants, both PR-1 expression and camalexin production seem to be under the control of SA. The *eds1* mutant also fails in the induction of defense responses after inoculation with virulent pathogens (Feys and Parker 2000). The *EDS1* and *PAD4* genes have been cloned and both encode proteins of the L-lipase class (Falk et al. 1999; Jirage et al. 1999). Both proteins seem to have a similar mode of action in plant defense although their function as lipases has not been demonstrated. NDR1 has also been cloned and encodes a novel membrane bound protein (Century et al. 1997). In addition, a number of mutants have been identified that show a constitutive or lesion-dependent activation of the SA biosynthesis pathway (reviewed in Glazebrook 1999; Alvarez 2000).

The Biosynthetic Pathway of SA

In the last few years, little progress has been made in characterizing the SA biosynthesis pathway itself. A number of experiments demonstrated that SA is synthesized from phenylalanine via cinnamic and benzoic acid (Lee et al. 1995; Coquoz et al. 1998). Mutants with a general block in SA biosynthesis have not been identified until quite recently and no genes have been isolated so far that encode proteins directly involved in SA biosynthesis.

Characterization of the *sid* Mutants

The SA-biosynthesis pathway was studied using a genetic approach in Arabidopsis. By screening directly for the amount of SA in a mutagenized plant population, two mutants were identified that did not accumulate SA after inoculation with *Pseudomonas syringae* carrying the *avrRpt2* gene (Nawrath and Métraux 1999). The mutants were called SA-induction deficient (*sid*). The *sid* mutants do not accumulate SA after inoculation with either virulent or avirulent *P. syringae* and *P. parasitica* strains nor after a number of abiotic stresses that have been shown to lead to SA accumulation, e.g. ozone, UV-C light and callus-inducing hormone treatments. The *sid* mutants most likely have a general block in the SA-biosynthesis, since they are not able to degrade exogenously applied SA.

Characterization of the *sid* mutants revealed that both *sid1* and *sid2* behave similarly in all experiments undertaken. Both *sid1* and *sid2* are hypersusceptible to virulent and avirulent strains of *Pseudomonas syringae* and *Peronospora parasitica* and immunization with avirulent *Pseudomonas* leads only to a very weak SAR. Interestingly, in all experiments the *sid* mutants were not as susceptible as NahG plants. Molecular analysis of the defense responses showed that *sid1* and *sid2* mutants are only strongly impaired in the expression of *PR-1* but not of the *PR-2* and *PR-5* genes. Furthermore, *sid* mutants accumulate high levels of camalexin unlike NahG plants, while having low amounts of SA similar to NahG plants.

The signal transduction pathway leading to camalexin accumulation and to the induction of *PR-2* and *PR-5* leaves open questions that have been addressed by constructing double mutants such as *sid1*NahG, *sid2*NahG as well as *sid1pad4* and *sid2pad4*. All 4 double mutants display both low SA and camalexin levels after pathogen infection with *P. syringae* demonstrating that *pad4* and NahG act epistatically to the *sid* mutations. A possible interpretation of these results is that *sid* mutants are only affected in SA-signaling and that PAD4 and NahG can also act independently of SA in other signaling pathways. Further investigations are currently been undertaken to fully understand these results.

Mapping of the *sid* mutations to the Arabidopsis genome located *SID1* on the bottom of chromosome 4 and *SID2* on the bottom of chromosome 1. The *sid1* gene was found to be allelic to *eds5*, a mutant reported earlier to have low amounts of PR-1 after inoculation with a virulent *P. syringae* strain (Rogers and Ausubel 1997), and *sid1* has been renamed *eds5-3* (Nawrath and Métraux 1999). Recently, *eds16*, a mutant susceptible to *Erysiphe orontii*, has been found to be allelic to *sid2* (Dewdney et al. 2000).

Cloning of the *EDS5* Gene

EDS5 has been cloned by a map-based cloning strategy (Nawrath et al. submitted). *EDS5* represents gene At4g39030 of the Arabidopsis genome. In contrast to the annotated sequence, *EDS5* has been found to have 4 more introns and thus covers a region of 3.5 kb. EDS5 encodes a protein of 543 amino acids. Computer programs predict that the major part of EDS5 protein might form 9-11 membrane-spanning domains and the hydrophilic domain at the N-terminus a coiled coil. EDS5 has a significant homology to members of the recently identified family of transporters that were named MATE (for multidrug and toxin extrusion) (Brown et al. 1999).

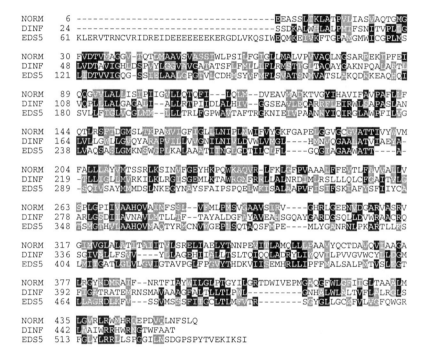

Fig. 1. Analyses of the protein sequence of EDS5.
Sequence alignment of the EDS5 protein (aa 61 to end) with the NORM protein of *V. parahaemolyticus* (aa 6 to end) and the DINF protein of *E. coli* (aa 24 to end). Invariant amino acids are highlighted in black, while similar amino acids are highlighted in grey.

In bacteria, NORM (for norfloxacin resistance M) of *Vibrio parahaemolyticus* and its homologs have been found to be multidrug transporters. NORM transports drugs in exchange for sodium (Morita et al. 2000). In addition, DINF (for DNA-damage inducible F) from *Escherichia coli* and other bacteria and archea belong to this transporter family (Brown et al. 1999). Although the transport function of DINF has not been characterized, it has been found that DINF is induced by UV-C light as SA-biosynthesis in plants (Kenyon and Walker 1980). The sequence alignment between EDS5, NORM and DINF is shown in Figure 1. Transporters of the MATE-family have also been found in the other kingdoms of life. In *Saccharomyces cerevisiae*, the MATE protein ERC1 (for ethionine resistance conferring1) has been proposed to transport ethionine to the vacuole (Shiomi et al. 1991). In Arabidopsis, the mutant *transparent testa 12* (*tt12*) blocked in flavonoid biosynthesis has recently been shown to be defective in a MATE protein that might be a vacuolar flavonoid-transporter (Debeaujon et al. 2001). Sequence comparisons have shown that EDS5 is more closely related to the bacterial proteins NORM and DINF than to ERC1 and TT12. In summary, MATE proteins are generally involved in the transport of organic molecules, and possibly in the transport of secondary metabolites in plants. EDS5 is therefore hypothesized to transport either a signaling molecule or a metabolite essential for SA biosynthesis.

Gene Expression Studies of *EDS5*

EDS5 transcript accumulates transiently after treatments that lead to SA accumulation, such as inoculation with different pathogens and UV-C light. Although a small basal amount of *EDS5* transcript is present in uninduced plants inducers of SA biosynthesis lead to a strong induction of *EDS5*. This induction in gene expression takes place before the first increase in the amounts of SA indicating that the transcriptional up-regulation may be necessary for the subsequent SA accumulation. However, the transient expression of EDS5 ceases already when the amounts of SA are still increasing possibly indicating a good stability the protein.

The expression of *EDS5* was analyzed after UV-C light exposure and inoculation with different pathogens in mutants blocked pathogen defense pathways. The expression of *EDS5* was reduced in *pad4*, *eds1* and *ndr1*, particularly when the plants were inoculated with pathogens to which these mutants have an enhanced susceptibility. This shows that EDS1, PAD4 and NDR1 are necessary for EDS5 expression after pathogen inoculation. EDS1, PAD4 and NDR1 are also involved in the induction of *EDS5* after UV-C light treatment.

EDS5 expression was found to be normal in the *sid2* mutant both after inoculation with pathogens or treatment with UV-C light. Therefore, SA does not seem to be essential for EDS5 expression. The fact that NahG plants express *EDS5* normally after UV-C light exposure, but show a strong reduction in reaction to pathogens might again indicate some unexpected epistatic effects of NahG on plant defence reactions. The *EDS5* gene expression is independent of *NPR1* expression as well as of the JA and ethylene signaling pathways as found by analysis the expression of *EDS5* in the *npr1*, *jar1*, and *etr1* mutants. A model for the transcriptional regulation of *EDS5* after inoculation with different strains of *P. syringae* is shown in Figure 2.

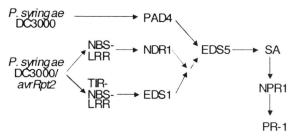

Fig. 2. Model for the transcriptional regulation of *EDS5* after inoculation with virulent and avirulent *P. syringae* strains

Concluding Remarks

The analysis of the *eds5* and *sid2* mutants has given new insights into the SA-dependent pathogen response pathway and uncovered hitherto unexpected complexities. The subsequent cloning of *EDS5* revealed that a transport step seems to be essential for the biosynthesis of SA. Future research will elucidate the chemical nature of the molecules that are transported by EDS5 and whether they are essential signaling molecules or precursors of SA biosynthesis. The elucidation of the SA-biosynthesis pathway and its regulation will further our understanding of the plant defense responses to pathogens.

Acknowledgment

The financial support of the Swiss National Science Fundation is gratefully acknowledged (grant 3100- 055662 to JPM).

Literature Cited

Aarts, N., Metz, M., Holub, E., Staskawicz, B. J., Daniels M. J., and Parker J. E. 1998. Different requirements for EDS1 and NDR1 by disease resistance genes define at least two R gene-mediated signaling pathways in Arabidoposis. Proc. Natl. Acad. Sci. USA 95: 10306-10311.

Alvarez, M. E. 2000. Salicylic acid in the machinery of hypersensitive cell death and disease resistance. Plant Mol. Biol. 44: 429-442.

Brown, M. H., Paulsen, I. T., and Skurray, R. A. 1999. The multidrug efflux protein NorM is a prototype of a new family of transporters. Mol. Microbiol. 31: 394-395.

Cameron, R. K. 2000. Salicylic acid and its role in plant defense responses: what do we really know? Physiol. Mol. Plant Pathol. 56: 91-93.

Century, K. S., Shapiro, A. D., Repetti, P., Dahlbeck, D., Holub, E., and Staskawicz, B. J. 1997. NDR1, a pathogen-induced component required for Arabidopsis disease resistance. Science 278: 1963-1965.

Coquoz, J-L, Buchala, A., and Métraux, J.-P. 1998. The biosynthesis of salicylic acid in potato plants. Plant physiol. 117: 1095-1101.

Debeaujon, I., Peeters, A.J.M., Léon-Kloosterziel, K. M., and Koorneef, M. 2001. The TRANSPARENT TESTA 12 gene of Arabidopsis encodes a multidrug Secondary Transporter-like Protein required for flavonoid sequestration in vacuoles of the seed coat endothelium. Plant Cell 13: 853-871.

Delaney, T. P., Uknes, S., Vernooij, B., Friedrich, L., Weymann, K., Negretto, D., Gaffney, T., Gut-Rella, M., Kessmann, H., Ward, E., and Ryals, J. 1994. A central role of salicylic acid in plant resistance. Science 266: 1247-1250.

Dewdney, J., Reuber, T., Wildermuth M. C., Devoto, A., Cui, J., Stutius, L. M., Drummond, E. P., and Ausubel, F. M. 2000. Three unique mutants of Arabidopsis identify eds loci required for limiting growth of a biotrophic fungal pathogen. Plant J. 24: 205-218.

Dong, X. 1998. SA, JA, ethylene, and disease resistance in plants. Curr. Opin. Plant Biol. 1: 316-323.

Falk, A., Feys, B. J., Frost, L. N., Jones, D. G., Daniels, M, J., and Parker, J. 1999. EDS1, an essential component of R-gene mediated disease resistance in Arabidopsis has homology to eukaryotic lipases. Proc. Natl. Acad. Sci. USA 96: 3292-3297.

Feys, B. J. and Parker, J. E. 2000. Interplay of signaling pathways in plant disease resistance. Trends Genetics 16:449-455.

Glazebrook, J. 1999. Genes controlling expression of defense responses in Arabidopsis. Curr. Opin. Plant Biol. 2: 280-286.

Jirage, D., Tootle, T. L., Reubener, T., Frost, L. N., Feys, B. J., Parker, J. E., Ausubel, F. M., and Glazebrook, J. 1999. Arabidopsis thaliana PAD4 encodes a lipase-like gene that is important for salicylic acid signaling. Proc. Natl. Acad. Sci. USA 96: 13583-13588.

Kenyon, C. J. and Walker, G.C. 1980. DNA-damaging agents stimulate gene expression at specific loci in Escherichia coli. Proc. Natl. Acad. Sci. USA 77: 2819-2823.

Lee H-I, Léon, J., and Raskin, I. 1995. Biosynthesis and metabolism of salicylic acid. Proc. Natl. Acad. Sci. USA 92: 4076-4079.

Morita, Y., Kataoka, A., Shiota, S., Mizushima, T., and Tsuchiya, T. 2000. NorM of *Vibrio parahaemolyticus* is an Na^+-driven multi drug efflux pump. J. Bacteriol. 182: 6694-6697.

Nawrath, C. and Métraux, J.-P. 1999. Salicylic acid induction-deficient mutants of Arabidopsis express *PR-2* and *PR-5* and accumulate high levels of camalexin after pathogen inoculation. Plant Cell 11: 1393-1404.

Rogers, E. E. and Ausubel, F. M. 1997. Arabidopsis enhanced disease susceptibility mutants exhibit enhanced susceptibility to several bacterial pathogens and alterations in *PR-1* gene expression. Plant Cell 9: 305-316.

Shiomi N., Fukuda, H., Fukuda, Y., Murata, K., and Kimura, A. 1991. Nucleotide sequence and characterization of a gene conferring resistance to ethionine in yeast *Saccharomyces cerevisiae*. J Ferment. Bioeng. 71: 211-215.

Zhao, J. and Last, R. L. 1996. Coordinate regulation of the tryptophan biosynthetic pathway and indolic phytoalexin accumulation in Arabidopsis. Plant Cell 8: 2235-2244.

Zhou, N., Tootle, T. L., Tsui, F., Klessig, D. F., and Glazebrook, J. 1998. PAD4 functions upstream from salicylic acid to control defense responses in Arabidopsis. Plant Cell 10: 1021-1030.

Challenges and Opportunities for Understanding Disease Resistance Signaling

Fumiaki Katagiri and Jane Glazebrook

Torrey Mesa Research Institute, San Diego, CA 92121 USA

Thorough understanding of a biological system can be defined as the ability to build a model that exactly simulates the biological system. The signal transduction network that controls activation of plant defense responses to microbial attack is one biological system that we would like to understand. Genetic analyses, primarily using Arabidopsis, have allowed identification of numerous genes that function in regulation of disease resistance responses. Phenotypic characterization of mutant plants with defects in these genes, together with biochemical analyses, has led to the identification of pathways required for signal transduction. These include gene-for-gene resistance responses, salicylic acid (SA)-dependent responses, jasmonic acid (JA)-dependent responses, and ethylene (ET)-dependent responses. However, as our analysis of these pathways grows more and more sophisticated, we are faced with many observations that are not easily explained by simple models. Mutants which seem to affect the same pathway generally have significant phenotypic differences incompatible with the idea that they are components of a simple linear signaling pathway, gene-for-gene resistance genes of very similar sequence require different sets of signaling genes for their function, and mutations that block one pathway (SA signaling, for example) affect signaling through other pathways (JA signaling, for example).

These days, we account for the difficulties in model building by saying that there must be a "complex" signaling "network". However, our way of describing complex networks so far is merely drawing complex arrangements of arrows connecting signaling components. See Glazebrook (2001), for a review of genetic analysis of defense-related signal transduction and an example of inadequate model-drawing. The major challenge we face is to evolve a mindset to handle concepts of complex networks, which could be totally different from our conventional, intuitive understanding. Some of the points we may need to consider if we are to fully understand the defense-response signaling network are discussed here.

Considerations Affecting Model Building

EPISTASIS

Using epistasis among mutants to determine the order of the steps corresponding to the mutations depends on the type model presumed to described the pathway. Let's consider a simple imaginary case. A loss-of-function mutation in gene A causes constitutive accumulation of SA, and a loss-of-function mutation in gene B inhibits accumulation of SA after infection of a pathogen. Both genes A and B appear to encode regulatory proteins (e.g., protein kinases or transcription factors). The phenotype of the double mutant is identical to that of the gene B mutant. Therefore, the gene B mutation is epistatic to the gene A mutation. Fig. 1 shows three simple models that can explain this observation. Correct placing of certain genes in the pathway depends on the pathway model having the correct structure, which we may not know.

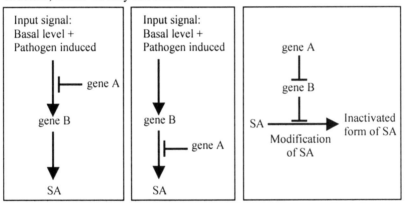

Fig. 1. Models to explain epistasis results. The two figures on the left describe signaling models, while the figure on the right describes a metabolic pathway model.

PHENOTYPIC ANALYSIS

Assessment of a broad spectrum of phenotypes for various mutants can help to determine the order of steps corresponding to mutations. If a signal transduction pathway has a structure in which a signal proceeds from top to bottom, with pathway branches at various intervals, genes that mediate steps closer to the top of the pathway affect more downstream events than genes closer to the bottom (Fig. 2A). Furthermore, the spectra of phenotypes of mutants affected in the downstream genes are subsets of the phenotypes of mutants with defects in the upstream genes. In fig. 2A, mutation #2 affects response B, a subset of the responses affected by mutation #1 (affects A and B), so mutation #2 is correctly presumed to act downstream from mutation #1. However, if cross-talk in the form of convergence of some branches has significant effects on the system, a mutation #2 that affects a subset of phenotypes affected by another mutation #1 does not necessarily lie downstream of mutation #1 in the signal transduction pathway. In fig 2B, the phenotypes of mutants #1 and #2 are the same as in fig. 2A, but mutation #2 does not lie downstream from mutation #1. Feedback pathways can also add complexity.

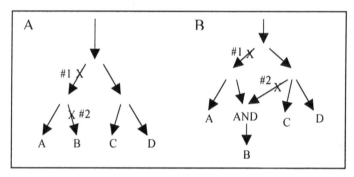

Fig. 2. Two possible signal transduction circuits.

Another point we should keep in mind is that the same phenotype can be caused by different mechanisms. For example, when two mutants both allow increased growth of *P. syringae*, the mechanisms that allowed the bacteria to grow better could be different. If wild-type plants use defense mechanisms A, B, C, and D, one mutant might be deficient in mechanism A and the other mutant might be deficient in mechanisms D. Thus, we cannot assume that the same signal transduction mechanism is responsible for indistinguishable phenotypes. Furthermore, the extent to which A, B, C, and D contribute to resistance could be affected by environmental factors. Relevant differences in environmental factors could be as subtle as different watering programs for plants or different light bulbs (hence different light spectra) in environment-controlled chambers. Such phenomena may explain why observations made in different laboratories are not consistent even when they are reproducible in specific laboratories.

SPATIAL AND TEMPORAL RESOLUTION

Our ability to design accurate models is hampered by lack of sufficient spatial and temporal resolution. Plant cells under direct attack by a pathogen presumably respond differently than neighboring cells not under direct pathogen attack. The situation changes over time as the pathogen spreads cells that were neighboring cells become targets of direct attack. Our assays for many signaling events do not have enough resolution to distinguish differences between neighboring cells. For example, in many experiments the SA and JA pathways appear to be mutually antagonistic. In spite of this, we often see both pathways activated after pathogen infection. Does this mean that all the cells have both the pathways active or that the measurements represent mixed populations of cells, some with the SA pathway active and some with the JA pathway active?

NON-LINEAR RESPONSES

A signaling network system composed of quantitatively non-linear steps with a single positive feedback loop could behave in a complex manner. We know that in general any single step in signal transduction is non-linear (e.g., it is saturable). It is very likely that there is at least one positive feedback loop in SA signaling. Including pathogens in the system creates another opportunity for a feedback loop. When the plant responds to the pathogen, the pathogen responds to the plant response – in this way it is easy to form a feedback loop in the system. Thus, there are many ways for the dynamics of the defense response signaling system to develop complexity without requiring complex relationships between individual steps. It is likely that consideration of system dynamics will be necessary to build a predictive model. In this case, experimental approaches quite different from those used conventionally will be required.

Beyond Genetics

Even if all the currently available methodologies were applied to study a biological system, the amount of knowledge we would obtain would be insufficient for thorough understanding of the system. It is therefore crucial that we do not limit our approaches, but rather emphasize studying a biological system from multiple angles, such as genomics, biochemistry, cell biology, biophysics, bioinformatics, and mathematics in addition to genetics. Here we discuss just one example of how a new approach, genomics, can broaden our understanding.

The recent completion of Arabidopsis genome sequencing (The Arabidopsis Genome Initiative 2000) and the imminent completion of *P. syringae* genome sequencing advance the Arabidopsis-*P. syringae* system from a genetically amenable system to a genomics-amenable system. Global mRNA profiling using microarrays is a powerful genomics technology that is already available for Arabidopsis (Zhu and Wang 2000). It has been used for identification of candidate genes that are involved in particular biological phenomena based on the notion of "guilt by association", that is, genes whose expression change in connection with a biological phenomenon could have a causal role in that phenomenon. These candidate genes provide good starting points for reverse genetic approaches. In combination with genome sequence information, reverse genetic approaches have the potential to handle functionally redundant genes and mutations that could cause severe growth or reproductive disadvantages. Furthermore, as exemplified by the case of benomyl-resistant mutants of yeast (Ross-MacDonald et al. 1999), systematic reverse genetics has the potential to identify a significant number of new genes that have escaped detection in apparently saturated forward genetic screens. Global expression profiling has also been used for identification of candidate cis-regulatory elements responsible for transcriptional regulation.

Another advantage of global expression profiling is that it is the equivalent of massive phenotyping. Generally, whenever the biological status of the cell changes, expression of some genes changes. This change may or may not have caused the altered cell status, but it serves as a marker of the alteration. Thus, global mRNA expression profiling provides sensitive quantitative measurements at numerous observation points in the biological system. This aspect of the technology, in combination with the concept of specific perturbation of the system and knowledge about parts of the system obtained by conventional reductionist approaches, is crucial when we try to understand the dynamics of a biological system. Global expression profiling-based phenotyping can be easily combined with phenotyping done by any other method.

Concluding Remarks

We should be aware that we are at the beginning of an era when we can apply powerful scientific approaches to understanding biological systems at a global level, in addition to understanding narrowly reduced, specific parts of systems. This will drastically change the way biological research can be done, the way we think about biology, and the level of understanding we have in biology. Use of a model biological system in which powerful genetics and genomics tools are available makes sense for a collective effort to achieve understanding of a system. For the study of plant-pathogen interactions, the Arabidopsis-*P. syringae* system is such a model system.

Literature Cited

Glazebrook, J. 2001. Genes controlling expression of defense responses in Arabidopsis - 2001 status. Curr. Opin. Plant Biol. 4:301-308.
Ross-MacDonald P., Coelho P.S., Roemer T., Agarwal S., Kumar A., Jansen R., Cheung K.H., Sheehan A., Symoniatis D., Umansky L.,

Heidtman M., Nelson F.K., Iwasaki H., Hager K., Gerstein M., Miller P.,
Roeder G.S., and Snyder M. 1999. Large-scale analysis of the yeast
genome by transposon tagging and gene disruption. Nature 402:363-363.

The Arabidopsis Genome Initiative. 2000. Analysis of the genome
sequence of the flowering plant Arabidopsis thaliana. Nature 408:796-
815.

Zhu T., and Wang X. 2000. Large-scale profiling of the Arabidopsis
transcriptome. Plant Physiol. 124:1472-1476.

SA- and NO-Mediated Signaling
in Plant Disease Resistance

Daniel F. Klessig[1,2], Pradeep Kachroo[1,2], David Slaymaker[2], Keiko
Yoshioka[1,2], DuRoy A. Navarre[2], Daniel Clark[1,2] Dhirendra Kumar[1,2], and
Jyoti Shah[2]

[1]Boyce Thompson Institute for Plant Research, Ithaca, N.Y., U.S.A.;
[2]Waksman Institute, Rutgers, The State University of New Jersey,
Piscataway, N.J., U.S.A.

Several defense signaling molecules have been identified during the past
several decades. These include ethylene, jasmonic acid (JA), salicylic acid
(SA) and nitric oxide (NO). Although the involvement of SA in several
defense responses has been rigorously demonstrated, its mechanism(s) of
action still remains poorly defined and/or controversial (Dempsey et. al.
1999). Evidence for the participation of NO in plant defense against
pathogens, while far less extensive, is beginning to build (Durner and
Klessig 1999; Wendehenne et al. 2001).

SA-Interacting Proteins in Tobacco

During the past decade, we have shown that several proteins in tobacco,
including catalase, ascorbate peroxidase and SA-binding protein 2
(SABP2), interact with SA (Chen et al. 1993; Durner and Klessig 1995; Du
and Klessig 1997). Catalase and ascorbate peroxidase are the major H_2O_2-
scavenging enzymes in plants. SA inhibits this activity. More recently, we
discovered two additional SABPs – the chloroplastic SABP3 and
mitochondrial SABP4. SABP3 was purified and its corresponding gene
cloned (Slaymaker et al. 2001). SABP3 is the chloroplastic carbonic
anhydrase, which reversibly hydrates CO_2 to form HCO_3^-. However, SA
binding to carbonic anhydrase does not alter this enzymatic activity.
Interestingly, in yeast this tobacco carbonic anhydrase exhibits antioxidant
activity. Thus, all three SA-interacting proteins identified to date have
antioxidant activity.

Analyses of the SA-Mediated Pathway through Arabidopsis Mutants

Through analyses of mutant Arabidopsis, we and several other groups have identified several potential components of the SA-mediated pathway leading to disease resistance. One class of mutants exhibits constitutive expression of PR genes (cpr) and enhanced disease resistance. Mutant $cpr22$ in addition contains elevated levels of SA and spontaneously develops lesions resembling the hypersensitive resistance response (HR) (Yoshioka et al. 2001). All of these phenotypes are dependent on SA, but only constitutive $PR-1$ gene expression requires NPR1, a key component of at least one branch of the SA signaling pathway. $cpr22$ also activates the JA and ethylene-mediated pathway leading to induction of the defensin gene $PDF1.2$. Based on these results, the $cpr22$ mutation appears to induce its associated phenotypes by activating NPR1-dependent and NPR1-independent branches of the SA pathway, as well as an ethylene/JA signaling pathway. Interestingly, the SA-dependent phenotypes, but not the SA-independent phenotypes, are suppressed when the $cpr22$ mutant is grown under high relative humidity.

A second class of mutants fails to induce PR genes and exhibits reduced resistance. Twelve mutants in this class, isolated in four labs, alter the same, ankyrin repeat-containing protein with homology to $I\kappa B\alpha$, termed NPR1. NPR1-interacting proteins have been characterized including members of the TGA family of bZIP transcription factors (Zhang et al. 1999; Zhou et al. 2000; Deprés et al. 2000). Several suppressors of the salicylate insensitive (ssi) phenotype of our $npr1-5$ mutant are being characterized and cloned (Shah et al. 1999, 2001).

The best characterized is the recessive $ssi2$ mutant, which exhibits constitutive PR gene expression, spontaneous lesion formation, and enhanced resistance to $Pseudomonas\ syringae$ and $Peronospora\ parasitica$ (Shah et al. 2001; Kachroo et al. 2001). By contrast, a subset of defense responses regulated by the JA signaling pathway, including $PDF1.2$ expression and resistance to $Botrytis\ cinerea$, is impaired in the $ssi2$ mutant. The $SSI2$ gene was cloned and shown to encode a stearoyl-ACP desaturase (S-ACP DES). S-ACP DES is the archetype member of a family of soluble fatty acid (FA) desaturases; these enzymes play an important role in regulating the overall level of desaturated FAs in the cell. The level of S-ACP-DES's substrate 18:0 FA was elevated while its product 18:1 FA was reduced in $ssi2$, consistent with the 10-20 fold lower activity of the mutant enzyme. Since reduced S-ACP DES activity leads to the induction of certain defense responses and the inhibition of others, we propose that a FA-derived signal modulates cross-talk between different defense signaling pathways. This FA signal may be 18:1 or a derivative of it.

Nitric Oxide and the Activation of Plant Defense Responses

NO has been shown to function as an important redox-active signal in the induction of innate immunity in animals. To determine whether it serves a similar defense function in plants, NO synthase (NOS) activity was monitored in TMV-infected resistant and susceptible tobacco plants. NOS activity was observed to increase dramatically in resistant but not susceptible plants (Durner et al. 1998). Moreover, treating tobacco suspension cells with recombinant mammalian NOS or various NO donors induced the expression of *PR-1* and the early defense gene *PAL*, while the NOS inhibitor L-NMMA blocked *PR-1* expression after TMV infection (Durner et al. 1998; Klessig et al. 2000). The expression of *PR-1* and *PAL* was also shown to be induced by cyclic GMP (cGMP) and cyclic ADP ribose (cADPR); these molecules are known to serve as second messengers for NO in mammals. These and other results argue that NO activates *PR-1* and *PAL* through a cGMP-dependent pathway. Using the SA-deficient NahG transgenic plants, SA could be placed within the NO-mediated pathway downstream of NO and its second messengers cGMP, cADP ribose and Ca^{2+}.

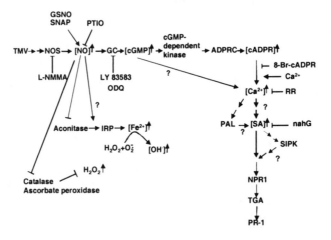

Fig. 1. Proposed pathways of NO signaling in tobacco

In addition to guanylate cyclase, which is activated post-translationally by NO to produce cGMP, three more direct targets (effector proteins) were identified in tobacco. Aconitase, catalase and ascorbate peroxidase are all inhibited by NO (Navarre et al. 2000; Clark et al. 2000). Interestingly, the activity of these enzymes are also blocked by SA, suggesting that these two secondary defense signals share common targets.

In animals NO converts the cytosolic aconitase into an iron regulatory protein (IRP) which binds iron responsive elements (IRE) in mRNAs encoding proteins involved in the homeostasis of free cellular iron. Preliminary results indicate that the tobacco cytosolic aconitase also has IRE-binding activity and thus may play a similar role in plants (Navarre, D. and Klessig, D.F., unpublished results).

Acknowledgments

This work was supported by Grants MCB 9723952/0196168 and MCB 9904660/0196046 from the National Science Foundation and Grant 98-35303-6664 from the USDA.

Literature Cited

Chen, Z., Silva, H., and Klessig, D.F. 1993. Active oxygen species in the induction of plant systemic acquired resistance by salicylic acid. Science 262: 1883-1886.

Clark, D., Durner, J., Navarre, D.A. and Klessig, D.F. 2000. Nitric oxide inhibition of tobacco catalase and ascorbate peroxidase. Mol. Plant-Microbe Interact. 13: 1380-1384.

Dempsey, D., Shah, J. and Klessig, D.F. 1999. Salicylic acid and disease resistance in plants. Critical Reviews in Plant Sciences 18: 547-575.

Després, C., DeLong, C., Glaze, S., Liu, E. and Fobert, P.R. 2000. The Arabidopsis NPR1/NIM1 protein enhances the DNA binding activity of a subgroup of the TGA family of bZIP transcription factors. Plant Cell 12:279-290.

Du, H. and Klessig, D.F. 1997. Identification of a soluble, high affinity salicylic acid-binding protein from tobacco. Plant Physiol. 113: 1319-1327.

Durner, J. and Klessig, D.F. 1995. Inhibition of ascorbate peroxidase by salicylic acid and 2,6-dichloroisonicotinic acid, two inducers of plant defense responses. Proc. Natl. Acad. Sci. 92: 11312-11316.

Durner, J. and Klessig, D.F. 1999. NO as a signal in plants. Curr. Opin. in Plant Biol. 2: 369-374.

Durner, J., Wendehenne, D. and Klessig, D.F. 1998. Defense gene induction in tobacco by nitric oxide, cyclic GMP and cyclic ADP ribose. Proc. Natl. Acad. Sci. USA 95: 10328-10333.

Kachroo, P., Shanklin, J., Shah, J., Whittle, E.J. and Klessig, D.F. 2001. A fatty acid desaturase modulates the activation of defense signaling pathways in plants. Proc. Natl. Acad. Sci. USA. 98(16):9448-9453.

Klessig, D.F., Durner, J., Zhou, J.M., Kumar, D., Navarre, R., Zhang, S., Shah, J., Wendehenne, D., Trifa, Y., Noad, R., Kachroo, P., Pontier, D., Lam, E. and Silva, H. 2000. NO and salicylic acid signaling in plant defense. Proc. Natl. Acad. Sci. USA. 97: 8849-8855.

Navarre, D., Wendehenne, D., Durner, J., Noad, R. and Klessig, D.F. 2000. Nitric oxide modulates the activity of tobacco aconitase. Plant Physiol. 122: 573-582.

Shah, J., Kachroo, P. and Klessig, D.F. 1999. The Arabidopsis *ssi1* mutation restores pathogenesis-related gene expression in *npr1* plants and renders defensin gene expression SA dependent. Plant Cell 11: 191-206.

Shah, J., Kachroo, P., Nandi, A. and Klessig, D.F. 2001. A loss-of-function mutation in the Arabidopsis *SSI2* gene confers SA- and *NPR1*-independent expression of *PR* genes and resistance against bacterial and oomycete pathogens. Plant J. 25:563-574.

Slaymaker, D.H., Navarre, D.A. and Klessig, D.F. 2001. The tobacco salicylic acid-binding protein (SABP)3 is the chloroplastic carbonic anhydrase which exhibits antioxidant activity. Proc. Natl. Acad. Sci. USA. In review.

Wendehenne, D., Pugin, A., Klessig, D.F, and Durner, J. 2001. Nitric oxide: comparative synthesis and signaling in animal and plant cells. Trends in Plant Sci. 4:177-183.

Yoshioka, K., Kachroo, P., Tsui, F., Sharma, S.B., Shah, J. and Klessig, D.F. 2001. Environmentally-sensitive, SA-dependent defense responses in the *cpr22* mutant of Arabidopsis. Plant J. 26:447-459.

Zhang, Y., Fan, W., Kinkema, M., Li, X. and Dong, X. 1999. Interaction of NPR1 with basic leucine zipper protein transcription factors that bind sequences required for salicylic acid induction of the *PR-1* gene. Proc. Natl. Acad. Sci. USA. 96:6523-6528.

Zhou, J.M., Trifa, Y., Silva, H., Pontier, D., Lam, E., Shah, J. and Klessig, D.F. 2000. NPR1 differentially interacts with members of TGA/OBF family of transcription factors which bind an element of the *PR-1* gene required for induction by salicylic acid. Mol. Plant-Microbe Interact. 13: 191-202.

G Protein Signaling in Disease Resistance of Rice

Ko Shimamoto, Utut Suharsono, Eiichiro Ono, Hann Ling Wong, and
Tsutomu Kawasaki

Laboratory of Plant Molecular Genetics, Nara Institute of Science and
Technology, Ikoma, Japan

Recently, important progress has been made in the molecular biological
study of rice-pathogen interactions (reviewed in Ronald 1997). Resistance
genes against bacterial blight (Song et al. 1995) and rice blast fungus (Wang
et al. 1999) were isolated, and lesion-mimic mutants were characterized at
the molecular level (Takahashi et al. 1999). Results of these recent studies
suggest that we are beginning to understand the molecular biology of
disease resistance in rice and that rice will become a useful model cereal for
studies of plant-microbe interactions in the future. Despite recent progress
in our understanding of molecular biology of rice-pathogen interactions,
very little is known about the signaling pathways underlying disease
resistance in rice. We have been focusing on two kinds of G proteins which
play important roles in disease resistance of rice.

Roles of the Small GTPase Rac in Disease Resistance of Rice

OsRac GENE FAMILY IN RICE

Rac belongs to the Rho subfamily of small GTPases and constitutes a
gene family in plants. Their functions in diverse signaling in plants are
recently becoming understood (Valster et al. 2000). Because Rac plays an
important role in the regulation of the NADPH oxidase in mammalian
phagocytic cells, we sought rice cDNAs having homology with human Rac
and found 3 such sequences, OsRac1, 2, and 3 (Kawasaki et al. 1999). Their
deduced amino acid sequences are ca. 60% identical with those of human
Rac proteins. More recently we isolated 4 more genes in rice that are
homologous with the human Rac genes. To date we identified four groups
of Rac genes in rice: OsRac1, 2, 3, 4 with OsRac2 having four closely
related members. Thus, in total, rice has at least 7 Rac-related genes and

most are expressed in both leaves and roots.

REGULATION OF ROS PRODUCTION BY OsRac1

The small GTPase such as Rac takes two forms within a cell; the GTP-bound form is an active form and it transmits signals to downstrean effectors and the GDP-bound inactive form is not active. These two forms cycle in the cell depending on presence or absence of various signals.

We made a constitutive active form of OsRac1 by substituting glycine at position 19 with valine and fusing the gene with the CaMV35S promoter. The construct was introduced into seed-derived calli of the wild type (cv. Kinmaze) and a lesion mimic-mutant of rice, *sl* (Sekiguchi lesion), by *Agrobacterium*-mediated transformation. In the transformed cell lines of the wild type and the *sl* mutant, H_2O_2 production was demonstrated by staining with diaminobenzidine (DAB). The observed H_2O_2 production was inhibited by diphenylene iodonium (DPI), an inhibitor of the neutrophil NADPH oxidase. These findings suggest that a NADPH oxidase similar to the neutrophil enzyme is involved in Rac-induced H_2O_2 production. Furthermore, DAB staining of leaf sheath cells of transgenic wild type plants showed H_2O_2 production, which appeared to be localized at the intercellular space (Kawasaki et al. 1999).

We produced a dominant negative form of OsRac1 by changing threonine at 24th position to asparagine. The mutant dominant-negative form is able to suppress activities of all Rac genes within the same cell. In untransformed *sl* cell cultures H_2O_2 production was induced by calyculin A (CA), a protein phosphatase inhibitor, and the induction was inhibited by DPI. In contrast, CA-induced H_2O_2 production was inhibited in the *sl* cells transformed with the dominant-negative OsRac1, indicating that OsRac was required for activation of H_2O_2 production in the *sl* cells (Kawasaki et al. 1999).

REGULATION OF CELL DEATH BY OsRac1

Terminal Deoxynucleotidyltransferase-Mediated UTP-End-Labeling (TUNEL) signals indicative of nuclear DNA cleavage were observed in the transformed *sl* cells expressing the constitutively active OsRac1. Electron microscopic analysis of the transformed *sl* cells indicated that cell death occurs in the transformed cells and that the observed cell death exhibits a set of morphological changes found in apoptosis in mammalian cells. Necrotic lesions were found in leaves of transgenic wild type plants. During maturation, discrete lesions developed in the leaves and they were frequently observed at the junction of the blade and the sheath of the leaves. These results indicate that the constitutive active OsRac1 can induce cell death in transgenic rice plants as well as cultured cells. Furthermore, the dominant negative OsRac1 suppresses lesion formation in *sl* plants

(Kawasaki et al. 1999).

ROLES OF OsRac1 FOR DISEASE RESISTANCE OF RICE

The japonica rice variety Kinmaze, which was used for the production of transgenic plants, carries the *Pi-a* resistance gene that is incompatible with the race 031 of the blast fungus. We infected the leaf blade of transgenic rice plants expressing the constitutively active OsRac1 with the compatible race 007 of the blast fungus by the punch infection method. Transgenic plants showed HR-like responses or a greatly reduced level of symptoms. These results indicate that rice plants transformed with the constitutive active OsRac1 acquire resistance to a compatible race of the rice blast fungus and exhibit HR-like OsRac1 responses (Ono et al. 2001).

We next asked whether HR caused by an avirulent race of the rice blast fungus is suppressed by expression of the dominant negative OsRac1. The leaf blades of transgenic plants expressing the dominant negative OsRac1 were infected with an avirulent race 031 of the blast fungus. Typical HR accompanied by cell death was observed in untransformed control plants. In contrast, in transgenic lines examined, HR was clearly suppressed in the leaf blade, and suppression was observed in repeated experiments, indicating that the dominant negative OsRac1 suppresses *R* gene-specific resistance against rice blast fungus (Ono et al. 2001).

We also tested a compatible race of bacterial blight on transgenic plants transformed with the constitutively active OsRac1 and the dominant negative OsRac1. We found that transgenic plants transformed with the constitutively active OsRac1 were more resistant to bacterial blight. Together, these results indicated that OsRac1 is a regulator of disease resistance in rice (Ono et al. 2001).

ACTIVATION OF PHYTOALEXIN PRODUCTION AND ALTERATION OF DEFENSE-RELATED GENE EXPRESSION IN TRANSGENIC RICE EXPRESSING THE CONSTITUTIVE ACTIVE OsRac1

We examined the amounts of momilactone A, a major phytoalexin of rice, in the leaves of transgenic rice expressing the constitutive active OsRac1. In all seven transgenic lines examined, the levels of momilactone A were highly elevated, and the increases were 19-180 fold higher than the levels of the untransformed control plants. These results indicate that constitutive active OsRac1 activates phytoalexin synthesis to confer resistance to the blast fungus. We next examined the expression of two genes which are closely associated with disease resistance in rice. Expression of D9 was highly activated in all lines examined. D9 was isolated from lesion-mimic mutants of rice (Takahashi et al. 1999) resistant to rice blast and found to be up-regulated in these mutants. One of the rice peroxidase genes, POX22.3, which was originally isolated as a gene activated during the resistance reactions of rice against *Xanthomonas oryzae* pv. *oryzae* (Chittoor et al. 1997), was shown to be strongly down-regulated in the transgenic rice expressing the constitutive active OsRac1 that acquired resistance to the blast disease.

Role of Heterotrimeric G Protein in Disease Resistance of Rice

Many studies using inhibitors and agonists of heterotrimeric G proteins in several plant species suggested that G proteins are involved in defense signaling (Legendre et al. 1993). Specifically, changes in cytosolic Ca^{2+} concentrations which are often observed in elicitor-treated plant cells are thought to be regulated by heterotrimeric G proteins (Blumwald et al. 1998). However, roles of heterotrimeric G protein in plant defense have not been directly tested using G protein mutants.

In rice, mutations in the a subunit of heterotrimeric G protein have been identified they were shown to cause dwarf phenotype of the mutants (Fujisawa et al. 1999). We used these mutations to address roles of heterotrimeric G protein in disease resistance of rice. We found that the lack of $G\alpha$ caused rice plants to be susceptible to infection by rice blast and bacterial blight, indicating that heterotrimeric G protein is essential for disease resistance of rice. The susceptible reaction of the rice Ga mutants to pathogens was correlated with delayed induction of defense genes in the mutants lacking heterotrimeric G protein. Furthermore, cell cultures derived from the rice $G\alpha$ mutants were not able to produce ROS or activate defense gene expression in response to sphingolipid elicitors derived from the membrane fractions of the rice blast fungus. Cell death induced by these elicitors were highly reduced by the mutations. These studies indicated that heterotrimeric G protein plays important roles in defense signaling of rice.

Conclusions

Our studies on interactions of rice plants with rice blast and bacterial blight indicate that two types of GTPases, the small GTPase Rac and heterotrimeric G protein, play important roles in disease resistance of rice.

Literature Cited

Blumwald,E., Aharon,G.S. and Lam,B.C-H. 1998. Early signal transduction pathways in plant-pathogen interactions. Trends Plant Sci. 3: 342-346
Chittoor,J.M., Leach,J.M. and White,F.F. 1997. Differential induction of a peroxidase gene family during infection of rice by *Xanthomonas oryzae*

Chittoor,J.M., Leach,J.M. and White,F.F. 1997. Differential induction of a peroxidase gene family during infection of rice by *Xanthomonas oryzae* pv. *oryzae*. Mol.Plant-Microbe Interact. 10: 861-871

Fujisawa,Y., Kato, T., Ohki, S., Ishikawa, A., Kitano, H., Sasaki,T., Asahi,T. and Iwasaki,Y. 1999. Suppression of the heterotrimeric G protein causes abnormal morphology, including dwarfism in rice. Proc. Natl. Acad. Sci. USA 96: 7575-7580

Kawasaki,T., Henmi,K., Ono,E., Hatakeyama,S., Iwano,M., Satoh,H. and Shimamoto,K. 1999. The small GTP-binding protein Rac is a regulator of cell death in plants. Proc. Natl. Acad. Sci. USA 96: 10922-10926

Legendre,L., Heinstein,P.F. and Low,P.S. 1992. Evidence for participation of GTP-binding proteins in elicitation of the rapid oxidative burst in cultured soybean cells. J. Biol. Chem. 267: 20140-20147

Ono,E., Wong, H.-L., Kawasaki,T., Hasegawa,M., Kodama,O. and Shimamoto,K. 2001. Essential role of the small GTPase Rac in disease resistance of rice. Proc. Natl. Acad. Sci. USA 98: 759-764

Ronald, P.C. 1997. The molecular basis of disease resistance in rice. Plant Mol Biol. 35: 179-86.

Song, W.Y., Wang, G.L., Chen, L.L., Kim, H.S., Pi, L.Y., Holsten, T., Gardner, J., Wang, B., Zhai, W.X., Zhu, L.H., Fauquet, C. and Ronald, P.C. 1995. A receptor kinase-like protein encoded by the rice disease resistance gene, Xa21. Science 270: 1804-1806.

Takahashi,A., Kawasaki,T., Henmi,K., Shii,K., Kodama,O., Satoh,H. and K. Shimamoto,K. 1999. Lesion-mimic mutants of rice with alterations in early signaling events of defense. Plant J. 17: 535-545

Valster, A.H., Hepler, P.K. and Chernoff, J. 2000. Plant GTPases: the Rhos in bloom. Trends in Cell Biol. 10: 141-146.

Wang, Z.X., Yano, M., Yamanouchi, U., Iwamoto, M., Monna, L., Hayasaka, H., Katayose, Y. and Sasaki, T. 1999. The Pib gene for rice blast resistance belongs to the nucleotide binding and leucine-rich repeat class of plant disease resistance genes. Plant J. 19: 55-64.

The Hypersensitive Response: Control and Function

Jeff Dangl, Daniel H. Aviv, Petra Epple, Saijun Tang, Aaron Wiig and
Mats Ellerstrom

Dept. of Biology and Curriculum in Genetics (JD and DHA), CB#3280
University of North Carolina at Chapel Hill
Chapel Hill, N. C. 27599-3280 USA

It has been recognized since 1915 that rapid, limited cell death at the site
of attempted pathogen ingress is a general feature of plant disease resistance.
This type of cell death (the hypersensitive reaction, or HR) is also
"programmed", since mutants exist in several plant species that mimic the
effect of infection in the absence of pathogens. Initiation of HR comes via
the action of disease resistance (R) genes that "recognize" specific pathogen
derived signals. During HR, signals emanate from cells destined to die.
These can lead to cell death in a tightly localized cluster of cells not directly
in contact with the pathogen. Thus, the propagation of cell death is also
under genetic control since the spread of HR must eventually be halted.
Little is known about the molecular basis of programmed cell death (PCD)
in higher plants. We wish to understand the relationship, if any, between
the mechanisms controlling HR and actual stop of pathogen growth. We
further wish to know if mechanisms regulating HR also regulate
developmental or cell-type specific cell death.

We address these issues by isolating mutants of Arabidopsis that are
disrupted in their control of cell death initiation and propagation. The
Arabidopsis genome is fully sequenced and there is little molecular
evidence for conservation of key regulators of animal PCD at the sequence
level. We identified and analyzed a series of mutants that mis-regulate HR-
like cell death in the absence of pathogen.

Cell Death and its Control in Plants

Plants express very sophisticated genetic strategies for recognition of
pathogens, most of which result in localized, very rapid, HR at the site of
attempted pathogen ingress. HR is found in nearly all responses mediated
by single, dominant or semi-dominantly acting plant "Disease Resistance

Genes" (*R*-genes; see Dangl and Jones 2001 for recent review). HR is also a hallmark of resistance to pathogens that are incapable of infecting any genotype of a certain host plant species (so-called "non-host" resistance). Other loci necessary for *R*-gene function (reviewed in Glazebrook 2001) and those with roles in control of cell death per se have also recently been defined.

Subsequent signal transduction includes rapid ion flux leading to alkalinization of the extracellular apoplast, generation of Reactive Oxygen Intermediates (ROI), generation of Nitric Oxide (NO), activation of signaling cascades involving MAP kinase pathway(s) and transcriptional activation of a broad range of "defense genes" (Wendehenne et al. 2001; Yang et al. 1997). The products of this transcriptional re-programming can be involved in biosynthesis or release of potential antimicrobial effector molecules and in the generation of signaling intermediates that will act distal to the infection site to establish Systemic Acquired Resistance (SAR). Salicylic Acid (SA) is required in Arabidopsis and tobacco locally at the primary infection site, and in the distal secondary tissue, for establishment and maintenance of SAR (reviewed in Ryals et al. 1996). SA is not generally required for *R* action in determining resistance at the infection site (Bittner-Eddy and Beynon 2001; McDowell et al. 2000). The nature of the systemic signal molecule remains elusive, but it is known genetically that establishment of SAR in distal tissue requires *NPR1/NIM1* function. This gene encodes an ankyrin repeat containing protein that may function as a transcriptional regulator. Global analysis of gene expression reveals that the SAR response is probably controlled by regulators of the WRKY class (Maleck et al. 2000), presumably in concert with other transcription factors such as the TGA class bZIP proteins that interact with NPR (Zhang et al. 1999; Zhou et al. 2000).

The extent of cell death during an HR can vary from one cell to tens of cells at the infection site in an *R*-dependent. It should also be stressed, however, that not all disease resistance reactions are accompanied by cell death (reviewed in Heath 2000). The HR may be a consequence of the mechanisms that halt pathogen growth in some cases. HR may, in fact, be the ultimate reflection of a local signal threshold, driven by the quantity of R and Avr proteins interacting to trigger resistance (Bendahmane et al. 1999). According to this model, the extent of cell death is a correlate of R protein "efficiency". An efficient R protein initiates resistance without the attendant HR, a less efficient R protein requires more signal flux and thus engenders HR. Current models for HR are based on the interplay, and positive mutual feedback regulation, of ROI and SA dependent signals. For example, sub-optimal doses of SA prime subsequent pathogen-dependent ROI production to induce HR in soybean cells. In each of these cases, the evolution of ROI plays a key role in signal amplification (Alvarez 2000). Genetic analyses support this model. SA and ROI levels, however, may not be the only signals required to set the cell death threshold. ROI and NO generated independently during the oxidative burst collaborate to initiate HR. NO and superoxide can form peroxynitrite (ONOO-), a very toxic compound in animal cells. However, Delledonne et al. (2001) demonstrate that ONOO- is inert in plant cells. These authors further demonstrate that a balance between hydrogen peroxide (made from dismutation of superoxide) and NO is required for HR. Thus, superoxide is a key regulator that can either scavenge NO into inert ONOO- or be dismutated to hydrogen peroxide. In this regard it is noteworthy that superoxide dismutase is rapidly induced by SA, and this induction is mis-regulated in one of our key cell death mutants (Kliebenstein et al. 1999). Other recent genetic analyses underscore the role of SA in not only cell death, but in decisions of cell growth (Rate et al. 1999). This work is particularly exciting as it strongly suggests that the poise between SA, and ROI, and the genes they regulate, is a linchpin between cellular live and die signals

The HR is a "programmed cell death", using as a definition the fact that plant-intrinsic signals are capable of initiating cell death in the absence of pathogen. In several plant species, mutants exist with visible phenotypes that resembles the lesions caused by pathogen attack, even when grown aseptically. These have been identified in corn (disease lesion mimics) tomato, and Arabidopsis (Dangl et al. 1996). The phenotypes associated with these mutants hint that they represent steps along normal disease resistance response pathways. In fact, mutations at *R* loci can exhibit cell death control phenotypes (Hulbert 1997). Alternatively, these mutant phenotypes could represent perturbations of normal metabolism, which the cell senses and translates into a commitment to rapid cell death, effectively removing the renegade cell from the metabolic pool. After commitment to a cell death pathway, the plant must have some mechanism to prohibit cell non-autonomous signals that might propagate cell death to neighboring cells. This is particularly true in plants because they have no scavengers to engulf the corpses of cells removed by PCD.

The Arabidopsis *LSD1* Gene: Control of Cell Death "Propagation"

The recessive *lsd1* null allele leads to a lowered threshold for pathogen, ROI-derived, or SA related signals entering the disease resistance pathway. The mutant phenotype is an inability to stop the spread of cell death once it is initiated (Dietrich et al. 1994; Dietrich et al. 1997; Jabs et al. 1996; Rustérucci et al. 2001). Developing foci of dead cells are initiated by local application of low concentrations of the plant signal molecule SA, or other chemicals which activate the syndrome of "systemic acquired resistance" (SAR), pathogenic bacteria and pathogenic fungi, or by a shift to non-permissive long day conditions. Both biotrophic and necrotrophic fungi will trigger these lesions. Each initiator induces "runaway cell death", or rcd, that spreads beyond the initial site of infection to kill the inoculated leaf. All other tissues and cell types can also exhibit this phenotype in long days. Thus, *lsd1* is conditionally lethal if young plants are shifted from short days to long days. It is important to note that only the inoculated leaf responds in these experiments. The *lsd1* mutation does not engender systemic cell death. This suggests that the initial signal for rcd does not propagate through the petiole. *lsd1* does trigger expression of genes correlated to the onset of SAR. It is important to note that neither wounding, nor inoculation with either heat killed bacteria or buffer induces cell death.

We demonstrated that accumulation of superoxide radical is both necessary and sufficient for lesion formation, and that evolution of superoxide precedes onset of obvious cell death after initiation using any of three means (Jabs et al. 1996). We used an extragenic suppressor mutation of *lsd1*, which restores all assayed phenotypes associated with *lsd1* back to wild type, to show that the effect of superoxide was directly tied to the *lsd1* mutation. Our interpretation of this data is as follows: The *lsd1* mutation allows accumulation of extracellular superoxide; *lsd1* cells are acutely sensitive to signals derived from extracellular superoxide, and cell death is initiated. This initiates subsequent superoxide formation in live neighboring cells, auto-amplifying a cell non-autonomous signal leading to runaway cell death. It is also important to note that the necrotroph *Botrytis cinerea*, a very important agronomic pathogen, is a superb inducer of rcd in *lsd1*. *B. cinerea* releases hydrogen peroxide, or superoxide that is rapidly dismutated into hydrogen peroxide. This stimulates the plant HR pathway. Thus, this fungus usurps HR signaling to invae dying tissue, and then further colonizes the plant by continued mimicry of HR signals (Govrin and Levine, 2000).

Acknowledgements

Supported by Syngenta, NIH 5RO1-GM057171-01 to JLD and the UNC Curriculum in Genetics and Molecular Biology NIH Training Grant T32 GM07092-26 to DHA. Fellowship support from the Swiss National Funds and Deutscher Akademischer Austauschdienst (DAAD) to PE and from the Wennergren Foundation, The Swedish Institute, and The Swedish Foundation for International Cooperation in Research and Higher Education (STINT) to ME is also gratefully acknowledged.

Literature cited

Alvarez, M. E. 2000. Salicylic acid in the machinery of hypersensitive cell death and disease resistance. Plant Molec Biol 44:429-442.

Bendahmane, A., Kanyuka, K., and Baulcombe, D. C. 1999. The *Rx* gene from potato controls separate virus resistance and cell death responses. Plant Cell 11:781-791.

Bittner-Eddy, P. D., and Beynon, J. L. 2001. The Arabidopsis downy mildew resistance gene, *RPP13-Nd*, functions independently of *NDR1* and *EDS1* and does not require the accumulation of Salicylic Acid. Mol Plant-Microbe Interact 14:416-421.

Dangl, J. L., Dietrich, R. A., and Richberg, M. H. 1996. Death Don't Have No Mercy: cell death programs in plant-microbe interactions. Plant Cell 8:1793-1807.

Dangl, J. L., and Jones, J. D. G. 2001. Plant pathogens and integrated defence responses to infection. Nature 411:826-833.

Delledonne, M., Zeier, J., Marocco, A., and J., L. C. 2001. Signal interactions between nitric oxide and reactive oxygen intermediates in the plant hypersensitive disease resistance response. Proc Natl Acad Sci, USA *in press*.

Dietrich, R. A., Delaney, T. P., Uknes, S. J., Ward, E. J., Ryals, J. A., and Dangl, J. L. 1994. Arabidopsis mutants simulating disease resistance response. Cell 77:565-578.

Dietrich, R. A., Richberg, M. H., Schmidt, R., Dean, C., and Dangl, J. L. 1997. A novel zinc-finger protein is encoded by the Arabidopsis *lsd1* gene and functions as a negative regulator of plant cell death. Cell 88:685-694.

Glazebrook, J. 2001. Genes controlling expression of defense responses in Arabidopsis -2001 status. Curr Opin Plant Biol *in press*.

Govrin, E., and Levine, A. 2000. The hypersensitive response facilitates plant infection by the necrotrophic pathogen *Botrytis cinerea*. Curr Biol 10:751-757.

Heath, M. C. 2000. Hyoersensitive response-related death. Plant Molec Biol 44:321-334.

Hulbert, S. H. 1997. Structure and evolution of the *rp1* complex conferring rust resistance in maize. Annu Rev Phytopathol 35:293-310.

Jabs, T., Dietrich, R. A., and Dangl, J. L. 1996. Initiation of runaway cell death in an Arabidopsis mutant by extracellular superoxide. Science 27:1853-1856.

Kliebenstein, D. J., Dietrich, R. A., Martin, A. C., Last, R. L., and Dangl, J. L. 1999. LSD1 regulates Salicylic Acid induction of copper-zinc superoxide dismutase in *Arabidopsis thaliana*. Molec Plant-Microbe Interact 12:1022-1026.

Maleck, K., Levine, A., Eulgem, T., Morgan, A., Schmid, J., Lawton, K., Dangl, J. L., and Dietrich, R. A. 2000. The transcriptome of Arabidopsis during systemic acquired resistance. Nature Genet 26:403-410.

McDowell, J. M., Cuzick, A., Can, C., Beynon, J., Dangl, J. L., and Holub, E. B. 2000. Downy mildew (*Peronospora parasitica*) resistance genes in Arabidopsis vary in functional requirements for *NDR1*, *EDS1*, *NPR1*, and Salicylic Acid accumulation. Plant J 22:523-530.

Rate, D. N., Cuenca, J. V., Bowman, G. R., Guttman, D. S., and Greenberg, J. T. (1999). The gain-of-function Arabidopsis *acd6* mutant reveals novel regulation and function of the Salicylic Acid signaling pathway in controlling cell death, defense, and cell growth. Plant Cell 11:1695-1708.

Rustérucci, C., Aviv, D. H., Holt III, B. F., Dangl, J. L., and Parker, J. E. 2001. The disease resistance signaling components *EDS1* and *PAD4* are essential regulators of the cell death pathway controlled by *LSD1* in Arabidopsis. Plant Cell *in press*.

Ryals, J. L., Neuenschwander, U. H., Willits, M. C., Molina, A., Steiner, H.-Y., and Hunt, M. D. 1996. Systemic acquired resistance. Plant Cell 8:1809-1819.

Wendehenne, D., Pugin, A., Klessig, D. F., and Durner, J. 2001. Nitric oxide: comparative synthesis and signaling in animal and plant cells. Trends Plant Sci 6:177-183.

Yang, Y., Shah, J., and Klessig, D. F. 1997. Signal perception and transduction in plant defense responses. Genes Dev 11:1621-1639.

Zhang, Y., Weihua, F., Kinkema, M., X., L., and X, D. 1999. Interaction of NPR1 with basic leucine zipper protein transcription factors that bind sequences required for salicylic acid induction of the PR-1 gene. Proc Natl Acad Sci, USA 96:6523-6528.

Zhou, J.-M., Trifa, Y., Silva, H., Pontier, D., Lam, E., Shah, J., and Klessig, D. F. 2000. NPR1 differentially interacts with members of the TGA/OBF family of transcription factors that bind an element of the *PR-1* gene required for induction by salicylic acid. Molec Plant-Microbe Interact 15:191-202.

Systemic Acquired Resistance in Arabidopsis

Weihua Fan, Mark Kinkema, Joseph Clarke, Xin Li, Yuelin Zhang, Meenu Kesarwani, Wendy Durrant, Becky Mosher, and Xinnian Dong

DCMB Group, Department of Biology, Duke University, Durham, NC 27708-1000, USA

Systemic acquired resistance (SAR) is a secondary resistance response in plants that can be induced after a local hypersensitive response (HR) to avirulent pathogens (Ryals et al. 1996). Establishment of SAR involves production of a systemic signal at the primary infection site, accumulation of salicylic acid (SA) in both local and systemic tissues, and activation of a battery of effector genes, some of which are known as pathogenesis-related (*PR*) genes. Such concerted gene expression results in resistance to a variety of pathogens.

My laboratory uses *Arabidopsis thaliana* as a model system to dissect the signal transduction pathway of SAR. Using one of the SAR-regulated genes as a reporter, we isolated Arabidopsis mutants that showed either constitutive SAR (*cpr* mutants) or diminished SAR (*npr* mutants). Interestingly, while many *cpr* and *cpr*-like mutants have been isolated in screens performed in both my laboratory and other laboratories, only one *npr* locus, *npr1* (also known as *nim1*), was identified in multiple mutant screens (Cao et al. 1997; Ryals et al. 1997).

In the *npr1* mutants, SA-induced gene expression and resistance are completely blocked. The recessive nature of the *npr1* mutations indicates that wild-type NPR1 is a positive regulator of SAR required for transducing the SA signal (Cao et al. 1994). Under SAR inducing conditions, *NPR1* gene expression is moderately enhanced. Overexpression of *NPR1* using the constitutive CaMV 35S promoter in transgenic Arabidopsis resulted in plants with significantly enhanced resistance to *Pseudomonas syringae* and *Peronospora parasitica* which are both virulent pathogens on wild-type Arabidopsis (Cao et al. 1997).

The NPR1 function seems to be conserved in plants. *NPR1* homologs have been found in other plant species such as tomato, tobacco, apple, and rice. Excitingly, overexpression of Arabidopsis *NPR1* gene in rice led to transgenic plants with enhanced resistance to *Xanthomonas oryzae* pv. *oryzae*, a pathogen that causes rice leaf blight (Chern et al. 2001).

Northern blot analysis performed on the *NPR1*-overexpressing plants showed that the SAR-regulated genes are not constitutively expressed but rather induced during a pathogen challenge. This indicates that the overexpressed NPR1 proteins are inactive prior to a pathogen challenge probably due to the low levels of endogenous SA. This active-upon-induction character of NPR1 is ideal for engineering plants with disease resistance. Unlike the *cpr* mutants where the SAR pathway is constitutively turned on, *NPR1*-overexpressing plants are not compromised in growth and development even when grown in the wild (Heidel and Dong, unpublished).

To determine the induction mechanism of the NPR1 protein, we conducted various molecular and genetic experiments. Since the NPR1 protein contains three putative nuclear localization sequences (NLSs), we suspected that NPR1 might be a nuclear protein. Indeed, when we fused NPR1 with GFP, the resulting fusion protein was detected in the nuclei of the transgenic plants, with much stronger fluorescence observed in plants treated with SA than without the treatment (Kinkema et al. 2000). Site-directed mutagenesis was then performed on the three NLSs and the npr1-GFP fusions carrying specific mutations were tested *in planta* for their effects on nuclear localization of the protein and NPR1 function. We found that one of the three NLSs is important for nuclear targeting of NPR1 and simultaneous mutations of five of the basic amino acids in this sequence are required to completely abolish its function. To demonstrate that nuclear localization of NPR1 is essential for its function, we fused wild-type NPR1 with the hormone binding domain (HBD) of rat glucocorticoid receptor (GR) to control the nuclear movement of NPR1. In the absence of its ligand (dexamethasone), the HBD is associated with the hsp90 protein, which masks the NLSs located in HBD, and the protein is retained in the cytoplasm. In the presence of dexamethasone, the hormone will replace hsp90 and allow the protein to translocate to the nucleus. In the *NPR1-HBD* transgenic plants (in the *npr1-3* mutant background), NPR1-regulated gene expression was detected only when treated with both SA and dexamethasone, indicating that nuclear localization of NPR1 is essential for its function in regulating gene expression. Since the presence of SA is also required to induce gene expression in the *NPR1-HBD* transgenic plants, we suspect that in addition to nuclear localization, other SA-mediated activation events must also occur before gene expression.

The mechanism by which NPR1 regulates gene expression is not completely understood. NPR1 contains an ankyrin-repeat domain and a BTB domain, which are both involved in protein-protein interactions. Indeed, in multiple yeast two-hybrid screens performed in my laboratory and in other laboratories, NPR1 was found to interact with the TGA subfamily of bZIP transcription factors (Zhang et al. 1999). This subfamily of transcription factors have been implicated in regulating SA-mediated gene expression by various promoter and gel mobility shift assays. Different TGA transcription factors showed different affinities to NPR1. In yeast, this interaction appears to involve the C-terminal half of TGA, which we named NPR1-interacting domain (NID), and the BTB and ankyrin-repeat domains of NPR1. To demonstrate that this NPR1-TGA interaction indeed occurs *in vivo*, we overexpressed the NID of TGA2 in wild-type plants. It was anticipated that the NID fragment which lacks the DNA binding and dimerization domain (bZIP domain) would bind to NPR1, sequester the protein, and cause an *npr1* mutant phenotype. Indeed, in transgenic plants which showed high levels of NID, NPR1-regulated gene expression was diminished. To further demonstrate that this observed dominant-negative effect of NID was due to *in vivo* interaction with NPR1, we also overexpressed NID in an *npr1* mutant (*npr1-2*) which carries a point mutation that disrupts the interaction with TGA in yeast. We found that NID had no effect on the residual activity of npr1-2. In other words, the low levels of *PR* gene expression detected in *npr1-2* were not further reduced as a result of NID overexpression.

The biological consequence of NPR1-TGA interaction has yet to be revealed. According to the promoter study conducted in the *PR1* promoter (Lebel et al. 1998), TGA transcription factors should be positive regulators of this gene. Considering the fact that NPR1 positively regulates SAR, it is reasonable to hypothesize that NPR1 binding to TGA may be important for its nuclear transport, DNA binding, or transactivation activity. Our data showed that TGA factors can be transported to the nucleus without interacting with NPR1. *In vitro* experiments performed by Després et al. (2000) implied that NPR1 binding may enhance TGA binding to DNA. Our own data suggest that the situation *in vivo* may be more complicated than that proposed by Després et al. We suspect that different TGA factors may play different roles in NPR1-mediated gene expression. To reveal the effect of each TGA factor, we systematically isolated knockout mutants of each *TGA* gene and are in the process of generating co-suppression lines using the RNAi technology. Phenotype characterization of these mutants will provide genetic information on the roles of these transcription factors.

We also utilized genetic approaches to identify additional regulatory components of SAR besides NPR1 and TGA. A suppressor screen was performed in the *npr1-1* mutant background. In this screen, we looked for mutants that restored the expression of genes activated during SAR. From this screen we identified the *sni1* mutant (suppressor of *npr1*, inducible 1) in which systemic induction of *PR* genes and disease resistance is restored (Li et al. 1999). The point mutation found in *sni1* causes a frame shift early in the coding region. The recessive phenotype of this loss-of-function mutant indicates that wild-type SNI1 is a negative regulator of SAR and NPR1 is probably required to alleviate SNI suppression . Unfortunately, no interaction between SNI1 and NPR1or between SNI1 and TGA was detected in yeast two-hybrid assays. Even though SNI1 encodes a pioneer protein, conserved domains have been identified through sequence alignment with homologs found in other plant species. Systematic mutagenesis is being carried out in my laboratory to define the functional domains of this protein and determine the mechanism by which NPR1 derepresses SNI1.

Through the *npr1* suppressor screen and double mutant analysis performed between *npr1* and *cpr* mutants which show constitutively enhanced disease resistance, we found that many *cpr*-like mutants can confer resistance in the SA-insensitive *npr1* mutant background (Clarke et al. 2000). Surprisingly, the effect of *npr1* is often less drastic than that caused by an SA deficiency. These results seem to be inconsistent with our finding that *npr1* mutations block SA-induced SAR completely. Taking this contradicting evidence into consideration, we propose that NPR1 is required for SAR in systemic tissues where SA is a sufficient signal, but NPR1 is not required in local tissues where other signaling molecules are also present in addition to SA. In many *cpr*-like mutants, SA and other signaling molecules accumulate leading to activation of both NPR1-dependent and NPR1-independent resistance. Through genetic analysis, we suspect that components in the ethylene and jasmonic acid signaling pathway may be involved in this NPR1-independent but SA-dependent resistance.

In summary, we have made good progress in understanding the induction mechanism of SAR using Arabidopsis as a model organism. We found that SAR is regulated by both positive regulators such as NPR1 and TGA and negative regulators such as SNI1. NPR1 is a nuclear protein that interacts with the TGA subclass of bZIP transcription factors and alleviates SNI1 repression through an unknown mechanism. NPR1-independent but SA-dependent resistance also exists in plants, which may be involved in conferring resistance at the site of pathogen infection.

Literature Cited

Cao, H., Bowling, S.A., Gordon, S., and Dong, X. 1994. Characterization of an Arabidopsis mutant that is nonresponsive to inducers of systemic acquired resistance. Plant Cell 6: 1583-1592.

Cao, H., Glazebrook, J., Clark, J.D., Volko, S., and Dong, X. 1997. The Arabidopsis NPR1 gene that controls systemic acquired resistance encodes a novel protein containing ankyrin repeats. Cell 88: 57-64.

Chern, M.-S., Fitzgerald, H.A., Yadav, R.C., Canlas, P.E., Dong, X., and Ronald, P.C. 2001. Evidence for a disease resistance pathway in rice similar to the NPR1-mediated signaling pathway in Arabidopsis. Plant J. In press.

Clarke, J.D., Volko, S.M., Ledford, H., Ausubel, F.M., and Dong, X. 2000. Roles of salicylic acid, jasmonic acid, and ethylene in cpr-induced resistance in Arabidopsis. Plant Cell 12: 2175-90.

Després, C., DeLong, C., Glaze, S., Liu, E., and Fobert, P.R. 2000. The Arabidopsis NPR1/NIM1 protein enhances the DNA binding activity of a subgroup of the TGA family of bZIP transcription factors. The Plant Cell 12: 279-290.

Kinkema, M., Fan, W., and Dong, X. 2000. Nuclear Localization of NPR1 Is Required for Activation of PR Gene Expression. Plant Cell 12: 2339-2350.

Lebel, E., Heifetz, P., Thorne, L., Uknes, S., Ryals, J., and Ward, E. 1998. Functional analysis of regulatory sequences controlling *PR-1* gene expression in Arabidopsis. Plant J 16: 223-33.

Li, X., Zhang, Y., Clarke, J.D., Li, Y., and Dong, X. 1999. Identification and cloning of a negative regulator of systemic acquired resistance, SNI1, through a screen for suppressors of npr1-1. Cell 98: 329-339.

Ryals, J., Weymann, K., Lawton, K., Friedrich, L., Ellis, D., Steiner, H.-Y., Johnson, J., Delaney, T.P., Jesse, T., Vos, P., and Uknes, S. 1997. The Arabidopsis NIM1 protein shows homology to the mammalian transcription factor inhibitor IkB. The Plant Cell 9: 425-439.

Ryals, J.A., Neuenschwander, U.H., Willits, M.G., Molina, A., Steiner, H.-Y., and Hunt, M.D. 1996. Systemic acquired resistance. Plant Cell 8: 1809-1819.

Zhang, Y.L., Fan, W.H., Kinkema, M., Li, X., and Dong, X. 1999. Interaction of NPR1 with basic leucine zipper protein transcription factors that bind sequences required for salicylic acid induction of the PR-1 gene. Proc Natl Acad Sci USA 96: 6523-6528.

Analysis of SAR and Identification of Other Pathogen-Induced Defense Responses in Arabidopsis

Terrence P. Delaney, Cristiana Argueso, Nicole Donofrio, Han Suk Kim, Jong-Hyun Ko, Joshua Malamy and Greg Rairdan

Cornell University, Ithaca, NY U.S.A.

Plants achieve resistance to disease through action of a number of pathogen-induced responses. One of these is systemic acquired resistance (SAR), which depends upon salicylic acid accumulation and function of the *NIM1/NPR1* gene. A number of labs have sought to elucidate the SAR regulatory pathway using molecular genetic approaches in *Arabidopsis thaliana*. For example, in yeast two-hybrid experiments, several groups have found bZIP family transcription factors that interact with the NIM1/NPR1 protein (Despres et al. 2000; Zhang et al. 1999; Zhou et al. 2000; H. Kim and T. Delaney, unpublished data). We have extended these studies using transgenic plants to assess whether these factors play a defense role *in planta*. In other work, we used genetic screens to identify additional components of the NIM1/NPR1 pathway or novel resistance determinants, by isolating suppressor mutations that restore *Peronospora parasitica* resistance to *nim1-1* plants. Four of our suppressor mutants appear distinct from those identified elsewhere (Li et al. 1999; Shah et al. 1999), based on their suppressed phenotypes, suggesting that mutations in several genes can activate resistance in *nim1/npr1* mutants. It is evident that SAR is just one component of the defense armamentarium, and that other defense pathways are essential for full expression of pathogen-induced resistance. To identify genes that contribute to SAR-independent resistance (SIR) mechanisms, we conducted both genetic screens and cDNA cloning experiments in SAR-defective hosts after pathogen inoculation. This article will present an overview of our findings in these areas.

Work with Arabidopsis mutants has shown SAR to play a crucial role in controlling disease caused by a number of virulent pathogens. The findings have come from studies of salicylate hydroxylase-expressing (NahG) plants, and mutants with lesions in the *NIM1/NPR1* gene (Cao et al. 1994; Delaney et al. 1995; Delaney et al. 1994). Investigation into the role of the SAR pathway in race-specific resistance also showed that this pathway contributes to but is not sufficient for full expression of resistance to some normally avirulent pathogens (Delaney et al. 1994). Because avirulent pathogens are still retarded in growth when inoculated onto *nim1/npr1* mutants, it is apparent that some determinants of race-specific resistance are not under control of the SAR pathway. This 'residual' resistance can be substantial, depending upon which pathogen species and race is tested, suggesting the existence of important SA and NIM1/NPR1-independent forms of resistance (Delaney et al. 1995; Delaney et al. 1994). We feel that learning the identity of these pathways is crucial for understanding the maintenance of plant health. Further, for the rational development of strategies for controlling plant disease, we feel that it will be essential to understand at the molecular level not only the regulation of SAR, but also SAR-independent resistance (SIR) mechanisms.

Sar Regulation 1 - TGA2 and TGA5 Transgenic Plants

The NIM1/NPR1 protein is a central regulator of SAR (Cao et al. 1994; Delaney et al. 1995). Our initial thoughts about NIM1/NPR1 function were based on analysis of the protein sequence, which showed the existence of several ankyrin repeats, and well as other regions with similarity to the mammalian ankyrin repeat protein Iκ-B (Cao et al. 1997; Ryals et al. 1997). Because ankyrin repeats are known to interact with other proteins, it was reasonable to hunt for Arabidopsis proteins that bound to NIM1/NPR1 in yeast two hybrid screens. That work led to the discovery that several bZIP family transcription factors in the TGA subfamily bind NIM1/NPR1 (Despres et al. 2000; Zhang et al. 1999; Zhou et al. 2000; HSK and TPD, unpublished results). To test whether TGA2 or TGA5 factors play a role in regulating resistance, we made transgenic plants that contain sense or antisense constructions of each gene under control of the CaMV35S promoter. We saw only moderate changes in PR gene expression in the TGA2 transgenics, but a striking phenotype in TGA5 plants. First, many TGA5 antisense plants accumulated more TGA5 mRNA than did the control transgenic or wild type plants. This observation was confirmed in several independent transformants, which were also subjected to PCR amplification of the transgene insert and DNA sequencing to insure the identity of the transgene. Plants accumulating excessive amounts of TGA5 mRNA also showed significant reduction in PR-1 inducibility by pathogen or INA (2, 6-dichloroisonicotinic acid), and were highly resistant to *P. parasitica*. Together, these observations indicate that overexpression of TGA5 can activate a defense pathway that is not part of the PR-1 regulon of genes, and is in fact distinct from SAR.

In mammals, Iκ-B binds through its ankyrin repeats to the Rel family transcription factor Nf-KB, preventing the latter from entering the nucleus and controlling gene expression. Iκ-B itself is regulated by phosphorylation, ubiquitination and ubiquitin-mediated proteolysis. Thus phosphorylation of Iκ-B plays an important role in the ability of Nf-κB to bind to and regulate target gene promoters. Because of this regulatory mechanism, and the potential homology between Iκ-B and NIM1/NPR1, we have investigated the role phosphorylation may play in NIM1/NPR1 activity.

SAR Regulation 2 - Phosphorylation of NIM1/NPR1

Like most proteins, NIM1/NPR1 has a number of potential phosphoryla-tion sites based on sequence analysis, and some of these are found within conserved regions of Iκ-B (Ryals et al. 1997). To investigate if these sites are phosphorylated, we cloned the *NIM1/NPR1* gene into a bacterial expression vector, and purified the protein product. Using extracts made from Arabidopsis leaves, we found that NIM1/NPR1 can act as a substrate for protein kinase activity in the preparation, and incorporate radioactive phosphate from γ-labeled ATP. The phosphorylated NIM1/NPR1 protein was analyzed by phosphoamino acid analysis, and the majority of the phosphate addition was found to occur on serine residues, with a minor component evident on threonine residues. To determine which amino acids were modified, we performed peptide mapping by digesting the phosphorylated protein with trypsin and fractionating the products by two-dimensional gel electrophoresis. Four distinct peptide fragments were resolved, indicating that at least this number of phosphorylation sites exist in NIM1/NPR1. To map the positions of these sites we created 22 site-directed mutations, replacing selected serine or threonine residues with alanine. Most of the mutant proteins have been subjected to peptide mapping, and two of the radiolabeled peptide fragments have been correlated with specific mutations, providing a tentative map position for some of the phosphorylation events caused by the plant extract.

To assign function to candidate phosphorylation sites, we developed a transient assay to measure function of NIM1/NPR1 or mutant derivatives of the protein. Arabidopsis *nim1-1* protoplasts were transiently transformed with plasmids containing a *PR-1* promoter-GUS reporter construct, a CaMV 35S promoter expressing luciferase as an internal positive control, and a CaMV 35S promoter expressing the wild type *NIM1/NPR1* gene or mutant test version of the gene. Using this assay, we observed a consistent doubling of GUS activity when the wild type *NIM1/NPR1* gene is introduced into *nim1-1* protoplasts, compared to protoplasts receiving no *NIM1/NPR1* gene. When the 22 alanine-substituted mutants were tested in this assay, several produced approximately 25% greater GUS activity than did the wild type protein, while one mutant failed to activate the reporter. In two cases, mutations that replace serine/threonine residues with alanine alter both the peptide mapping profile as well as change the performance of the protein in the functional assay.

The aim of these studies is to determine whether phosphorylation plays a regulatory role for NIM1/NPR1. By correlating phosphorylation of certain sites with function of those sites, we can begin to learn whether this modification is essential for regulation of SAR. Additional work will be needed to assess the *in vivo* phosphorylation events that occur on NIM1/NPR1, and to learn whether this modification occurs coincident with signaling through the NIM1/NPR1 pathway.

SAR Regulation 3 - Genetic Suppressors of *nim1-1* Mutants

To identify additional components of the NIM1/NPR1 pathway, we conducted genetic suppressor screens to find second site mutations that masked the *nim1-1* phenotype. We exploited the highly susceptible phenotype of *nim1-1* (Ws-0 accession) to *P. parasitica* isolate Emwa2, and searched for resistant mutants. Our rationale for using pathogen resistance as a phenotype was that we could potentially recover a wider range of mutations that affected this trait, than if we had used a *PR* gene promoter-reporter strategy. The latter strategy may restrict the scope of the screen to genes that affect gene induction, and possibly fail to recover mutants that affect resistance without causing a change in PR gene expression.

Our suppressor screens yielded five mutants that displayed enhanced *P. parasitica* resistance despite harboring *nim1-1* mutations. Upon further analysis, the suppressors were found to fall into several phenotypic classes based on their defense gene expression phenotype and responsiveness to SA or INA; one is inherited as a dominant trait and four are recessive. Other groups have also reported suppressors of *nim1/npr1* mutants. Shah et al. (1999) described the *ssi1* mutation that restores PR gene expression in *npr1-5* plants, while Li et al. (1999) described and cloned *SNI1*, which when mutated restores INA and SA inducibility to *npr1-1* plants. We believe that most or all of our suppressors are not *ssi1* or *sni1* alleles, based on differences between the molecular phenotype and allele specificity of the mutants. For example *son2* (*SUPPRESSOR OF nim1-1*) shows restored PR-1 inducibility by INA, as does *sni1*, yet unlike *sni1*, *son2* is allele-specific, suppressing just some of the *nim1* alleles we have tested. Our *son1* suppressor is also noteworthy, because it expresses a high level of resistance to *P. parasitica*, yet shows no accumulation of PR-1,PR-2, PR-5 or PDF1.2 transcripts compared to wild type, genes whose expression is often correlated with resistance due to SAR or other responses. Using positional cloning techniques, we have localized *SON1* to a small region on chromosome 2, and identified a novel open reading frame at the locus that is polymorphic between *son1* and its parent, indicating that we may have cloned the gene. It will be interesting to learn the nature of the *SON1* gene, because it potentially may encode a regulator or effector of a novel *P.*

parasitica resistance mechanism.

Because disruption of SAR diminishes but does not eliminate resistance to most avirulent pathogens, other defense systems must exist that do not require SA accumulation and are independent of NIM1/NPR1. We believe that these pathways are accessible to genetic analysis and control expression of novel effector genes. Therefore, we have conducted genetic and molecular screens to identify genes required for SAR-independent resistance (SIR).

Novel Induced Defense Pathways 1 - SIR Mutant Screens

We previously showed that some normally avirulent pathogens display partial but not complete virulence on *nim1-1* plants (Delaney et al. 1995), implying that a form of NIM1/NPR1-independent resistance (NIR) functions in these plants. To identify putative *NIR* genes that control this resistance, we used EMS to mutagenize *nim1-1* plants and screened their M2 progeny for enhanced susceptibility to a normally avirulent *P. parasitica* strain. Approximately 108,000 M2 plants were examined, and two mutants recovered, currently designated 3-3-3 and 8-3-1. To eliminate the possibility that they derive from contaminating seed or pollen, both have been examined using molecular markers and shown to be homozygous for markers derived from the expected (Ws-O) parent. Mutant 3-3-3 exhibits s high susceptibility to the normally avirulent *P. parasitica* isolate Noco2, and is also more susceptible to the ascomycete pathogen *Erysiphe orontii* (MHG), which causes powdery mildew disease. Mutant 8-3-1 also shows high susceptibility to *P. parasitica*; progeny from this plant segregate for size and susceptibility, suggesting either a pleiotropic phenotype from this mutation, or that multiple mutant loci produce the observed phenotype. Additional work is underway to better understand these mutants.

Novel Induced Defense Pathways 2 - cDNA-AFLP
Screens in SAR Mutant Plants

We speculate that the residual resistance against avirulent pathogens that is expressed in SAR-compromised genotypes has some basis in differential gene expression. Therefore, identification of pathogen-induced genes in *nim1/npr1* mutants or NahG plants may reveal molecular markers of NIR or SIR pathways. Using cDNA-AFLP, we examined mRNA accumulation profiles in wild type, *nim1-1* and NahG plants one and four days following inoculation with a normally avirulent isolate of *P. parasitica*. cDNA fragments that showed a differential expression pattern after pathogen exposure were selected and reexamined using RNA blot analysis. Fifteen of the most promising gene fragments were further analyzed for expression properties after inoculation with Noco2, the virulent *P. parasitica* Emco5 and treatment with synthetic SAR inducer INA. Analysis of the genes' expression profiles in the three host genotypes showed that two had expression patterns typical for SAR-associated genes, such as PR-1, while four showed a NIM1/NPR1-independent response (NIR) pattern, and nine were expressed both in *nim1-1* and NahG plants, exhibiting an SA-independent response (SIR) behavior (Rairdan et al. 2001).

This approach led to identification of a number of pathogen-induced genes with different requirements for NIM1/NPR1 or SA accumulation in induction. The genes may prove to be useful molecular markers for NIR and SIR pathways, or possibly be regulators of resistance pathways or the effectors themselves. Historically, it has been difficult to identify the effectors that produce a disease resistance phenotype, despite substantial effort by many investigators. A few regulatory genes have been discovered using pathogen susceptibility assays or defense-associated gene promoter-reporter fusion approaches. In this regard, we feel it is unlikely that the genes identified in our cDNA-AFLP screens will be essential effectors of resistance, but they may prove to have great value as sources of promoters for the design of mutant screens to identify plants unable to activate novel NIR and SIR pathways. The recovery of *nir* and *sir* regulatory mutants will enable testing to determine the role, if any, such pathways have in defense, much like *nim1/npr1* mutants have been essential for demonstrating the role of the SAR pathway in defense.

Summary

Our yeast two-hybrid and *nim1-1* suppressor studies were aimed at learning the identity of other genes in the *NIM1/NPR1* pathway whose products contribute to the regulation of SAR. When this work is concluded, we may find that both approaches were successful in attaining that goal. However, an unanticipated result of our investigations was the discovery of resistance mechanisms that appear to be independent of SAR, based on the lack of SAR gene expression in *P. parasitica*-resistant *son1* mutants and transgenic TGA5 RNA over-accumulator plants. This suggests that the signaling pathways that control SAR and SIR may converge at certain points, possibly sharing some regulatory components. This concept has already been suggested by work with induced systemic resistance (ISR), which has been shown to be distinct from SAR yet dependent upon the NIM1/NPR1 gene product (Pieterse et al. 1998). Further, SA responsive defense pathways can be inhibited by flux through a jasmonate responsive pathway (Thomma et al. 1998), suggesting interference between the two pathways.

The elucidation of SAR-independent resistance mechanisms is essential for a complete understanding of plant immune and disease recovery systems. The development of disease resistant agricultural crops will require harnessing SAR as well as SAR-independent resistance pathways.

Acknowledgments

We apologize to those whose work could not be cited due to space restrictions. TPD acknowledges support of the NSF CAREER program (No. IBN-9722377) and USDA NRICGP (No. 9802134).

Literature Cited

Cao, H., Bowling, S. A., Gordon, A. S., and Dong, X. 1994. Characterization of an Arabidopsis mutant that is nonresponsive to inducers of systemic acquired resistance. Plant Cell 6:1583-1592.

Cao, H., Glazebrook, J., Clarke, J. D., Volko, S., and Dong, X. 1997. The Arabidopsis *NPR1* gene that controls systemic acquired resistance encodes a novel protein containing ankyrin repeats. Cell 88:57-63.

Delaney, T. P., Friedrich, L., and Ryals, J. A. 1995. Arabidopsis signal transduction mutant defective in chemically and biologically induced disease resistance. Proc. Natl. Acad. Sci. USA 92:6602-6606.

Delaney, T. P., Uknes, S., Vernooij, B., Friedrich, L., Weymann, K., Negrotto, D., Gaffney, T., Gut-Rella, M., Kessmann, H., Ward, E., and Ryals, J. 1994. A central role of salicylic acid in plant disease resistance. Science 266:1247-1250.

Despres, C., DeLong, C., Glaze, S., Liu, E., and Fobert, P. R. 2000. The Arabidopsis NPR1/NIM1 protein enhances the DNA binding activity of a subgroup of the TGA family of bZIP transcription factors. Plant Cell 12:279-290.

Li, X., Zhang, Y., Clarke, J. D., Li, Y., and Dong, X. 1999. Identification and cloning of a negative regulator of systemic acquired resistance, SNI1, through a screen for suppressors of *npr1-1*. Cell 98:329-339.

Pieterse, C. M. J., van Wees, S. C. M., van Pelt, J. A., Knoester, M., Laan, R., Gerrits, N., Weisbeek, P. J., and van Loon, L. C. 1998. A novel signaling pathway controlling induced systemic resistance in Arabidopsis. Plant Cell 10:1571-1580.

Rairdan, G. J., Donofrio, N. M., and Delaney, T. P. 2001. Salicylic acid and NIM1/NPR1-independent gene induction by incompatible *Peronospora parasitica* in Arabidopsis. Mol. Plant-Microbe Interact. 14(10):1235-1246.

Ryals, J., Weymann, K., Lawton, K., Friedrich, L., Ellis, D., Steiner, H. Y., Johnson, J., Delaney, T. P., Jesse, T., Vos, P., and Uknes, S. 1997. The Arabidopsis NIM1 protein shows homology to the mammalian transcription factor inhibitor I kappa B. Plant Cell 9:425-439.

Shah, J., Kachroo, P., and Klessig, D. F. 1999. The Arabidopsis *ssi1* mutation restores pathogenesis-related gene expression in *npr1* plants and renders defensin gene expression salicylic acid dependent. Plant Cell 11:191-206.

Thomma, B., Eggermont, K., Penninckx, I., Mauch-Mani, B., Vogelsang, R., Cammue, B. P. A., and Broekaert, W. F. 1998. Separate jasmonate-dependent and salicylate-dependent defense- response pathways in Arabidopsis are essential for resistance to distinct microbial pathogens. Proc. Natl. Acad. Sci. USA 95:15107-15111.

Zhang, Y., Fan, W., Kinkema, M., Li, X., and Dong, X. 1999. Interaction of NPR1 with basic leucine zipper protein transcription factors that bind sequences required for salicylic acid induction of the PR-1 gene. Proc. Natl. Acad. Sci. USA 96:6523-6528.

Zhou, J. M., Trifa, Y., Silva, H., Pontier, D., Lam, E., Shah, J., and Klessig, D. F. 2000. NPR1 differentially interacts with members of the TGA/OBF family of transcription factors that bind an element of the *PR-1* gene required for induction by salicylic acid. Mol. Plant-Microbe Interact. 13:191-202.

Cross-talk Between Salicylate- and Jasmonate-Dependent Induced Defenses in Arabidopsis

Corné M.J. Pieterse, Steven Spoel, Jurriaan Ton, Saskia C.M. Van Wees, Johan A. Van Pelt, and L.C. Van Loon

Section of Phytopathology, Utrecht University, The Netherlands

Plants possess inducible defense mechanisms to effectively combat invasion by microbial pathogens or attack by herbivorous insects. Research on defense signaling pathways revealed that induced defenses against pathogens and herbivores are regulated by a network of interconnecting signaling pathways in which the plant signal molecules salicylic acid (SA), jasmonic acid (JA) and ethylene (ET) play a dominant role (Glazebrook 2001; Pieterse and Van Loon 1999). In many cases, attack by pathogens or herbivores is associated with enhanced production of these hormones and a concomitant activation of distinct sets of defense-related genes (Maleck et al. 2000; Reymond et al. 2000; Schenk et al. 2000). Moreover, exogenous application of SA, JA or ET often results in an enhanced level of resistance (Van Wees et al. 1999).

Little is known about how plants integrate signals generated by different inducers of resistance into specific defense responses. An well-accepted hypothesis is that this is accomplished by modulation of different signaling pathways. There is ample evidence that SA-, JA-, and ET-dependent defense pathways can affect each other's signaling, either positively or negatively (for review see Pieterse et al. 2001a). This so-called cross-talk between pathways provides a great regulatory potential for activating multiple resistance mechanisms in varying combinations and may help the plant to prioritize the activation of a particular defense pathway over another, thereby providing an optimal defense against the invader encountered. It is often assumed that SA-dependent defenses and JA/ET-dependent defenses are mutually exclusive due to negative cross-talk (Felton and Korth 2000). This may have an enormous impact on crop plants that gained improved resistance to certain diseases or pests, either through genetic engineering of key factors of defense-signaling pathways, or upon treatment with chemical plant protectants that mimic the action of specific defense signaling molecules.

SA, JA and ET: Important Signals in Induced Resistance

A classic example of systemically induced resistance is activated after primary infection with a necrotising pathogen, rendering distant, uninfected plant parts more resistant towards a broad spectrum of virulent pathogens. This form of induced resistance is often referred to as systemic acquired resistance (SAR). The onset of SAR is associated with increased levels of SA (Métraux 2001), and the coordinate activation of a specific set of genes encoding pathogenesis-related (PR) proteins (Van Loon 1997). Transgenic NahG plants that cannot accumulate SA are incapable of developing SAR and do not show *PR* gene activation upon pathogen infection indicating that SA is a necessary intermediate in the SAR signaling pathway (Gaffney et al. 1993). Another key component in the SAR pathway is the regulatory protein NPR1. Mutants affected in the *NPR1* gene accumulate normal levels of SA in response to pathogen infection but fail to mount SAR (Cao et al. 1994). Upon induction of SAR, NPR1 activates *PR-1* gene expression by physically interacting with a subclass of basic leucine zipper protein transcription factors that bind to promoter sequences required for SA-inducible *PR* gene expression (Zhang et al. 1999), suggesting a direct link between NPR1 activity and regulation of *PR* gene expression.

Another type of induced resistance is triggered by selected strains of non-pathogenic, biological control bacteria that colonize plant roots. Similar to pathogen-induced SAR, the induced resistance is systemically activated and is effective against various pathogens. This type of induced disease resistance is often referred to as rhizobacteria-mediated induced systemic resistance (ISR; for reviews see Van Loon et al. 1998; Pieterse *et al.*, 2001b). In Arabidopsis, ISR has been shown to function independently of SA and *PR* gene activation (Pieterse et al. 1996; Van Wees et al. 1997). Instead, ISR signaling requires an intact response to both JA and ET (Pieterse et al. 1998; Ton et al. 2001a). The state of ISR is not associated with increases in the expression of known defense-related genes (Van Wees et al. 1999). However, upon challenge with a pathogen, ISR-expressing plants show an enhanced expression of certain JA-responsive genes, suggesting that ISR-expressing tissue is primed to activate specific JA-inducible genes faster or to a higher level upon attack (Van Wees et al. 1999). This phenomenon of priming has also been described for other types of induced resistance (Conrath et al. 2001; Zimmerli et al. 2000).

Although SAR and ISR follow distinct signaling pathways, they are both blocked in mutant *npr1* plants. Elucidation of the sequence of ISR-signaling events revealed that NPR1 functions downstream of the JA and the ET response (Pieterse et al. 1998). Evidently, NPR1 is not only required for the

SA-dependent expression of *PR* genes that are activated during SAR, but also for the JA- and ET-dependent activation of so far unidentified defense responses in rhizobacteria-mediated ISR.

Differential Effectiveness of SAR and ISR

SA, JA and ET are involved to different extents in basal resistance against specific pathogens. Mutant analyses in Arabidopsis showed that basal resistance against *Peronospora parasitica* and turnip crinkle virus (TCV) is controlled predominantly by a SA-dependent pathway (Delaney et al. 1994; Kachroo et al. 2000; Thomma et al. 1998). By contrast, basal resistance against *Alternaria brassicicola* is dependent on JA (Thomma et al. 1998), whereas basal resistance against *Pseudomonas syringae* pv. *tomato* (*Pst*) and *Xanthomonas campestris* pv. *armoraciae* was found to be controlled by a combined action of SA, JA and ET (Pieterse et al. 1998; Ton et al. 2001b). Comparison of the effectiveness of SA-dependent SAR and JA/ET-dependent ISR against these different Arabidopsis pathogens, revealed that SAR is predominantly effective against pathogens that in non-induced plants are resisted through SA-dependent basal resistance mechanisms, whereas ISR is predominantly effective against pathogens that in non-induced plants are resisted through JA/ET-dependent basal resistance responses (Ton et al. 2001b).

No Cross-talk Between SAR and ISR

Negative interactions between SA- and JA/ET-dependent defense pathways have been repeatedly demonstrated, feeding the notion that SA- and JA/ET-dependent defenses are mutually exclusive (for reviews see Felton and Korth 2000; Pieterse et al. 2001a). To investigate the possibility of negative cross-talk between the SAR and the ISR signaling pathway, we activated both pathways simultaneously and determined the level of protection against *Pst*, which is sensitive to both SAR and ISR. Simultaneous activation of SAR and ISR resulted in an additive effect on the level of induced protection against this pathogen. In Arabidopsis genotypes that are blocked in either SAR or ISR, this additive effect was not evident. Moreover, induction of ISR did not affect the expression of the SAR marker gene *PR-1* in plants expressing SAR. Together, these observations demonstrate that the SAR and the ISR pathway are compatible and that there is no significant cross-talk between these pathways (Van Wees et al. 2000). Therefore, combining SAR and ISR provides an attractive tool for improvement of disease control.

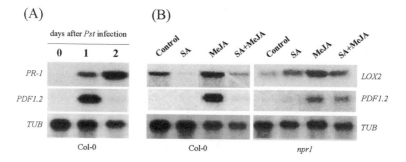

Fig. 1. (A) The JA-responsive *PDF1.2* gene is down-regulated in later stages of *Pst* infection when the SA-inducible *PR-1* gene is highly expressed. (B) Exogenous application of SA suppresses both steady-state and MeJA-induced mRNA levels of the JA-responsive genes *LOX2* and *PDF1.2* in wild-type Col-0 plants but not in mutant *npr1 plants.* The blots were also hybridized with a probe for β-tubulin (*TUB*) to check for equal loading.

Negative Cross-talk Between SA- and JA-Dependent Defenses

Although Van Wees et al. (2000) demonstrated that SA- and JA-dependent defenses are not necessarily mutually exclusive, other studies have shown that activation of the SAR pathway can negatively affect certain JA-dependent resistance responses. This negative cross-talk is thought to be caused by SA-mediated suppression of JA-responsive gene expression, possibly through the inhibition of JA biosynthesis and action (see Pieterse et al. 2001a and references herein). Previously, Van Wees et al. (1999) showed that the JA-responsive genes *PDF1.2*, *VSP*, and *LOX2* are transiently expressed upon infection with *Pst*. After a strong induction in early stages of infection, the genes were significantly down-regulated in the later stages when SA-inducible *PR*-genes were maximally expressed (see Fig. 1A for results of *PDF1.2* and *PR-1*). From this it was postulated that cross-talk between SA- and JA-dependent pathways is involved in the orchestration of the defense response against the invading pathogen.

To investigate the molecular mechanism of SA-mediated suppression of JA signalling, we monitored biosynthesis of JA and the expression of JA-responsive genes in Arabidopsis genotypes Col-0, NahG and *npr1*. Upon infection with *Pst*, NahG plants accumulated 32-fold more JA than wild-type Col-0 plants (1990 versus 61 ng/g FW), suggesting that JA biosynthesis was significantly suppressed by SA in wild-type plants. Consistent with this, infected NahG plants accumulated significantly higher levels of transcripts of the JA-responsive genes *PDF1.2*, *VSP*, and *LOX2*.

Furthermore, exogenous application of SA inhibited steady-state and/or MeJA-induced *PDF1.2*, *VSP*, and *LOX2* mRNA levels in wild-type Col-0 plants. However, in mutant *npr1* plants this inhibition was not apparent (see Fig. 1B for results of *PDF1.2* and *LOX2*), indicating that SA-mediated inhibition of JA-inducible gene expression functions via NPR1.

LOX2 encodes a key enzyme in the octadecanoid pathway leading to biosynthesis of JA. Thus, SA-mediated inhibition of *LOX2* gene expression might be sufficient to inhibit JA production. To investigate this we monitored JA production in *Pst*-infected transgenic S-12 plants, which have severely reduced levels of the LOX2 isozyme due to co-suppression of the *LOX2* gene (Bell et al. 1995). The reduced LOX2 levels in S-12 plants had no effect on the steady-state JA level, but the wound-induced production of JA is blocked (Bell et al. 1995). Two days after *Pst* infection, infected Col-0 leaves showed an 8-fold increase in JA levels compared to the water control (115 versus 15 ng/g FW). In contrast, water-treated and *Pst*-infected S-12 plants showed similar, low basal levels of JA (8 versus 19 ng/g FW), indicating that suppression of the *LOX2* gene is sufficient to block pathogen-induced production of JA (Pieterse et al. 2000).

In view of the above mentioned results we hypothesize that SA-mediated inhibition of JA signaling is based on an NPR1-dependent suppression of JA-responsive gene expression. Consequently, suppression of the JA-responsive *LOX2* gene, and possibly also other JA-responsive genes involved in JA biosynthesis, leads to an inhibition of JA biosynthesis. The mode of action of the NPR-dependent down-regulation of JA-responsive gene expression by SA is currently being investigated.

Literature Cited

Bell, E., et al. 1995. Proc. Natl. Acad. Sci. USA 92:8675-8679.
Cao, H., et al. 1994. Plant Cell 6:1583-1592.
Conrath, U., et al. 2001. Eur. J Plant Pathol. 107:113-119.
Delaney T.P., et al. 1994. Science 266:1247-1250.
Felton, G.W. and Korth, K.L. 2000. Curr Opinion Plant Biol 3:309-314.
Gaffney, T., et al. 1993. Science 261:754-756.
Glazebrook, J. 2001. Curr Opinion Plant Biol. 4: 301-308.
Kachroo, P., et al. 2000. Plant Cell 12:677-690.
Maleck, K. et al. 2000. Nature Genetics 26:403-410.
Métraux J.-P. 2001. Eur. J Plant Pathol. 107:13-18.
Pieterse, C.M.J. and Van Loon, L.C. 1999. Trends Plant Sci. 4:52-58.
Pieterse, C.M.J. et al. 1996. Plant Cell 8:1225-1237.
Pieterse, C.M.J. et al. 1998. Plant Cell 10:1571-1580.
Pieterse, C.M.J. et al. 2000. Physiol. Mol. Plant Pathol. 57:123-134.
Pieterse, C.M.J. et al. 2001a. AgBiotechNet, in press.
Pieterse,C.M.J. et al. 2001b. Eur. J Plant Pathol. 107:51-61.

Reymond, P. et al. 2000. Plant Cell 12:707-719.

Schenk, P.M. et al. 2000. Proc. Natl. Acad. Sci. USA 97:11655-11660.

Thomma, B.P.H.J. et al. 1998. Proc. Natl. Acad. Sci. USA 95:15107-15111.

Ton, J. et al. 2001a. Plant Physiol. 125:652-661.

Ton, J. et al. 2001b. manuscript submitted.

Van Loon, L.C. 1997. Eur. J Plant Pathol. 103:753-765.

Van Loon, L.C. et al. 1998. Annu. Rev. Phytopathol. 36:453-483.

Van Wees, S.C.M. et al. 1997. Mol. Plant-Microbe Interact. 6:716-724.

Van Wees, S.C.M. et al. 1999. Plant Mol. Biol. 41:537-549.

Van Wees, S.C.M. et al. 2000 Proc. Natl. Acad. Sci. USA 97:8711-8716.

Zhang, Y. et al. 1999. Proc. Natl. Acad. Sci. USA 96: 6523-6528.

Zimmerli, L. et al. 2000. Proc. Natl. Acad. Sci. USA 97: 12920-12925.

Mechanism of Local and Systemic Oxidative Bursts Induced by Infection or Elicitor in Potato

Noriyuki Doke, Hirofumi Yoshioka, Kazuhito Kawakita, Kenichi Sugie, Kouji Sunazaki and Hae Jun Park

Graduate School of Bioagricultural Sciences, Nagoya University

Local and systemic oxidative bursts (OXB) were firstly demonstrated in relation to a signal mechanism for induction of local and systemic resistance in potato plants (Doke 1983a, 1983b and Chai and Doke 1987a, respectively). Local OXB is a common reaction in the early process of hypersensitive resistance response of tissues, suspension-cultured cells or protoplasts of many kinds of plant species against infection with incompatible pathogens or non-pathogenic pathogens, or by treatment with elicitors of the hypersensitive reaction (Doke 1997). Systemic OXB was induced by local OXB at a distant tissue in relation to a novel systemic signaling system for induction of systemic acquired resistance (SAR) (Park et al. 1998a, 1998b, Sunazaki et al. 1999, 2000).

In the present review, we describe phenomena and mechanisms of local and systemic OXB based on our recent work using potato plants.

Mechanism of Local OXB

PHARMACEUTICAL INVESTIGATION ON MECHANISM

Doke (1985) showed that infection- or fungal elicitor-stimulated local OXB was dependent on an O_2^--generating NADPH oxidase in plasma membrane of potato tissues. The mechanism of the OXB had been investigated using leaves, wounded-tissues, suspension-cultured cells or protoplasts, and evaluated and discussed on the basis of experimental results using specific metabolic inhibitors (Doke 1997). Extracellular Ca^{2+}-chelator, Ca^{2+}-channel blockers and inhibitors of calmodulin or protein kinase blocked the fungal wall elicitor-induced local OXB (Miura et al.

1995). Calcium ionophore or ionomycin, that caused Ca^{2+} influx, stimulated local OXB similar to that with the elicitor. Inhibitors of protein phosphatase, calyculin A also induced local OXB (Kanai et al. Unpublished data). Inhibitors of calmodulin or protein kinase also inhibited the induction of local OXB by these reagents. Simultaneous treatment of the tissue with elicitor or ionomycin and calyculin A caused a synergistic enhancement of local OXB. An inhibitor of human neutrophil NADPH oxidase inhibited the elicitor-stimulated local OXB. These pharmacological studies provided an idea that Ca^{2+} influx through channel, and then Ca^{2+}, calmodulin-dependent protein kinase may be involved in activation of an O_2^--generating NADPH oxidase responsible for local OXB. Furthermore, the tissue or cells with latent potential for OXB might be in an active state of the OXB system by balancing activation and inactivation through Ca^{2+}-calmodulin-dependent phosphorylation and dephosphorylation of some key proteins for the activity.

The OXB potential of potato tissue was nil on fresh sliced-tissue within 3 hrs after slicing, and then increased depending on new protein synthesis with time of aging (Komatsubara et al. Unpublished data). Fresh wounded-surface cells did not show the OXB response to elicitor as well as Ca^{2+} ionophore, ionomycin or calyculin A, although the basic level of *in vitro* activity of the O_2^--generating NADPH oxidase in isolated plasma membrane was not significantly different between aged and fresh wounded-tissues. These observations suggested that plant tissues might have a cell priming process for the OXB response after wounding.

O_2^--GENERATING NADPH OXIDASE IN PLASMA MEMBRANE

Enhanced activity of O_2^- generating NADPH oxidase had been obtained in the plasma membrane fraction isolated from potato tuber tissues with local OXB caused by infection (Doke 1985). Diphenyliodonium (DPI), a specific inhibitor of O_2^--generating NADPH oxidase in human leucocytes, also inhibited the NADPH-dependent O_2^--generating activity in the plasma membrane fraction.

An *in vitro* activation of the O_2^--generating NADPH oxidase in plasma membrane isolated from non-stimulated potato tuber tissue was achieved by stimulation with HWC or a detergent, digitonin in a reaction mixture consisting of Ca^{2+} and ATP (Doke and Miura 1995). Ca^{2+} chelator and inhibitors of calmodulin and protein kinase also inhibited the *in vitro* activation (Miura et al. Unpublished data).

Molecular Basis of Local OXB System

GP91*PHOX* HOMOLOG OF NADPH OXIDASE

According to the homology of NADPH oxidase with a human O_2^--generating NADPH oxidase consisted of gp91^{phox}, p47, p67, and rac, we cloned two gp91phox homologues, StrbohA and StrbohB, from potato tuber (Yoshioka et al. 2000). These proteins were estimated to have 6 transmenbrane-spanning domains, flavin adenine dinucleotide, NADPH-ribose, and NADPH-adenine binding sites at the C-terminus similar to human neutrophil NADPH oxidase gp91^{phox}, and two Ca^{2+} binding domains (EF hand) at the N-terminal region similar to plant gp91^{phox} homologue from Arabidopsis (Keller et al. 1998).

EXPRESSION OF STRBOHA AND STRBOHB

Northern analysis of expression of StrbohA and StrbohB genes in aged wound tuber tissue following elicitor treatment suggested differential expression of these genes. The former was constitutively expressed without induction by elicitor treatment, but the latter was inductively expressed from about 6 h with a maximum at 9 h after elicitor treatment (Yoshioka et al. 2000). Long-term assay of OXB after elicitor treatment showed two phases of early and late OXB. StrbohA and StrbohB may be responsible for the early and late OXB, respectively.

Mechanism Of Induction Of Systemic OXB

In a potato tuber with aged sliced-surface at both basal and topside, induction of local OXB on one side by treatment with elicitor was followed within several minutes by an OXB on the other side. This phenomenon had been proposed as a systemic OXB in a plant tissue (Park et al. 1998a). Elicitor treatment together with inhibitors of local OXB or scavengers of AOS resulted in no occurrence of local or systemic OXB (Park et al.1998b). The reaction of systemic OXB was suppressed by most of inhibitors of induction of local OXB, suggesting that systemic OXB might be induced by some systemic signals that activate the $O2^-$-generating NADPH oxidase (Park et al. 1998b). The inhibitory effect of catalase on induction of systemic OXB suggested that H_2O_2 generated during local OXB might play an important role in dispatching of a systemic signal. Application of H_2O_2 on aged, but not fresh, sliced-tissues induced the systemic OXB (Sunazaki et al. 2000).

In a thin rectangular tissue with aged, sliced surfaces on both sides as shown in Fig. 1, elicitor treatment at one aged, sliced-surface showed occurrence of local OXB to about 2 mm depth (ca. 30 cells) from the treated surface, followed by systemic OXB at ca. 2 mm depth from the other aged, sliced-surface. No OXB was observed on the freshly cut surface between the area showing local and systemic OXB (Sunazaki et al. 2000). In this experimental system, application of a Ca^{2+} chelator and Ca^{2+} channel blocker, but not inhibitors of calmodulin or protein kinase, in the pathway of the systemic signal stopped the induction of systemic OXB. Monitoring the change in fluorescence due to Fluo-3, a Ca^{2+} indicator, or pyranine, a pH indicator, which were loaded in the tissue along the pathway of the systemic signal, indicated the occurrence of a rapid Ca^{2+} influx from cell to cell and an increase in the pH outside of these cells (Sunazaki et al. 2000).

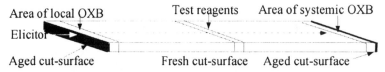

Area of local OXB   Test reagents   Area of systemic OXB

Elicitor

Aged cut-surface   Fresh cut-surface   Aged cut-surface

Fig. 1. A model tissue system for determination of the mechanism of systemic signalling of the systemic oxidative burst. Elicitor treatment causes a local OXB followed by systemic OXB in restricted areas. The signal passes through tissue with no potential for OXB.

Concluding Remarks

The OXB based on an O_2^--generating NADPH in the plasma membrane may be involved in induction of not only local, but also systemic induction of disease resistance. We assumed that their activation was regulated through Ca^{2+}, calmodulin dependent protein kinase. H_2O_2 generated during local OXB may stimulate a systemic signaling system consisted of a chain reaction of Ca^{2+} influx from cell to cell.

The molecular basis of the local and systemic OXB and the systemic signaling system remains to be further investigated to understand their mechanism and function in relation to both local and systemic induced resistance in plants.

Acknowledgements

The work was supported in part by Grant-in-aid for Scientific Research (A) and for Scientific Research on Priority Areas (A) from the Ministry of Education, Science, Sports and Culture.

Literature Cited

Doke, N. 1983a. Involvement of superoxide anion generation in hyper-sensitive response of potato tuber tissues to infection with an incompatible race of *Phytophthora infestans*. Physiol. Plant Pathol. 23:345-357.

Doke, N. 1983b. Generation of superoxide anion by potato tuber proto-plasts upon the hypersensitive response to hyphal wall compo-nents of *Phytophthora infestams* and specific inhibition of the reaction by suppressors of hypersensitivity. Physiol. Plant. Pathol. 23: 359-367.

Doke. N. 1997. The oxidative burst: roles in signal transduction and plant stress. Pages 785-813 in: Oxidative Burst and the Molecular Biology of Antioxidant Defenses, Scandalios, J. G. ed. CSH Laboratory Press.

Chai. H. B. and Doke, N. 1987. Systemic activation of O_2- generating reaction, superoxide dismutase and peroxidase in potato plant in relation to systemic induction of resistance to *Phytophthora infestans*. Ann. Phytopath. Soc. Jpn 53:585-590.

Keller, T., Damude, H. G., Werner, D., Doerner, P., Dixon, R. A., and Lamb, C. 1998. A plant homologue of the neutrophil NADPH oxidase gp91phox subunit gene encodes a plasma membrane protein with $Ca2^+$ binding motifs. Plant Cell 10:255-266.

Miura, Y., Yoshioka, Y. and Doke, N. An autographic determination of the active oxygen generation in potato tuber slices during hypersensitive response to fungal infection or elicitor. Plant Sci. 105:45-52.

Park. H.-J., Doke, N., Miura, Y., Kawakita, K., Noritake, T. and Komatsubara, H. 1998a. Induction of a sub-systemic oxidative burst by elicitor-stimulated local oxidative burst in potato plant tissues: a possible systemic signaling in systemic acquired resistance. Plant Sci. 138:197-208.

Park, H.-J., Miura, Y., Kawakita, K., Yoshioka, H. and Doke, N. 1998b. Physiological mechanisms of a sub-systemic oxidative burst triggered by elicitor-induced local oxidative burst in potato tuber slices. Plant Cell Physiol. 39:1218-1225.

Sunazaki, K., Ban, S., Park, H.-J., Yoshioka, H., Kawakita, K. and Doke, N. 1999. Induction of local and systemic oxidative bursts in plants by elicitors and plant activators. Ann. Phytopath. Soc. Jpn. 65:690 (abst.).

Sunazaki, K., Yoshioka, H., Kawakita, K. and Doke, N. 1999. Signal mechanisms for induction of systemic oxidative burst in plant tissues: involvement of calcium ion. Ann Phytopath. Soc. Jpn 66:110 (abst.).

Yoshioka, H., Sugie, K., Park, H. J., Maeda, H., Tsuda, N., Kawakita, K. and Doke, N. 2001. Induction of plant gp91 *phox* homologue by fungal cell wall, arachidonic acid, salicylic acid in potato. Mol. Plant-Microbe Interact. 14:725-736.

The Identity and Function of Cyst Nematode-Secreted Proteins in Pathogenesis

Ling Qin, Geert Smant, Jaap Bakker, Johannes Helder

Wageningen University, Graduate School for Experimental Plant Sciences, Laboratory of Nematology, Wageningen, The Netherlands

INTIMATE PLANT-PATHOGEN INTERACTIONS

Evolution of communities of organisms has resulted in many kinds of interactions varying from peaceful, separate co-existence (= non-interaction) to symbiotic or parasitic relationships. Some pathogens have developed sophisticated mechanisms to interact with their hosts and start a durable relationship. Durable parasitic relationships are fascinating and scientifically interesting as they illustrate the maximal impact of co-evolution. Often these pathogens have evolved the ability to recognize individual compounds unintentionally released by their hosts. These signals will then trigger the production and / or the release of an array of pathogenicity factors from the parasites. The comprehension of the molecular events underlying the resulting intimate interactions will lead to the better understandings of the basic biology as well as development of new approaches to elegantly and specifically control harmful pathogens.

Nematodes, members of the phylum Nematoda, are present in almost all the imaginable habitats on earth. Most nematodes are free-living and relatively few nematode species developed into parasites of plants or animals. Among these parasitic nematodes, sedentary endoparasitic nematodes of plants have evolved complex relationships with their hosts and they complete the whole life cycle by extracting nutrients solely from a fixed feeding site inside the host plant root. Economically, the families *Heteroderidae* including cyst (*Heterodera* and *Globodera* spp.) and *Meloidogyne*, root knot nematodes, are the most important.

NEMATODE SECRETIONS

As compared to nematodes that feed on bacteria, plant parasitic nematodes have relatively enormous esophageal glands. Cyst nematodes have one dorsal and two subventral esophageal secretory glands. The secretory proteins produced in these glands are thought to play key roles in the parasitism of host plants (Davis et al., 2000).

The morphologies of the subventral and dorsal esophageal glands are highly different during the parasitic process, which could point at different functions. During migration through the plant root, the two subventral secretory glands are large and packed with secretory granules. The onset of parasitism, feeding-site initiation, is accompanied by a rapid decrease in size of the two subventral glands, whereas the dorsal gland shows a remarkable enlargement. These changes were observed for both the cyst and root knot nematodes (Hussey and Mims 1990; Wyss et al. 1992). These morphological changes suggest an important role of subventral gland secretions during migration. To date, a small number of subventral gland proteins have been identified: β-1,4-endoglucanases (Smant et al. 1998) and a pectate lyase (Popeijus et al. 2000). The nature of these proteins suggests that the subventral gland proteins indeed play a role during migration through the plant root. Feeding site initiation is accompanied by an activation of the dorsal gland and, as such, dorsal gland proteins could be functional during the onset of parasitism and are likely to be important for the induction and maintenance of the syncytium.

STRATEGIES TO CLONE NEMATODE SECRETORY GENES

Because of the small sizes of infective juveniles, their obligatory plant parasitic nature and their relatively long life cycle, it is a formidable challenge to collect pure nematode secretions essentially free from other microbial contaminants and perform protein analysis. Several alternative approaches can be used to circumvent this problem.

Monoclonal antibodies. Monoclonal antibodies (mAb's) were raised against nematode secretions. One mAb reacting with the subventral glands of the potato cyst nematode was used to immunopurify proteins for sequence analysis and the first subventral gland secretory proteins, β-1,4-endoglucanases, were identified in this way (Smant et al. 1998). Several mAb's have been raised that specifically recognized the dorsal glands of cyst and root knot nematodes (Atkinson et al. 1988; Davis et al. 1994). However, the corresponding genes could not be identified. The mAb approach is time-consuming and appeared to be biased towards immuno-dominant proteins.

Expressed sequence tags. Expressed sequence tags (EST) are single pass sequences of cDNA clones selected randomly from a library. When high throughput sequencing facility is available, a large number of nematode genes can be discovered rather quickly.

A novel cDNA-AFLP-based stategy. Most pathogenicity factors are not expressed constitutively, but in a highly coordinated way. cDNA-AFLP is a novel RNA fingerprinting technique to display differentially expressed genes, which can also distinguish between highly homologous genes from individual gene families. In our laboratory, this robust and relatively cheap technique has been applied to monitor the gene expression of five distinct life stages of the potato cyst nematode (Qin et al. 2000). Three enzyme combinations of cDNA-AFLP experiments have been performed covering approximately 70% of the expressed genes. Dozens of putative pathogenicity factors have been identified and *in situ* hybridization experiments have revealed that most of these genes are specifically expressed in the esophageal glands (Ling Qin, unpublished). In fact, a survey of the expression patterns of the genes representing a significant part of the genome can be achieved with relatively small investment both in time and financial resources.

IDENTIFICATION OF A RANBPM-LIKE GENE FAMILY

Using this novel cDNA-AFLP-based strategy, we have identified a multiple gene family from the potato cyst nematode *Globodera rostochiensis*, which shares significant homology with RanBPMs (Ran-Binding Protein in Microtubule organizing center) from various organisms. These genes were up-regulated in the infective second-stage juvenile (J2), preceded by a predicted signal peptide for secretion, and specifically expressed in the dorsal glands of infective juveniles (Table 1).

Table 1. Overview of eight cDNAs of a RanBPM-like gene family predominantly expressed in pre-parasitic second stage juveniles of the potato cyst nematode *G. rostochiensis*.

Gene name	TDF No.	EST No.	Full length cDNA (bp)	Length partial cDNA	*In situ* hybridization
GR-*dgl-2A*	A41	-	871	-	Dorsal gland
GR-*dgl-2B*	A18	-	845	-	Dorsal gland
GR-*dgl-2C*	E19	GE2075	885	-	n.d
GR-*dgl-2D*	A29	-	-	246	Dorsal gland
GR-*dgl-2E*	A30	GE1855	-	193	n.d
GR-*dgl-2F*	NA16	-	-	192	Dorsal gland
GR-*dgl-2G*	-	GE1156	-	470	n.d
GR-*dgl-2H*	-	GE1519	-	244	n.d

n.d.: not determined.

Using the homology search programs BLASTP, GR-DGL-2B was shown to be homologous to the N terminal parts of a number of RanBPMs (Ran-Binding Protein in microtubule organizing center) from *Xenopus laevis* (38% identity, 50% similarity, and an E value of $3e^{-15}$), from fission yeast (*Schizosaccharomyces pombe*) (31% identity, 45% similarity, and an E value of $7e^{-14}$), from *Caenorhabditis elegans* (hypothetical protein Y54E5A.7): 31% identity, 45% similarity, E value of $2e^{-12}$) and from *Homo sapiens* (40% identity; 50% similarity, E value of $5e^{-12}$). Only the function of the *Homo sapiens* RanBPM protein has been studied in some more detail. Currently, we are investigating the possible roles of these RanBPM-like proteins in syncytium induction.

ASSESSING THE IMPORTANCE OF PATHOGENICITY FACTORS

To infect their hosts, plant parasitic nematodes produce a range of pathogenicity factors. There is a need for reliable methods that would allow us to evaluate the relative importance of the putative parasitism genes.

Nematode transformation. A transformation protocol of the potato cyst nematode would be very useful either to knockout one putative pathogenicity factor or test whether one protein may function as an avirulence factor. Unfortunately, for plant parasitic nematodes, due to the long life cycle, obligatory parasitic nature and lack of selective markers, an efficient transformation protocol has not been established yet. As a first step, we have cloned the promoter of GAPDH gene from the potato cyst nematode and fused it to a reporter gene green fluorescence protein. After microinjection, this promoter was shown to be functional in *C. elegans* (Qin et al. 1998).

Double-stranded RNA. Introduction of double-stranded RNA (dsRNA) has been shown to specifically disrupt the activity of genes containing homologous sequences in *C. elegans* (Fire et al. 1998). dsRNA can be delivered by micro-injection, bacteria feeding or soaking in solutions containing dsRNA. This technique can be adapted to silence genes from plant parasitic nematodes. For example, host plants could be transformed with constructs encoding dsRNA. When nematodes are feeding on the transformed plants, they will automatically take up dsRNA.

Inhibitory antibodies. An ingenious approach is to use so-called 'plantibodies'; the expression *in planta* of single chain antibodies (scAb) that have high binding affinity to the candidate pathogenicity factors in order to inactivate these nematode proteins (Schots et al. 1992). In this way, the functionality of putative pathogenicity factors could be assessed. It is probably feasible and likely to be beneficial to express both scAb and dsRNA at the same time and in the same nematode feeding sites in order to achieve the maximum silencing effect.

Given the enormous efforts implicated in the sequencing of eukaryotes,
it is unlikely that pathogens such as the potato cyst nematode or any other
plant parasitic nematode will be sequenced within the near future. An
alternative way to discover a large number of genes with a modest
investment is the expressed sequence tag (EST) approach. Because many
genes are developmentally regulated, preferably cDNA libraries should be
used from several distinct life stages, especially from the young parasitic
stages. A good quality gland-specific library would lead to the sequencing
of a higher percentage of parasitism-related genes. The limitation of EST
approach is that it will not reveal the potential functions of the genes if they
do not share homologies with functionally annotated genes in the database.
It is therefore necessary to link ESTs with functional genomics techniques.
We have developed software GenEST to link ESTs with cDNA-AFLP
expression profiles (Qin et al. 2001). Using GenEST, ESTs, which are
predicted by the program to have interesting expression patterns, can be
quickly identified. Alternatively, identifiers of a band displayed on a
cDNA-AFLP gel can be used to obtain the DNA sequence(s) corresponding
to this band. The expression pattern of ESTs can also be analyzed using
cDNA microarray technique. Equally, if not even more informative, is the
proteomics approach which can provide profiles of a large number of
proteins. The amino acid sequences from minute amounts of proteins, for
instance the mixture of proteins that is secreted by potato root diffusate-
exposed infective juveniles, can be readily determined by mass-
spectrometry technology. Proteomics of plant nematology will certainly
become an interesting research area in the next few years.

Literature Cited

Atkinson, H. J., P. D. Harris, E. J. Halk, C. Novitski, J. Leighton-Sands, P.
Nolan, P. C. Fox, and J. L. Sands. 1988. Monoclonal antibodies to the
soybean cyst nematode, *Heterodera glycines*. Ann. Appl. Biol. 112:459-
469.
Davis, E. L., R. Allen, and R. S. Hussey. 1994. Developmental expression
of esophageal gland antigens and their detection in stylet secretions of
Meloidogyne incognita. Fundam. Appl. Nematol. 17:255-262.
Davis, E. L., R. S. Hussey, T. J. Baum, J. Bakker, A. Schots, M. N. Rosso,
and P. Abad. 2000. Nematode parasitism genes. Ann. Rev. Phytopathol.
38:365-396.
Fire, A., S. Xu, M. K. Montgomery, S. A. Kostas, S. E. Driver, and C. C.
Mello. 1998. Potent and specific genetic interference by double-stranded
RNA in *Caenorhabditis elegans*. Nature 391:806-811.

Hussey, R. S. and C. W. Mims. 1990. Ultrastructure of esophageal glands and their secretory granules in the root-knot nematode *Meloidogyne incognita*. Protoplasma 156:9-18.

Popeijus, H., H. Overmars, J. Jones, V. Blok, A. Goverse, H. Helder, A. Schots, J. Bakker, and G. Smant. 2000. Degradation of plant cell walls by a nematode. Nature 406:36-37.

Qin, L., H. Overmars, J. Helder, H. Popeijus, d. V. van, Jr., W. Groenink, P. van Koert, A. Schots, J. Bakker, and G. Smant. 2000. An efficient cDNA-AFLP-based strategy for the identification of putative pathogenicity factors from the potato cyst nematode *Globodera rostochiensis*. Mol. Plant-Microbe Interact. 13:830-836.

Qin, L., P. Prins, J. T. Jones, H. Popeijus, G. Smant, J. Bakker, and J. Helder. 2001. GenEST, a powerful bidirectional link between cDNA sequence data and gene expression profiles generated by cDNA-AFLP. Nucleic Acids Res. 29:1616-1622.

Qin, L., G. Smant, J. Stokkermans, J. Bakker, A. Schots, and J. Helder. J. 1998. Cloning of a *trans*-spliced glyceraldehyde-3-phosphate-dehydrogenase gene from the potato cyst nematode *Globodera rostochiensis* and expression of its putative promoter region in *Caenorhabditis elegans*. Mol.Biochem.Parasitol. 96:59-67.

Schots, A., J. M. De Boer, A. Schouten, J. Roosien, J. F. Zilverentant, H. Pomp, L. Bouwman, H. Overmars, F. J. Gommers, B. Visser, W. J. Stiekema, and J. Bakker. 1992. 'Plantibodies': a flexible approach to design resistance against pathogens. Neth. J. Pl. Path. Supplement 2: 183-191.

Smant, G., J. P. Stokkermans, Y. Yan, J. de Boer, T. J. Baum, X. Wang, R. S. Hussey, F. J. Gommers, B. Henrissat, E. L. Davis, J. Helder, A. Schots, and J. Bakker. 1998. Endogenous cellulases in animals: isolation of beta-1, 4-endoglucanase genes from two species of plant-parasitic cyst nematodes. Proc. Natl. Acad. Sci. U.S.A 95:4906-4911.

Wyss, U., F. M. W. Grundler, and A. Munch. 1992. The parasitic behaviour of second-stage juveniles of *Meloidogyne incognita* in roots of *Arabidopsis thaliana*. Nematologica 38:98-111.

Type I Secretion and Sulfation are Required for *avrXa21* Avirulence Activity of *Xanthomonas oryzae* pv. *oryzae*

Yuwei Shen, Francisco Goes da Silva, Christopher Dardick, Parveen Sharma, Ram Yadav, Pamela Ronald

Department of Plant Pathology, University of California Davis, Davis, CA 95616, USA

Many plant disease resistance (*R*) genes encode intracellular receptors that recognize type III secreted effectors (avirulence gene products) (Staskawicz et al. 2001). In contrast to most cloned *R* genes, the extracellular leucine-rich-repeat (LRR) domain of the receptor kinase encoded by the rice *R* gene, *Xa21,* determines race specific recognition of *Xanthomonas oryzae* pv. *oryzae* (*Xoo*) (Song et al. 1995; Wang et al. 1998). To elucidate the molecular basis for this extracellular recognition, we have undertaken experiments to isolate the relevant genes from *Xoo* controlling *avrXa21* effector activity. By using two approaches, Tn5 transposon mutagenesis of the avirulent *Xoo* Philippine race 6 (PR6) and complementation of the virulent Korean race 1 (KR1) with a PR6 genomic library, we isolated two loci, *raxPQ* and *raxSTAB*, respectively, containing five genes that are essential for the race specific recognition. Furthermore, we have isolated another *Xoo* gene, *raxC*, which is also required for the race- specific recognition.

raxP, raxQ and *raxST* Encode Enzymes for Sulfation

raxP and *raxQ* were isolated from a virulent Tn5 mutant of PR6. The deduced protein products of *raxP* and *raxQ* have similarity to ATP sulfurylases and APS (adenosine-5'-phosphosulfate) kinases from other organisms. These enzymes convert sulfate into the activated forms, APS and 3'-phosphoadenosine-5'-phosphosulfate (PAPS). APS or PAPS are used for synthesis of L-cysteine while PAPS is also the sole sulfuryl group donor for sulfation of various types of molecules including proteins and oligosaccharides (Leyh 1993). Proteins similar to RaxP include NodP from the symbiotic bacteria *Sinorhizobium meliloti* and *Escherichia coli* CysD whereas proteins resembling RaxQ include *S. meliloti* NodQ, *E. coli* CysN and *E. coli* CysC (Leyh 1988; Shwedock and Long 1990). NodP and CysD encode the small subunit of ATP sulfurylases. CysN and the N-terminal domain of NodQ encode the large subunit of ATP sulfurylase whereas CysC and the C-terminal domain of NodQ encode APS kinases.

The functions of RaxP and RaxQ as ATP sulfurylase and APS kinase were verified by complementation of *E. coli cysD⁻, cysN⁻C⁻* and *cysC⁻* mutants with *raxP* and *raxQ*. Furthermore ^{35}S-labeled APS and PAPS were detected in the wild-type PR6 strain but not in the raxP and raxQ knockout strains. Unlike the *E. coli cysD⁻, cysN⁻* and *cysC⁻* mutants, the *Xoo raxP* and *raxQ* mutants were not cysteine auxotrophic. Since the *raxPQ* mutants block APS and PAPS synthesis, these mutants must adopt an alternative pathway for cysteine synthesis. Therefore the role of *raxPQ* in avrXa21 activity is not related to cysteine synthesis, but rather to sulfation of a molecule required for recognition by the rice XA21 receptor kinase.

Transfer of the activated sulfuryl group from PAPS to a target molecule requires the presence of a sulfotransferase. For instance, *Rhizobium* sp. NGR234 NoeE and *S. meliloti* NodH transfer a sulfuryl group from PAPS to a fucose or glucose residue on the lipo-chito-oligosaccharide Nod factor, respectively (Quesada-Vincens et al. 1998; Ehrhardt et al. 1994). Interestingly the *raxSTAB* locus isolated using the KR1 complementation approach, carries the gene *raxST* that encodes a protein showing similarity to NodH, NoeE and human tyrosyl protein sulfotransferases in two PAPS binding motifs. Based on its similarity to these sulfotransferases, we predict that RaxST encodes a sulfotransferase that uses PAPS produced by RaxPQ for sulfation of a molecule required for host recognition.

raxA, raxB and *raxC* Encode Components of a Type I Secretion System

The predicted *raxA* and *raxB* products have similarity to membrane fusion proteins and inner membrane ATP binding cassette (ABC) transporter proteins of bacterial type I secretion systems (Holland and Blight 1999). Type I secretion systems secrete proteins from the bacterial cytoplasm directly to the bacterial cell surface or the extracellular environment in contrast to type III secretion systems which deliver effector molecules directly into host cells. Sequence analysis indicates that RaxB belongs to a specific family of ABC transporters that contain, in addition to the membrane spanning and ATPase domains, an N-terminal proteolytic domain of approximately 150 amino acids (Michiels et al. 2001). These ABC transporters secrete peptides (called bacteriocin-like peptides) with a characteristic double-glycine-type leader sequence of 15-20 amino acids that is cleaved off during secretion.

In addition to the ABC transporter and membrane fusion protein, Type I secretion systems require an outer membrane protein. The gene encoding the outer membrane protein is usually located in a separate chromosomal region although the genes encoding the ABC transporter and MFP are typically in the same operon. To determine if an outer membrane component is also required for the *Xoo* host recognition, we isolated a gene, called *raxC*, from PR6. The *raxC* encoded protein shares 33% identity with the *E. coli* TolC outer membrane protein required for secretion of the bacteriocin colicin V (Wandersman et al. 1990). Like PR6Δ*raxA* and PR6Δ*raxB*, the raxC knockout strain, PR6Δ*raxC*, also became virulent on *Xa21* plants.

To test if the *raxA*, *raxB*, and *raxC* encode proteins that function in secretion of bacteriocin-like peptides, we tested whether these genes could complement *E. coli cvaA, cvaB* (encoding the ABC transporter), and *tolC* mutants for colicin V secretion (Hwang et al. 1997). *raxA* and *raxB* failed to complement *cvaA* and *cvaB*, respectively. This result is not surprising as it is known that ABC transporters and MFPs are highly specific for the substrate to be secreted (Van Belkum et al. 1997). Nevertheless the *raxC* gene complemented the *tolC⁻* mutant to secrete colicin V based on a growth inhibition assay of the colicin V sensitive *E. coli* strain BL21 confirming its role in secretion of bacteriocin-like peptides.

The requirement of RaxA, RaxB and RaxC for avrXa21 activity and their similarities with components of type I secretion systems led us to search for a gene encoding a bacteriocin-like peptide that may confer avirulence on *Xa21* plants. However, a bacteriocin-like ORF could not be found adjacent to either the *raxSTAB*, *raxC* or *raxPQ* loci. We speculate that RaxA/B and RaxC secrete a peptide encoded elsewhere in the *Xoo* genome. Furthermore, the organization of the *raxSTAB* locus suggests that *raxST* may be involved in the modification of the RaxABC secreted molecule. Many bacteriocins, such as *E. coli* microcin B17, are known to undergo a variety of post-translational modifications that mediate their activity and the enzymes responsible for modification are usually encoded by genes closely linked to the MFP and ABC ORFs (Baba and Schneewind 1998).

Although the avrXa21 effector has not yet been isolated, dependence on the *raxABC* encoded type I secretion system supports our hypothesis that the recognition of *Xoo* cells containing *avrXa21* by the rice Xa21 receptor kinase occurs extracellularly. Based on our results, we predict that a molecule, possibly a bacteriocin-like peptide, is sulfated and then secreted through the RaxABC type I system (Fig.1). Further experiments are planned to study the role of sulfation, identify the type I secreted molecule (s), and investigate its role in the Xa21-mediated resistance response.

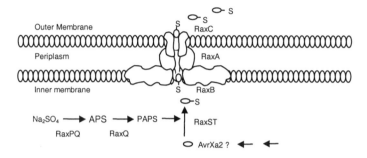

Fig.1. Proposed model for functions of *Xoo* proteins encoded by *rax* genes.

Acknowledgements

This work was funded by NIH, NSF and a Guggenheim Fellowship to P. R., Y. S., P. S. and R. Y. were supported by the Rockefeller Foundation Postdoctoral Fellowships.

Literature Cited

Baba, T. and Schneewind, O. 1998. Instruments of microbial warfare: bacteriocin synthesis, toxicity and immunity. Trends in Microbiol. 6:66-71.

Ehrhardt, D.W. *et al.* 1995. In vitro sulfotransferase activity of NodH, a nodulation protein of *Rhizobium meliloti* required for host-specific nodulation. J. Bacteriol. 177:6237-6245.

Holland, I. B. and Blight, M. A. 1999. ABC-ATPases, adaptable energy generators fuelling transmembrane movement of a variety of molecules in organisms from bacteria to humans. J. Mol. Biol. 293:381-399.

Hwang, J., Hong, X., and Tai, P. C. 1997. Interactions of dedicated export membrane proteins of the colicin V secretion system: *cvaA*, a member of the membrane fusion protein family, interacts with *cvaB* and *tolC*. J. Bacteriol. 179:6264-6270.

Leyh, T. S. 1993. The physical biochemistry and molecular genetics of sulfate activation. Crit. Rev. Biochem. Mol. Biol. 28:515-542.

Leyh, T. S., Taylor, J. C., and Markham, G.D. 1988. The sulfate activation locus of *Escherichia coli* K12: Cloning, genetic and enzymatic characterization. J. Biol. Chem. 263:2409-2416.

Michiels, J., Dirix, G., Vanderleyden, J., and Xi, C. 2001. Processing and export of peptide pheromones and bacteriocins in Gram-negative bacteria. Trends in Microbiol. 9:164-168.

Quesada-Vincens, D., Hanin, M., Broughton, W. J., and Jabbouri, S. 1998. In vitro sulfotransferase activity of NoeE, a nodulation protein of *Rhizobium* sp.NGR234. *Mol.* Plant-Microbe Interact. 11:592-600.

Schwedock, J. S., Liu, C., Leyh, T. S., and Long, S. R. 1994. *Rhizobium meliloti* NodP and NodQ form a multifunctional sulfate-activating complex requiring GTP for activity. J. Bacteriol. 176:7055-7064.

Schwedock, J. and Long, S. R. 1990. ATP sulphurylase activity of the *nodP* and *nodQ* gene products of *Rhizobium meliloti*. Nature 348:644-647.

Song, W.Y. *et al.* 1995. A receptor kinase-like protein encoded by the rice disease resistance gene, *Xa21*. Science 270:1804-1806.

Staskwicz, B., Mudgett, M. B., Dangle, J. L., and Galan, J. E. 2001. Common and contrasting themes of plant and animal diseases. Science 292:2285-2289.

Van Belkum, M. J., Worobo, R. W., and Stiles, M. E. 1997. Double-glycine-type leader peptides direct secretion of bacteriocins by abc transporters: colicin v secretion in *lactococcus lactis*. Mol. Microbiol. 23:1293-1301.

Wandersman, C. and Delepelaire, P. TolC, 1990. An *Escherichia coli* outer membrane protein required for hemolysin secretion. Proc. Natl. Acad. Sci. USA 87:4776-4780.

Wang, G.L. *et al.* 1998. *Xa21*d encodes a receptor-like molecule with a leucine-rich repeat domain that determines race-specific recognition and is subject to adaptive evolution. Plant Cell 10:765-779.

Weinshilboum, R. M. *et al.* 1997. Sulfotransferase molecular biology: cDNAs and genes. The FASEB J. 11:3-13.

The Molecular Basis of *Pseudomonas syringae* Pathogenesis in Susceptible *Arabidopsis thaliana* Plants

Sheng Yang He, Qiao-Ling Jin, Roger Thilmony, Kinya Nomura, Julie Zwiesler-Vollick, Sruti Bandyopadhyay, Paula Hauck, Wenqi Hu, Anne Plovanich-Jones, Mingbo Lu, and Elena Bray

Department of Energy Plant Research Laboratory, Michigan State University, East Lansing, MI 48824, USA.

With the exception of the gall-forming *Agrobacterium tumefaciens*, the molecular basis of bacterial pathogenesis in susceptible plants is not understood. Hypersensitive reaction and pathogenicity (*hrp*) genes appear to play an essential role in the pathogenesis of most bacterial pathogens (reviewed by Lindgren 1997). A key function of *hrp* genes is assembly of a type III secretion system for presumed injection of bacterial virulence/ avirulence proteins into plant cells (reviewed by He 1998; Galan and Collmer 1999). However, the actual mechanism of type III protein delivery, the identities of delivered virulence proteins, and the effects of bacterial virulence proteins on host signaling or metabolic pathways are not known. The goal of our research is to reveal how *P. syringae* delivers various virulence factors to modulate plant susceptibility. This report summarizes our recent work on the characterization of the function of a pilus (the Hrp pilus) in type III protein secretion and our analysis of *Arabidopsis* nuclear response to infection by *P. syringae* pv. *tomato* strain DC3000.

The Hrp Pilus: A Secretion Pilus

The *hrp* genes were first discovered in *P. syringae* pv. *phaseolicola* (Lindgren et al. 1986). After more than a decade of molecular characterization by a number of research groups, the *P. syringae hrp*-encoded type III secretion system has become one of the best studied in plant pathogenic bacteria. The entire *hrp* gene locus of *P. syringae* spans a chromosomal region of about 25 kb and contains 27 open reading frames

(He 1998). The *hrp* region is flanked by an exchangeable effector locus (EEL) on the left and a conserved effector locus (CEL) on the right (Alfano et al. 2000), constituting a functional pathogenicity island. In the *hrp* region, eight *hrp* genes (renamed *hrc* genes) share sequence similarity with flagellar assembly genes and are conserved among all plant, animal, and human pathogenic bacteria that contain type III secretion systems. The widespread conservation of these eight genes suggests similar mechanisms in type III protein secretion and flagellum assembly (He 1997).

The Hrp secretion system of *Pseudomonas syringae* assembles an *hrp*-dependent pilus (named the Hrp pilus) in minimal medium and *in planta* (Roine et al. 1997; Hu et al. 2001) and secretes two families of proteins: Hrp proteins, such as HrpA, HrpZ, and HrpW (e.g., Yuan and He 1996), and Avr proteins (e.g., Mudgett and Staskawicz, 1999; van Dijk et al., 1999). The HrpA protein has been shown to be the structural protein of the Hrp pilus (Roine et al. 1997). Genetic analysis shows that HrpA is required for *Pst* DC3000 to secrete Hrp and Avr proteins (Wei et al. 2000), to cause disease in Arabidopsis, and to elicit the hypersensitive response (HR) in tobacco and tomato (Roine et al. 1997), suggesting an essential role of the Hrp pilus in plant-*Pst* DC3000 interactions.

Pili have also been shown to be required for two other macromolecular trafficking systems: T-DNA transfer by *Agrobacterium tumefaciens* (Fullner et al. 1996) and bacterial conjugation (Willetts and Skurray 1980). However, it has never been shown directly that the secreted proteins and DNA are localized along or inside the pili, a key prediction of the 'conduit/guiding filament' model, in which the pilus directly guides protein or DNA traffic. We have now visualized localization of HrpW and AvrPto proteins along the Hrp pilus. The localization of HrpW and AvrPto along the Hrp pilus was specific because these effectors were not found randomly in the intercellular space or along the flagellum. The Hrp pilus-specific localization was also observed for two type III effectors, HrpN and DspA/E, of *Erwinia amylovora* (the causal agent of fire blight disease of apple and pear). In contrast, PelE, a pectate lyase secreted via the *Erwinia* type II protein secretion system, was not localized to the Hrp pilus (Jin et al. 2001). Furthermore, by conditionally expressing AvrPto from a plasmid, we found that AvrPto is secreted from the tip of a growing pilus, but not at the base of the Hrp pilus. These results provide direct evidence that the Hrp pilus serves as a conduit for protein delivery.

How Many Type III Virulence Effectors?

Most type III effector proteins in plant pathogenic bacteria have been identified based on their avirulence phenotype in resistant plants as a result of recognition by the corresponding host resistance proteins (Mudgett and Staskawicz 1998; Kjemtrup et al. 2000). Consequently, they are called Avr proteins. It is believed, however, that the original functions of Avr proteins are to promote bacterial parasitism and to establish a compatible interaction with a susceptible host. To identify type III effector genes in DC3000 we used 15 known *avr* genes previously cloned from other *P. syringae* strains as DNA probes to identify homologous genes in *Pst* DC3000. We found that three *avr* genes, *avrPpiB*, *avrPphE*, and *virPphA*, hybridized to the chromosomal DNA of *Pst* DC3000. We have now cloned and sequenced these three *avr* genes from DC3000 and produced transposon mutants of the homologues of *avrPphE*, *avrPpiB* and *virPphA*. Preliminary pathogenesis assays showed that these three *avr* genes do not contribute to DC3000 virulence in Arabidopsis, presumably due to functional redundancy or lack of corresponding host targets in Arabidopsis.

The recent release of the DC3000 genomic sequence by The Institute for Genomic Research, Rockville, MD (part of the tomato-*P. syringae* functional genomics project led by Alan Collmer, Cornell University), has made it possible to estimate the total number of potential type III effector genes in this pathogen. In *P. syringae*, all known *avr* genes are co-regulated with *hrp* genes owing to the presence of a conserved 'harp box' in the promoter region (e.g., Shen and Keen 1993). We used the 'harp box' motif as a search tool and have identified about 70 genes/operons, some of which may be co-regulated with *hrp* genes. Among these genes/operons are all known *hrp*-regulated genes/operons in DC3000 and a dozen *avr* genes known to be present in other *P. syringae* strains.

Defining *Arabidopsis* Nuclear Response to Virulence Factors

A major roadblock to rapid progress in the study of host susceptibility and functions of type III virulence proteins is lack of host cellular and molecular markers (in contrast to plant resistance). To identify these molecular markers, we examined the expression of about 11,000 *Arabidopsis* cDNA clones (representing about 8,000 unique sequences) from the Arabidopsis Functional Genomic Consortium (AFGC) during infection by *Pst* DC3000 vs. the *hrpS* mutant, which is defective in type III secretion (Yuan and He 1996). About 290 clones reproducibly showed differential expression in four independent experiments. In these experiments, we used pooled RNA samples isolated from pre-symptomatic *Arabidopsis* plants at 12, 24, and 36 h post-inoculation (hpi) with 10^6 cfu/ml bacteria. Disease symptoms (necrosis and chlorosis) appeared at 72 hpi in DC3000-inoculated plants. We did not include the 72-hpi sample to reduce nonspecific host responses from cell death and other stresses.

The most notable *Pst* DC3000-induced genes in our current slide pool include jasmonic acid (JA)-responsive genes, known defense genes (but not classical *PR* genes), and genes encoding sugar transporters, putative transcription factors, signal-transduction components, chlorophyll-degrading enzymes, and cell-wall-modifying enzymes. The induction of these genes is consistent with the fact that *Pst* DC3000 (i) produces a JA-mimicking toxin, coronatine, (ii) presumably releases sugars from the host cell, and (iii) causes tissue chlorosis symptoms. The repressed genes include a family of the water channel genes, several defense genes, and genes encoding sugar-sensing proteins. The repression of these genes is likely related to *Pst* DC3000-caused defense suppression, water trapping in the apoplast ('water soaking' symptom), and sugar production and release. Therefore, we believe that the observed changes in the expression of the 290 host genes represent a molecular signature of DC3000 infection in susceptible *Arabidopsis* plants.

A Type III Effector Putatively Involved in Overcoming A Salicylic Acid-Mediated *Arabidopsis* Response

A DC3000 mutant strain (named ΔCEL), carrying a large deletion in the CEL region (*avrE-orf2-3-4-hrpW-orf5*; Alfano et al. 2000), elicited HR in tobacco but no longer caused disease symptoms in wild-type *Arabidopsis* plants (ecotype Columbia). We found that the multiplication of the CEL mutant was severely restricted (by 500-fold) compared with that of DC3000 in Columbia plants. Unexpectedly, the ΔCEL multiplied almost like DC3000 and caused disease symptoms in *nahG* plants, which are defective in salicylic acid-mediated host responses. As a control, the *hrcC* mutant of DC3000 did not multiply significantly in either Columbia or *nahG* plants. These results suggest that the CEL is involved in overcoming an SA-mediated host response in the wild-type host plants, possibly by suppressing or evading host defense. Complementation analysis of the ΔCEL mutant revealed that *orf3* and *orf4* are responsible for the CEL mutant phenotype. *orf3* and *orf4* encode unique 65-kDa and 18-kDa proteins, respectively. An Orf3-AvrRpt2 fusion, but not an Orf4-AvrRpt2 fusion, triggers an HR in *RPS2*[+] *Arabidopsis* plants, suggesting that Orf3 is targeted into the host cell cytoplasm. Yeast two-hybrid analysis showed that Orf3 and Orf4 interact with each other, implicating an effector protein-chaperone relationship.

Acknowledgments

This research is funded by the DOE, USDA and NSF.

Literature Cited

Alfano, J. R., Charkowski, A. O., Deng, W. L., Badel, J. L., Petnicki-Ocwieja, T., van Dijk, K., and Collmer, A. 2000. The *Pseudomonas syringae hrp* pathogenicity island has a tripartite mosaic structure composed of a cluster of type III secretion genes bounded by exchangeable effector and conserved effector loci that contribute to parasitic fitness and pathogenicity in plants. Proc. Natl. Acad. Sci. USA 97:4856-4861.

Fullner, K. J., Lara, J. C., and Nester, E. W. 1996. Pilus assembly by *Agrobacterium* T-DNA transfer genes. Science 273:1107-1109.

Galan, J. E., and Collmer, A. 1999. Type III secretion machines: Bacterial devices for protein delivery into host cells. Science 284:1322-1328.

He, S. Y. 1997. Hrp-controlled interkingdom protein transport: learning from flagellar assembly? Trends Microbiol. 5:489-495.

He, S. Y. 1998. Type III secretion systems in animal and plant pathogenic bacteria. Annu. Rev. Phytopathol. 36:363-392.

Hu, W., Yuan, J., Jin, Q. L., Hart, P., and He, S. Y. 2001. Immunogold labeling of Hrp pili of *Pseudomonas syringae* pv. *tomato* DC3000 in minimal medium and *in planta*. Mol. Plant-Microbe Interact. 14:234-241.

Jin, Q.-L., Hu, W., Brown, I., McGhee, G., Hart, P., Jones, A., and He, S. Y. 2001. Visualization of effector Hrp and Avr proteins along the Hrp pilus during type III secretion in *Erwinia amylovora* and *Pseudomonas syringae*. Mol. Microbiol. 40:1129-1139.

Kjemtrup, S., Nimchuk, Z., and Dangl, J. L. 2000. Effector proteins of phytopathogenic bacteria: bifunctional signals in virulence and host recognition. Curr. Opin. Microbiol. 3:73-78.

Lindgren, P. B. 1997. The role of *hrp* genes during plant-bacterial interactions. Annu. Rev. Phytopathol. 35:129-152.

Lindgren, P. B., Peet, R. C., and Panopoulos, N. J. 1986. Gene cluster of *Pseudomonas syringae* pv. '*phaseolicola*' controls pathogenicity of bean plants and hypersensitivity on nonhost plants. J. Bacteriol. 168:512-522.

Mudgett, M. B., and Staskawicz, B. J. 1998. Protein signaling via type III secretion pathways in phytopathogenic bacteria. Curr. Opin. Microbiol. 1: 109-114.

Mudgett, M. B., and Staskawicz, B. J. 1999. Characterization of the *Pseudomonas syringae* pv. *tomato* AvrRpt2 protein: demonstration of secretion and processing during bacterial pathogenesis. Mol. Microbiol. 32:927-941.

Roine, E., Wei, W., Yuan, J., Nurmiaho-Lassila, E.-L., Kalkkinen, N., Romantschuk, M., and He, S. Y. 1997. Hrp pilus: An *hrp*-dependent bacterial surface appendage produced by *Pseudomonas syringae* pv. *tomato* DC3000. Proc. Natl. Acad. Sci. USA 94:3459-3464.

Shen, H., and Keen, N. T. 1993. Characterization of the promoter of avirulence gene D from *Pseudomonas syringae* pv. *tomato*. J. Bacteriol. 175:5916-5924.

van Dijk, K., Fouts, D. E., Rehm, A. H., Hill, A. R., Collmer, A., and Alfano, J. R. 1999. The Avr (effector) proteins HrmA (HopPsyA) and AvrPto are secreted in culture from *Pseudomonas syringae* pathovars via the Hrp (type III) protein secretion system in a temperature- and pH-sensitive manner. J. Bacteriol. 181:4790-4797.

Wei, W., Plovanich-Jones, A., Deng, W.-L., Collmer, A., Huang, H.-C., and He, S. Y. 2000. The gene coding for the structural protein of the Hrp pilus is required for type III secretion of Hrp and Avr proteins in *Pseudomonas syringae* pv. *tomato*. Proc. Natl. Acad. Sci. USA 97:2247-2252.

Willetts, N., and Skurray, R. 1980. The conjugation system of F-like plasmids. Annu. Rev. Genet. 14:41-76.

Yuan, J., and He, S. Y. 1996. The *Pseudomonas syringae* hrp regulation and secretion system controls the production and secretion of multiple extracellular proteins. J. Bacteriol. 178:6399-6402.

Role of Type III Effector Proteins from *Xanthomonas* in the Interaction with the Plant

Thomas Lahaye, Boris Szurek, Eric Marois, Sebastian Schornack, Tina Jordan, Daniela Büttner, Lucia Escolar, Frank Thieme, Laurent Noël and Ulla Bonas

Dept. of Genetics, Martin-Luther University, 06099 Halle, Germany

Virulence of most phytopathogenic Gram-negative bacteria depends on a molecular syringe, the type III protein secretion system (TTSS), which secretes and probably translocates proteins into the plant cell (Staskawicz et al. 2001). Driven by evolutionary forces, plants have evolved sophisticated defense systems, targeted against individual type III-secreted proteins. Despite recent advances, little is known about how type III effector proteins initiate disease or resistance. Our lab investigates (i) secretion, (ii) virulence and (iii) avirulence functions of type III effectors employing the type III secretion in the model organism *Xanthomomonas campestris* pv. *vesicatoria* (*Xcv*), the causal agent of bacterial spot in pepper and tomato.

cDNA-AFLP analysis unravels a genome-wide *hrpG* regulon

Expression of bacterial *hrp* (*h*ypersensitive *r*esponse and *p*athogenicity) genes, which encode a TTSS, is induced during infection of the plant. Regulation of *hrp* genes is controlled by *hrpG* and *hrpX* (Wengelnik and Bonas 1996; Wengelnik et al. 1996). To characterize the *hrpG* regulon in more detail and to identify new genes, we performed a cDNA-AFLP (Noël et al. 2001). The *hrpG* virulon is composed of at least 4 *hgr* genes (*hrpG*-repressed) and 21 *hgi* genes (*hrpG*-induced) which are scattered over the *Xcv* chromosome and plasmids (Fig. 1). Interestingly, a region flanking the *hrp* gene cluster, which does not contain *hrp* genes, nevertheless contributes to virulence (Noël et al. 2001). Recent study of two particular *hgi* genes revealed that they encode Xops (*Xanthomonas* outer proteins), which are secreted by the TTSS (Noël and Bonas unpublished; Noël et al. 2001). XopB belongs to a novel class of type III effectors, which includes the *Pseudomonas syringae* AvrPphD avirulence protein (Arnold et al. 2001). XopJ is a member of the AvrBsT/YopJ family of effector proteins, which are conserved among plant and animal pathogens (Noël and Bonas unpublished Galán 1998; Noël et al. 2001). The identification of the entire gamut of Xop proteins and their plant targets will lead to a better understanding of *Xcv* virulence strategies.

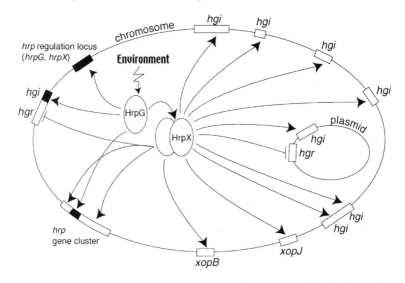

Fig. 1. HrpG and HrpX control the expression of a genome-wide virulon coding for the TTSS, Xop proteins and other *hgi* and *hgr* genes. The exact position of the genes is not known.

A Yeast Two-Hybrid Screen Identifies AvrBs3-Interacting Plant Proteins

Xcv strains expressing the avirulence gene *avrBs3* are specifically recognized by the pepper genotype ECW-30R, which carries the resistance gene *Bs3* (Bonas et al. 1989). The 122 kDa AvrBs3 protein is a member of a large family of proteins which share 90-97% sequence identity at the amino acid level and are secreted via the Hrp type III pathway (Ballvora et al. 2001; Rossier et al. 1999). Structural hallmarks of AvrBs3-like proteins are the presence of functional nuclear localization signals (NLS) and an acidic activation domain (AAD) in the C-terminus (Szurek et al. 2001; Van den Ackerveken et al. 1996; Zhu et al. 1998). In a search for AvrBs3-interacting pepper proteins using the yeast two-hybrid system, we have isolated eight different classes of cDNA inserts including two genes for importin α. Importin α is part of the nuclear import machinery and interacts with AvrBs3 preferentially through NLS2, both in yeast and *in vitro*. The mechanism of AvrBs3 recognition was further studied by analysis of the putative transcription activation domain. The AAD was shown to be required for AvrBs3 HR-inducing activity and could be functionally replaced by the VP16 AAD from the herpes simplex virus. Altogether these data support the model in which AvrBs3 localizes to the nucleus, where the *Bs3*-mediated surveillance system of resistant plants detects AvrBs3 through its interference with host gene transcription (Fig. 2).

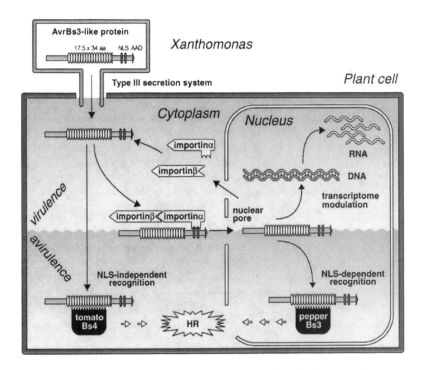

Fig. 2. Model of molecular mechanisms determining virulence and avirulence of AvrBs3-like effector proteins. AvrBs3-like proteins are translocated into the plant cell via the bacterial type III secretion system. NLSs interact with importin α which catalyzes together with importin β transport of AvrBs3-like proteins into the nucleus. Modulation of the host's transcriptome is achieved by direct or indirect interaction of AvrBs3 with DNA. Recognition of AvrBs3 and its homologs is often dependent on NLSs, which leads us to speculate that corresponding R proteins (e.g. pepper Bs3) are localized in the nucleus. However, some R proteins probably recognize AvrBs3-like proteins in the cytoplasm (prototype: tomato Bs4).

One cDNA identified in the two-hybrid screen encodes a protein with homology to an *Arabidopsis* ankyrin-motif-containing protein of unknown function. Interestingly, this interaction depends on the presence of the repeat region that determines avirulence specificity (Herbers et al. 1992). Yet, the interaction is not repeat-specific since this interactor interacts also with AvrBs3Δrep16, an AvrBs3-deletion derivative which lacks four repeats and is not recognized by the pepper *Bs3* resistance (*R*) gene (Herbers et al. 1992).

Isolation and Characterization of Plant Resistance Genes Determining Recognition Specificity to Different Variants of the AvrBs3 Family

AvrBs3 and AvrBs4 (97% sequence identity) are members of the AvrBs3 family and differ mainly in the repeat domain (Bonas et al. 1993). Analysis of deletion derivatives demonstrated repeat-specific recognition mediated by *Bs3* and *Bs4* gene products, respectively (Ballvora et al. 2001). Although recognizing highly similar Avr proteins, *Bs3* and *Bs4* differ with respect to their dependence on NLSs in the Avr protein. Mutations in the C-terminal NLSs of AvrBs3 and AvrBs4 abolished *Bs3*-mediated but not *Bs4*-mediated recognition (Ballvora et al. 2001; Van den Ackerveken et al. 1996) which may indicate that Bs3 and Bs4 act in different plant cell compartments (Fig. 2). We are working towards the molecular isolation and comparative functional analysis of both *R* genes to gain insights into the principle of recognition specificity.

The pepper *Bs3* locus has been genetically mapped to a 2.1 cM target interval by an amplified fragment length polymorphism (AFLP)-bulked segregant approach (Pierre et al. 2000). In order to generate a high-resolution genetic map at the *Bs3*-locus, we analysed 2445 additional F_2-segregants. Recombinants were employed to assemble new DNA bulks for a *Sac*I/*Taq*I-based AFLP marker screen, yielding new *Bs3*-linked AFLP markers. The most closely *Bs3*-linked AFLPs will be used to isolate large insert genomic clones, which possibly span the *Bs3* target locus.

Genetic mapping located the tomato *Bs4* locus on tomato chromosome 5 (Ballvora et al. 2001). Within the *Bs4*-cosegregating area we identified a TIR-NBS-LRR encoding resistance gene analog (RGA) which is most homologous to the tobacco *N* disease resistance gene (Whitham et al. 1994). Transient and stable complementation analysis in tomato have shown that the identified RGA confers AvrBs4-specific recognition capacity. This indicates that the identified RGA is indeed the *Bs4* resistance gene.

Acknowledgements

Our research is supported by grants from the Deutsche Forschungsgemeinschaf to U.B. and T.L. (SFB 363 and LA 1338/1-1).

138

Literature Cited

Arnold, D. L., Gibbon, M. J., Jackson, R. W., Wood, J. R., Brown, J., Mansfield, J. W., Taylor, J. D., and Vivian, A. 2001. Molecular characterization of *avrPphD*, a widely-distributed gene from *Pseudomonas syringae* pv. *phaseolicola* involved in non-host recognition by pea (*Pisum sativum*). Physiol. Mol. Plant Pathol. 58: 55-62.

Ballvora, A., Pierre, M., Van den Ackerveken, G., Schornack, S., Rossier, O., Ganal, M., Lahaye, T., and Bonas, U. 2001. Genetic mapping and functional analysis of the tomato *Bs4* locus, governing recognition of the *Xanthomonas campestris* pv. *vesicatoria* AvrBs4 protein. Mol. Plant-Microbe Interact. 14:629–638.

Bonas, U., Conrads-Strauch, J., and Balbo, I. 1993. Resistance in tomato to *Xanthomonas campestris* pv *vesicatoria* is determined by alleles of the pepper-specific avirulence gene *avrBs3*. Mol. Gen. Genet. 238:261-269.

Bonas, U., Stall, R. E., and Staskawicz, B. 1989. Genetic and structural characterization of the avirulence gene *avrBs3* from *Xanthomonas campestris* pv. *vesicatoria*. Mol. Gen. Genet. 218:127-136.

Galán, J. E. 1998. 'Avirulence genes' in animal pathogens? Trends Microbiol. 6:3-6.

Herbers, K., Conrads-Strauch, J., and Bonas, U. 1992. Race-specificity of plant resistance to bacterial spot disease determined by repetitive motifs in a bacterial avirulence protein. Nature 356:172-174.

Noël, L., Thieme, F., Nennstiel, D., and Bonas, U. 2001. cDNA-AFLP analysis unravels a genome-wide *hrpG*-regulon in the plant pathogen *Xanthomonas campestris* pv. *vesicatoria*. Mol. Microbiol. 41:271-281.

Pierre, M., Noël, L., Lahaye, T., Ballvora, A., Veuskens, J., Ganal, M., and Bonas, U. 2000. High-resolution genetic mapping of the pepper resistance locus *Bs3* governing recognition of the *Xanthomonas campestris* pv. *vesicatoria* AvrBs3 protein. Theor. Appl. Genet. 101:255-263.

Rossier, O., Wengelnik, K., Hahn, K., and Bonas, U. 1999. The *Xanthomonas* Hrp type III system secretes proteins from plant and mammalian pathogens. Proc. Natl. Acad. Sci. U.S.A. 96:9368-9373.

Staskawicz, B. J., Mudgett, M. B., Dangl, J. L., and Galan, J. E. 2001. Common and contrasting themes of plant and animal diseases. Science 292:2285-2289.

Szurek, B., Marois, E., Bonas, U., and Ackerveken, G. V. d. 2001. Eukaryotic features of the *Xanthomonas* type III effector AvrBs3: protein domains involved in transcriptional activation and the interaction with nuclear import receptors from pepper. Plant J. 26:523-534.

Van den Ackerveken, G., Marois, E., and Bonas, U. 1996. Recognition of the bacterial avirulence protein AvrBs3 occurs inside the host plant cell. Cell 87:1307-1316.

Wengelnik, K., and Bonas, U. 1996. HrpXv, an AraC-type regulator, activates expression of five of the six loci in the *hrp* cluster of *Xanthomonas campestris* pv. vesicatoria. J. Bacteriol. 178:3462-3469.

Wengelnik, K., Marie, C., Russel, M., and Bonas, U. 1996. Expression and localization of HrpA1: A protein of *Xanthomonas campestris* pv. vesicatoria essential for pathogenicity and induction of the hypersensitive reaction. J. Bacteriol. 178:1061-1069.

Whitham, S., Dinesh-Kumar, S. P., Choi, D., Hehl, R., Corr, C., and Baker, B. 1994. The product of the tobacco mosaic virus resistance gene *N* : Similarity to Toll and the Interleukin-1 receptor. Cell 78:1101-1115.

Zhu, W. G., Yang, B., Chittoor, J. M., Johnson, L. B., and White, F. F. 1998. AvrXa10 contains an acidic transcriptional activation domain in the functionally conserved C terminus. Mol. Plant-Microbe Interact. 11:824-832.

Suppression of RNA Silencing in Plants

Allison Mallory, Trent Smith, Braden Roth, Gail Pruss, Lewis Bowman
and Vicki Vance

Department of Biological Sciences, University of South Carolina,
Columbia, South Carolina 29208 USA

RNA silencing is an inducible mechanism for destroying specific RNA molecules in the cell. Though it was first discovered in transgenic plants, related processes have been found in a number of animal species including humans (see Ding 2001; Cogoni and Macino 2000; and Vance and Vaucheret 2001 for recent reviews of RNA silencing). In plants, it has evolved as an anti-viral defense and many plant viruses encode suppressors of RNA silencing. One such suppressor of silencing is the helper component proteinase (HC-Pro) encoded by plant potyviruses (Anandalakshmi et al. 1998; Brigneti et al. 1998; Kasschau and Carrington 1998). HC-Pro has proven to be a powerful tool for understanding the mechanism of RNA silencing.

HC-Pro and Viral Synergism

The idea that plant viruses might suppress RNA silencing comes from research on synergistic diseases of plants. Plants are commonly infected with more than one virus at the same time and sometimes the interaction between viruses results in a dramatic increase in disease symptoms. Interestingly, nearly all the reported synergistic diseases involve a potyvirus as one member of the pair of co-infecting viruses. In each case, the nonpotyvirus of the pair accumulates to a much higher level than in the equivalent single infection (Vance 1991; Pruss et al. 1997).

Our studies have used a classic synergism between potato virus X (PVX) and potato virus Y (PVY, a potyvirus) as a model to understand the molecular basis of synergism. We found that both the increased symptoms and the increased accumulation of PVX associated with synergism are mediated by a single potyvirus protein - HC- Pro (Vance et al. 1995). Furthermore, transgenic plants expressing HC-Pro display dramatic symptoms when infected with a broad range of heterologous viruses and this is correlated with a dramatic increase in accumulation of the virus (Pruss et al. 1997). These results led us to hypothesize that expression of HC-Pro blocks a general antiviral defense pathway and thus allows many viruses to accumulate past the normal host-imposed limits. RNA silencing was proposed to be the general antiviral defense blocked by HC-Pro (Pruss et al. 1997).

HC-Pro Suppresses RNA Silencing

Several approaches were used to test the idea that HC-Pro interferes with RNA silencing. First, a number of transgenic plants had been shown to be silenced for a reporter gene by an RNA silencing mechanism. These silenced transgenic lines were crossed with a transgenic line expressing HC-Pro and the offspring were assayed for expression of the previously silenced transgene. In all cases it was found that HC-Pro could suppress this kind of transgene-induced gene silencing (Ananadalakshmi et al. 1998; Kasschau and Carrington 1998). In addition, HC-Pro could reverse an already established RNA silencing (Brigneti et al. 1998) and prevent silencing induced by a virus (Ananadalakshmi et al. 1998). Thus, HC-Pro is a suppressor of both transgene-induced and virus-induced RNA silencing. Later work determined that many plant viruses encode such suppressors of silencing (Voinnet et al. 1999).

HC-Pro as Tool to Understand RNA Silencing

The finding that HC-Pro suppresses RNA silencing has practical implications. RNA silencing limits expression of transgenes and interferes with a number of biotechnological applications. HC-Pro can be used to directly counter RNA silencing to give consistent , high level expression of transgenes. More importantly, HC-Pro is a powerful tool to understand the mechanism of RNA silencing so that this process can be manipulated in plants as well as in other organisms.

Our recent studies have placed HC-Pro suppression of silencing with regard to important benchmarks of the process. In particular, it is known that RNA silencing is associated with methylation of the transcribed region of the silenced transgene and with accumulation of small RNAs representative of the silenced RNA (about 25 nucleotides and of both polarities; Hamilton and Baulcombe 1999). These small RNAs are thought to incorporate into a ribonuclease complex and provide the sequence specificity in targeting of RNAs (Hammond et al. 2000). Furthermore, RNA silencing can be induced locally and then spread via production of a mobile silencing signal (Palaqui et al. 1997; Voinnet and Baulcombe 1997). The identity of the mobile signal is currently unknown, but it is thought to include a nucleic acid component to account for the sequence specificity of the process.

We tested the point of HC-Pro interference using a well characterized tobacco transgenic line (line 6b5; Elmayan and Vaucheret 1996) in which the reporter gene GUS is silenced by an RNA silencing mechanism. We found that HC-Pro suppressed RNA silencing in 6b5 at a step that prevented accumulation of the small RNAs (Mallory et al. 2001). A similar result was obtained by another group using a different GUS-silenced transgenic line (Llave et al. 2000). However, HC-Pro did not interfere with methylation of the transgene in line 6b5. Furthermore, grafting experiments to examine the mobile silencing signal showed that 6b5 plants in which silencing was suppressed by HC-Pro were still able to produce and send the mobile silencing signal (Mallory et al. 2001). In contrast, a grafted plant expressing HC-Pro could not silence in response to the mobile signal. These experiments demonstrate that HC-Pro suppresses silencing by preventing the accumulation of the small RNAs (and thus, presumably preventing the assembly of a functional sequence-specific silencing complex). The suppression occurs downstream of transgene methylation and the mobile silencing signal because plants in which silencing is suppressed by HC-Pro remain methylated and able to transmit the mobile signal (Mallory et al. 2001).

Cellular Proteins Involved in Silencing

Our current hypothesis is that HC-Pro suppresses RNA silencing by interacting with host proteins that are either components of the silencing machinery or regulators of the pathway. To investigate this possibility, we used HC-Pro as bait in a yeast two hybrid system and this approach identified several putative HC-Pro-interacting tobacco proteins. To determine if any of these proteins are involved in RNA silencing, we have begun experiments to alter their expression.

One of the HC-Pro interacting proteins is a calmodulin-related protein which we have named rgs-CaM. Several lines of evidence suggest that rgs-CaM suppresses silencing(Anandalakshmi et al. 2000). Transgenic tobacco plants that over express rgs-CaM show delayed and reduced virus-induced gene silencing. In addition, rgs-CaM expressed from a PVX vector is able to reverse silencing of a GFP transgene. In general calmodulins act indirectly as intermediates in calcium regulated signal transduction pathways. The molecule binds calcium and changes conformation allowing subsequent binding to and activation of specific target proteins. Experiments are in progress to identify the target protein(s) for rgs-CaM.

Literature Cited

Anandalakshmi, R. Pruss, G.J., Xin, G., Marathe, R., Mallory, A.C., Smith, T.H., and Vance, V.B. 1998. A viral suppressor of gene silencing in plants. Proc. Natl. Acad. Sci. USA 95:13079-13084.

Anandalakshmi, R., Marathe, R., Xin, G., Herr, J.M., Jr., Mau, C., Mallory, A.C., Pruss, G., Bowman, L., and Vance, V.B. 2000. A calmodulin-related protein suppreses post-transcriptional gene silencing in plants. Science 290:142-144.

Brigneti, G., Voinnet, O., Li, W-X., Ji, L-H., Ding, S-W., and Baulcombe, D.C. 1998. Viral pathogenicity determinants are suppressors of transgene silencing in *Nicotiana benthamiana*. EMBO J. 17: 6739-6746.

Cogoni, C., and Macino, G. 2000. Post-transcriptional gene silencing across kingdoms. Curr. Opin. Genet. Devel. 10:638-643.

Ding, S.W. 2000. RNA silencing. Curr. Opin. Biotechnol. 11: 152-156.

Elmayan, T., and Vaucheret, H. 1996. Expression of single copies of a strongly expressed 35S transgene can be silenced post-transcriptionally. Plant J. 9: 787-797.

Hamilton, A.J., and Baulcombe, D.C. 1999. A species of small antisense RNA in posttranscriptional gene silencing in plants. Science 286:950-952.

Hammond, S.M., Bernstein, E., Beach, D., and Hannon, G.J. 2000. An RNA-directed nuclease mediates post-transcriptional gene silencing in Drosophila cells. Nature 404:293-296.

Kasschau, K.D., and Carrington, J.C. 1998. A counterdefensive strategy of plant viruses suppression of posttranscriptional gene silencing. Cell 95: 461-470.

Llave, C., Kasschau, K.D., Carrington, J.C. 2000. Virus-encoded suppressor of posttranscriptional gene silencing targets a maintenance step in the silencing pathway. Proc. Natl. Acad. Sci. U S A. 97:13401-6.

Mallory, A.C. Ely, L. Smith, TH. Marathe, R. Anandalakshmi, R. Fagard, M. Vaucheret, H. Pruss, G. Bowman, L., and Vance, VB. 2001. HC-Pro suppression of transgene silencing eliminates the small RNAs but not transgene methylation or the mobile signal. Plant Cell 13:571-583.

Palauqui, J-C., Elmayan, T., Pollien, J-M., and Vaucheret, H. 1997. Systemic acquired silencing: Transgene-specific posttranscriptional silencing is transmitted by grafting from silenced stocks to non-silenced scions. EMBO J. 16:4738-4745.

Pruss, G., Ge, X., Shi, X.M., Carrington, J.C., and Vance, V.B. 1997. Plant viral synergism: The potyviral genome encodes a broad-range pathogenicity enhancer that transactivates replication of heterologous viruses. Plant Cell 9:859-868.

Vance, V.B. 1991.Replication of potato virus X RNA is altered in coinfections with potato virus Y. Virology. 182:486-94.

Vance, V.B., Berger, P.H., Carrington, J.C., Hunt, A.G., and Shi, X.M. 1995. 5' proximal potyviral sequences mediate potato virus X/potyviral synergistic disease in transgenic tobacco. Virology 206:583-90.

Vance, V., and Vaucheret, H. 2001. RNA silencing in plants--defense and counterdefense. Science 292:2277-80.

Voinnet, O. and Baulcombe, D.C. 1997. Systemic signalling in gene silencing. Nature 389: 553.

Voinnet, O., Pinto, Y.M. and Baulcombe, D.C. 1999. Suppression of gene silencing: a general strategy used by diverse DNA and RNA viruses of plants. Proc. Natl. Acad. Sci. USA 96: 14147-14152

Host Compatibility Functions During Virus Infection

James C. Carrington, Kristin D. Kasschau, Andrew D. Lellis, Cesar Llave-Correas, Lisa K. Johansen, and Zhixin Xie

Center for Gene Research and Biotechnology, and Department of Botany and plant Pathology, Oregon State University, Corvallis, OR 97331-7303 USA

Compatibility and Incompatibility Functions

Viruses of plants require sets of host proteins, structures and processes for genome replication, cell-to-cell movement and long-distance movement. These factors and processes form a basis for virus-host compatibility. Superimposed on basic compatibility is the capacity of plants to mount innate and adaptive defense responses to block one or more stages of infection. Thus, whether or not a plant is susceptible to systemic infection by any given virus depends on the net effects of compatible and incompatible interactions. Virus-host interactions governing compatibility may affect any of three general processes: genome expression/replication at the single-cell level, cell-to-cell movement, and long-distance movement (Carrington and Whitham 1998). Genome replication of positive-strand RNA viruses requires enzymatic viral proteins, such as RNA-dependent RNA polymerase, as well as a membrane substratum, such as the endoplasmic reticulum. Host proteins contribute essential functions for replication or transcription complex activity, and several genes encoding such factors were recently identified (Diez et al. 2000; Noueiry et al. 2000; Yamanaka et al. 2000). Cell-to-cell movement requires interactions between one or more viral proteins, the viral genome and intra- and intercellular trafficking pathways. An obvious point of interaction occurs at plasmodesmata connecting cells, although equally important interactions may also occur at the intracellular level to facilitate transit of new genomes from sites of replication to plasmodesmata. Long-distance movement requires virus-host interactions between specialized cells around vascular tissue and in phloem sieve elements.

Virus-host interactions leading to resistance may occur in many ways. Innate resistance involving a hypersensitive or cell death response occurs when a cellular receptor-like protein complex [containing a dominant resistance (R) gene product] interacts directly or indirectly with a viral protein (avirulence factor) to trigger local and systemic signaling cascade. RNA silencing is an adaptive antiviral defense response. Sequence-specific RNA silencing occurs during the course of infection by most, if not all, viruses in plants (Al-Kaff et al. 1998; Ratcliff et al. 1997; Ratcliff et al. 1999). In many cases, plants can recover from the effects of infection through development of new tissue that lacks symptoms, is largely devoid of virus, and exhibits a sequence-specific silenced state. This response also explains some of the features of classical cross-protection. Many or most plant viruses encode suppressors of RNA silencing (Carrington et al. 2001). In some cases, silencing suppressors have general pathogenicity enhancing activities. Plant viral silencing suppressors are structurally and functionally diverse, with some targeting cell autonomous steps and others targeting systemic signaling steps (Carrington et al. 2001).

POTYVIRUS P1/HC-PRO SILENCING SUPPRESSOR

Numerous functions have been assigned to the potyviral HC-Pro protein. It has a cysteine-type proteinase domain, which catalyzes autoproteolytic cleavage between HC-Pro and the neighboring protein within the large viral polyprotein. Among other functions, HC-Pro is required for long-distance movement through the phloem and for maintenance of genome amplification (Kasschau et al. 1997). TEV mutants with defects in the central region of HC-Pro are able to move cell to cell, but are restricted to initial infection foci in inoculated leaves. At the single cell level, these mutants are unable to maintain genome amplification, which shuts down prematurely. In addition, HC-Pro enhances pathogenicity and amplification levels of heterologous viruses (Pruss et al. 1997). Each of these properties is likely the consequence of the RNA silencing suppressing function of HC-Pro (Kasschau and Carrington 2001). HC-Pro targets a cell autonomous step that is necessary for maintenance of silencing triggered by both replicating viruses and transgenes (Llave et al. 2000). RNA silencing is reversed in cells that express HC-Pro, regardless of whether HC-Pro is delivered by injection of a transgene, by a virus vector, or by a genetic cross. The silencing-associated small RNAs from a silenced transgene are absent when HC-Pro is introduced, suggesting that HC-Pro targets a step coincident with, or upstream of, production of small RNAs. One possibility is that HC-Pro directly or indirectly inhibits the dsRNase, or a factor required for dsRNase activity, that is required for small RNA production from both silenced transgene and viral RNAs. Recently, HC-Pro was shown to interact with a calmodulin-related cellular protein, which itself functions as an RNA silencing suppressor (Anandalakshmi et al. 2000). This raises the possibility that HC-Pro functions indirectly by influencing a calcium-dependent regulator of RNA silencing. Several virus groups, including the sobemoviruses, encode suppressors that are functionally equivalent to HC-Pro based on analysis of suppression activities.

Genetics in the Potyvirus-Arabidopsis System

As a group, the potyviruses cause a large proportion of important viral diseases in most major crops around the world. Our work has focused on virus-host interactions between potyviruses and model hosts. Both tobacco etch virus (TEV) and turnip mosaic virus (TuMV) genomes are amenable to genetic modification for insertion of reporter genes or selectable markers. The selectable viruses encode proteins that enable either positive selections (bar gene) or negative selections ($P450_{sul}$)(Whitham et al. 1999). These are useful in genetic selections for Arabidopsis mutants with either gain-of-susceptibility or loss-of-susceptibility phenotypes. Selectable TEV strains and high-throughput inoculation techniques were developed for identification of altered susceptibility mutants of *Arabidopsis thaliana*. These strains conferred conditional-survival phenotypes to Arabidopsis based on systemic expression of herbicide resistance (TEV-bar) or pro-herbicide sensitivity (TEV-$P450_{sul}$) genes, allowing selections for Arabidopsis mutants that enhance or suppress TEV replication, cell-to-cell movement or long-distance movement. The use of TEV-bar as a positive selection tool to recover gain-of-susceptibility mutants was validated by isolation of several Arabidopsis Col-0 mutants with defects in *RTM1*, *RTM2* and *RTM3* (Whitham et al., 1999). These three genes, two of which were isolated by map-based cloning methods (Chisholm et al. 2000; Whitham et al. 2000), are required for a TEV-specific restriction of long-distance movement in certain Arabidopsis ecotypes, such as Col-0.

In C24 plants, TuMV induces mosaic symptoms and severe stunting. However, TuMV also causes remarkable, ecotype-specific developmental defects in infected plants. These include deeply serrated leaves and increased trichome numbers in vegetative and reproductive organs. TuMV also causes severe developmental abnormalities of flowers, including homeotic-like transformations of organ identity, split carpels, narrow sepals and aborted pollen formation. Arabidopsis C24 plants that are systemically infected by TuMV are sterile. Importantly, these phenotypes are due primarily to P1/HC-Pro. Transgenic, non-infected plants containing a 35S-TuMV P1/HC-Pro gene show all of the phenotypes characteristic of TuMV infection. Whether or not they are due to the silencing suppression function is not known. The fact that P1/HC-Pro, introduced by TuMV infection or a transgene, induces such major effects formed the basis for a new round of selections and screens for mutants with altered responses to HC-Pro.

Approximately 200,000 EMS-mutagenized M2 plants (C24) were inoculated with TuMV using high-throughput, high-efficiency procedures.

Any plants that failed to respond to P1/HC-Pro with the severe developmental defects, that were non-susceptible, or that restricted TuMV to inoculated leaves were easily scored as fertile survivors at 21 days post inoculation. Systemically infected individuals that responded like wild-type plants were severely symptomatic, stunted, and sterile. M3 plants from candidate mutants were tested for TuMV susceptibility or response. Eleven bona fide, recessive mutants were isolated.

Genetic analysis of four of the mutants revealed two complementation groups (group 1, C12-21 and C15-8; group 2, C13-3 and C13-7). C12-21 and C15-8 were completely immune with no infection foci in inoculated leaves (data not shown), whereas C13-3 and C13-7 exhibited a slow systemic infection phenotype. The susceptibility defects were identical using the heterologous potyvirus, TEV. However, each mutant was highly susceptible to the unrelated virus, turnip crinkle virus, indicating that the defects were potyvirus-specific. We termed these mutants *loss-of-susceptibility to potyviruses* (*lsp*) – complementation group 1 mutants were designated *lsp1-1* (C12-21) and *lsp1-2* (C15-8), and complementation group 2 mutants were termed *lsp2-1* (C13-3) and *lsp2-2* (C13-7). Crosses between each mutant and the susceptible ecotype, La-er, were done for purposes of mapping the *LSP1* and *LSP2* loci. Most progress was made with *LSP1*, which was mapped in the middle of chromosome V to a ~150 kb interval that is spanned by five overlapping bacterial artificial chromosomes. This was done by a reiterative process of developing PCR-based markers and scoring genotypes of nonsusceptible (*lsp1/lsp1*) individuals from the F2 progeny of the *lsp1-1* x La-er cross.

Acknowledgments

Work in the authors' laboratory is funded by grants from the national Institutes of Health (AI27832 and AI43288) and the U.S. Department of Agriculture (98-35303-6485).

Literature Cited

Al-Kaff, N. S., Covey, S. N., Kreike, M. M., Page, A. M., Pinder, R., and Dale, P. J. 1998. Transcriptional and posttranscriptional plant gene silencing in response to a pathogen. Science 279:2113-2115.

Anandalakshmi, R., Marathe, R., Ge, X., Herr, J. M., Mau, C., Mallory, A., Pruss, G., Bowman, L., and Vance, V. B. 2000. A calmodulin-related protein that suppresses posttranscriptional gene silencing in plants. Science 290:142-144.

Carrington, J. C., Kasschau, K. D., and Johansen, L. K. 2001. Activation and suppression of RNA silencing by plant viruses. Virology, in press.

Carrington, J. C., and Whitham, S. A. 1998. Viral invasion and host defense: strategies and counter-strategies. Curr. Opin. Plant Biol. 1:336-341.

Chisholm, S. T., Mahajan, S. K., Whitham, S. A., Yamamoto, M. L., and Carrington, J. C. 2000. Cloning of the Arabidopsis *RTM1* gene, which controls restriction of long-distance movement of tobacco etch virus. Proc. Natl. Acad. Sci. USA 97:489-494.

Diez, J., Ishikawa, M., Kaido, M., and Ahlquist, P. 2000. Identification and characterization of a host protein required for efficient template selection in viral RNA replication. Proc. Natl. Acad. Sci. USA 97:3913-3918.

Kasschau, K. D., and Carrington, J. C. 2001. Long-distance movement and replication maintenance functions correlate with silencing suppression activity of potyviral HC-Pro. Virology 285:71-81.

Kasschau, K. D., Cronin, S., and Carrington, J. C. 1997. Genome amplification and long-distance movement functions associated with the central domain of tobacco etch potyvirus helper component-proteinase. Virology 228:251-262.

Llave, C., Kasschau, K. D., and Carrington, J. C. 2000. Virus-encoded suppressor of posttranscriptional gene silencing targets a maintenance step in the silencing pathway. Proc. Natl. Acad. Sci. USA 97:13401-13406.

Noueiry, A. O., Chen, J., and Ahlquist, P. 2000. A mutant allele of essential, general translation initiation factor DED1 selectively inhibits translation of a viral mRNA. Proc. Natl. Acad. Sci. USA 97:12985-12990.

Pruss, G., Ge, X., Shi, X. M., Carrington, J. C., and Vance, V. B. 1997. Plant viral synergism: the potyviral genome encodes a broad-range pathogenicity enhancer that transactivates replication of heterologous viruses. Plant Cell 9:859-868.

Ratcliff, F., Harrison, B. D., and Baulcombe, D. C. 1997. A similarity between viral defence and gene silencing in plants. Science 276:1558-1560.

Ratcliff, F. G., MacFarlane, S. A., and Baulcombe, D. C. 1999. Gene silencing without DNA. RNA-mediated cross-protection between viruses. Plant Cell 11:1207-1216.

Whitham, S., Yamamoto, M., and Carrington, J. C. 1999. Selectable viruses and *Arabidopsis thaliana* gain-of-susceptibility mutants. Proc. Natl. Acad. Sci. USA 96:772-777.

Whitham, S. A., Anderberg, R. J., Chisholm, S. T., and Carrington, J. C. 2000. Arabidopsis *RTM2* gene is necessary for specific restriction of tobacco etch virus and encodes an unusual small heat shock-like protein. Plant Cell 12:569-582.

Yamanaka, T., Ohta, T., Takahashi, M., Meshi, T., Schmidt, R., Dean, C., Naito, S., and Ishikawa, M. 2000. *TOM1*, an *Arabidopsis* gene required for efficient multiplication of a tobamoviruses, encodes a putative transmembrane protein. Proc. Natl. Acad. Sci. USA 97:10107-10112.

Microarray Analysis to Identify Common
Gene Expression Changes Induced by RNA Viruses

Steven A. Whitham[1], Yu-Ming Hou[2], Sheng Quan[2], Tong Zhu[2], Hur-Song Chang[2], and Xun Wang[2]

[1]Iowa State University, Department of Plant Pathology, Ames, IA 50011;
[2]Torrey Mesa Research Institute, 3115 Merryfield Row, San Diego, CA 92121

Viral infection can cause dramatic changes in plant morphology, pigmentation, growth and development and fertility. These macroscopic changes may be the direct result of viruses interfering with host-signaling networks in order to promote infection. Viruses encode a variety of proteins that enable them to infect their hosts. These proteins are generally categorized by their roles in replication, cell-to-cell and long-distance movement, capsid formation and vector transmission. Although the functions of viral proteins have been the subject of intense scrutiny for many years, we are continuing to learn about their multifunctional roles in viral lifecycles. Not only do viral proteins directly mediate replication and movement, but they can also alter the cellular environment to create a favorable state for infection. Viral proteins can directly interfere with key host processes to promote infection either by inducing required proteins (host factors) or by suppressing host defense responses (reviewed in Carrington and Whitham 1998). Examples of each of these cases are provided by geminiviruses (reviewed in Gutierrez 2000) and by viral encoded suppressors of posttranscriptional gene silencing (Anandalakshmi et al. 1998; Brigneti et al. 1998; Kasschau and Carrington 1998), respectively.

The complete chain of signaling events that lead to diseased states has not been characterized in detail for any plant-virus interaction. One approach to characterizing the molecular events that occur during viral infection is to monitor the expression levels of host genes as the infection proceeds. The sets of host genes whose expression levels become induced or repressed provide information about the signaling pathways that are altered by viruses or other stimuli (Eisen et al. 1998; Harmer et al. 2000; Maleck et al. 2000)).

DNA microarrays (Lockhart et al. 1996; Schena et al. 1995) provide platforms to study the expression of thousands of genes in parallel in response to stimuli such as virus infection. We have used DNA microarrays to define some host gene expression changes that occur in inoculated *Arabidopsis thaliana* leaves during infection by five different positive-strand RNA viruses. Here, we summarize a subset of genes that are induced in response to all five viruses at some time point during the infection time course.

Results and Discussion

VIRUS INFECTION, RNA EXTRACTION AND MICROARRAY HYBRIDIZATION

To identify gene expression changes triggered by virus infection, *Arabidopsis thaliana* plants (Columbia-0 ecotype) were infected with cucumber mosaic cucumovirus (CMV), turnip vein clearing tobamovirus (TVCV), tobacco rattle tobravirus (TRV), turnip mosaic potyvirus (TuMV) and oilseed rape mosaic tobamovirus (ORMV). Infections were performed by dusting leaves with carborundum, pipetting 10 µl of virus solution onto leaf surface and rubbing with a gloved finger. At the time of inoculation, the plants were 3.5 weeks old and had been grown in a growth chamber at 22 degrees C and a 14-hour photoperiod. The inoculated leaves were harvested at 1, 2, 4 and 5 days after inoculation as were mock-inoculated sets of leaves that provided baseline gene expression levels for each time point. Total RNA was extracted from each of the 24 leaf samples by the RNA*wiz* method (Ambion). RT-PCR was performed with virus-specific primers to verify that each virus was present in appropriate inoculated samples (Figure 1). The RNA was then used as template for the synthesis of labeled copy RNA, which was hybridized to Arabidopsis GeneChips (Affymetrix) containing sequences corresponding to approximately 8,100 unique Arabidopsis genes (Zhu and Wang 2000).

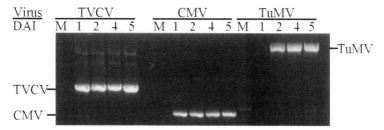

Figure 1. Examples of RT-PCR to confirm virus infection in samples used for microarray analysis. DAI, days after inoculation; TVCV, turnip vein clearing virus; CMV, cucumber mosaic virus; TuMV, turnip mosaic virus.

Table 1. Summary of commonly induced gene expression changes
identified during the infection time course

Days after inoculation	Number of genes induced
1	6
2	10
4	44
5	75
2,4	1
2,4,5	4
2,5	2
4,5	10
Total[a]	114

[a]Total number of unique genes identified.

114 GENES INDUCED BY FIVE RNA VIRUSES

Affymetrix GeneChip Analysis Software was used to calculate the
relative expression level of each gene for each virus treatment and time
point. The software was also used to calculate the fold change in the
expression level of each gene, by using the appropriate mock-infected
sample as the baseline. The output of this analysis was sorted in a
spreadsheet to yield several sets of genes. The set described here includes
all genes that were expressed at least 2-fold above the baseline during
infection by all five viruses at one time point or more. For example, a gene
included in this set could have an expression level of 100 in all virus
treatments at day 2 and an expression level of 50 in the corresponding
mock-infected baseline. The gene may or may not have a significant fold
change from the baseline at other time points. Collectively, this set of genes,
of which there are 114, is referred to as "commonly induced". Table 1
summarizes the number of genes in the commonly induced set, the number
induced at each day and the number induced on subsequent days. In
general, the number of induced genes unique to each time point increased as
the time course proceeded, as did the number of genes induced at
subsequent time points. It seems logical that as the infection proceeded and
more cells became infected that a more complex gene expression profile
would have been observed. This is because many early gene expression
changes may have been diluted and not detectable until a sufficient number
of cells became infected. Another factor that would add complexity would
be the effects of viruses on host signaling pathways that may require some
lag time before gene expression changes occur or before expression changes
reach a magnitude at which they were detectable by the method used in this
study.

Table 2. Functional classification of commonly induced genes

Function[a]	Number of genes in class
Cell rescue, defense, cell death & ageing	35
Unclassified	21
Signal transduction	17
Metabolism	16
Protein destination	10
Transcription	8
Cellular biogenesis	4
Energy	3
Total	114

[a]Functional classifications are according to the MIPS functional catalogue
(http://mips.gsf.de/proj/thal/db/tables/tables_func_frame.html) and were determined based on
known functions or putative functions that were derived from homology to genes of known
function.

FUNCTIONAL CLASSIFICATION OF COMMONLY INDUCED GENES

The DNA sequences of the commonly induced genes were subjected to
TBLASTX analysis (Altschul et al. 1990) against the non-redundant
GenBank protein database. Each gene was classified based on its actual
function or its putative function deduced by homology to other genes of
known function. The results are summarized in Table 2. The largest class of
these genes have known or predicted roles in cell rescue, defense, cell death
or ageing. The majority of them are known to be involved in biotic and
abiotic stress responses. Examples of these genes include; PR1, PR5, β-1,3
glucanases, chitinases, glutathione metabolism and heat shock proteins. The
second largest class contains unclassified genes that possess no significant
homology to genes of known function or lack structural or functional motifs
that could also provide clues as to function. The third largest class contains
genes involved in signal transduction of which most possess a kinase motif.
Metabolism is the fourth largest and the broadest class including amino acid
synthesis, secondary metabolism, small molecules and nucleotide synthesis.
The transcription class primarily contains known or putative transcription
factors that possess homology to known transcription factors and DNA
binding proteins. The signal transduction and transcription classes may
contain good candidates for regulatory genes that could control some of the
transcriptional responses that were observed. If this hypothesis is correct,
then it will be informative to investigate the functions of these genes by
identifying T-DNA insertion mutations (Sussman et al. 2000) or creating
lines that over express or silence their expression by double stranded RNA
(RNAi) synthesis (Smith et al. 2000). Insertion or RNAi knockouts of the
regulatory genes could disrupt viral induction of groups of responsive genes
or pathways and/or effect viral virulence and host susceptibility.

Acknowledgments

The authors thank Torrey Mesa Research Institute (San Diego, CA USA) for support of this work.

Literature Cited

Altschul, S. F., Gish, W., Miller, W., Myers, E. W., and Lipman, D. J. 1990. Basic local alignment search tool. J Mol Biol 215:403-410.

Anandalakshmi, R., Pruss, G. J., Ge, X., Marathe, R., Mallory, A. C., Smith, T. H., and Vance, V. B. 1998. A viral suppressor of gene silencing in plants. Proc Natl Acad Sci USA 95:13079-13084.

Brigneti, G., Vionnet, O., Li, W.-X., Ji, L.-H., Ding, S.-W., and Baulcombe, D. C. 1998. Viral pathogenicity determinants are suppressors of transgene silencing in *Nicotiana benthamiana*. EMBO J 17:6739-6746.

Carrington, J. C., and Whitham, S. A. 1998. Viral invasion and host defense: strategies and counter-strategies. Curr Opin Plant Biol 1:336-341.

Eisen, M. B., Spellman, P. T., Brown, P. O., and Botstein, D. 1998. Cluster analysis and display of genome-wide expression patterns. Proc Natl Acad Sci U S A 95:14863-14868.

Gutierrez, C. 2000. DNA replication and cell cycle in plants: learning from geminiviruses. EMBO J 19:792-799.

Harmer, S. L., Hogenesch, J. B., Straume, M., Chang, H. S., Han, B., Zhu, T., Wang, X., Kreps, J. A., and Kay, S. A. 2000. Orchestrated transcription of key pathways in arabidopsis by the circadian clock. Science 290:2110-2113.

Kasschau, K. D., and Carrington, J. C. 1998. A counter-defensive strategy of plant viruses: Suppression of posttranscriptional gene silencing. Cell 95:461-470.

Lockhart, D., Dong, H., Byrne, M., Folleettie, M., Gallo, M., Chee, M., Mittmann, M., Wang, C., Kobayashi, M., Horton, H., and Brown, E. 1996. Expression monitoring by hybridization to high-density oligonucleotide arrays. Nature Biotechnology 14:1675-1680.

Maleck, K., Levine, A., Eulgem, T., Morgan, A., Schmid, J., Lawton, K. A., Dangl, J. L., and Dietrich, R. A. 2000. The transcriptome of arabidopsis thaliana during systemic acquired resistance. Nat Genet 26:403-410.

Schena, M., Shalon, D., Davis, R. W., and Brown, P. O. 1995. Quantitative monitoring of gene expression patterns with a complementary DNA microarray. Science 270:467-470.

Smith, N. A., Singh, S. P., Wang, M. B., Stoutjesdijk, P. A., Green, A. G., and Waterhouse, P. M. 2000. Total silencing by intron-spliced hairpin RNAs. Nature 407:319-320.

Sussman, M. R., Amasino, R. M., Young, J. C., Krysan, P. J., and Austin-Phillips, S. 2000. The Arabidopsis knockout facility at the University of Wisconsin-Madison. Plant Physiol. 124:1465-1467.

Zhu, T., and Wang, X. 2000. Large-scale profiling of the arabidopsis transcriptome. Plant Physiol. 124:1472-1476.

Control of Root Nodule Organogenesis

A. Kondorosi, C. Charon, A. Cebolla, J.-M. Vinardell, F. Frugier, F. Roudier, C. Sousa, M. Crespi, E. Kondorosi

Institut des Sciences du Végétal, CNRS, 91198 Gif-sur-Yvette, France

Under nitrogen-limited conditions rhizobia induce the formation of a new organ, the nitrogen-fixing nodule on the roots of their leguminous host plants. First, flavonoids exuded by the host plant roots turn on the nodulation genes in the microsymbionts. The lipochito-oligosaccharide Nod factors subsequently produced induce the expression of the early nodulin genes, leading to the activation of the cell cycle in the nodulation sensitive root zone. In *Medicago sativa* roots, the G0-arrested cortical cells dedifferentiate and reenter the cell cycle in front of the protoxylem poles. These cells undergo the G1/S transition, however, the cell cycle is completed by cell division only in the inner cortex. Maintenance of mitotic activity and recruitment of the neighbouring cells lead to extensive but localized cell proliferation and formation of the nodule primordium. Then, the nodule primordium differentiates. In *Medicago*, an autonomous meristem is established in the apical region whereas submeristematic cells develop to various nodule cell types. Cell differentiation necessitates exit from the cell cycle, followed by terminal differentiation of cells which are then invaded by the nitrogen-fixing bacteroids. These non-dividing cells continue to replicate their genome (referred as endoreduplication or endocycles), undergo a gradual enlargement and constitute the nitrogen fixation zone (Schultze and Kondorosi 1998; Foucher and Kondorosi 2000).

The molecular bases controlling nodule organogenesis are poorly understood. In our laboratory, we have been taking several different approaches to elucidate these processes in *Medicago sativa* and in the model legume *Medicago truncatula*. One approach is to identify key regulatory genes controlling different steps of nodule development. This type of analysis may permit the dissection of regulatory networks involved in different nodule developmental stages. Since plant organ development is a constant interplay between cell cycle and differentiation programs, we have been focusing our studies on genes regulating these processes. Below we show for three regulatory genes that they are required at different stages of nodule development. Moreover, their proposed functions are discussed.

enod40 is Required for Inducing Cell Division in the Inner Cortex of Medicago Roots

The *enod40* gene is expressed very early after infection of the leguminous plant by *Rhizobium*. An increase in the accumulation of *enod40* transcripts is detected first in the root pericycle opposite to the protoxylem pole, then in the dividing cortical cells and in all differentiating cells of the growing nodule primordia (Fang and Hirsch 1998 and references therein). Under nitrogen-limited conditions, its overexpression from the constitutive 35S promoter resulted in a significant increase of cortical cell divisions in *M. truncatula* roots (Charon et al. 1997). This was accompanied by the accumulation of amyloplasts in the dividing cells. In nodulation assays using transgenic plants carrying this construct, activation of cortical cell division was observed earlier and at a higher frequency than in the control plants. These results suggested that expression of *enod40* in the cortex is required for nodule initiation (Charon et al. 1999). These effects of *enod40* expression were observed only under nitrogen-limited conditions, indicating that this gene does not control cell division directly. Moreover, in several transgenic plant lines a likely co-suppression phenomenon (gene silencing) for *enod40* was observed. As a consequence, nodule development was arrested, indicating that *enod40* expression is required for appropriate development of the nodule primordium (Charon et al. 1999). These results suggest a role of *enod40* in cell-to-cell communication between the vascular tissue and the specific cells of the inner cortex that may allow proper development of the nodule primordia.

The *enod40* genes have been found in all leguminous plants tested as well as in numerous other non-legumes but not in *Arabidopsis thaliana*. Interestingly, they code for about a 0.7 kb RNA containing only short ORFs (Cohn et al. 1998; Schultze and Kondorosi 1998). Modeling predicted that *enod40* RNA sequences have the tendency to form stable secondary structures, a property shared with several biologically active RNAs (Crespi et al. 1994). A very small ORF corresponding to 10 to 13 amino acids in the 5' end of the transcripts is common among these genes and has been proposed to be the active gene product (van de Sande et al. 1996). By measuring GUS activity, we have demonstrated that several small ORFs of *enod40* were translated when fused to the *uidA* reporter gene. To carry out a structure-function study of this gene a biological assay was developed. By microtargetting of the *Mtenod40* gene into *Medicago* roots a cell-specific growth response, the division of cortical cells was induced. This assay was suitable to test different gene derivatives containing specific point mutations and deletions (Sousa et al. 2001). Translation of two sORFs present in the conserved 5' and in the 3' *enod40* regions was required for activity. Moreover, a gene construct carrying a small deletion in the region between the two sORFs and spanning the predicted RNA structure, exhibited significantly decreased activity, without affecting translation of the two sORFs. Our data revealed a complex regulation of *enod40* action, suggesting a role of the two sORF-encoded peptides and the structural RNA in the cellular function of this gene.

Differentiation of Nodule Cells: CCS52 Mediates Cell Division Arrest and Endocycles

The most critical steps of nodule development, *de novo* meristem formation and cell differentiation, are controlled at the level of the cell cycle. Our aim is at identifying cell cycle components and regulators which switch the cell fate either from the quiescent state to proliferation or from proliferation to differentiation programs during nodule development in *M. truncatula.*

Cell differentiation requires division arrest. In plants, this is frequently linked to the duplication of the genome without mitosis. Endoreduplication can contribute to higher metabolic activity and is likely required for the formation of large cells which takes place in nodule zone II (Truchet 1978). Factors controlling transition from mitotic cycles to differentiation programs or conversion of mitotic cycles to endocycles have not been identified previously in plants. We isolated a cDNA, *ccs52* coding for a 52 kDa WD40-repeat protein, a homolog of yeast and animal cell cycle regulatory proteins providing substrate-specific activation of the anaphase promoting complex (APC) and involved in ubiquitin-dependent proteolysis of mitotic cyclins. By overexpression of *ccs52* in *Schizosaccharomyces pombe* we demonstrated that CCS52 provokes degradation of the mitotic cyclin CDC13, leading to growth arrest, endocycles and elongation and enlargement of cells (Cebolla et al. 1999).

In *Medicago* nodules, expression of *ccs52* was localized by *in situ* hybridization in zone I where cells exit from proliferation and in zone II which is the major site for endoreduplication and cell differentiation. RT-PCR analysis of *ccs52* expression during nodule development revealed activation of the gene 4-5 days after inoculation with *Sinorhizobium meliloti*. To study the temporal and spatial expression pattern of *ccs52* in *M. truncatula*, the genomic region was isolated and the promoter region was cloned in front of the *uidA* reporter gene (Vinardell et al. unpublished). The construct was introduced in *M. truncatula* by *Agrobacterium tumefaciens*-mediated transformation and the *ccs52* promoter-driven GUS activity was tested in the transgenic roots as well as during different stages of nodule development. The GUS staining was absent in the growing primordia whereas gene expression was switched on prior to differentiation of primordia in different nodule zones (Vinardell et al. unpublished). The *ccs52* promoter-driven GUS activity and the expression pattern were consistent with the *in situ* hybridization results and with the predicted function of *ccs52* in mitosis arrest and in endocycles.

M. *truncatula* displays a systemic endoploidy with the exception of leaves which are diploid. Northern analysis demonstrated that the *ccs52* transcripts were present also in other tissues. This indicated that the *ccs52* function might not be restricted to nodulation and could be involved in the development of other polyploid tissues and organs. To demonstrate this function in *M. truncatula*, transgenic plants, carrying the *ccs52* cDNA either in sense or antisense orientation downstream of the 35S promoter, were produced. By testing more than 30 transgenic plants obtained from two independent transformations, no overexpression of the sense *ccs52* cDNA was found. This result indicates that the inhibitory effect of *ccs52* on cell proliferation likely interferes with callus formation and somatic embryogenesis. The antisense expression in 3 lines out of 75 transgenic plants resulted in slight downregulation of *ccs52*. The lack of knock-out phenotype and the significant reduction of *ccs52* transcript levels suggests that the absence of gene function might be lethal and the level of gene expression might vary within a narrow window. However, even a 40% reduction in the mRNA level compared to the wild type was sufficient to reduce the degree of ploidy in the polyploid organs, such as petioles, roots and hypocotyls. Moreover, the reduced ploidy correlated with the formation of smaller cells demonstrating that this change in the expression level of *ccs52* affects directly both the degree of endoploidy and the size of the cell volume. Downregulation of *ccs52* expression affected also nodule development. Though nodule primordia were formed with the same kinetics and number as on the control plants, the late stage of nodule development was halted. The ploidy level was significantly reduced, invasion of plant cells was less efficient and maturation of symbiotic cells was not completed that induced early senescence and cell death.

Our results indicate that formation of highly polyploid cells is an integral part of nodule development. CCS52 appears to act as a key regulator of endocycles. Though its highest expression level correlates with the highest ploidy level in the nodule, *ccs52* is likely to have a general role in plant development, particularly in organs containing polyploid cells.

CCS52, like its orthologs in yeast and animals, acts as substrate-specific activator of the Anaphase-Promoting Complex (APC), a cell cycle regulated ubiquitin ligase. At different stages of the cell cycle, these WD40-repeat proteins may target a great variety of proteins carrying D-box or KEN-box motifs to APC for ubiquitination and then degradation by the 26S proteasome. Moreover, plants compared to other eukaryotes have evolved a multigenic family for these WD40-repeat proteins that likely regulate cell function and fate by fast and irreversible destruction of regulatory proteins.

The *ccs52* gene appears to be conserved in the plant kingdom. It consists of a gene family and members of this family may differ in their temporal and spatial expression patterns which could control differently the APC activity during the cell cycle and contribute to the degradation of different substrates. Elucidation of these specific mechanisms may provide a means to manipulate the size of specialized cells or organs of agronomic interest.

A Krüppel-Like Zinc Finger Protein is Required for the Differentiation of the Nitrogen-Fixing Zone

To identify potential regulatory genes for nodule organogenesis, a cold-plaque screening method was developed for low abundance transcripts (Frugier et al. 1998). In this way, we identified several genes containing regulatory motifs or similarities to regulatory genes, including *Mszpt2-1*, a Krüppel-like zinc finger protein. This gene belongs to a class of transcription factors involved in many animal developmental processes. It was expressed in the vascular bundles of roots and nodules. Antisense *M. truncatula* plants developed non-functional nodules where differentiation of the nitrogen-fixing zone and bacterial invasion were arrested. These results suggest that this gene expressed in the vascular tissue is involved in a non-cell autonomous process, required for the formation of the central nitrogen-fixing zone (Frugier et al. 2000). The gene was able to confer salt tolerance to yeast cells, as it was shown for a homologous gene in *Arabidopsis*. Moreover, this transcription factor is strongly and rapidly induced after application of salt stress to roots and nodules, suggesting that it may participate in osmotic stress responses in plant cells. We suggest that *Mtzpt2-1* may be involved in the osmotic adaptation of the nodule vascular tissues to support nitrogen fixation.

Literature Cited

Cebolla A. et al. 1999. EMBO J. 18 :4476-4484.
Charon C. et al. 1997. Proc. Natl. Acad. Sci. USA 94:8901-8906.
Charon C. et al. 1999. Plant Cell 11 :1953-1965.
Cohn J. et al. 1998. Trends Plant Sci. 3:105-110.
Crespi, M.D. et al. 1994. EMBO J. 13:5099-5112.
Fang Y. and Hirsch A.M. 1998. Plant Physiol. 116:53-68.
Foucher F. and Kondorosi E. 2000. Plant Mol. Biol., 43, 773-786.
Frugier F. et al. 1998. Mol. Plant-Microbe Interact. 11:358-366.
Frugier F. et al. 2000. Genes Dev. 14 :475-482.
Kondorosi E. et al. 2000. Curr. Opin. Plant Biol. 3 :488-492.
Schultze, M. and Kondorosi A. 1998. Annu. Rev. Genet. 32:33-57.
Sousa et al. 2001. Cell. Biol. 21 :354-366.

Truchet G. et al. 1989. Mol. Gen. Genet. 219:65-68.
Van de Sande K. et al. 1996. Science 273:370-373.

Avirulence Factors from Symbiotic Bacteria

M.R. Bladergroen and H.P. Spaink

Leiden University, Leiden, the Netherlands

In the early stages of the symbiosis between rhizobia and plants, when the host plant does not yet benefit from the symbiosis, the rhizobia can be considered as parasites and potential plant pathogens. The virulence of the bacteria during these stages is determined by various factors. The Nod factors (lipo-chitin oligosaccharides), which elicit many infection and nodulation related processes in the host plants can be considered as unique virulence factors which distinguish rhizobia from non-symbiotic pathogens. The structural features of the Nod factors are highly host-specific: various plant species respond only to Nod factors which are modified with substituents such as acetyl, fucosyl or sulphate groups or that contain a highly unsaturated fatty acyl moiety. Such substituents can also have negative effects on symbiotic interactions in particular bacterium-plant combinations and in these cases can be regarded as avirulence factors. An example of this is the sulphate moiety on the Nod factors of *S.meliloti* that prevents nodulation on *Vicia* plants (Faucher et al. 1989; Roche et al. 1991). Another example is the highly unsaturated fatty acyl moieties of *R.leguminosarum* bv. *trifolii* that prevents nodulation on pea plants (Bloemberg et al. 1995). In addition to these specific avirulence traits more general avirulence responses can be caused by a general effect of genes on the production or secretion of Nod factors as exemplified by the recently discovered homologs of NodI and NodJ which are discussed below.

Specific avirulence responses can also be caused by rhizobial genes which are related to pathogenic avirulence factors. As an example, we summarize in this paper the data obtained on a avirulence locus of *R. leguminosarum* bv. *trifolii* which is involved in temperature-dependent protein secretion and thereby blocks nodulation on pea plants.

Characterization of a NodIJ-Related Rhizobial Type I Secretion System Interferring with Nod Factor Production

The establishment of the symbiosis between rhizobia with leguminous plants is initiated by an extensive signal exchange. In the secretion process of the above mentioned lipo-chitin oligosaccharides, two proteins, NodI and NodJ, have been shown to be involved. Mutation of these genes results in a delayed LCO secretion and nodulation, but not abolishment of these processes (Spaink et al. 1995). Recent experiments performed in our lab have been set up, to identify homologous proteins with a putative LCO secretion activity. We have identified seven potential candidates. Extensive examination of one of them, HndIJ, showed that this system was not involved in LCO secretion, but was relevant for nodulation, since it interfered with LCO synthesis. Mutation of *hndI* resulted in an increased nodulation and nitrogen fixation, while overproduction of this protein resulted in an abolishment of LCO synthesis and the production of a relatively hydrophilic compound with a TLC retention time similar to that of NodBC intermediates. Sequence analysis of the flanking genes suggested that these genes were involved in the production and secretion of a lipo-carbohydrate compound, as we found carbohydrate and fatty acid metabolizing genes. The putative functions of the encoded proteins indicate lipo-polysaccharides as the synthesized substrate. On the basis of these experiments we hypothesize that HndIJ secrete a substrate needed for the LCO synthesis proteins (possibly containing a fatty acyl moiety) resulting in a depletion of the acyl-donor pool and consequently can be regarded as an avirulence factor.

A Pathogen-Type Avirulence Operon in
R. leguminosarum Strain RBL5523

Rhizobium leguminosarum strain RBL5523 is able to form nodules on pea, but these nodules are ineffective for nitrogen fixation. The impairment in nitrogen fixation appears to be caused by a defective infection of the host plant and is temperature dependent and host-specific. A Tn5 mutant of this strain, RBL5787, isolated by Roest and coworkers (Roest et al. 1997), forms effective nodules on pea. Recently, we have sequenced a 32 kb region around the phage transducible Tn5 insertion in which we identified genes belonging to the family of type III secretion systems. This locus was called *imp*, for impaired in nitrogen fixation. Several highly similar gene clusters of unknown function are present in *Pseudomonas aeruginosa* and *Vibrio cholerae*. Two dimensional gel electrophoretic analysis of the secreted proteins in the supernatant fluid of cultures of RBL5523 and RBL5787 showed the absence in the mutant strain of at least four proteins with molecular masses of around 27 kDa and pI's between 5.5 and 6.5. The production of these proteins in the wild type strain is temperature

165

dependent. Inoculation of RBL5787 on pea plants in the presence of supernatant of RBL5523 caused a reduced ability of RBL5787 to nodulate pea and fix nitrogen. Boiling of this supernatant before inoculation restored the formation of effective nodules to the original values, suggesting that the *imp* avirulence locus is a type III secretion system involved in the secretion of proteins which cause avirulence specifically during infection of pea plants.

Literature Cited

Bloemberg, G. V., Kamst, E., Harteveld, M., van der Drift, K. M. G. M., Haverkamp, J., Thomas-Oates, J. E., Lugtenberg, B. J. J. and Spaink, H. P. 1995. A central domain of *Rhizobium* NodE protein mediates host specificity by determining the hydrophobicity of fatty acyl moieties of nodulation factors. Mol. Microbiol. 16:1123-1136.

Faucher, C., Camut, S., Dénarié, J. and Truchet, G. 1989. The *nodH* and *nodQ* host range genes of *Rhizobium meliloti* behave as avirulence gens in *Rhizobium leguminosarum* bv. *viciae* and determine changes in the production of plant-specific extracellular signals. Mol. Plant-Microbe Interact. 2:291-300.

Roche, P., Debellé, F., Maillet, F., Lerouge, P., Faucher, C., Truchet, G., Dénarié, J. and Promé, J. C. 1991. Molecular basis of symbiotic host specificity in *Rhizobium meliloti*: *nodH* and *nodPQ* genes encode the sulfation of lipooligosaccharides signals. Cell 67:1131-1143.

Roest, H. P., Mulders, I. H., Spaink, H. P., Wijffelman, C. A. and Lugtenberg, B. J. 1997. A *Rhizobium leguminosarum* biovar *trifolii* locus not localized on the sym plasmid hinders effective nodulation on plants of the pea cross-inoculation group. Mol. Plant-Microbe Interact. 10:938-941.

Spaink, H. P., Wijfjes, A. H. M. and Lugtenberg, B. J. J. 1995. *Rhizobium* NodI and NodJ proteins play a role in the efficiency of secretion of lipochitin oligosaccharides. J. Bacteriol. 177:6276-6281.

Genetic Dissection of Nod Factor Signalling
in *Medicago truncatula*

R Catoira[1], C Galera[1], T Timmers[1], F de Billy[1], F Maillet[1], V Penmetsa[2], R Wais[3], G Oldroyd[3], C Rosenberg[1], S Long[3], D Cook[4], J Dénarié[1] and C Gough[1]

[1]LBMRPM, CNRS-INRA, France. [2]Texas A&M University, USA. [3]Stanford University, USA. [4]University of California, USA.

Rhizobial Nod factors are lipo-chitooligosaccharides that act as symbiotic signalling molecules to initiate nodule development (Dénarié et al. 1996; Long 1996). Nod factors also play a key role in the control of specificity of infection and nodulation, due to particular substitutions present on the backbone of the molecule. Purified Nod factors can elicit in roots of legume hosts, many of the plant responses characteristic of the bacteria themselves, including root hair deformations, the activation of plant genes that are specifically induced during early stages of nodulation (early nodulin genes), the initiation of cortical cell division and the triggering of a plant organogenic programme leading to nodule formation. The induction by Nod factors of cellular, molecular and developmental responses in several tissues of the root, indicates a high level of complexity in Nod factor signal transduction. Moreover, rhizobia need to be producing Nod factors to be able to infect host plants. This indicates that rhizobial infection also involves Nod factor signalling.

Using plant (*Medicago truncatula*) and bacterial (*Sinorhizobium meliloti*) genetics, we are studying the mechanisms controlling Nod factor perception and signalling leading to nodulation. We first exploited nodulation mutants of *M. truncatula* (Sagan et al. 1995, 1998; Penmetsa and Cook 2000), in order to identify plant genes involved in the signal transduction of purified Nod factors. Our strategy was to identify mutants blocked at an early stage of the symbiotic interaction and then to test their abilities to respond to Nod factors. We looked specifically for mutants pleiotropically affected in Nod factor responses, as such mutants are likely to be affected in genes controlling Nod factor signal transduction.

Characterisation of a Nod Factor-Activated
Signal Transduction Pathway

Following large scale ethylmethane sulphonate (EMS) (Penmetsa and Cook 2000), and gamma-ray (Sagan et al. 1995 and 1998) mutageneses of *M. truncatula*, mutants were identified that were devoid of both rhizobial infection and the induction of nodule primordia. Allelism tests performed on a group of nine such mutants (six EMS and three gamma-ray mutants), led to the identification of four complementation groups (*DMI1*, *DMI2*, *DMI3* and *NSP*) (Sagan et al. 1998; Catoira et al. 2000).

Following detailed analyses of Nod factor responsiveness, these mutants could be divided into two phenotypic classes. One included *dmi1*, *dmi2* and *dmi3* mutants, which showed no induction of the early nodulin genes *MtENOD11* and *MtENOD40*, a greatly reduced level of *rip1* induction, no cell divisions and were affected in Nod factor-induced root hair branching, showing root hair swelling instead; and the other included *nsp* mutants, which were similarly defective for Nod factor-induced *MtENOD40* induction and cell divisions, and showed a greatly reduced level of *MtENOD11* and *rip1* induction, but still responded to Nod factors by root hair branching. These mutants all being affected in the transcription of early nodulin genes in different tissues, (the epidermis, the cortex and the pericycle), and in cortical cell divisions are clearly pleiotropic and correspond to multiple response mutants. Furthermore, the analysis of different alleles and co-segregation studies provided genetic evidence that a single mutated gene was responsible in each locus for the multiple defects. It is therefore probable that these mutations alter genes involved in a signal transduction pathway activated by Nod factors and leading to nodulation (Fig. 1) (Catoira et al. 2000).

In response to Nod factors, root hairs of legume host plants display sharp oscillations of cytoplasmic calcium ion concentration, termed calcium spiking (Ehrhardt et al. 1996; Downie and Walker 1999). When *dmi* and *nsp* mutants were tested for this response, *dmi1* and *dmi2* mutants were unable to induce calcium spiking in response to Nod factors; while *dmi3* and *nsp* mutants showed calcium spiking comparable to wild type plants (Wais et al. 2000). *DMI1* and *DMI2* are therefore required for Nod factor-induced calcium spiking, suggesting that calcium spiking is part of the Nod factor-activated signal transduction pathway controlled by the *dmi* and *nsp* genes and leading to nodulation (Fig. 1). These data also indicate that *DMI1* and *DMI2* lie upstream of *DMI3* in the pathway (Fig. 1).

dmi1, *dmi2* and *dmi3* mutants are also unable to establish a symbiotic association with arbuscular endomycorrhizal fungi. In *M. truncatula* there are therefore at least three common steps to the establishment of nodulation and endomycorrhization, all of which are involved in a Nod factor-activated signal transduction pathway leading to the induction of symbiotic responses such as nodulin gene expression and cortical cell division. These data suggest conservation of signal transduction pathways between the *Rhizobium*-legume symbiosis and endomycorrhization (Fig. 1).

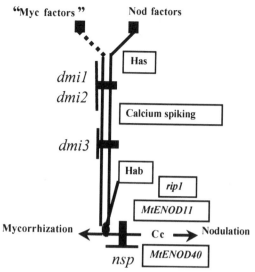

Fig. 1. Model for the role of *DMI1*, *DMI2*, *DMI3* and *NSP* in a Nod factor-activated signal transduction pathway leading to *rip1*, *MtENOD11* and *MtENOD40* expression, cortical cell division and nodulation. As deduced by mutant phenotypes, *DMI1* and *DMI2* would intervene at one or more steps of the pathway upstream of *DMI3*, which would in turn be upstream of *NSP*. The part of the signalling pathway controlled by *DMI1*, *DMI2* and *DMI3* would be induced both by Nod factors and by potential mycorrhization signals ("Myc factors"). Has, root hair swelling; Hab, root hair branching; Ccd, cortical cell division.

Rhizobial Positional Signalling and Infection

nsp mutants show Nod factor-induced root hair branching comparable to wild type plants, while *dmi* mutants are apparently blocked for this response, showing mainly root hair swelling instead (Catoira et al. 2000). These data suggest that, during root hair branching, Nod factors have a dual effect on the polarity of root hair growth by first inhibiting endogenous root hair tip growth (swelling) and then initiating Nod factor-dependent polar growth. This ability of Nod factors to redirect root hair tip growth is likely to be involved in the formation of marked root hair curls, which constitute an early stage of rhizobial infection in most legumes. Moreover, the *DMI* and *NSP* genes are necessary for root hair curling, since *dmi* and *nsp* mutants are completely blocked for rhizobial infection.

In order to identify additional plant genes required for this early stage of infection we studied further *M. truncatula* EMS mutants deficient for root hair curling and identified the *HCL* gene (Catoira et al. 2001). We first tested the Nod factor responsiveness of *hcl* mutants and showed that they respond to Nod factors by wild-type epidermal nodulin gene expression, root hair deformation and calcium spiking (Catoira et al. 2001; Wais et al. 2000). The block in root hair curling is therefore apparently not due to a defect in Nod factor responsiveness in the epidermis of *hcl* mutants.

We next studied the microtubular cytoskeleton of *hcl* mutants, since cytoskeleton rearrangements occur prior to infection in wild-type plants (Timmers et al. 1999). In response to *S. meliloti*, *hcl* mutants showed altered re-orientation of the microtubule cytoskeleton in root hairs and outer cortical cells, with typical *Rhizobium*-related polarity changes no longer being induced in either cell type (Catoira et al. 2001).

In wild-type plants, these cytoskeleton rearrangements clearly reflect spatial information, suggesting that positional signalling is required for infection. Since *hcl* mutants are unable to reorient the microtubular cytoskeleton network in epidermal and cortical cells in response to rhizobia, *hcl* mutations appear to alter the formation of signalling centres or *infection organisers*, that normally provide positional information for polarity changes in these tissues. We propose that this spatial signalling mechanism determines the position both of the curling site and of infection, and is set up by the local production of signals from a microcolony of rhizobia on the root hair surface.

Finally, root hair curling requires Nod factor-producing rhizobia in temperate legumes such as *M. truncatula*. This suggests that the positional signalling mechanism is Nod factor-mediated, but we cannot determine from our data whether or not *HCL* is involved in Nod factor signalling.

Nod Factor Signalling and Infection Thread Initiation

Characterisation of the symbiotic phenotype of an *S. meliloti nodFL* mutant, that produces Nod factors lacking the O-acetyl group and N-acylated by a modified fatty acid chain, revealed that Nod factor structural requirements are more stringent for infection thread initiation than for marked root hair curling in *M. truncatula* (Catoira et al. 2001). In order to dissect this particular Nod factor signalling mechanism, we are adopting two strategies. First, we are trying to identify plant genes that control infection thread initiation, by characterising *M. truncatula* mutants blocked at this stage of infection. Second, we have screened natural populations of *M. truncatula* with rhizobial mutants producing modified Nod factors, with the aim of identifying plant genes involved in Nod factor recognition and infection thread initiation.

Literature Cited

Catoira, R., Galera, C., De Billy, F., Penmetsa, R.V., Journet, E.P., Maillet, F., Rosenberg, C., Cook, D., Gough, C., and Dénarié, J. 2000. Four genes of *Medicago truncatula* controlling components of a Nod factor transduction pathway. Plant Cell 12:1647-1666.
Catoira, R., Timmers, A.C.J., Maillet, F., Galera, C., Penmetsa, R.V.,

Cook, D., Dénarié, J., and Gough, C. 2001. The *HCL* gene of *Medicago truncatula* controls *Rhizobium*-induced root hair curling. Development 128:1507-1518.

Dénarié, J., Debellé, F., and Promé, J.C. 1996. Rhizobium lipo-chitooligosaccharide nodulation factors: signalling molecules mediating recognition and morphogenesis. Annu. Rev. Biochem. 65:503-535.

Downie, J.A., and Walker, S.A. 1999. Plant responses to nodulation factors. Curr. Opin. Plant Biol. 2:483-489.

Ehrhardt, D.W., Wais, R., and Long, S.R. 1996. Calcium spiking in plant root hairs responding to Rhizobium nodulation signals. Cell 85:673-681.

Long, S.R. 1996. Rhizobium symbiosis: Nod factors in perspective. Plant Cell 8:1885-1898.

Penmetsa, R.V., and Cook, D.R. 2000. Production and characterization of diverse developmental mutants of *Medicago truncatula*. Plant Physiol. 123:1387-1397.

Sagan, M., Morandi, D., Tarenghi, E., and Duc, G. 1995. Selection of nodulation and mycorrhizal mutants in the model plant *Medicago truncatula* (Gaertn) after gamma-ray mutagenesis. *Plant Sci.* 111:63-71.

Sagan, M., de Larambergue, H., and Morandi, D. 1998. Genetic analysis of symbiosis mutants in *Medicago truncatula*. Pages 317-318 in: Biological Nitrogen Fixation for the 21st Century, C. Elmerich, A. Kondorosi, and W.E.Newton, eds. Kluwer Academic Publishers.

Wais, R.J., Galera, C., Oldroyd, G., Catoira, R., Penmetsa, R.V., Cook, D., Gough, C., Dénarié, J. and Long, S.R. 2000. Genetic analysis of calcium spiking responses in nodulation mutants of *Medicago truncatula*. Proc. Natl. Acad. Sci. USA 97:13407-13412.

Genes Involved in Nodulation and Mycorrhization of the Model Legume *Lotus japonicus*

Madsen LH[1], Borisov AY[2], Umehara Y[1], Tsyganov VE[2], Voroshilova VA[2] Batagov AO[2], Radutoiu S, Schauser L[1], Sandal N[1], Ellis N[3], Tikhonovich IA[2], Parniske M[4] and Stougaard J[1]

1. Laboratory of Gene Expression, Department of Molecular and Structural Biology, University of Aarhus, Denmark.
2. All-Russia Research Institute for Agricultural Microbiology, St.-Petersburg-Pushkin, Russia.
3. John Innes Centre, Norwich, UK.
4. Sainsbury Laboratory, Norwich UK.

The observation that some non-nodulating pea mutants were not colonized by arbuscular mycorrhizal fungi suggested common steps in the pathways leading to these two different forms of endosymbiosis (Duc et al. 1989). In *Lotus japonicus* there is at least six genetically defined loci controlling both nodulation and mycorrhization (Wegel et al. 1998; Bonfante et al. 1999; Parniske et al. 2000). In order to define the common steps in the endosymbiotic pathways mutants were phenotypically characterized with respect to root hair response to *Rhizobium*, mycorrhization, and cortical cell division. On this phenotypic basis an overview of the early symbiotic events can be made. Two loci, *LjSym1* and *LjSym5* appear to be required for rhizobial symbiosis but not for mycorrhizal colonisation. Lack of root hair response with *Rhizobium* indicates that these genes may be involved in Nod-factor perception or related signalling. In *Lotus* the *LjSym2*, *LjSym3*, *LjSym4*, *LjSym15*, *LjSym23* and *LjSym30* mutants are blocked in both rhizobial and mycorrhizal invasion (Parniske et al. 2000) and these loci define steps in the common pathway. A common feature of mutants in the shared pathway is the lack of extensive root hair deformation. Characterization of the *Ljsym4* mutants indicated for example that the *LjSym4* gene is necessary for passage of *Rhizobium* and *Glomus* through the epidermal cell layer. Molecular characterisation of common pathway genes will soon provide insight into the commonalities of symbiotic plant-microbe interactions. At present the *LjSym1*, *LjSym2*, *LjSym3*, *LjSym4* and *LjSym5* are under map based cloning.

Normal mycorrhization and extensive root hair deformation phenotypes of *Ljnin* mutants suggest that NIN has a function in the early nodule organogenic process (Schauser et al. 1999). The previously cloned and characterised *Nin* gene encoding a putative transcriptional regulator is not required for colonization of the plant root by mycorrhizal fungi. The *Ljnin* mutants have a characteristic phenotype with excessive root hair deformation in the absence of infection thread formation and cortical cell division. This phenotype including the normal mycorrhization was also observed for the pea *Pssym35* mutants (Tsyganov et al. 1999) and a comparative molecular analysis of the *LjNin* and the *PsNin* genes was therefore initiated. First a fragment of the *PsNin* gene from the parents of a *Pssym35* mapping population was amplified by PCR and sequenced. Parent specific PCR markers were then used for cosegregation analysis in homozygous *Pssym35* and *PsSym35* plants. This analysis demonstrated a close linkage of the *PsNin* gene and the *Pssym35* mutants. In order to confirm that the *PsSym35* locus encodes the *PsNin* gene the *PsNin* gene was amplified and sequenced from the three available *Pssym35* mutant alleles. An amino acid substition was found in one allele while the two others carried stop codons leading to truncated protein products.

This demonstrates that the *PsSym35* locus corresponds to the *PsNin* gene and shows the potential for comparative phenotype analysis and comparative genetics in the symbiotic interactions.

Literature Cited

Bonfante P, Genre A, Faccio A, Martini I, Schauser L, Stougaard J, Webb J, and Parniske M. 2000. The *Lotus japonicus LjSym4* gene is required for the successful symbiotic infection of root epidermal cells. Mol. Plant Microbe Interact. 13:1109-1120.

Duc G, Trouvelot A, Gianinazzi-Pearson V, and Gianinazzi S. 1989. First report of non-mycorrhizal Mutants (Myc-) obtained in pea (*Pisum sativum* L.) and Fababean (*Vicia faba* L.). Plant Sci. 60:215-222.

Parniske M, Coomber S, Kistner C, Mulder L, Pitzschke A, Stougaard J, Szczyglowski K, Webb J, and Stracke S. 2000. Plant genetics of symbiosis. Pages 40- in: Molecular Genetics of Model Legumes. Impact for Legume Biology and Breeding, Parniske M and Ellis N., eds. Keely Print, Beccles.

Schauser L, Roussis A, Stiller J, and Stougaard J. 1999. A plant regulator controlling development of symbiotic root nodules. Nature 402:191-195.

Tsyganov VE, Voroshilova VA, Kukalev AS, Azarova TS, Yakobi LM, Borisov AY, and Tikhonovich IA. 1999. *Pisum sativum* L. Genes *Sym14* and *Sym35* control infection thread growth initiation during the development of symbiotic nodules. Russian J. Genetics 35:284-291.

Wegel E, Schauser L, Sandal N, Stougaard J, and Parniske M. 1998. Mycorrhiza mutants of *Lotus japonicus* define genetically independent steps during symbiotic infection. Mol. Plant Microbe Interact. 11:933-936.

Molecular Basis of Co-evolution Between *Cladosporium fulvum* and Tomato

Pierre J.G.M. de Wit[1], B.F. Brandwagt[1], H.A. van den Burg[2], X. Cai[1], R.A.L. van der Hoorn1, C.F. de Jong[1], J. van 't Klooster[1], M.J.D. de Kock[3], M. Kruijt[1], W.H. Lindhout[3], R. Luderer[1], F.L.W. Takken[1], N. Westerink[1], J.J.M. Vervoort[2] and M.H.A.J. Joosten[1]

Wageningen University, Graduate School Experimental Plant Sciences, [1]Laboratory of Phytopathology, [2]Laboratory of Biochemistry, [3]Laboratory of Plant Breeding, Wageningen, The Netherlands

Cladosporium fulvum is a semi-biotrophic pathogen, which causes leaf mold of tomato (*Lycopersicon* sp.). In our laboratory this pathosystem serves as a model to study gene-for-gene interactions between plants and pathogenic fungi (Joosten and De Wit 1999). Many avirulence (*Avr*) genes and matching resistance (*Cf*) genes have been cloned and we are now beginning to understand how their products induce an array of plant defense responses, including the classic hypersensitive response (HR). Here we will discuss the latest results of our molecular studies on this interaction, including the discovery of new *Avr* genes, specificity determinants of *Cf* genes and the polymorphism in AVR9-responsive *Cf* genes occurring in natural populations of *L. pimpinellifolium*. We also describe an efficient method to identify early HR-related genes.

Virulence and Avirulence Factors of *C. fulvum*

In planta, *C. fulvum* secretes many stable cysteine-rich elicitors of which some are known to facilitate infection of tomato. Tomato has an efficient surveillance system to recognise these peptides and to subsequently mount an HR, which is the most efficient defense mechanism of plants against biotrophic and obligate pathogens. Altogether, we have now cloned eight genes encoding such elicitors (e.g. four *Avr* genes; *Avr2*, *Avr4*, *Avr4E* and *Avr9* and four extracellular protein (*Ecp*) genes; *Ecp1*, *Ecp2*, *Ecp4* and *Ecp5*). The recently isolated genes, *Avr2* and *Avr4E*, will be discussed in more detail. The *Avr2* gene was identified by functional screening of a cDNA library of *C. fulvum* on tomato containing the *Cf-2* gene (Takken et al. 2000). It encodes a mature peptide of 58 amino acids including eight cysteines. Avoidance of recognition of the AVR2 protein by *Cf2* plants is caused by single nucleotide deletions and insertions in the *Avr2* gene, and in a few cases large transposon insertions have been found in virulent alleles of this gene (Luderer et al., unpublished). Dixon et al. (2000) found that *Rcr3* is required for *Cf-2*-mediated HR. It will be interesting to determine whether the Rcr3 protein physically interacts with AVR2. The *Avr4E* gene, which matches the *Hrc9-4E* homologue present at the *Cf-4* locus, was isolated by reverse genetics. It encodes a mature peptide of 101 amino acids which contains six cysteine residues (Westerink et al., unpublished). Avoidance of AVR4E recognition produced by strains of *C. fulvum* that are virulent on tomato plants containing the *Cf-4E* gene, is caused by two base pair mutations in the *Avr4E* gene. So far, no other mutations leading to virulence have been found in this gene. Plants from the genus *Lycopersicon* responding to individual ECPs with HR have been reported (Laugé et al. 2000). In addition to ECP1 and ECP2, the other ECPs are probably also virulence factors and are produced by all strains of *C. fulvum*. All ECPs are cysteine-rich peptides and the role of the cysteine residues in stability and biological activity of the ECPs has been studied (Luderer et al. unpublished). Presently we are cloning resistance gene *Cf-ECP2* which mediates ECP2 recognition (De Kock et al., unpublished).

Specificity of Cf-4 and Cf-9 Resistance Proteins

Cf-4 differs from Cf-9 at 67 amino acid positions and by three deletions. Cf-4 lacks two LRRs when compared with Cf-9. The role in specificity of these differences was studied by mutational analysis. The absence of the two LRRs in Cf-4 is essential for its function, whereas their presence is essential for Cf-9 function (Van der Hoorn et al.; 2001a; Wulff et al. 2001). For Cf-4 function its B domain is also essential, whereas this is less so for Cf-9 function. In Cf-9, the specificity determinants are scattered throughout the LRR domain, while for Cf-4 they are confined to three solvent-exposed amino acid residues in three adjacent LRRs (van der Hoorn et al. 2001a; Wulff et al. 2001). Keeping the overall structure of the Cf-4 protein intact, all Cf-9- specific amino acid residues could be introduced in the Cf-4 protein without affecting Cf-4 specificity, with the exception of the three solvent-exposed amino acid residues mentioned above. This indicates that many of the different amino acids present in both proteins are not essential for specificity but could serve as a potential reservoir to generate new specificities.

In addition to the targeted mutations we have created in the *Cf-9* gene in laboratory experiments, we were interested to study the polymorphism in

AVR9-responsive genes occurring in natural populations of *L. pimpinellifolium* (*Lp*) which served as the progenitor of the *Cf-9* locus introgressed in commercial cultivars of tomato. For this purpose we screened a collection of 231 *Lp* accessions for the ability to mount a HR after injection with AVR9. AVR9 recognition occurred frequently throughout the *Lp* population, and in addition to *Cf-9*, a second gene designated *9DC* was found to confer AVR9 recognition. Compared to *Cf-9*, *9DC* is more polymorphic, occurs more frequently and is more widely spread throughout the *Lp* population, suggesting that *9DC* is older than *Cf-9*. The second half of the *9DC* gene is nearly identical to the second half of *Cf-9* (*Hcr9-9C*), while the first half is nearly identical to *Hcr9-9D*, a *Cf* homologue adjacent to *Cf-9* at the *Cf-9* locus (Van der Hoorn et al. 2001b). This suggests that *Cf-9* has evolved by intragenic recombination between *9DC* and another *Cf* homologue. The fact that *9DC* and *Cf-9* proteins both confer recognition of AVR9 but differ in 61 amino acid residues indicates that *Cf* proteins allow much variation without affecting recognition specificity, as has also been observed in our targeted mutational analyses described above.

Cf proteins are expected to be extracellular membrane-anchored receptor-like proteins. Both *Cf-4* and *Cf-9* contain a dilysine motif in the G-domain (KKRY), which could serve as an ER retrieval signal. We found that exchanging the KK residues in the G domain by AA did not affect the ability of *Cf-9* to mediate an HR after AVR9 treatment. This suggests that the dilysine motif is not functional or is masked by interacting proteins allowing targeting of the *Cf-9* protein to the plasma membrane, where it mediates recognition of AVR9 as a component of a receptor complex (Van der Hoorn et al. 2001c). These findings support the suggestions made by Piedras et al. (2000), who concluded that functional *Cf-9* resides in the plasma membrane but do not support the suggestion made by Benghezal et al. (2000) who concluded that *Cf-9* resides in the ER.

Early HR-Related Gene Expression in Tomato

Cell suspensions of MM-*Cf9* tomato do not respond to AVR9, while suspensions generated from transgenic *Cf-9*-expressing tobacco plants show specific defense responses upon AVR9 treatment (De Jong et al. 2000). Despite extensive research, our understanding of the role of the various components of the signal transduction pathway, eventually leading to HR, that is triggered after elicitor treatment, is still fragmentary.

To get further insight on plant defense signalling, Durrant et al. (2000) performed cDNA-AFLP analysis to identify transcripts of which the abundance rapidly changes upon elicitation of transgenic *Cf-9* tobacco cells by AVR9. Various differentially-induced cDNA fragments were identified, of which several showed sequence similarity to genes encoding proteins involved in signal transduction, such as protein kinases, transcription factors and phosphatases. However, a large number of the induced genes is also induced in response to general stresses, such as wounding. We set out to unravel *Cf*-mediated signalling in intact tomato plants that contain both *Avr4* and *Cf-4*. Cotyledons from *Cf-4/Avr4* seedlings start to show necrotic symptoms soon after emergence from the soil, concomitant with transcriptional activation of various defense-related genes (Cai et al. 2001). Subsequently, an extensive systemic HR develops resulting in plant death. We have recently discovered that HR development in *Cf-4/Avr4* seedlings is temperature-sensitive (De Jong et al. 2001, submitted). *Cf-4/Avr4* seedlings quickly develop systemic HR at 23°C, but at 33°C those seedlings grow normally without any sign of HR or HR-related gene expression. Thus, when plants are grown at 33°C and subsequently transferred to 23°C they synchronously start a cell death program within minutes after the temperature-shift. In cooperation with KeyGene, an extensive differential cDNA-AFLP analysis was performed on RNA isolated from wild-type MM-*Cf-4* plants and *Cf-4/Avr4* tomato plants, before and after the temperature-shift. About 50,000 cDNA fragments were screened, of which 420 showed differential expression upon the onset of HR. About 25% of the fragments were found to decrease in abundance (some up to 20-fold) whereas 75% of the fragments were up-regulated (some as high as 100-fold). All 420 fragments were subcloned and sequenced, and Blast searches revealed that 45% show no homology to any gene present in databases. About 30% show homology to ESTs (mainly from tomato and Arabidopsis) with unknown function, whereas 25% show homology to genes from tomato and Arabidopsis with known function, most of which appear to be involved in signalling (Takken et al. unpublished). We are now studying the role of these early, differentially expressed genes by functional screens. Genes will be silenced by virus-induced gene silencing (VIGS; Baulcombe, 1999), after which the plants will be assayed for the ability to mount a HR upon treatment with AVR4 elicitor. We routinely use Potato Virus X (PVX), both as an expression vector (Takken et al. 2000) and as a vector to induce VIGS. Currently we are also testing a Tobacco Rattle Virus (TRV)-based gene silencing system, which is expected to be more efficient on tomato and to induce silencing faster, to a higher level and more homogeneously throughout the plant (Ratcliff et al. 2001).

Literature Cited

Baulcombe, D.C. 1999. Fast forward genetics based on virus-induced gene silencing. Curr.Op. Plant Biol. 2:109-113.

Benghezal, M., Wasteneys, G. O., and Jones, D. A. 2000. The C-terminal dilysine motif confers endoplasmic reticulum localisation to type I membrane proteins in plants. Plant Cell 12:1179-1201.

Cai, X., Takken, F.L.W., Joosten, M.H.A.J., and De Wit, P.J.G.M. 2001. Specific recognition of AVR4 and AVR9 results in distinct patterns of hypersensitive cell death in tomato, but similar patterns of defense-related gene expression. Mol. Plant Pathol. 2:77-86 .

De Jong, C.F., Honée, G., Joosten, M.H.A.J., and De Wit, P.J.G.M. 2000. Early defense responses induced by AVR9 and mutant analogues in tobacco cell suspensions expressing the *Cf-9* resistance gene. Physiol. Mol. Plant Pathol. 56:169-177.

Dixon, M.D., Golstein, C., Thomas, C.M., Van der Biezen, E.A., and Jones, J.D.G. 2000. Proc. Natl. Acad. Sci. USA. 97:8807-8814.

Durrant, W.E., Rowland, O., Piedras, P., Hammond-Kosack, K.E., and Jones, J.D.G. 2000. cDNA-AFLP reveals striking overlap in race-specific resistance and wound response gene expression profiles. Plant Cell 12:963-977.

Joosten, M.H.A.J., and De Wit, P.J.G.M. 1999. The tomato-*Cladosporium fulvum* interaction: a versatile experimental system to study plant-pathogen interactions. Annu. Rev. Phytopathol. 37:335-367.

Laugé, R., Goodwin, P.H., De Wit, P.J.G.M. and Joosten, M.H.A.J. 2000. Specific HR-associated recognition of secreted proteins from *Cladosporium fulvum* occurs in both host and non-host plants. Plant J. 23:735-645.

Piedras, P., Rivas, S., Dröge, S., Hillmer, S., and Jones, J. D. G. 2000. Functional, c-myc-tagged *Cf-9* resistance gene products are plasma-membrane localized and glycosylated. Plant J. 21:529-536.

Ratcliff, F., Montserrat Martin-Hernandez, A., and Baulcombe, D.C. 2001. Tobacco rattle virus as a vector for analysis of gene function by silencing. Plant J. 25:237-245.

Takken, F.L.W., Luderer, R., Gabriëls, S.H.E.J., Westerink N., Riu L., De Wit, P.J.G.M., and Joosten, M.H.A.J. 2000. A functional cloning strategy, based on a binary PVX-expression vector, to isolate HR-inducing cDNAs of plant pathogens. Plant J. 24:2000, 275-283.

Van der Hoorn, R.A.L., Roth, R., and De Wit, P.J.G.M. 2001a. Identification of distinct specificity determinants in resistance protein Cf-4 allows construction of a *Cf-9* mutant that confers recognition of avirulence protein AVR4. Plant Cell 13:273-285.

Van der Hoorn, R.A.L., Kruijt, M., Roth, R., Brandwagt, B.F., Joosten, M.H.A.J. and De Wit, P.J.G.M. 2001b. Intragenic recombination generated two distinct *Cf* genes that mediate AVR9 recognition in natural population of *Lycopersicon pimpinellifolium*. Proc. Natl. Acad. Sci. USA. 98:10493-10498.

Van der Hoorn, R.A.L., Van der Ploeg, A., De Wit, P.J.G.M. de Wit, and Joosten, M.H.A.J. 2001c. The c-terminal dilysine motif for targeting to the endoplasmic reticulum is not required for *Cf-9* function. Mol. Plant-Microbe Interact. 14:412-415.

Wulff, B.B.H., Thomas, C.W., Smoker, M., Grant, M., Jones, J.D.G. 2001.

Domain swapping and gene shuffling identify sequences required for induction of *Avr*-dependent hypersensitive response by tomato *Cf-4* and *Cf-9* proteins. Plant Cell 13: 255-272.

The *Lml* Gene from *B. nigra* and Interactions Between *L. maculans* and *A. thaliana*

Sofia Wretblad, Svante Bohman and Christina Dixelius

Dept. of Plant Biology, Swedish Univ. Agr. Sci, Uppsala, Sweden

Leptosphaeria maculans (Desm.) Ces. & de Not. (anamorph: *Phoma lingam* (Tode ex Fr.) Desm.) causes blackleg disease or stem canker of oilseed *Brassica* crops worldwide, including *B. napus, B. rapa* and *B. juncea.* The disease is of major economic importance in the main oilseed rape growing areas of Australia, Canada and Europe and severe epidemics have periodically occurred (Gladders et al. 1998). The taxonomy of this fungus is complicated, as *L. maculans* appears to comprise several closely related species that are morphologically similar (Balesdent et al. 1998). Over the last ten years several molecular approaches have been applied to aid in the classification of *L. maculans* isolates and further subgroupings have been suggested (Purwantara et al. 2000; Howlett et al. 2001). The rapid evolution of new and more virulent isolates demand a more efficient use of resistance sources within the *Brassica* gene pool (Ballinger et al. 1996). Resistance to *L. maculans* is mainly found in *Brassica* species containing the B-genome, i. e. *Brassica nigra, B. juncea* and *B. carinata* (Sjödin and Glimelius 1988). Conventional breeding programs are utilizing this type of germplasm as a source of resistance, but transferring genes from interspecific hybrids is very laborious. Recent reports of resistance breakdown highlight the need of identifiying new genetic sources as well as a more fundamental understanding of function and regulation of genes conferring resistance to *L. maculans.*

Cloning and Characterization of the *Lml* Gene

With the objective to clone potential blackleg resistance genes from *B. nigra*, we utilized a degenerated PCR primer strategy based on *R*-gene sequence similarities. Degenerated sequence motifs from the previously cloned tomato gene *Pto*, conferring resistance to *Pseudomonas syringae*

(Martin et al. 1993) were used for amplification. One of the obtained sequences was used to screen a cDNA library, prepared from *L. maculans* inoculated *B. nigra* plants. Positive cDNA clones were transferred into a binary vector, using the cauliflower mosaic virus 35S promoter to drive expression, and a spectinomycin resistance marker (*aadA*) for selection of transformed plants. The binary vectors were transferred to *Agrobacterium tumefaciens*, and transgenic *B. napus* plants were generated.

The symptoms after inoculation with *L. maculans* spores were markedly reduced in the *Lm1* transformants as compared to untransformed plants. Decreased symptoms were observed using four different *L. maculans* isolates representing three different pathogenicity groups.

Sequencing of the *Lm1* cDNA yielded a 2385 bp sequence, containing no previously known typical R-gene motifs. A BLAST search revealed striking similarities with genes of unknown function in both *Arabidopsis thaliana* and rice (*Oryza sativa*). In *A. thaliana*, homeologous genes were identified on both chromosomes 1 and 4, and predicted exons of these genomic sequences perfectly matched the 3' half of the *Lm1* cDNA. No sequences with homology to the 5' half were identified. A BLAST search using the deduced protein sequence of *Lm1* identified more than ten significantly similar proteins (Fig. 1). All identified proteins were of unknown function, except the nodule inception (*nin*) protein of *Lotus japonicus*. Interestingly, this protein is involved in the nodulation processes induced by the bacterial symbiont *Mezorhizobium loti*. In addition, two putative trans-membrane regions were identified within the *Lm1* sequence.

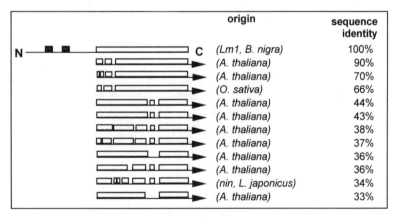

Fig. 1. Schematic presentation of proteins showing amino acid sequence homology to *Lm1*, including species origin and percentage sequence identity on the amino acid level. Shaded boxes represent stretches of relatively high homology. Black boxes represent putative transmembrane regions of *Lm1*.

To confirm the presence and localization of *Lm1* in the *B. nigra* genome, genetic mapping and Southern analysis were carried out (Fig. 2). Linkage analysis revealed that *Lm1* is located on linkage group 8, within a region to which adult leaf resistance of *B. nigra* and cotyledon resistance of *B. carinata* have previously been mapped (Dixelius and Wahlberg 1999). Furthermore, a second locus with *Lm1* homology was found to coincide with a region on linkage group 3 linked to stem resistance to *L. maculans* in *B. nigra* (Struss et al. unpublished). These results further support the role of *Lm1* in blackleg resistance. Presence of homologous sequences in Arabidopsis and other *Brassica* species was also assayed by Southern analysis. Interestingly, the results show that both susceptible (*B. napus*) and resistant (*B. nigra, B. carinata* and *B. juncea*) cultivars carry sequences with homology to *Lm1*. Southern analysis also confirmed the finding of *Lm1* homologous sequences in the *A. thaliana* database. In addition, Southern analysis revealed presence of sequences homologous to the 5' half of *Lm1* in *A. thaliana*, although no such sequences were identified in the database. These results suggest that *Lm1*-like sequences could represent members of a gene family, possibly wide spread within the plant kingdom.

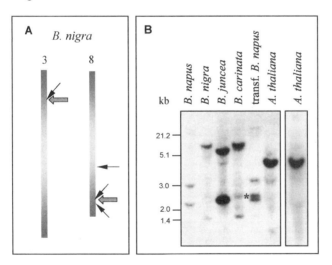

Fig. 2. (a) Large arrows indicate map positions of *Lm1* in the *B. nigra* genome, and small arrows indicate positions for previously mapped loci conferring resistance to *L. maculans*. (b) Large panel shows Southern blot hybridisation with a fragment corresponding to part of the 3' half of *Lm1* to four different Brassica species and *A. thaliana*. Small panel represents hybridisation with a fragment from the 5' half of *Lm1*, showing presence of this sequence in *A. thaliana* although no homology was found in the database. (*) indicates the unique *Lm1* fragment found in the transformed *B. napus*.

The exact role of *Lm1* in resistance to *L. maculans* is presently unclear. Studies of interacting proteins, expression patterns and activation of other defense related genes are underway as an attempt to understand the function of this gene.

L. maculans and *A. thaliana* Interactions

We have put a lot of effort into creating an *Arabidopsis* model system as a tool to study the interaction with *L. maculans*. *A. thaliana* is naturally resistant to *L. maculans*, but a number of susceptible EMS mutants have been identified by screening an *A. thaliana* (Ler) population. The mutant with the clearest phenotype has been used in crosses with Ws to create mapping populations. Preliminary results indicate a location of this mutation on chromosome 2. In a parallell mapping study, utilizing the genetic variation found between ecotypes, locations on chromosomes 4 and/or 5 are of interest.

A new set of interesting mutants were identified by screening a T-DNA tagged *A. thaliana* population. Sequencing flanking regions revealed that one of these lines was mutated in a *RacGTPase* gene. This mutant is susceptible to both *L. maculans* and *V. longisporum* and recent complementation confirmed its role in biotic stress signalling (Bohman et al., in prep.). The *RacGTPase* gene family is rather well studied in animal systems (Sternweis, 1996), where it is involved in many processes, e.g. apoptosis. In plants it has been suggested to take part in cell polarity formations, cell wall synthesis and programmed cell death (Kawasaki et al., 1999). However, the role of *RacGTPase* in plants is far from clear.

A number of *A. thaliana* mutants impaired at defined postitions in signalling pathways related to pathogen induced plant stress are available. The following have been screened with *L. maculans*: *eds1-1, 1-2, 4-1, 8; ndr1-1, npr1, npr1-2, npr1-3; cpr1, cpr5, lsd-1, dnd1; pad1, 2-1, 3-1, 4-1, 5; etr1-1, ein3-1, jar1-1* and finally a *nahG* transgene. Only *pad3-1*, defective in camalexin production, gave a clear susceptible phenotype. Production of camalexin alone is not responsible for resistance to *L. maculans*, as one of the susceptible EMS mutants isolated does produce camalexin. Our results further indicate that there is no requirement for functional SA, JA or ethylene pathways respectively. However, *L. maculans* does stimulate both SA and JA pathways, since PR-1 and PDF1.2 are expressed 48 h after inoculation. Thus, resistance to *L. maculans* appears complex, with different pathways mediating defense signalling. Future work will focus on further mapping and cloning, knockouts, complementation and global gene expression analysis using microarrays.

Literature Cited

Balesdent, M.H., Jedryczka, M., Jain, L., Mendes-Pereira, E., Bertrandy, J., Rouxel, T. 1998. Conidia as a substrate for internal transcribed spacer-based PCR identification of members of the *Leptosphaeria maculans* species complex. Phytopathology 88:1210-7.

Ballinger, D.J., Salisbury, P. A. 1996. Seedling and adult plant evaluation of race variability in *Leptosphaeria maculans* on Brassica species in Australia. Austr. J. Exp. Agric. 36:485-488.

Dixelius, C., Wahlberg, S. 1999. Resistance to Leptosphaeria maculans is conserved in a specific region of the Brassica B-genome. Theor. Appl. Genet. 99:368-372.

Gladders P., Symonds B.V., Hardwick N.V., Sansford C.E. 1998. Opportunities to control canker (*Leptosphaeria maculans*) in winter oilseed rape by improving spray timing. International Organization for Biological Control Bullentin 21:111-20.

Howlett, B.J., Idnurm, A., Pedras, M.S.C. 2001. *Leptosphaeria maculans* the causal agent of blackleg disease of Brassicas. Fungal Genetics and Biology (accepted).

Kawasaki, T., Henmi, K., Ono, E., Hatakeyama, S., Iwano, M., Satoh, H., Shimamoto, K. 1999. The small GTP-binding protein rac is a regulator of cell death in plants. Proc. Natl. Acad. Sci. USA 96:10922-10926.

Martin, G.B., Brommonschenkel, S. H., Chunwongse, J., Frary A., Ganal, M. W., Spivey, R., Wu, T., Earle, E. D., Tanksley, S. D. 1993. Map-based cloning of a protein kinase gene conferring disease resistance in tomato. Science 262:1432-1436.

Purwantara A., Barrins J.M., Cozijnsen A.J., Ades P.K., Howlett B.J. 2000. Genetic diversity of isolates of the *Leptosphaeria maculans* species complex from Australia, Europe and North America using amplified fragment length polymorphism analysis. Mycological Research 104:772-81.

Sjödin, C., Glimelius, K. 1988. Screening for resistance to blackleg, *Phoma lingam* (Tode ex Fr.)Desm. within *Brassicaceae. J. Phytopathol.* 123:322-332.

Sternweis, P.C. 1996. G proteins in signal transduction. In: C-H Hedin, M Purton eds. Signal Transduction. Chapman & Hall, London pp. 285-301.

Lipid Mediated Signaling in
the *Aspergillus*/Seed Interaction

Dimitrios I. Tsitsigiannis, Richard A.Wilson, Nancy P. Keller

University of Wisconsin, Madison, WI, USA

Oil seed crops are susceptible to infestation by the filamentous fungi *Aspergillus flavus* and *Aspergillus parasitcus*. Asexual *Aspergillus* spores, called conidia, are wind-borne structures that land on and penetrate lipid-rich seed. While metabolizing the fat-stores of seed, *Aspergillus* produces more conidia (e.g. secondary inocula) and also the mycotoxin aflatoxin (AF), the most potent natural carcinogen known. AF contamination of crops results in substantial crop loss in developed countries and significant AF associated health problems in those countries unable to implement detection and decontamination strategies. Because traditional plant protection and breeding methods are not sufficient to prevent this disease, research efforts have turned to deciphering the molecular events regulating the *Aspergillus*/seed interaction as a means to develop effective control measures. Here we present data suggesting that fatty acid signaling molecules derived from the metabolism of both plant and *Aspergillus* unsaturated fatty acids are mediators of this plant/fungal/mycotoxin relationship.

Review of Fatty Acid Pathway in Plants and Fungi

Lipids are important constituents of all living cells, for example the cell membrane is a fluid barrier consisting mainly of saturated and unsaturated lipids. In addition to their role as membrane constituents, fatty acids and other lipids are often utilized as signal transduction components. Figure 1 illustrates the metabolic pathway of fatty acid metabolism in both plants and fungi. Palmitic, stearic, oleic, linoleic and linolenic acids are important cell membrane components, and in oilseed crops, they represent a major store of energy available to the germinating plant embryo. In plants, lipoxygenase enzymes convert linoleic acid and linolenic acids into oxygenated derivatives utilized in stress/defense signaling in the plant. In

Aspergillus, oleic, linoleic and linolenic acid are enzymatically converted into the extracellular signaling psi factors.

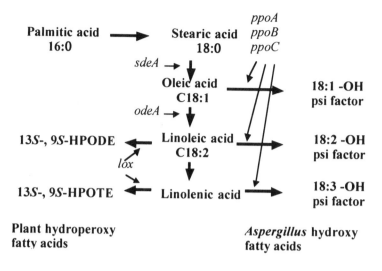

Fig. 1 The pathway of fatty acid metabolism in plants and *Aspergillus* spp.

Physiological Evidence of the Role of Fatty Acids as Extracellular Sporogenic Factors and Mycotoxin Regulators

Due to the importance of spores in initiating an infection and establishing a fungal colony, there has been considerable focus on identifying factors regulating spore production in a number of Ascomycetes and Imperfect Fungi. Identification of environmental factors that affect morphological differentiation in fungi would be useful for designing strategies to control *Aspergillus* infestation of seeds and seed products.

Although great progress has been made in elucidating the role of an intracellular camp-dependent G protein transduction pathway in governing *Aspergillus* asexual spore production (Shimizu and Keller 2001; Hicks et al. 1997), very little is known about the specific extracellular signals that play a role in spore development. One of the few extracellular signals known to regulate both asexual and sexual spore development is psi factor (Fig. 1). Psi factor is a mixture of hydroxylated linoleic, oleic, and linolenic acid derivatives (termed psiAα,β & γ, psiBα,β & γ and psiCα,β & γ, respectively) produced by *A. nidulans* (Champe et al. 1989, Calvo et al. 2001) and other *Aspergillus* spp. The proportion of psiA to psiB and psiC is postulated to regulate the ratio of asexual to sexual development in *A. nidulans* (Champe et al. 1989). Considering that the α forms of psi factor are derived from linoleic acid and that *Aspergillus* spp.

typically colonize oil seed high in linoleic acid content, we asked if seed fatty acids would have a sporogenic effect on *Aspergillus* spp.

As summarized in Table 1, we found that linoleic acid and two plant lipoxygenase derivatives of linoleic acid, 9*S*- and 13*S*-hydroperoxylinoleic acid (9*S*- and 13*S* - HPODE) had a significant effect on spore production in *A. nidulans, A. flavus* and *A. parasiticus.* In contrast palmitic acid and oleic acid (the other two major seed fatty acids) had no sporogenic effect on these fungi (Calvo et al. 1999). Although all of the 18 C polyunsaturated fatty acids promoted asexual sporulation, there was a notable difference of their effects on mycotoxin production as well as on sclerotial (*A. flavus*) and cleistothecial (*A. nidulans*) development. Linoleic acid and 9*S*-HPODE both stimulated sexual spore production in *A. nidulans* (Calvo et al. 1999) and stimulated mycotoxin production in liquid shake media (Burow et al. 1997). On the other hand 13*S*-HPODE inhibited sexual spore production in *A. nidulans,* inhibited production of sclerotia in *A. flavus* and inhibited mycotoxin production.

Table 1. Effect of polyunsaturated fatty acids on asexual spore production, production of cleistothecia, and sterigmatocystin gene expression in *A. nidulans* and asexual spore production, production of sclerotia and aflatoxin gene expression in *A. flavus.*

Fatty acid	Asexual Spore	Sexual Spores	Sclerotia	AF/ST
Palmitic acid (16:0)	NE	NE	NE	ND[a]
Oleic acid (18:1)	NE	NE	NE	ND
Linoleic acid (18:2)				+(1)[c]
1.0 mg	+[a]	-[a]	NE	
0.1 mg	- (+ *A. flavus*)[b]	+	NE	
9S-HPODE (18:2)				+(1)
1.0mg	+	-	NE	
0.1mg	- (+ *A. flavus*)	+	NE	
13S-HPODE (18:2)				-(1)
1.0 mg	+	-	-	
0.1 mg	+	-	NE	

[a] NE =no effect. ND=not done. (+) = induction of morphological structure or AF/ST genes compared to control. (-) = inhibition of morphological structure or AF/ST genes compared to control.
[b] (+ *A. flavus*) = at 0.1 mg LA and 9S-APODE, asexual sporulation was induced in *A. flavus.* Sexual sporulation was induced and asexual sporulation repressed in *A. nidulans* at these concentrations (Calvo et al. 1999).
[c] (1) = results from liquid shake culture (Burow et al. 1997).

The above results coupled with studies from other fungal research groups (Nukima 1981) suggest that linoleic acid and its derivatives, such as psi factor, are conserved signal molecules modulating fungal sporulation and other aspects of fungal differentiation processes.

Aspergillus Fatty Acid Mutants are Defective in Sporulation

To genetically address the importance of linoleic acid and psi factor in *Aspergillus*, we created a mutant lacking the Δ12-oleic acid desaturase gene (*odeA*, see Fig. 1) which is required for the conversion of oleic acid to linoleic acid (Calvo et al. 2001). This strain produces large amounts of oleic acid and oleic acid-derived psi factor, but only trace amounts of linoleic acid. It produces less asexual spores but more sexual spores than the wild type. Most recently we have created a mutant lacking a putative Δ9-stearic acid desaturase gene (*sdeA*) proposed to convert stearic acid to oleic acid. This strain presumably synthesizes no psi factors due to lack of substrate material. The phenotype of the Δ*sdeA* strain is similar to the Δ*odeA* strain although more extreme in its loss of asexual spore production. We are currently examining the ability of these strains to colonize seed. Preliminary data suggests they are complemented - at least in part - by growth on seed.

We have also cloned putative oxygenase genes (*ppoA*, *ppoB* and *ppoC*) likely to be required for psi formation (Fig. 1). A thorough examination and comparison of *Aspergillus* strains lacking these five genes should provide us with insight as to the signaling molecule(s) required for developmental processes in the Aspergilli.

Plant Lipoxygenases Play a Role in the *Aspergillus* / Seed Interaction

Lipoxygenases are plant defense/stress enzymes thought to play a role in plant-microbe interactions. They catalyze the dioxygenation of *cis*, *cis* 1,4 pentadiene moieties of fatty acids to produce 9*S* and 13*S* fatty acid hydroperoxides (e.g. 9*S*-HPODE and 13*S*-HPODE). As seen in Table 1, both of these products have profound effects on *Aspergillus* spore, production of sclerotia and mycotoxin production. We have shown that peanut seed and corn seed lipoxygenase (*lox*) genes are induced by *Aspergillus* infection and, in the case of peanut seed, that 9*S*-HPODE levels increase during *Aspergillus* colonization of the seed (Burow et al. 2000, Wilson et al. in press). Furthermore, the corn seed *lox* gene, which encodes a 9*S*-HPODE producing enzyme, is highly expressed in corn lines susceptible to AF but is not expressed - or expressed only at low levels - in corn lines with some resistance to AF (Wilson et al. in press). These results together with the physiological data (Table 1) support a hypothesis that 9*S*-HPODE promotes sporulation and AF production in *Aspergillus* spp. This observation suggests that seed *lox* could be used as biomarkers denoting resistance or susceptibility to AF contamination in the field.

189

Conclusions

Based on our accumulated data there is considerable evidence for a lipid-mediated interaction between *Aspergillus* spp. and host seed. Due to the structural and functional similarities between seed lipid metabolites and psi factor (Fig. 1), it is possible that seed linoleic acid and seed linoleic acid derivatives could be mimicking and/or interfering with endogenous *Aspergillus* psi factors and thus directing developmental processes in the fungus. We hypothesize that these seed lipids affect at least two developmental pathways in *Aspergillus*. One pathway leads to the production of conidia. The other pathway, possibly linking aflatoxin and production of sclerotia in the asexual Aspergilli and production of cleistothecia, and sterigmatocystin production in *A. nidulans*, is inhibited by a subset of fatty acids (i.e. 13S-HPODE). Asexual sporulation in *Aspergillus* spp. is stimulated by increasing amounts of linoleic acid. This fatty acid is both endogenously produced in *Aspergillus* and also can be obtained from seed during fungal ingress, derived by fungal lipase activity on triaglycerols found in fat bodies in the seed. It is possible that the overproduction of conidia and the occurrence of secondary disease cycles require the increased levels of linoleic acid released by seed colonization. Concurrently with the morphological development of *Aspergillus* on the seed, secondary metabolism of the fungus (i.e. AF production) is also affected by seed lipoxygenase products dependent on which metabolite is produced. If the primary metabolites are 13S hydroperoxides, there will be an inhibition of aflatoxin biosynthesis and possibly reduction of production of sclerotia. If a substantial amount of the primary metabolites are 9S hydroperoxides, there will be an increase in aflatoxin production.

Literature Cited

Burow, G. B., Nesbitt, T. C., Dunlap, J., and Keller, N. P. 1997. Seed lipoxygenase products modulate *Aspergillus* mycotoxin biosynthesis. Mol. Plant-Microbe Interact. 10:380-387.

Burow G. B., Gardner H. W and, Keller N. P. 2000. A peanut seed lipoxygenase responsive to *Aspergillus* colonization. Plant Mol. Biol. 42:689-701.

Calvo, A. M., Hinze, L. L., Gardner H. W., and Keller, N. P. 1999. Sporogenic effect of polyunsaturated fatty acids on development of *Aspergillus* spp. Appl. Environ. Microbiol. 65:3668-3673.

Calvo, A. M., Gardner H. W., and Keller, N. P. 2001. Genetic connection between fatty acid metabolism and sporulation in *Aspergillus nidulans*. J. Biol. Chem. 276:25766-25774.

Champe, S. P., and El-Zayat, A. A. E. 1989. Isolation of a sexual sporulation hormone from *Aspergillus nidulans*. J. Bacteriol. 171:3982-3988.

Hicks, J. K., Yu, J. H., Keller, N. P., and Adams, T. H. 1997. *Aspergillus* sporulation and mycotoxin production both require inactivation of the

FadA G alpha protein-dependent signaling pathway. EMBO J. 16:4916-4923.

Nukima, M. T., Sassa, T., Ikeda, M., and Takahashi, K. 1981. Linoleic acid enhances perithecial production in *Neurospora crassa*. Agric. Biol. Chem. 45:2371-2373.

Shimizu, K., and Keller, N. P. 2001. Genetic involvement of a cAMP-dependent protein kinase in a G protein signaling pathway regulating morphological and chemical transitions in *Aspergillus nidulans*. Genetics. 157:591-600.

Towards the Identification of Membrane Proteins from Arbuscular Mycorrhizas Formed Between *Medicago truncatula* and *Glomus versiforme*

Huda J. Mussa, Lloyd W. Sumner and Maria J. Harrison

The Samuel Roberts Noble Foundation, Plant Biology Division, 2510 Sam Noble Parkway, Ardmore, OK, 73402, USA

Introduction

Most vascular flowering plants are able to form symbiotic associations with arbuscular mycorrhizal (AM) fungi. These associations, which develop in the roots, are called arbuscular mycorrhizas and are highly beneficial for both the plant and the fungus. A central feature of the AM symbiosis is the bi-directional exchange of nutrients between the symbionts; the plant provides the fungus with carbon while the fungus transports phosphate to the plant. Little is known about the transport processes involved in carbon and phosphate movement between the symbionts; however, this process has been suggested to occur at the interface between fungal hyphae termed arbuscules and the root cortical cells. At the arbuscular/cortical cell interface, the symbionts are separated by a specialized membrane of plant origin, termed the peri-arbuscular membrane, as well as the fungal plasma membrane of the arbuscule. Phosphate and carbon transport in and out of the plant may occur across the peri-arbuscular membrane. Analysis of the peri-arbuscular membrane is hampered by its location deep within the root and by the lack of membrane markers that might be used in biochemical analyses.

Proteomic analysis of membrane proteins present in mycorrhizal roots may permit the identification of proteins from this membrane. With recent advances in two-dimensional gel electrophoresis and mass spectrometry analyses coupled with the complete sequences of a number of genomes, expression proteomics has become a powerful tool for the analysis of cellular behaviour. Here we summarize some initial investigations of the use of proteomic approaches to identify microsomal proteins from *M. truncatula/G.versiforme* mycorrhizal roots.

Materials and Methods

PLANT GROWTH CONDITIONS AND INOCULATION OF *M. TRUNCATULA* ROOTS
WITH *G. VERSIFORME*

M. truncatula plants were grown and inoculated with *G. versiforme* as described previously (Harrison 1996). Mycorrhizal roots were harvested at 28 days post-inoculation and a random sample was stained for evaluation of colonization. The remainder of the root sample was frozen immediately in liquid nitrogen and stored at –80°C. The extent of colonization was evaluated via a grid-line intersect method. Samples in which the colonization was estimated to be 50% (root length colonized) or greater were used in subsequent analyses.

EXTRACTION OF PROTEINS

Microsomal proteins were extracted from mycorrhizal root samples based on the method described by Larsson et al.(1987). All extractions were carried out on ice and all centrifugation steps were performed at 4°C. Frozen roots were ground to a fine powder, suspended in 0.5M sucrose, 5mM ascorbic acid, 50 mM Hepes-KOH pH 7.4, 10 mM DTT, 0.6% PVPP and a protease inhibitor cocktail, (Complete^{TM}, Roche Diagnostics) and filtered through a 240 μm nylon mesh. The filtered suspension was subjected to centrifugation at 10,000g for 10 minutes and then the supernatant was subjected to a second centrifugation at 100,000 g for 1 hour. Microsomes were pelleted while cytosolic proteins remained in the supernatant. The microsomal proteins were solubilized in protein extraction buffer (100mM TrisHCl pH 8.4, 20% glycerol, 4% SDS and 10mM DTT) by incubating at 80^{0}C for 10 minutes. Microsomal proteins were then concentrated and desalted by chloroform methanol precipitation where 400μl of methanol was added to 400μl of protein extract and 300μl of chloroform was added to this mixture. The mixture was vortexed and then subjected to centrifugation at 10,000 g at room temperature for 30 minutes. Microsomal proteins collect at the interphase between the organic and aqueous solvents. The aqueous phase was removed and the microsomal proteins were precipitated by the addition of 300μl of methanol followed by centrifugation at 10,000g for 10 minutes. The microsomal proteins were then dried under vacuum.

SEPARATION OF PROTEINS VIA 2D SDS-PAGE

The microsomes were solubilized in IEF buffer consisting of 9M urea, 1.2% carrier ampholyte (17-6000-87, Pharmacia), 4% CHAPS, 60mM DTT and 0.01% bromophenol blue. Proteins were separated in the first dimension by isoelectric focusing on 11 cm immobilized Bio-Rad IPG strips (pI 3-10). The strips were focussed at 250V for 1 hour, followed by 8000V for 3.5 hours or until 22000 V/hours had been acheived. Proteins were separated in the second dimension on Bio-Rad Criterion 10-20% SDS-PAGE gels and were stained with colloidal blue (Pierce, GelCode). Protein spots were excised and digested in-gel with sequencing grade modified trypsin (Promega, Madison, WI) according to Shevchenko et al., (1996). Digested products were dissolved in 0.1% TFA, mixed with an equal volume of a 20 mg/mL solution of α-cyano-4-hydroxy-cinnamic acid in acetonitrile/water (50% v/v), 1% formic acid and subjected to mass analysis using a PE Biosystem DE-STR MALDI-TOF-MS. Positive-ion MALDI mass spectra were obtained in the delayed extraction and reflected-ion mode, yielding a resolution of approximately 15,000. Mass spectra were internally mass calibrated using observed trypsin autolytic digestion product ions. Data base searching was performed using Mascot (http://www.matrixscience.com) or MS-FIT (http://prospector.ucsf.edu).

Results and Discussion

Methods for extracting microsomal proteins from mycorrhizal roots of *Medicago truncatula* and their subsequent separation by isoelectric focussing were optimized. Following separation of proteins in the second dimension on SDS-polyacrylamide gels, microsomal proteins were resolved (Figure 1).

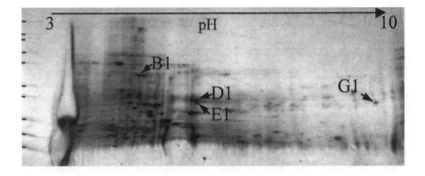

Fig. 1. Two-dimensional polyacrylamide gel showing microsomal proteins from mycorrhizal roots of *M. truncatula /G. versiforme*. Markers shown to the left of the gel have the following molecular weights:200, 116.3, 97.4, 66.3, 55.4, 36.5, 31, 21.5, 14.4 and 6 kD.

In-gel digestion of proteins followed by MALDI-TOF-MS analysis yielded mass spectra (Figure 2) that were used to search the Genbank protein database. In general, queries of the Genbank protein database were successful only 20% of the time. Of the four proteins shown in Figure 1, a significant match was obtained only for protein B1, where 4 of the 14 peptides queried matched calreticulin from *Beta vulgaris* (g11131631). In an effort to improve our identification rate, we also searched the EST databases. Recent sequencing efforts from Stanford University, TIGR (NSF funded project), INRA-CNRS (France) and The Noble Foundation have generated approximately 122,000 ESTs for *M. truncatula*, including 7689 ESTs from *M. truncatula/G. versiforme* mycorrhizal roots. Searching the EST databases increased the success rate. For example, microsomal protein E1 (Figure 1) yielded the mass spectra shown in Figure 2.

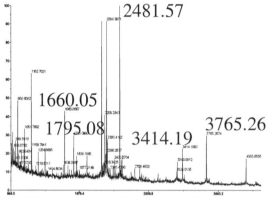

Fig. 2. MALDI-TOF mass spectra of protein E1. The peaks corresponding to peptides that were matched in a database search are underlined.

When this spectra was used to query the plant EST databases, 6 of the 21 peptides submitted matched those of a protein predicted from a *M. truncatula* EST (N100540e). The matching peptides corresponded to the strongest peaks in the spectra (Figure 2). Additional analyses of the EST suggested that it represents a gene encoding a non-seed lectin. The EST is not full length but over a 238 amino acid region, the predicted protein shares 66% similarity with *PsNlec*1, a lectin from pea. Interestingly, the pea protein is located within the symbiosomes of pea nodules where it is suggested to play a role as a transient storage protein. In the AM symbiosis there is an equivalent location, between the peri-arbuscular membrane and the arbuscule. It is unclear whether *PsNlec*1 is associated with membranes but it is glycosylated and therefore expected to be found within the endomembrane system during processing. There is evidence for modification of the *M. truncatula* protein in that the adjacent protein, D1 (Figure 1) also matches this EST, however it is not known if the modification is due to glycosylation.

Table 1. Identification of proteins from mycorrhizal roots (*M. truncatula/G. versiforme*).

Protein spot	# masses matched	MW / pl [1]	Identity [2] (*M. truncatula* EST)
B1	4/13	13419 / 5.19	MtBA 56-E07 (calreticulin)
D1	6/9	19553.1 / 5.77	MHRP- 8B9 (non-seed lectin)
E1	7/30	19553.1 / 5.77	MHRP – 8B9 (non-seed lectin)
G1	5/15	24814.2 / 8.32	PGVN-64-K7 (ion channel)

[1] Experimental molecular weight and isoelectric point.
[2] Only the top match is shown

Other proteins identified from this gel via analysis of the EST databases included protein B1, (Figure 1) which is similar to calreticulin, a calcium binding protein located within the ER and protein G1, (Figure 1), which is similar to a volatage-dependant anion channel from the mitochondrial membrane.

These results are encouraging as they suggest that membrane proteins can be resolved and that identification via the EST databases is possible. Approaches to enrich for proteins associated with the peri-arbuscular membrane, such as comparative analyses including mutants unable to form arbuscules, will be considered.

Acknowledgements

This work was supported by The Samuel Roberts Noble Foundation.

Literature Cited

Harrison, M. J. 1996. A sugar transporter from *Medicago truncatula*: altered expression pattern in roots during vesicular-arbuscular (VA) mycorrhizal associations. Plant J. 9:491-503.

Larsson, C., Widell, S. and Kjellbom, P. 1987. Preparation of high purity plasma membranes. Meth. Enzymol. 148:558-568.

Shevchenko, A., Wim, M., Vorm, O. and Mann, M. 1996. Mass spectrometric sequencing of proteins from silver-stained polyacrylamide gels. Analytical Chemistry 68:850-858.

Molecular Genetics of Appressorium-Mediated Plant Infection by *Magnaporthe grisea*

Nicholas J. Talbot, Andrew J. Foster, Pascale V. Balhadère, Sara L. Tucker, Lucy J. Holcombe, Joanna L. Jenkinson, Eckhard Thines and Roland W.S. Weber

Univeristy of Exeter, School of Biological Sciences, Exeter EX4 4QG, UK

The rice blast fungus *Magnaporthe grisea* brings about plant infection by elaboration of a specialised infection structure, the appressorium. Formation of appressoria is fundamental to the ability of the fungus to cause one of the most devastating diseases of rice and understanding how these infection structures form and function has been the subject of considerable study. This chapter will review recent advances in understanding appressorium development in *M. grisea* and then discuss future areas for study.

Conidiogenesis and Conidial Germination

M. grisea reproduces asexually by production of spores called conidia. These spores are borne on aerial conidiophores, which each produce a whorl of sympodially-arrayed conidia. Conidiophores emerge from the centre of disease lesions and in this way each lesion can generate 2000-6000 conidia per day in order to propagate blast disease to new rice plants. Each conidium is itself composed of three cells and is tear-drop shaped (pyriform). The conidium contains a special glycoprotein adhesive in an apical compartment, which is released as soon as the spore become hydrated and sticks the conidium tightly to the leaf surface. Once attached, germination is rapid and a germ tube emerges, normally from one of the terminal cells. Germination is accompanied by breakdown of storage products such as glycogen, trehalose, lipid and perhaps mannitol. These act as energy sources to enable elongation of the germ tube across the leaf surface. Conidia in *M. grisea* are short-lived cells and are not dormant resting structures found in related fungal species. Breaking dormancy requires nothing more than the presence of water, and germ tubes emerge in as little as one hour. To over-winter, fungal hyphae can withstand desiccation and exposure to low temperatures. The fungus can remain viable as dried mycelium at $-20°C$ for many years. Rice straw probably represents the source of most new season inoculum, sporulating rapidly as soon as sufficient moisture is encountered.

Appressorium Differentiation

Germ tube extension proceeds for little more than four hours before the apex become swollen and flattened. This process is accompanied by a pronounced hooking as the germ tube apex bends at its tip. During this period mitosis occurs and one daughter nucleus migrates to the incipient appressorium, while the other migrates back to the conidial cell from which the germ tube emerged. Appressorium differentiation follows with a thickening of the cell wall, and laying down of a layer of melanin. Melanin biosynthesis in the appressorium is a characteristic shared by *Magnaporthe* and *Colletotrichum* species and is fundamental to the action of their appressoria (Bechinger et al. 1999). *M. grisea* appressoria generate enormous turgor during this period, of up to 8.0MPa. This is the result of synthesis of large quantities of compatible solute in the appressorium. The major solute, glycerol, has been measured in concentrations of up to 3.0 M (de Jong et al. 1997). Turgor is translated into mechanical force and forces a thin penetration hypha into the plant cuticle. Once within the initial cell, the narrow penetration hypha thickens to become bulbous and branched. Within four days, disease lesions become visible and in heavy infections, lesions coalesce and whole leaves become necrotic.

Genetic Control of Appressorium Differentiation

A number of genes have been identified which encode proteins that act during appressorium formation, or directly control development. These genes have been identified using a combination of techniques, including random mutagenesis, differential expression, or by identification of signaling components based on homology to yeast genes (for review see Tucker and Talbot 2001).

The surface-acting hydrophobin protein MPG1 is abundantly produced during appressorium formation and involved in the ability of *M. grisea* appressoria to perceive hydrophobic surfaces (see Tucker and Talbot 2001). In its absence Δ*mpg1* mutants do not form appressoria efficiently on hydrophobic surfaces. The *mpg1* mutant phenotype can be readily overcome by addition of cAMP indicating that the surface-acting protein causes efficient transmission of a surface signal for appressorium formation that acts through accumulation of cAMP. How this signal is transduced from the cell periphery, however, is not completely clear. A potential receptor has been identified in the form of the PTH11 protein, a putative membrane protein. *Pth11* mutants fail to develop appressoria on hydrophobic surfaces and are non-pathogenic (DeZwaan et al. 1999). Similarly *magB* which encodes an inhibitory Gα-protein also influences appressorium development as *ΔmagB* mutants fail to produce appressoria (Liu and Dean 1997). Significantly *magB* mutants can be remediated by addition of AMP indicating that the heterotrimeric G-protein of which it is a component acts upstream of adenylate cyclase. The *MAC1* gene which encodes adenylyl cyclase in *M. grisea* has been identified and *mac1* mutants fail to make appressoria as predicted. However, this phenotype can be overcome spontaneously in some strain backgrounds by suppressor mutations in the regulatory sub-unit of cAMP-dependent protein kinase A. These mutants, named *mac1:sum1*-99, produce appressoria but are not completely restored in their ability to cause rice blast disease (Adachi and Hamer 1998). Downstream of the cAMP signal it is likely that protein kinase A transduces the signal for appressorium morphogenesis, but the only identified PKA catalytic sub-unit-encoding gene *CPKA* is dispensable for appressorium morphogenesis, although appressoria are misshapen, non-functional, and form far later than in wild type strains of *M. grisea*.

In addition to cAMP signalling, mitogen-activated protein kinases also play a significant role in regulating appressorium morphogenesis. The central pathway involves the PMK1, which is functionally related to FUS3 from yeast. The PMK1 pathway affects appressorium development significantly and *pmk1* mutants fail to make appressoria, or to develop further after inoculation of plant tissue. The fact that cAMP appears to influence behaviour of *pmk1* germlings suggests that the MAP kinase

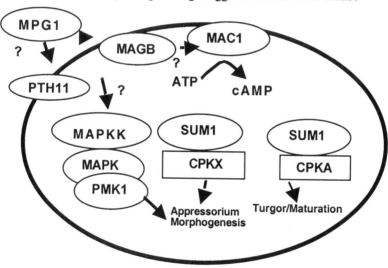

Fig. 1. Signaling pathways implicated in appressorium formation in *M. grisea*

cascade operates downstream (or parallel to) of the cAMP signal, although the effects on morphogenesis are more pronounced than any of the single components of the cAMP response pathway (Xu and Hamer 1996). A schematic representation of the putative signaling pathway for appressorium morphogenesis is given above.

Appressorium Function

Once formed, the appressorium develops enormous turgor in a process driven by solute accumulation. To investigate this process, we have investigated the sources from which appressorial glycerol might be synthesised. Glycogen and lipid are both degraded during conidial germination and lipid bodies translocate rapidly to the germ tube tip during appressorium morphogenesis (Thines et al. 2000). The process of lipid movement appears to be dependent on the presence of *PMK1* as lipid bodies are evenly dispersed in germ tubes of *pmk1* mutants. Glycogen and lipid both accumulate in the appressorium prior to turgor generation and are degraded at its onset. Lipid bodies coalesce during appressorium formation and are then taken up by vacuoles which coalesce to form a large central vacuole in fully mature appressoria (Weber et al. 2001). Lipolysis occurs rapidly during turgor generation and induction of intracellular lipase activity can be detected during this period.

In addition to lipid and glycogen, trehalose is present in spores at high concentrations, trehalose synthesis and breakdown appear both to be important for plant infection by *M. grisea* and trehalose synthesis in particular appears to be required for turgor generation.

Taken together, it seems likely that glycerol production occurs through the action of a number of degradative pathways involving triacylglycerol lipase, glycogen, and trehalose and perhaps also mannitol which is present in conidia and serves as a major storage carbohydrate in the fungus (Thines et al. 2001). The interplay between these potential glycerol sources may well turn out to be important for definition of the control mechanisms for appressorium function.

Penetration Peg Formation

How turgor is translated into the physical force necessary for plant cuticle penetration is still a poorly understood process, although recently three potential candidate genes playing roles in this process have been identified. The *PLS1* gene putatively encodes a tetraspanin protein, an unusual membrane-spanning protein not previously reported in fungi (Clergeot et al. 2001). An insertional *pls1* mutant was non-pathogenic and unable to penetrate intact plant cuticles, in spite of apparently normal cellular turgor. The phenotype suggests a role in regulation of penetration peg emergence. The MPS1 MAP kinase has a similar mutant phenotype with respect to pathogenicity and cuticle penetration, although the loss of this MAP kinase-encoding gene- related to SLT2 from yeast –has many other pleiotropic effects on cell wall integrity, cell wall biosynthesis and sporulation. It seems likely that MPS1 is essential for large scale re-modeling of the cell wall during appressorium maturation and penetration peg formation (Tucker and Talbot 2001). Finally, the *PDE1* gene, was recently identified as a penetration-defective mutant in a REMI screen. *Pde1* mutants fail to produce penetration hyphae efficiently and do not expand infection hyphae beyond the first epidermal cell encountered. As a result they are severely attenuated in disease symptom development. PDE1 encodes a P-type ATPase belonging to the aminophospholipid translocase family. These enzymes translocate aminophospholipid across the plasma or organellar membranes. Such movement is essential for maintenance of phospholipid asymmetry which is fundamental to membrane characteristics such as fluidity and rigidity. It may be that the severe membrane stress that is likely to accompany penetration peg formation in *M. grisea*, requires the *PDE1*-encoded enzyme at this critical stage of development (Balhadère and Talbot 2001).

In summary, a group of the principal components of signaling pathways involved in appressorium development have been identified. The significant challenge now, will be to determine the interplay between these pathways and downstream morphogenetic targets in order to gain a full understanding of plant infection in this significant cereal pathogen.

Literature Cited

Adachi, K., and Hamer, J.E. 1998. Divergent cAMP signaling pathways regulate growth and pathogenesis in the rice blast fungus *Magnaporthe grisea*. Plant Cell 10:1361-1373.

Bechinger, C., Giebel, K.-F., Schnell, M., Leiderer, P., Deising, H. B., and Bastmeyer, M. 1999. Optical measurements of invasive forces exerted by appressoria of a plant pathogenic fungus. Science 285:1896-1899.

Balhadère, P.V., and Talbot, N.J. 2001. *PDE1* encodes a P-type ATPase involved in appressorium-mediated plant infection by *Magnaporthe grisea*. Plant Cell:13(9):1987-2004.

Clergeot, P.H, Gourges, M., Cots, J., Laurans, F. et al. 2001 *PLS1*, A gene encoding a tetrapanin-like protein is required for penetration of rice leaf by the fungal pathogen *Magnaporthe grisea*. Proc. Natl. Acad. Sci. USA 98: 6963-6968.

de Jong, J.C., McCormack, B.J., Smirnoff, N., and Talbot, N.J. 1997. Glycerol generates turgor in rice blast. Nature 389:244-245.

DeZwaan, T.M., Carroll, A.M., Valent, B., and Sweigard, J.A. 1999. *Magnaporthe grisea* Pth11p is a novel plasma membrane protein that mediates appressorium differentiation in response to inductive surface cues. Plant Cell 11:2013-2030.

Liu, S., and Dean, R.A. 1997. G protein α-sub-unit genes control growth, development and pathogenicity of *Magnaporthe grisea*. Mol. Plant-Microbe Interact. 10:1075-1086.

Thines, E., Weber, R.W.S., Talbot, N.J. 2000. MAP kinase and protein kinase A-dependent mobilization of triacylglycerol and glycogen during appressorium turgor generation by *Magnaporthe grisea* Plant Cell 12:1703-1718.

Tucker, S.L., and Talbot, N.J. 2001. Surface attachment and pre-penetration stage development by plant pathogenic fungi. Annu Rev. Phytopathol. 39:385-417.

Weber, R.W.S., Wakley, G.E., Thines, E., and Talbot, NJ. 2001. The vacuole as central element of the lytic system and sink for lipid droplets in maturing appressoria of *Magnaporthe grisea*. Protoplasma 216:101-112.

Xu J.-R., and Hamer J.E. 1996. MAP kinase and cAMP signalling regulate infection structure formation and pathogenic growth in the rice blast fungus *Magnaporthe grisea*. Genes Dev. 10:2696-2706.

Mechanisms of Nematode Parasitism: A Genetic Approach

Charles H. Opperman

Plant Nematode Genetics Group, North Carolina State University
Raleigh, NC USA

The soybean cyst nematode, *Heterodera glycines* Ichinohe (SCN), occurs throughout all major soybean-growing regions of the United States, and causes substantial yield reduction. Planting of resistant soybean cultivars is the most widely used method for limiting yield losses caused by this nematode. SCN populations are dynamic with respect to their ability to parasitize resistant cultivars thus, resistance-breaking genotypes may be selected over time in soybean-production fields, resulting in nondurable resistance (Young 1994).

SCN is an obligate cross-fertile species and a sedentary endoparasitic plant nematode. The life cycle consists of six stages; the egg, 4 larval stages and the sexually dimorphic adults. The second stage larva (L2) is the infective form, and is arrested in development until successful feeding site initiation. After the L2 penetrates the root, it migrates to an area near the vascular cylinder, where it establishes a complex feeding site (Endo 1992; Jones 1981). Nematode sexuality is established during the late second stage L2. There is some evidence that the environment, particularly host resistance, plays a role in determining sexual fate. SCN males migrate out of the root for mating within 15-20 days after infection. The adult female nematode produces 200-400 eggs, which remain primarily in her swollen, hardened body, forming a cyst (Triantaphyllou and Hirschmann 1962). Each life cycle takes 25-40 days and there may be several generations per growing season. The nematode egg is able to survive in the cyst for a number of years under very harsh environmental conditions.

Genetic Analysis of SCN Parasitism

During the past several years, we have completed a comprehensive analysis of the genetics of SCN parasitism. It is generally believed that both major and minor genes (including dominant, partially dominant and recessive alleles) are all involved to some degree in conferring resistance to SCN (Triantaphyllou 1987), although it is not clear which genes are essential and which are specific to certain nematode genotypes, if any. Interpretation is complicated by the use of SCN field populations to evaluate resistant soybean; field populations are highly heterogeneous, both among, and within isolates (Triantaphyllou 1987). Results from population measurements usually are biased by this genetic variability, and the frequency of certain genes for parasitism (nematode genes necessary to overcome host resistance) may affect phenotypic designation of either parasitism or the levels of reproduction (Leudders 1983; Opperman et al. 1994).

We developed inbred lines of SCN that carry single genes for parasitic ability on soybeans, and used them to demonstrate that SCN contains unlinked dominant and recessive genes for parasitism of various host genotypes (Dong and Opperman 1997). A nonparasitic SCN line, which fails to reproduce on the resistant soybean lines PI88788 and PI90763, was used as the female and recurrent parent, and was crossed to a parasitic line that does reproduce on these resistant hosts. The segregation ratio of the progeny lines developed by single female inoculation revealed that parasitism to these soybean lines is controlled by independent, single genes in the nematode. We have defined these genes as *ror*(s) with the meaning of *r*eproduction *o*n a *r*esistant host (Dong and Opperman 1997). Both OP20 and OP50 carry dominant *Ror-1* alleles for parasitism of PI 88788. In contrast, OP50 carries a recessive *ror-2* allele for parasitism of PI 90763 and a recessive *ror-3* allele for parasitism of Peking. Finally, linkage analysis has confirmed that *Ror-1*, ror-2, and *ror-3* are separate, unlinked loci. One inbred line, OP20, carries two separate *Ror-1* loci, either of which is sufficient for parasitism of PI88788. It appears that the two genes in OP20 controlling parasitism of PI 88788 may be acting additively. Examination of F1 data from controlled crosses reveals that the presence of 2 genes (from OP20) results in twice as many females being formed on PI 88788 as when only one gene is present (from OP50). Although not verified, this is an intriguing possibility, and may explain varying levels of aggressiveness between different nematode populations on the same host genotype. These genes, however, remain to be isolated and characterized.

Functional and Comparative Genomic Approaches

Gene discovery in plant-parasitic nematodes is being driven by a number of EST sequencing projects for several economically important plant-, animal- and human-parasitic nematodes, and these will be valuable for comparative purposes. We anticipate that it will be possible to organize sets of SCN genes into classes such as: nematode-specific; parasite-specific; plant-parasite-specific; SCN-specific; and perhaps SCN-pathotype-specific.

However, it is still difficult to assign functions to genes identified in this manner, as methods for gene knockouts and forward mutagenesis are currently lacking for the parasitic species.

Nonetheless, a functional genomics approach to examine SCN development is possible because of the availability of a complete genomic sequence for the free-living nematode, *C. elegans* (*C. elegans* Genome Consortium 1998). A complete sequence of a reference nematode is necessary for several reasons. First, it permits the identification of orthologues between the parasitic and free-living form. In a pilot experiment, we compared 5,555 random EST sequences from a human-parasitic nematode (*Brugia*) against the database of 19,099 predicted *C. elegans* proteins, and found that the deduced proteins from 86% of the ESTs showed a match (Bird et al. 1999). This not only confirms the utility of the *C. elegans* sequence as a tool for brute-force gene discovery in parasitic nematodes, but points to a gene set (14%) with no clear orthologue. Having the complete *C. elegans* sequence also allows one to say with certainty that sequences we identify in SCN that don't match sequences in *C. elegans* truly are absent from the model nematode, or are so diverged as to be unrecognizable; there is no possibility of the match not yet being sequenced.

Classical genetic approaches to parasitism permit the mapping and hence isolation of any genes that exhibit a scorable and viable phenotype, and this strategy will prove to be a powerful tool to characterize some aspects of the host-parasite interaction. Unfortunately, since many genes in parasites are essential for parasitic behavior, it is difficult to perform classical mutagenesis on an obligate parasite with any degree of success. A complementary approach is based on a physical map of SCN, currently under development (Opperman, unpubl.). The construction of a physical map will enable rapid mapping and isolation of genes with scorable phenotypes in the absence of a mutagenesis system. Although gene isolation based solely on a genetic location (i.e., map-based cloning) is quite possible, it may be a formidable task. Because the *C. elegans* genome sequence has been completed, one tool that might readily be exploited is that of conserved synteny. The genome size and complexity of SCN is similar to that of *C. elegans*, and despite evolutionary distance it may be possible to find synteny between the two nematode species.

Conserved Synteny

Conserved synteny describes the co-linearity of homologous loci between different species. The closer the evolutionary distance between species, the lower the likelihood that linkage disruptions will have occurred to break synteny for any given genes. However, synteny is also strikingly conserved across wider evolutionary distances. Rice, maize and wheat, species believed to share a monophyletic origin more than 70 million years ago, exhibit sufficient co-linearity to permit the reconstruction of a hypothetical, ancestral grass genome (Bennetzen and Freeling 1997), and significant blocks of synteny have been conserved during the 400 million years since vertebrate diversification (Elgar et al. 1996). Just as evolutionary relationships can be reconstructed by comparing the DNA sequence of homologous loci, mapping the chromosomal rearrangements that have led to breakage of synteny might prove to be a powerful tool in understanding nematode evolution and phylogenetic relationships. Both the genetic and physical maps for SCN will permit these types of analyses to be performed for a parasitic nematode. A more compelling motive in searching for synteny is to be able to make predictions about gene position in SCN based on the location of the homologous gene in *C. elegans*. This approach will be especially powerful for the identification of homologous genes with low levels of DNA sequence identity.

Conclusions

The genetic basis of parasitism in SCN has revealed several genes involved in parasitism of resistant soybean plants, however isolation of these genes has so far proved elusive. A burgeoning number of EST projects are identifying genes from plant parasitic nematodes at a high rate, and will provide the basis for both functional analysis of various genes and also higher order genomic comparisons. In the future, it is likely that many essential functions in parasite development will be determined by comparative genomics with *C. elegans*. Of course, many parasite-specific behaviors and functions will also be uncovered that will not be amenable to the comparative approach. The challenge for the future is to develop the tools and databases to unravel the functions of genes that make a nematode a nematode, and those that then enable it to be a parasite.

Literature Cited

Bennetzen, J. L., and M. Freeling. 1997. The unified grass genome: synergy in synteny. Genome Research 7:301-306.

Bird, D.M. and C.H. Opperman. 1998. *Caenorhabditis elegans*: A Genetic Guide to Parasitic Nematode Biology. J. Nematol. 30: 299-308.

Bird, D.M., Opperman, C.H., Jones, S.J.M. and Baillie, D.L. 1999. The *Caenorhabditis elegans* genome: A guide in the post genomics age. *Annu. Review Phytopathology* 37:247-265.

The *C. elegans* Genome Consortium. 1998. Genome sequence of the nematode *C. elegans*: a platform for investigating biology. Science 282:2012-2018.

Dong, K., and C. H. Opperman. 1997. Genetic analysis of parasitism in the soybean cyst nematode Heterodera glycines. Genetics 146:1311-1318.

Dong, K., K. R. Barker, and C. H. Opperman. 1997. Genetics of soybean-*Heterodera glycines* interaction. Journal of Nematology 29:509-522.

Elgar, G., R. Sanford, S. Aparicio, A. Macrae, B. Venkatesh, and S. Brenner. 1996. Small is beautiful: comparative genomics with the pufferfish (Fugu rubripes). Trends in Genetics 12:145-150.

Endo, B. Y. 1992. Cellular responses to infection. Pages 37-49 in: Biology and management of the soybean cyst nematode, Riggs, R. D., and J. A. Wrather, eds. APS Press, St. Paul, MN.

Johnsen, R. C., and D. L. Baillie.. Mutation. Pp. 79-95 in D. L. Riddle, T. Blumenthal, B. J. Meyer, and J. R. Priess, eds. C. elegans II. Cold Spring Harbor: Cold Spring Harbor Laboratory Press, 1997.

Jones, M. G. K. 1981. The development and function of plant cells modified by endoparasitic nematodes. Pages 255-279 in: Plant Parasitic Nematodes, Vol. 3., Zuckerman, B. M., and R. A. Rohde, eds. Academic Press, New York.

Luedders, V. D. 1983. Genetics of the cyst nematode-soybean symbiosis. Phytopathology 73:944-948.

Opperman, C.H. and D.M. Bird. 1998. The soybean cyst nematode, *Heterodera glycines*: a genetic model system for the study of plant-parasitic nematodes. Current Opinion Plant Biol. 1: 342-346.

Opperman, C.H., K. Dong and S. Chang. 1994. Genetic analysis of the soybean-*Heterodera glycines* interaction. Pages 65-75 in: Advances in Molecular Plant Nematology, F. Lamberti, C. De Giorgi, and D. McK. Bird, eds. New York: Plenum Press

Schuler GD, Boguski MS, Stewart EA, Stein LD, Gyapay G, Rice K, White RE, Rodriguez-Tome P, Aggarwal A, Bajorek E, Bentolila S, Birren BB, Butler A, Castle AB, Chiannilkulchai N, Chu A, Clee C, Cowles S, Day PJ, Dibling T, Drouot N, Dunham I, Duprat S, East C, Hudson TJ, et al. 1996. A gene map of the human genome Science 274:540-6.

Triantaphyllou, A.C. 1987. Genetics of nematode parasitism on plants. Pages 354-363 in: Vistas on Nematology, Veech, J. A., and D. W. Dickson, eds. Society of Nematologists, Hyattsville, MD.

Triantaphyllou, A.C., and H. Hirshmann. 1962. Oogenesis and mode of reproduction in the soybean cyst nematode, *Heterodera glycines*. Nematologica 7: 235.

Waterston, R. H., J. E. Sulston, and A. R. Coulson. 1997. The genome. Pages 23-45 in: C. elegans II, D. L. Riddle, T. Blumenthal, B. J. Meyer, and J. R. Priess, eds. Cold Spring Harbor Laboratory Press, Cold Spring Harbor.

Young, L. D. 1992. Reproduction of differentially selected soybean cyst nematode populations on soybeans. Crop Science 22:385-388.

The Tomato *Rme1* Gene is Required for *Mi-1*-Mediated Resistance

Isgouhi Kaloshian and Oscar Martinez de Ilarduya

Department of Nematology, University of California, Riverside, CA 92521, USA.

Root-knot nematodes are obligate endoparasites of a large number of plant hosts. The infective stage, the second-stage juvenile (J2), is attracted to the plant roots and penetrates the root tips. Root-knot nematode J2s move intercellularly causing minimal injury, until they reach the differentiating vascular cylinder. In response to signals from the nematode, repeated nuclear division without cytokinesis is initiated within the developing vascular cylinder. These multinucleate cells, known as giant cells, are metabolically active and serve as a source of nutrients for the nematode. In most plant species, concurrent hyperplasia and hypertrophy in the cortical tissues surrounding the giant cells lead to the formation of root knots, characteristic of *Meloidogyne* spp. infections. After feeding is initiated, the nematode becomes sedentary and then undergoes three molts to develop into the adult stage. Adult females are bulbous and non-motile and the common mode of reproduction is by mitotic parthenogenesis. About three weeks after the initial infection, females lay eggs in a protective gelatinous sac protruding from the surface of the root.

Resistance in tomato to three species of root-knot nematodes *M. arenaria*, *M. incognita* and *M. javanica*, is conferred by the *Mi-1* gene. In addition to conferring resistance to root-knot nematodes, *Mi-1* also confers resistance to certain biotypes of the potato aphid, *Macrosiphum euphorbiae* (Rossi et al. 1998). In the incompatible interaction, nematodes penetrate tomato roots and migrate towards the developing vascular cylinder, however, no feeding site is established. Instead, a localized region of necrotic cells or hypersensitive response (HR) is observed near the head of the feeding J2 (Dropkin 1969). In contrast, no visible HR is seen in the incompatible interaction with the potato aphid. The resistance profoundly alters aphid feeding behavior where aphids are able to reach the phloem tissue but are unable or unwilling to feed (Kaloshian et al. 2000). Aphids confined to resistant plants seem to die because of starvation (Kaloshian et al. 1997).

Mi-1 belongs to the largest class of known resistance genes, encoding amino acid sequences predicted to contain nucleotide binding site (NBS) and leucine rich repeat (LRR) motifs (Milligan et al. 1998). It is not known how Mi-1 protein mediates recognition to two distinct organisms, nor how this recognition is transduced. In addition, very little is known about plant defense related gene induction in the nematode compatible interaction, and no information is available about the aphid interaction. To understand the role of *Mi-1* in these interactions, and to identify other members in the resistance signal transduction pathway, we initiated a mutational analysis of *Mi-1*-mediated resistance to *M. javanica*.

Mutational Analysis of *Mi-1*-Mediated Resistance to Root-Knot Nematodes

Towards this goal we developed four mutagenized populations of tomato. Seeds of resistant tomato cultivars Motelle and VFN were mutagenized with two different doses each of ethyl methanesulfonate or fast neutrons. M_2 seed families from individual M_1 plants were collected and processed separately to minimize the number of M_2 seedlings screened and to ensure that mutants isolated from individual seed lots were independently generated. Our primary screen seeks mutants showing susceptibility or reduced resistance to nematodes. The phenotype of *Mi-1*-mediated resistance to root-knot nematodes is extremely tight and very easy to score. In our system, resistant tomato roots infected with 500 infective juveniles usually develop 0-2 egg masses while susceptible tomato roots develop at least 60 egg masses. To minimize use of space in the greenhouse and to streamline nematode inoculation, we developed nematode assays in seedling trays and assembled a modified needle for accurate and uniform J2 delivery around the root system. From each M_2 family, twenty-five seeds were sown and the resulting seedlings were individually inoculated with nematodes. Six to eight weeks after inoculation, plants were checked for nematode infection, measured as number of egg masses developed on the root system. A total of 1,100 M_2 tomato families have been screened and four mutants have been identified. One mutant, *rme1* (for resistance to *Meloidogyne*), isolated from fast neutron irradiated seeds, showed complete susceptibility and was chosen for further analysis. Genetic analysis indicated that the *rme1* mutant has a single recessive mutation in a gene different from *Mi-1*.

THE RME1 GENE IS REQUIRED FOR MI-1-MEDIATED RESISTANCE

Since *Mi-1* confers resistance against 3 species of root-knot nematodes and the potato aphid, we analyzed the infection levels of these organisms on *rme1* plants. Plants were challenged with three different inoculum levels of *M. incognita*, *M. javanica* and *M. arenaria*. Six weeks after inoculation, no significant difference in the rate of nematode reproduction compared to susceptible tomato was detected with the 3 species tested. Similarly, aphid infestation experiments resulted in a similar number of aphids on *rme1* plants compared to susceptible tomato, indicating that *Rme1* is required for *Mi-1*-mediated resistance to both root-knot nematodes and the potato aphid.

THE RME1 MUTATION HAS NO EFFECT ON RESISTANCE MEDIATED BY THE I-2 GENE

To assess whether *rme1* mutation is specific to the *Mi-1*-mediated resistance or compromises other resistance pathways, we assessed the effect of this mutation on one other resistance gene, *I-2*, present in the wild-type tomato Motelle. *I-2* encodes a NBS-LRR protein that confers resistance against the fungus *Fusarium oxysporum* f.sp. *lycopersici* race 2 (Simons et al. 1998). The *rme1* mutation was found to have no effect on the *I-2*-mediated resistance. This indicates that *rme1* mutation might be specific to *Mi-1*-mediated resistance and that Rme1 might directly or indirectly interact with Mi-1. It is not known whether Mi-1 interacts directly with nematode or aphid avirulence factors since these factors have not yet been identified. It is conceivable that Rme1 and Mi-1 bind to the avirulence factor(s) in a complex formation.

It is not clear whether *Rme1* is specific for the *Mi-1* signal transduction pathway or is a conserved component of the root-knot nematode resistance pathway. Several genes conferring resistance to root-knot nematodes have been identified in different accessions of *Lycopersicon peruvianum* (Veremis and Roberts 1996a,b; Yaghoobi et al. 1995; Cap et al. 1993). These genes either confer resistance to *Mi-1* virulent *M. javanica* and *M. incognita* or to avirulent root-knot nematodes at soil temperatures above 30°C, at which the resistance mediated by *Mi-1* is not functional. Because of cross incompatibility between *L. peruvianum* and *L. esculentum*, it is not straightforward to test whether *Rme1* is required for the function of these resistance genes.

Future Directions

Mapping and cloning *Rme1* is our next priority. Towards this goal we have generated a mapping population by crossing *rme1* to *L. pennellii*. F1 population of this cross was resistant to *M. javanica* indicating that the *L. pennellii* allele could complement the *rme1* mutation. One of these F1 has been backcrossed to *rme1* and progeny of this backcross are being evaluated for nematode infection.

Acknowledgements

This research was supported by the United States Department of Agriculture NRI grant No 98-35302-6660 and 2000-02876.

Literature Cited

Cap, G. B., Roberts, P. A., and Thomason, I. J. 1993. Inheritance of heat-stable resistance to *Meloidogyne incognita in Lycopersicon peruvianum* and its relationship to the *Mi* gene. Theor. Appl. Genet. 85:777-783.

Dropkin, V.H. 1969. The necrotic reaction of tomatoes and other hosts resistant to *Meloidogyne:* reversal by temperature. Phytopathol. 59:1632-1637.

Kaloshian, I., Kinsey, M. G., Ullman, D. E., and Williamson, V. M. 1997. The impact of *Meu-1*-mediated resistance in tomato on longevity, fecundity and behavior of the potato aphid, *Macrosiphum euphorbiae*. Entomol. Exp. Appl. 83:181-187.

Kaloshian, I., Kinsey, M.G,, Williamson, V.M., and Ullman, D.E. 2000. *Mi*-mediated resistance against the potato aphid *Macrosiphum euphorbiae* (Hemiptera : Aphididae) limits sieve element ingestion. Environ. Entomol. 29:690-695.

Milligan, S. B., Bodeau, J., Yaghoobi, J., Kaloshian, I., Zabel, P., and Williamson, V. M. 1998. The root-knot nematode resistance gene *Mi* from tomato is a member of leucine zipper, nucleotide binding, leucine-rich repeat family of plant genes. Plant Cell 10:1307-1319.

Rossi, M., Goggin, F. L., Milligan, S. B., Kaloshian, I., Ullman, D. E., and Williamosn, V. M. 1998. The nematode resistance gene *Mi* of tomato confers resistance against the potato aphid. Proc. Natl. Acad. Sci. USA 95:9750-9754.

Simons, G., Groenendijk, J., Wijbrandi, J., Reijans, M., Groenen, J., Diergaarde, P., VanderLee, T., Bleeker, M., Onstenk, J., deBoth, M., Haring, M., Mes, J., Cornelissen, B., Zabeau, M., and Vos, P. 1998. Dissection of the *Fusarium I2* gene cluster in tomato reveals six homologs and one active gene copy. Plant Cell 10:1055-1068.

Veremis, J.C. and Roberts, P.A. 1996a. Identification of resistance to *Meloidogyne javanica* in the *Lycopersicon peruvianum* complex. Theor. Appl. Genet. 93:894-901.

Veremis, J.C. and Roberts, P.A. 1996b. Relationships between *Meloidogyne incognita* resistance genes in *Lycopersicon peruvianum* differentiated by heat sensitivity and nematode virulence. Theor. Appl. Genet. 93:950-959.

Yaghoobi, J., Kaloshian, I., Wen, Y. and Williamson, V.M. 1995. Mapping a new nematode resistance locus in *Lycopersicon peruvianum*. Theor. Appl. Genet. 91:457-464.

Large-Scale Identification of Parasitism Genes of the Soybean Cyst Nematode

Bingli Gao[1], Rex Allen[1], Tom Maier[2], Eric L. Davis[3], Thomas J. Baum[2], and Richard S. Hussey[1]

[1]Department of Plant Pathology, University of Georgia, Athens, GA 30602, U.S.A; [2]Department of Plant Pathology, Iowa State University, Ames, IA 50011, U.S.A.; [3]Department of Plant Pathology, North Carolina State University, Raleigh, NC 27695, U.S.A.

Plant-parasitic nematodes possess three large esophageal gland cells, one dorsal and two subventral, which are the principal sources of secretions involved in nematode infection and parasitism of plants. Sedentary endoparasitic nematodes, which are the most damaging plant parasitic nematodes, synthesize secretory proteins in their esophageal gland cells and release these proteins through a hollow, protrusible stylet during migration within plant roots and subsequent modification of root cells into discrete feeding cells (Hussey and Grundler 1998). The two subventral gland cells are the most active gland cells in infective second-stage juveniles while the single dorsal gland cell becomes the predominate source of secretions released through the stylet in subsequent parasitic stages of sedentary endoparasites (Hussey 1989). Research on nematode stylet secretions has been greatly hindered by the minute quantities of secretions available from these small biotrophs. Therefore, cloning parasitism genes encoding proteins secreted from the esophageal gland cells is the key to understanding the molecular basis of nematode parasitism of plants.

Several molecular approaches recently have revealed secretion genes of the esophageal gland cells of plant-parasitic nematodes (Davis et al. 2000). However, even with these recent successes, a more efficient selection system is desirable to achieve the goal of obtaining a complete profile of the secretion genes expressed in the nematode esophageal gland cells during the parasitic cycle.

In this study, we combined microaspirating the contents of esophageal gland and intestinal cells (to provide mRNA for RT-PCR) with a suppression subtractive hybridization (SSH) approach. In other words, cDNAs generated from microaspirated contents from the intestinal region of *H. glycines* were subtracted from cDNAs generated from gland cell cytoplasm to prepare a library enriched in esophageal gland cell secretory protein cDNAs. New putative parasitism genes expressed in the esophageal gland cells were identified, and their full-length clones were obtained from a gland-cell long distance (LD) PCR cDNA library generated from the same microaspirated esophageal gland cell cytoplasm (Gao et al. 2001).

Results

Template mRNA from 10 *H. glycines* gland cells was immobilized on oligo $(dT)^{25}$ magnetic beads and used for LD RT-PCR. An aliquot of the PCR product was used to create the gland-cell LD PCR cDNA library. This approach enabled the isolation of full-length clones of cDNAs identified in the gland cell SSH cDNA library.

We utilized a SSH protocol (Clontech Laboratories, Inc., Palo Alto, CA) to subtract intestinal region (driver) cDNAs from gland cell (tester) cDNAs to enrich for cDNAs only found in the tester sample. The subtracted product was used to construct a cDNA library (referred to as the SSH cDNA library).

Macroarraying the SSH gland cell cDNA library on nylon membranes was an efficient method for further analyses of the SSH cDNAs. A combination of sequence analyses, in situ hybridization, and subsequent hybridization screening with already identified clones, identified a total of 23 unique cDNA sequences (Table 1). Nine unique clones produced specific in situ hybridization signals within the esophageal gland cells of *H. glycines*, of which two clones hybridized exclusively with the subventral gland cells (Fig. 1A) and seven clones hybridized specifically within the dorsal gland cell (Fig. 1B). Three clones specifically hybridized with the *H. glycines* intestinal region (Fig. 1C), while nonspecific hybridization signals were observed within *H. glycines* for 11 clones. In Southern blot hybridizations at high stringency, all 23 cDNAs hybridized with genomic DNA from *H. glycines* and none hybridized with genomic DNA from *Meloidogyne incognita*, *C. elegans*, soybean, or tomato (data not shown).

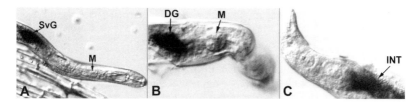

Fig. 1. *In situ* hybridization of antisense cDNA probes (dark staining) to *H. glycines*. **A**, GSB9 hybridizes to the subventral esophageal gland cells (SvG), **B**, SB89 hybridizes to the dorsal esophageal gland cell (DG), **C**, SB91 hybridizes to intestinal cells (INT). M, metacorpus.

Table 1. Summary of twenty-three unique cDNA clones from *Heterodera glycines* isolated by suppressive subtractive hybridization.

Clone Name/ Accession #	Highest Homology	SP	In- Situ	PSORT
GSB9/AF343567	Hyp. prot. *C. elegans*	yes	svg	ec
GSB10/AF344866	Allergen *Ascaris suum*	nd	ns	nd
GSB23/AF273728	Secretory protein *H. glycines*	yes	dg	ec
GSB6/AF344868	Hyp. prot. *C. elegans*	yes	ns	ec
GSB21/AF345801	Pioneer[g]	yes	dg	m
GSB3/AF345800	Pioneer	yes	svg	n
GSB17/AF345802	ATPase *C. elegans*	no	ns	c
GSB15/AF345794	Dynein *C. elegans*	no	ns	c
GSB13/AF345798	Pioneer	no	ns	n
GSB18/AF345799	Pioneer	no	ns	n
GSB24/AF344862	Salivary glycoprotein *Rattus*	yes	dg	ec
GSB25/AF345793	Hyp. prot. *C. elegans*	no	ns	c
GSB26/AF344864	Hyp. prot. *C. elegans*	no	ns	c
SB59/Y09499	Cysteine proteinase *H. glycines*	yes	int	ec
SB91/AF345792	Cysteine proteinase *C. elegans*	yes	int	ec
SB4/AF344867	Protease *Necator americanus*	yes	int	ec
SB89/AF344863	Pioneer	yes	dg	ec
SB76/AF344869	Histone *Emericella nidulans*	no	dg	c
SB26/AF344870	Pioneer	no	dg	c
SB84/AF344865	Pioneer	no	dg	c
SB93/AF345795	Hyp. prot. *C. elegans*	no	ns	c
SB61/AF345796	Hyp. prot. *C. elegans*	no	ns	c
SB3/AF345797	Pyruvate dehydrogenase *C. elegans*	no	ns	mt

SP, signal peptide; **In Situ**, in situ hybridization; **PSORT**, cellular localization; *Hyp. prot.*, hypothetical protein; *Pioneer*, no homologues; *svg*, subventral gland; *dg*, dorsal gland; *ns*, non specific; *int*, intestine; *ec*, extracellular; *nd*, not determined; *m*, membrane; *n*, nuclear; *c*, cytoplasmic; *mt*, mitochondrial

Screening of the LD PCR gland cell library identified full-length cDNAs for 21 clones. The predicted protein sequences encoded by these cDNAs were analyzed by BLASTP for similarity to known proteins, by Signal P for the presence of signal peptides, and by PSORT II for predicting subcellular localizations (Table 1). Ten of the analyzed proteins were preceded by a signal peptide. PSORT II analyses predicted eight of the proteins with a signal peptide to be extracellular, one to be a plasma membrane protein, and one to be nuclearly localized. Eight of the predicted extracellular proteins had homologies with known proteins based on BLASTP analysis, and only SB89 lacked homology with any known protein. The protein encoded by GSB9 had high similarity with a hypothetical protein from *C. elegans*. GSB10, while not full-length, was similar to a surface-associated glycoprotein from *Brugia pahangi*. The protein encoded by GSB24 was similar to a salivary proline-rich glycoprotein precursor from rat. Three of the predicted extracellular proteins (SB4, SB59, SB91) had significant homology with proteinases (SB4, lysosomal aspartic protease precursor from *Necator americanus*; SB91, cathepsin S-like cysteine proteinase from *H. glycines*; GSB6, cysteine proteinase from *C. elegans*). GSB23 was identical to a dorsal gland cell protein of unknown function previously cloned from *H. glycines*. Clone GSB6 was similar to a hypothetical protein from *C. elegans*.

We also have initiated large-scale sequence analysis of the LD PCR gland cell library and have sequenced over 400 expressed sequence tags. Of these, 12% coded for proteins with predicted signal peptides. In situ hybridizations showed that 40% of these putative secretory proteins were expressed specifically in the esophageal glands of *H. glycines*.

Discussion

The predicted amino acid sequence of the full-length cDNA of GSB9 had strong similarity to the venom allergen antigen 5 family of secreted proteins from hymenopteran insect venom and proteins found in several other nematode species (Ding et al. 2000). In *Ancylostoma caninum*, the AG-5 like proteins, AC-ASP-1 and AC-ASP-2, are the major excretory/secretory proteins released by infective third-stage larvae stimulated to feed in vitro (Hawdon et al. 1999). The secretion of these proteins is coupled with the transition to parasitism and the invasion of the host by the larvae. The in situ localization of GSB9 in the subventral gland cells may be indicative of a role for this protein in the interaction of *H. glycines* with its host plant.

The predicted protein for the full-length cDNA of GSB24 had strong similarity to salivary proline-rich glycoproteins from rat and human. These extracellular proteins contain many proline-rich repeating peptides, and while present in saliva, their functions remain unknown. The localization of GSB24 mRNA exclusively in the dorsal gland cell, i.e., the gland cell presumably involved in the late stages of parasitism, indicates that this protein also may have a role in plant parasitism.

Of the other two cDNA clones (GSB23 and SB89) that encoded proteins with putative signal peptides and that were specifically expressed within the dorsal gland cell, GSB23 was previously cloned from the dorsal gland cell of parasitic stages of *H. glycines*. Nevertheless, its function remains unknown (Wang et al. 2001). SB89, also predicted by PSORT II to be extracellular, had no significant matches with any proteins in the databases.

Interestingly, gland-expressed GSB3, which contained a signal peptide, was predicted by PSORT II to be localized in the nucleus. This protein, therefore, may enter the plant nucleus if secreted into a root cell.

Characterizing the nature and number of different secretory proteins packaged in the secretory granules of nematode esophageal gland cells and the temporal changes in the kinds of proteins secreted during the parasitic cycle is a prerequisite for understanding what makes a nematode a plant parasite. The procedure outlined herein provides a novel strategy for rapidly cloning parasitism genes encoding these secretory proteins.

Acknowledgment

Support for this research was provided by the United Soybean Board, the Iowa Soybean Promotion Board, and by Hatch Act Funds.

Literature Cited

Davis, E. L., Hussey, R. S., Baum, T. J., Bakker, J., Schots, A., Rosso, M.-N., and Abad, P. 2000. Nematode Parasitism Genes. Annu. Rev. Phytopathol. 38:365-396.

Ding, X., Shields, J., Allen, R. and Hussey, R. S. 2000. Molecular cloning and characterization of a venom allergen AG5-like cDNA from *Meloidogyne incognita*. Int. J. Parasitol. 30:77-81.

Gao, B., Allen, R., Maier T., Davis, E. L., Baum, T. J., and Hussey, R. S. 2001. Identification of putative parasitism genes expressed in the esophageal gland cells of the soybean cyst nematode, *Heterodera glycines*. Mol. Plant-Microbe Interact. 14:in press.

Hawdon, J. M., Narasimhan, S., and Hotez, P. J. 1999. *Ancylostoma* secreted protein 2: Cloning and characterization of a second member of a family of nematode secreted proteins from *Ancylostoma caninum*. Mol. Biochem. Parasitol. 99:149-166.

Hussey, R. S., and Grundler, F. M. 1998. Nematode parasitism of plants. Pages 213-243 in: Physiology and biochemistry of free-living and plant parasitic nematodes. R. N. Perry and D. J. Wright, eds. CAB International Press, England

Hussey, R. S. 1989. Disease-inducing secretions of plant-parasitic nematodes. Annu. Rev. Phytopathol. 27:123-141.

Wang, X., Allen, R., Ding, X., Goellner, M., Maier, T., de Boer, J. M., Baum, T. J., Hussey, R. S., and Davis, E. L. 2001. Signal peptide-selection of cDNA cloned directly from the esophageal gland cells of the soybean cyst nematode, *H. glycines*. Mol. Plant-Microbe Interact. 14:536-544.

Functional Analysis of the Nematode Resistance Gene *Mi-1*

Valerie Moroz Williamson and Chin-Feng Hwang

Center for Engineering Plants for Resistance Against Pathogens, University of California, Davis, CA, USA

The tomato gene *Mi-1* confers resistance against root-knot nematodes and aphids. Root-knot nematodes (RKN; genus, *Meloidogyne*) are obligate endoparasites that infect a large number of crop plants and cause severe losses in yield worldwide (Williamson and Hussey 1996). The resistance against RKNs is characterized by an apparent hypersensitive response (HR) on the part of the host. A localized region of necrosis occurs around the anterior end of the invading nematode (Ho et al. 1992). The earliest visible indications of the HR occur about 12 h after inoculation of roots (Dropkin et al. 1969; Paulson and Webster 1972). The nematode juveniles do not elicit an HR while migrating through the root tissue, but do so while attempting to establish a feeding site (Paulson and Webster 1972). *Mi* dramatically alters aphid feeding in a manner consistent with a rapidly induced plant defense associated with the phloem sieve element. However, we have so far seen no evidence for an HR. Whether *Mi* induces the same set of signaling pathways and defense responses (*e.g.* HR, release of preformed substances, cell wall fortification, oxidative burst, defense-related protein induction) in the leaves to aphids and in root tissues in response to nematodes is not known.

Molecular Characterization of *Mi-1*

The availability of a clone of *Mi-1* has permitted exploration of the role of the encoded protein in host recognition and signaling (Milligan et al. 1998). The predicted protein is 1257 amino acids in length. Highest sequence similarity is to the tomato gene *Prf*, which is required for resistance to specific isolates of *Pseudomonas syringae* mediated by the R-gene *Pto* (Loh and Martin 1995; Salmeron et al. 1996). The predicted *Mi-1* gene product, Mi-1, contains a putative nucleotide binding (NB) site and carboxy terminal leucine rich repeat (LRR) domain. Compared to other NB-LRR proteins, *Mi-1* and *Prf* encode long N-terminal extensions. The N-terminal region (amino acids 1-541) of Mi-1 does not strongly resemble other sequences found in protein databases including that of Arabidopsis. Analysis of the protein for particular motifs indicates the possible presence of two alpha-helical coiled coils in the N-terminal region (Williamson et al., 2000).

DNA blots probed with *Mi-1* at high stringency, indicate that there are 6-7 homologs in both resistant and susceptible tomato (Milligan et al., 1998). The majority of these copies are clustered in the 650 kb region of chromosome 6 where the functional copy, *Mi-1.2*, is located. Transcript analysis has revealed that, in addition to *Mi-1.2* at least three different homologs are expressed in roots of resistant plants (Milligan et al., 1998). This includes *Mi-1.1* a homolog which, despite a high sequence similarity to *Mi-1.2* does not confer resistance against nematodes. RNA blots showed that highly similar genes are also transcribed in susceptible tomato. We have isolated clones of most of the homologs from both resistant and susceptible tomato. DNA sequence of these homologs shows they have from 92% to 95% similarity with *Mi-1.2* (Seah and Williamson, unpublished).

Dissecting the Function

Mi-1 and other R-genes are thought to encode receptors that are involved in recognition of pathogens and initiation of signaling defense responses against pathogens (Yang et al. 1997; Martin 1999). One approach to investigating the role of *Mi-1.2* has been to generate *in vitro* alterations in the gene and to determine the phenotype produced by these changes. The availability of the highly similar gene *Mi-1.1* has provided an excellent substrate for a series of domain swap experiments (Figure 1). Using available or introduced restriction enzyme cleavage sites we exchanged the N-terminal 161 amino acid regions (B in Figure 1) and the LRR regions (D) of *Mi-1.1* and *Mi-1.2* (Hwang et al. 2000).

The nematode-resistance phenotypes of the domain swap constructs were tested using *Agrobacterium rhizogenes*-based tomato transformation. *A. rhizogenes* transfers to plant cells, in addition to the T-DNA of the binary vector, a second T-DNA region that results in transformed roots with a highly branched or "hairy" phenotype (Tepfer 1990). We found that the response of the *A. rhizogenes*-transformed roots to nematodes mirrors that of standard roots with regard to *Mi* phenotype (Hwang et al. 2000). With this assay, we can ascertain nematode resistance within 6 weeks of transformation. While constructs *Mi-DS1* and *Mi-DS2* resulted in loss of resistance, we found that, surprisingly, constructs *Mi-DS3* and *Mi-DS4* did

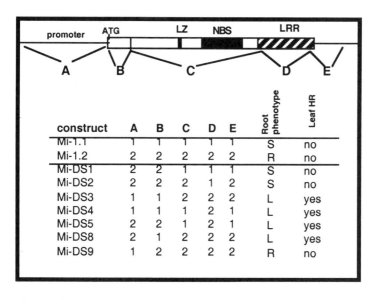

construct	A	B	C	D	E	Root phenotype	Leaf HR
Mi-1.1	1	1	1	1	1	S	no
Mi-1.2	2	2	2	2	2	R	no
Mi-DS1	2	2	1	1	1	S	no
Mi-DS2	2	2	2	1	2	S	no
Mi-DS3	1	1	2	2	2	L	yes
Mi-DS4	1	1	1	2	1	L	yes
Mi-DS5	2	2	1	2	1	L	yes
Mi-DS8	2	1	2	2	2	L	yes
Mi-DS9	1	2	2	2	2	R	no

Fig. 1. The *Mi-1* gene product and domain swap constructs. Predicted protein structure of Mi is shown as a wide bar. Regions of the gene A-E are indicated. In the table, *Mi-1.1* regions are indicated as "1" whereas those from *Mi-1.2* are indicated as "2." The column labeled "root phenotype" shows the response to nematodes of *A. rhizogenes*-transformed root cultures after introduction of each construct, "S" for a susceptible response, "R" for resistant response; "L" indicates "lethal", *i.e.*, no viable, transformed roots were obtained. The 'Leaf HR' column shows the phenotype after *A. rhizogenes* infiltration of *N. benthamiana* leaves with indicated constructs. "No" indicates there is no cell death visible, and "yes" indicates tissue collapse and cell death. For additional details see Hwang et al. (2000).

not yield transformed roots, suggesting that they produced a lethal phenotype. To confirm the lethality, *A. rhizogenes* with these constructs were infiltrated into *Nicotiana benthamiana* leaves. The resulting transient expression produced a localized cell death resembling the HR for *Mi-DS3* and *DS4*, but not for *Mi-1.1* or *Mi-1.2*. We also carried out RT-PCR assays to determine *Mi* expression from the introduced genes. These assays showed that *Mi-DS1* and *Mi-DS2* were expressed and suggested that the inability of these constructs to confer resistance in transgenic roots was not due to lack of expression.

All constructs with the LRR of *Mi-1.2*, and none with the LRR of *Mi-1.1*, resulted in a resistant or lethal response suggesting that the LRR region of *Mi-1.2* has a role in the transmission of a signal for cell death that cannot be replaced by the corresponding region from *Mi-1.1*. The phenotype of the exchanges of the N-terminal 161 amino acid regions suggested a model in which the N-terminus of Mi-1.2, but not that of Mi-1.1, acts to repress the signaling of an HR, allowing release only in the presence of the pathogen (Hwang et al. 2000).

There are 40 amino acid differences among the 250 amino acid residues spanning most of the LRR region of *Mi-1.1* and *Mi-1.2* distributed throughout the region. We have recently completed site-directed *in vitro* mutagenesis to introduce each of these amino acid differences individually into the *Mi-1.2* LRR. The phenotype of these alterations in *Mi*-DS3 using the transient expression assay revealed that 62% of the alterations resulted in loss of the localized necrosis triggered by this construct after transient expression in *N. benthamiana* leaves (Hwang and Williamson, unpublished). Each of these changes in the LRR region has been introduced into *Mi-1.2* and transferred into tomato roots using *A. rhizogenes*, and the effects of these single amino acid changes on resistance will be determined. Comparing results of the two assays will determine if there is a correlation between changes that result in localized cell death in construct *Mi-DS3* and those that affect nematode resistance. These experiments may differentiate amino acids required for transmitting the resistance response from those that are involved in pathogen recognition. For example, amino acid changes that result in loss of resistance in *Mi-1.2*, but that still confer the HR in *Mi-DS3* would be candidates for sequences important in pathogen recognition. This strategy will be continued with the remainder of the gene.

Plant parasitic nematodes and aphids are important pests with broad host ranges and cause major economic damage worldwide. Control of aphids and nematodes with pesticides negatively impacts the environment and is being severely restricted. Our hope is that an increase in the basic and broad understanding of the defense mechanisms and signaling pathways required for resistance against nematodes and aphids will enable future manipulation or enhancement of not only the R-gene itself, but also the individual defense responses and signaling components to maximize R-gene efficacy and durability in crop protection.

Literature Cited

Dropkin, V. H., Helgeson, J.P. and Upper, C.D. 1969. The hypersensitivity reaction of tomatoes resistant to *Meloidogyne incognita*: reversal by cytokinins. Journal of Nematology 1: 55-60.

Ho, J.-Y., Weide, R., Ma, H.M., Wordragen, M.F., Lambert, K.N., Koornneef, M., Zabel, P. and Williamson, V.M. 1992. The root-knot nematode resistance gene (*Mi*) in tomato: Construction of a molecular linkage map and identification of dominant cDNA markers in resistant genotypes. The Plant Journal 2: 971-982.

Hwang, C., Bhakta, A., Truesdell G., Pudlo, W., and Williamson, V.M. 2000. Evidence for a role of the N terminus and leucine-rich repeat region of the *Mi* gene product in regulation of localized cell death. Plant Cell 12: 1319-1329.

Loh, Y.-T. and Martin, G.B. 1995. The disease-resistance gene *Pto* and the fenthion-sensitivity gene *Fen* encode closely related functional protein kinases. Proc. Natl. Acad. Sci. USA 92: 4181-4184.

Martin, G. B. 1999. Functional analysis of plant disease resistance genes and their downstream effectors. Current Opinion in Plant Biology 2: 273-279.

Milligan, S., Bodeau, J., Yaghoobi, J., Kaloshian, I, Zabel, P., and Williamson, V.M. 1998. The root knot nematode resistance gene *Mi* from tomato is a member of the leucine zipper, nucleotide binding, leucine-rich repeat family of plant genes. Plant Cell 10: 1307-1319.

Paulson, R. E. and Webster, J.M. 1972. Ultrastructure of the hypersensitive reaction in roots of tomato, *Lycopersicon esculentum* L., to infection by the root-knot nematode, *Meloidogyne incognita*. Physiological Plant Pathology 2: 227-234.

Salmeron, J. M., Oldroyd, G.E.D. Rommens, C.M.T, Scofield, S.R., Kim, H.S., Lavelle, D.T., Dahlbeck, D., and Staskawicz, B.J. 1996. Tomato *Prf* is a member of the leucine-rich repeat class of plant disease resistance genes and lies embedded within the *Pto* kinase gene cluster. Cell 86: 123-133.

Tepfer, D. 1990. Genetic transformation using *Agrobacterium rhizogenes*. Physiologia Plantarum 79: 140-146.

Williamson, V.M. and Hussey, R.S. 1996. Nematode pathogenesis and resistance in plants. The Plant Cell 8: 1735-1745.

Williamson, V.M., Hwang, C.F., Truesdell, G., Bhakta, A.V., and Fort, K.P. 2000. The nematode resistance gene, *Mi. in* Biology of Plant-Microbe Interactions, Vol. 2. P.J.M. de Wit, T. Bisseling, and W.J. Stiekema, eds., International Society for Molecular Plant-Microbe Interactions, St. Paul. MI, USA, pp. 88-92.

Yang, Y., Shah, J. and Klessig, D. (1997). Signal perception and transduction in plant defense responses. Genes and Development 11: 1621-1639.

Pathogen Fitness and Resistance Gene Durability

Jan E. Leach[1], Kimberly Webb[1,2], Grisel Ponciano[1], Jianfa Bai[1], Isabelita Oña[2], M. Madamba[2], Hei Leung[2], and Casiana Vera Cruz[2]

[1]Department of Plant Pathology, Kansas State University, Manhattan, KS, USA. [2]Division of Entomology and Plant Pathology, International Rice Research Institute, Metro Manila, Philippines.

Resistance governed by single dominant resistance (*R*) genes has been widely and effectively used as a strategy to control disease in many crop species. The basis for this resistance is the genetic interaction of the host *R* genes and the pathogen avirulence (*avr*) genes (Flor 1971). In many cases, resistance governed by single *R* genes is not long-lasting or durable due to rapid changes in the pathogen population. Although frustrating for plant breeders, this has not raised the death knell for the use of single *R* genes in breeding programs because there are several examples demonstrating that durable resistance can be conferred by single genes (for review, see Leach et al. 2001). The key problem facing plant breeders is that currently there is no easy way to predict the durability of an *R* gene prior to its deployment. Thus, if we knew how to identify the *R* genes that would be durable, the chances to achieve long-lasting resistance would improve.

The means to predict durable resistance may come from an understanding of the relationships between *R* and *avr* genes. Based on genetic analyses, Flor (1958, 1971) suggested that easily mutated *avr* genes in pathogen populations were likely less critical to pathogenic fitness than those which were rarely mutated. This and other observations led Van der Plank (1975) to predict that pathogen fitness and the quality of a corresponding resistance are intimately linked. While studies such as these provided the conceptual basis for linking the quality or durability of resistance with pathogen fitness, the microbial and plant molecular genetic tools to experimentally confirm this relationship were not available until recently. Using a well-characterized rice/bacterial disease interaction (bacterial blight of rice, caused by *Xanthomonas oryzae* pv. *oryzae*), we describe laboratory and field approaches to evaluate the relationship between the quality of bacterial blight *R* genes and the fitness contribution of *avr* genes and discuss the application of these findings to practical disease control.

Avirulence and Fitness in *X. oryzae* pv. *oryzae*

If, as Flor and Van der Plank predicted, pathogen fitness is directly linked to *avr* gene function, and easily mutated *avr* genes are measures of poor *R* genes, then assessment of an *avr* gene's contribution to fitness might allow prediction of the durability of the corresponding *R* gene. Several bacterial *avr* genes have been shown to contribute to pathogen virulence and/or fitness (for review, Gabriel 1999; Leach et al. 2001; Staskawicz et al. 2001). To determine if *avr* genes from *X. oryzae* pv. *oryzae* contributed to pathogen fitness, Bai et al (2000) generated mutants with insertions in one or more *avr* gene and assessed one component of fitness, that is, the amount of disease (aggressiveness) caused by the mutants. The known *avr* genes (*avrxa5, avrXa7,* and *avrXa10*) from *X. oryzae* pv. *oryzae* are members of the highly conserved *avrBs3* family of *avr* genes (Hopkins et al. 1992). The genomes of various *X. oryzae* pv. *oryzae* contain at least 12 different copies of *avrBs3* gene family members. Mutations were created in the three known *avr* genes as well as four homologs with unknown function. Bai et al (2000) found that the amount of contribution to pathogen fitness varied, depending on the *avr* homolog. For example, mutation in *avrXa7* caused the largest reduction in pathogen aggressiveness (shorter lesions and reduced bacterial numbers compared to wild type) whereas mutation in *avrXa10* had no detectable effect. Mutation in the individual *avr* gene homologs whose avirulence function has not been determined also substantially reduced pathogen fitness. Another intriguing finding was that despite the high degree of sequence similarity among these *X. oryzae* pv. *oryzae avr* genes, their aggressiveness functions were not interchangeable. The reduction in aggressiveness due to *avrXa7* mutation could only be restored by complementation with the wild type *avrXa7* and was not restored by other gene homologs, including those that exhibited an aggressiveness function (Bai et al. 2000).

Epidemiological Consequences of Avirulence Gene Mutation

The above laboratory studies indicated that at least some *X. oryzae* pv. *oryzae avr* genes contribute to pathogen fitness, and that the contributions of different family members are not equal. This would suggest that, unless the fitness function could be compensated by other *avr* genes, the relative 'ease' of mutating to overcome an *R* gene would be a reflection of the fitness contribution of the corresponding *avr* gene.

Since *avrXa7* contributed more than *avrxa5*, and *avrXa10* showed no measurable contribution to aggressiveness (Bai et al. 2000), we predicted that the bacterial blight resistance gene *Xa7,* which corresponds to *avrXa7*, would be more durable than *Xa10*, which corresponds to *avrXa10*. To test these predictions and to determine if, under field conditions, the fitness cost associated with *avr* gene mutation was measurable, a field experiment was designed at two sites endemic for bacterial blight in the Philippines (Vera Cruz et al. 2000). The *Xa10* and *Xa7* genes had not been deployed in the Philippines prior to this time. Rice lines near-isogenic for the *Xa10* and *Xa7 R* genes and the recurrent parent were planted for six consecutive cropping seasons (two crops per year).

Disease assessment data suggested that *Xa10* was more easily overcome than *Xa7*. Over 3 years, very little disease was observed on the rice line with *Xa7* (<1% diseased leaf area, DLA and <5-10% incidence), whereas severe disease was observed on the line with *Xa10* in all three years (>40% DLA and 99-100% incidence) (Vera Cruz et al. 2000). Although disease is always detected on the line with *Xa7,* which was planted in these experimental sites through 1999, the amounts of disease are still very low and have not significantly increased (< 10% incidence, authors, unpublished results).

Strains virulent to *Xa7* were detected at both sites in all three years. Based on the lesion lengths they caused on plants with *Xa7,* these strains were grouped into two groups, those that had completely lost *avrXa7* avirulence function and those that had partially lost *avrXa7* function. Two trends related to the fitness of these groups of strains are significant. First, as *avrXa7* avirulence function decreased, the overall amount of disease (aggressiveness, measured by lesion lengths) caused by the strains decreased on both the line with *Xa7* and the susceptible recurrent parent. Second, strains that had completely lost *avrXa7* avirulence function (virulent to rice with *Xa7*) did not increase nor did they persist in the population. In fact, strains that had completely lost *avrXa7* avirulence function were not detected in the third year of the study.

The results from field study supported the prediction of the laboratory studies that there is a fitness cost associated with the loss of *avrXa7* function, but not of *avrXa10,* and that *Xa7* would be relatively more durable than *Xa10*. The fact that strains that had completely lost the *avrXa7* avirulence function did not persist in the population provided strong evidence that the mutation in *avrXa7* had imposed a significant cost on the overall fitness of the pathogen in the field.

Molecular analysis of *avrXa7* mutations in field strains of *X. oryzae* pv. *oryzae*

The group of strains that had completely lost *avrXa7* avirulence function exhibited two types of mutations at the *avrXa7* locus: 1) an undetermined genetic rearrangement that caused a polymorphism in the *avrXa7* fragment, and 2) a four base pair change that resulted in a two amino acid change in the carboxy terminus of the protein (Vera Cruz et al. 2000). Complementation studies confirmed that the four base pair change was responsible for the loss of both avirulence and aggressiveness function in the mutant *avrXa7* allele. As these changes in the carboxy terminus are upstream of structural features already known to be important for avirulence (e.g., the nuclear localization signal sequences and the transcriptional activation domain, for review, see White et al. 2000), the functional significance of these mutations is not yet understood.

The group of strains that show partial loss of *avrXa7* avirulence function and little or no loss of aggressiveness to susceptible rice are particularly intriguing because they persisted and increased in the field population during the study, yet did not cause an epidemic on *Xa7* rice. Significantly, continued samplings from one site for an additional 3 years show that this group of strains is increasing in proportion to other groups, and yet, still does not cause epidemic on *Xa7* (authors, unpublished). Sequence analysis of three strains from this group revealed a point mutation that occurs at the beginning of the transcriptional activation domain located in the C-terminus; site-directed mutagenesis of the *avrXa7* gene confirms that this mutation results in partial loss of the *avrXa7* avirulence function (authors, unpublished).

Conclusions and Applications to Disease Control

Our results from field and laboratory studies involving interactions between *X. oryzae* pv. *oryzae* and rice support the hypothesis that if the fitness penalty associated with adaptation of a pathogen to overcome an *R* gene is high, then the *R* gene would be predicted to be durable. However, the application of these findings to disease control depends on whether the relationship between fitness and durability of resistance can be generalized. Several questions are yet to be answered. Is the fitness attributed to an *avr* gene affected by other *avr* genes or by different pathogen genetic backgrounds? What is the frequency and impact of *avr* gene mutation and/or horizontal movement in the pathogen population? The fitness conferred by *avrXa7* has only been tested in Philippine strains, albeit from two distinct genetic lineages. It remains unknown if the same mutation would cause a loss of aggressiveness in other genetically distinct strains. Although complementation analyses indicated that loss of fitness function of one *X. oryzae* pv. *oryzae avr* gene could not be compensated by another (Bai et al. 2000), it is possible that in other cases there could be functional redundancy such that defects in one gene can be compensated by other genes. From the perspective of the *R* gene, although *Xa7* is predicted to be an effective resistance gene due to its impact on the pathogen (Bai et al. 2000; Vera Cruz et al. 2000), the actual performance of this gene remains to be tested when it is deployed widely. To test the performance of this and other genes, studies involving single *Xa* genes and pyramids containing multiple *Xa* genes (including *Xa7*) are currently underway in different countries (authors, unpublished).

Acknowledgments

This work was supported by the Rockefeller Foundation and by USDA-AID.

Literature Cited

Bai, J., Choi, S. H., Ponciano, G., Leung, H., and Leach, J. E. 2000. *Xanthomonas oryzae* pv. *oryzae* avirulence genes contribute differently and specifically to pathogen aggressiveness. Mol. Plant-Microbe Interact. 13:1322-1329.

Flor, H. H. 1958. Mutation to wider virulence in *Melampsora lini*. Phytopathology 48:297-301.

Flor, H. H. 1971. Current Status of the Gene-For-Gene Concept. Annu. Rev. Phytopathol. 9:275-296.

Gabriel, D. W. 1999. Why do pathogens carry avirulence genes? Physiol. Mol. Plant Pathol. 55:205-214.

Hopkins, C. M., White, F. F., Choi, S.-H., Guo, A., and Leach, J. E. 1992. Identification of a family of avirulence genes from *Xanthomonas oryzae* pv. *oryzae*. Mol. Plant-Microbe Interact. 5:451-459.

Leach, J. E., Vera-Cruz, C. M., Bai, J. F., and Leung, H. 2001. Pathogen fitness penalty as a predictor of durability of disease resistance genes. Annu. Rev. Phytopathol. 39:In Press.

Staskawicz, B. J., Mudgett, M. B., Dangl, J., and Galan, J. E. 2001. Common and contrasting themes of plant and animal diseases. Science 292:2285-2289.

Van der Plank, J. E. 1975. Principles of Plant Infection. Academic Press, New York.

Vera Cruz, C. M., Bai, J., Oña, I., Leung, H., Nelson, R. J., Mew, T. W., and Leach, J. E. 2000. Predicting durability of a disease resistance gene based on an assessment of the fitness loss and epidemiological consequences of avirulence gene mutation. Proc. Natl. Acad. Sci. USA 97:13500-13505.

White, F. F., Yang, B., and Johnson, L. B. 2000. Prospects for understanding avirulence gene function. Curr. Opin. Plant Biol. 3:291-298.

Host Diversity, Epidemics, and Pathogen Evolution

Christopher C. Mundt

Oregon State University, Corvallis, OR, USA

Genes for plant disease resistance can be deployed in mixed populations, e.g., as multiline cultivars (mixtures of lines bred to be phenotypically uniform for important agronomic traits) or cultivar mixtures (mixtures of cultivated varieties with no attempt to breed for phenotypic uniformity). Such mixtures have been shown to be effective in reducing disease, and in increasing and stabilizing crop yield (Browning and Frey 1969; Mundt and Browning 1985; Wolfe 1985; Finckh 2000). I will focus on pathogens that attack foliage through multiple cycles of reproduction during a cropping season, and interact in a gene-for-gene manner with their hosts.

Mechanisms of Disease Reduction in Host Mixtures

The dilution of inoculum that occurs due to increased distance between plants of the same genotype appears to be the most important mechanism of disease reduction in mixtures (Wolfe 1985). For example, in a 50:50 mixture of susceptible:resistant plants, the predicted disease level on susceptible plants in mixture will be one-half in the first generation of secondary spread, one-fourth in the second generation, one-eighth in the third generation, etc. The usual pattern seen in the field is for disease levels to initially diverge over time, and then to converge as the host's carrying capacity for disease is approached (e.g., Wolfe and Barrett 1980). The rate at which the carrying capacity is approached will impact the effectiveness of mixtures for disease control (Garrett and Mundt 1999).

Mixtures and Spatial Scale of Deployment

The efficacy of mixtures for disease control is affected by spatial scale, with mixtures performing better in commercial production than in small scale experimental plots (Wolfe 1985; Mundt 1994; Mundt et al. 2001), for several reasons.

Nearly all field experiments incorporate some type of "untreated" control, which will have higher disease levels and produce greater amounts of inoculum than other plots. In the case of mixtures, untreated controls are usually monocultures of susceptible host genotypes. Mixture experiments are especially vulnerable to interplot interference, and mixture effects on disease can sometimes be obliterated by interplot interference (Wolfe 1985; Mundt 1994).

Excessive inoculum levels in plots can sometimes arise from outside of the experiment itself. For example, in the humid highland tropics of Ecuador near Quito, year-round potato (*Solanum tuberosum*) production results in large amounts of inoculum that apparently overwhelmes the mixture effect on late blight, caused by *Phytophthora infestans*. On the other hand, late blight reduction due to mixing was observed at the site most distant from commercial potato production (Garrett et al. 2001) and in more temperate areas of Peru (Garrett et al. in preparation) and the USA (Garrett and Mundt 2000).

Initiating epidemics through high levels of artificial inoculation in experimental plots can reduce the number of generations of pathogen increase that occur before the crop's carrying capacity for disease is reached, thus reducing the impact of mixtures on disease (Garrett and Mundt 1999).

Epidemic velocity measures the rate at which a given level of disease severity moves in space per unit of time from an initial focus of infection, and has units of m day-1. Minoque and Fry (1983) and van den Bosch et al. (1988a,b) developed models to describe the movement of disease as a travelling wave. Due to assumptions and model construction, both models will always predict a constant velocity of epidemic increase. Later, Ferrandino (1993) presented an analysis suggesting that epidemic velocity may increase in time and space.

If disease spreads as a wave of constant velocity, then differences between monoculture and mixture (or any other disease control practice that reduces epidemic rate) will be constant in both time and space, assuming a constant environment. If epidemic velocity increases in time and space, however, then the difference in velocity between monoculture and mixture will increase as epidemics expand (Mundt et al. 2001). Preliminary studies with wheat (*Triticum aestivum*) yellow rust (caused by *Puccinia striiformis*) in 2001 suggest that epidemic velocity does in fact increase exponentially in time, and that this rate of increase is greater for a monoculture than for a mixture (Mundt unpublished).

Spatial scale may be of importance to the epidemiological impacts of diversity even when initial inoculum is more uniformly dispersed. Given the steep nature of pathogen dispersal gradients, there may often be only a small amount of dispersal between any two genotype units (independent units containing plants of the same genotype), be they plants, rows, or fields. However, the number of genotype units increases with the square of the radius of the geographic area in question. In larger areas, the overlap of gradient "tails" may contribute significantly to the total inoculum load and, thus, may be impacted by mixtures (Mundt and Brophy 1988), though this is difficult to test in the field (Mundt et al. 1996).

There are two examples where the epidemiological impact of mixtures has been well studied at large spatial scale. The percentage of the barley (*Hordeum vulgare*) area sown to cultivar mixtures in the former East Germany increased from 0 in 1980 to 92% by 1990. Correspondingly, mildew severity gradually declined from 50% in 1980 to 10% in 1990, while fungicide use declined about three-fold (Wolfe 1992). In a second example, mixtures of sticky rice (*Oryzae sativa*) cultivars highly susceptible to blast (caused by *Magnaporthe grisea*) were mixed with more resistant non-glutinous cultivars. Mixtures were deployed in all rice fields in five townships of Yunnan Province, China in 1998 (812 ha of rice) and 10 townships in 1999 (3,342 ha of rice). Mixtures reduced the severity of blast on susceptible sticky rice cultivars by 94% as compared to small pure stand observation plots of the same cultivars (Zhu et al. 2000).

Pathogen Evolution and Resistance Durability in Mixtures

A pertinent question is whether a given number of resistance genes will be more durable if deployed in a mixture as compared to the same number of genes deployed sequentially in monoculture. Observation of both agricultural and natural ecosystems have not detected strong selection for highly fit complex races in either agricultural or natural ecosystems (Mundt and Browning 1985; Wolfe 1985), though data are scant. Most mathematical models have assumed that there is a fitness cost associated with virulence alleles (more properly in most cases, a lack of avirulence alleles). Thus, the advantage of being able to attack multiple host genotypes in a mixture could be countered by a fitness reduction associated with lack of avirulence alleles corresponding to the matching resistance alleles.

Parlevliet (1981) provided a thorough review of the literature regarding the cost of virulence concept, which showed no consistent association of virulence with fitness for plant pathogens. Parlevliet explained this lack of association by selection for fitness modifiers that ameliorate the initial fitness cost, a process that has been seen with antibiotic resistance in non plant pathogenic bacteria (e.g., Cohan et al. 1994; Morrell 1997). There is also a strong need to examine alternative mechanisms (Mundt and Browning 1985; Lannou and Mundt 1997) that may prevent complex races from dominating the pathogen population. One such mechanism is disruptive selection caused by complex races cycling between multiple host genetic backgrounds in a mixture, which may have very substantial impacts on pathogen fitness (Chin and Wolfe 1984; Lannou and Mundt 1997; Mundt et al. 1999).

Literature Cited

Browning, J.A., and Frey, K.J. 1969. Multiline cultivars as a means of disease control. Annu. Rev. Phytopathol. 14:355-382.

Chin, K.M., and Wolfe, M.S. 1984. Selection on *Erysiphe graminis* in pure and mixed stands of barley. Plant Pathol. 33:535-546.

Cohan, F.M., King, E.C., and Zawadzki, P. 1994. Amelioration of the deleterious pleiotropic effects of an adaptive mutation in *Bacillus subtilis*. Evolution 48:81-95.

Ferrandino, F.J. 1993. Dispersive epidemic waves: I. Focus expansion within a linear planting. Phytopathology 83:795-802.

Finckh, M.R., Gacek, E.S., Goyeau, H., Lannou, C., Merz, U., Mundt, C.C., Munk, L., Nadziak, J., Newton, A.C., de Vallavieille-Pope, C., and Wolfe, M.S. 2000. Cereal variety and species mixtures in practice. Agronomie 20:813-837.

Garrett, K.A., and Mundt, C.C. 1999. Epidemiology in mixed host populations. Phytopathology 89:984-990.

Garrett, K.A., and Mundt, C.C. 2000. Host diversity can reduce potato late blight severity for focal and general patterns of primary inoculum. Phytopathology 90:1307-1312.

Garrett, K.A., Nelson, R.J., Mundt, C.C., Chacon, G., Jarmillo, R.E., and Forbes, G.A. 2001. The effects of host diversity and other management components on epidemics of potato late blight in the humid highland tropics. Phytopathology 91:in press.

Lannou, C., and Mundt, C.C. 1997. Evolution of a pathogen population in host mixtures: Rate of emergence of complex races. Theor. Appl. Genet. 94:991-999.

Minogue, K.P., and Fry, W.E. 1983. Models for the spread of disease: Model description. Phytopathology 73:1168-1173.

Morrell, V. 1997. Antibiotic resistance: Road of no return. Science 278:575-576.

Mundt, C.C. 1994. Use of host genetic diversity to control cereal diseases: Implications for rice blast. Pages 293-307 in: Proceedings of the International Symposium on Rice Blast Disease, R.S. Zeigler, S. Leong, and P.S. Teng, eds. CABI International, Cambridge.

Mundt, C.C., and Browning, J.A. 1985. Genetic diversity and cereal rust management. Pages 527-560 in: The Cereal Rusts, Vol. 2. A.P. Roelfs and W.R. Bushnell, eds. Academic Press, Orlando.

Mundt, C.C., and Brophy, L.S. 1988. Influence of number of host genotype units on the effectiveness of host mixtures for disease control: A modeling approach. Phytopathology 78:1087-1094.

Mundt, C.C., Brophy, L.S., and Kolar, S.C. 1996. Effect of genotype unit number and spatial arrangement on severity of yellow rust in wheat cultivar mixtures. Plant Pathol. 45:215-222.

Mundt, C.C., Cowger, C., and Hoffer, M.E. 1999. Disease management using variety mixtures. Pages 111-116 in: M. van Ginkel, A. McNab, and J. Krupinsky, eds. Septoria and Stagonospora Diseases of Cereals: A Compilation of Global Research. CIMMYT, Mexico, D.F.

Mundt, C.C., Cowger, C., and Garrett, K.A. 2001. Relevance of integrated disease management to resistance durability. Euphytica 50:in press.

Parlevliet, J.E. 1981. Stabilizing selection in crop patho-systems: An empty concept or a reality? Euphytica 30:259-269.

van den Bosch, F., Zadoks, J.C., and Metz, J.A.J. 1988a. Focus expansion in plant disease. I: The constant rate of focus expansion. Phytopathology 78:54-58.

Wolfe, M.S. 1985. The current status and prospects of multiline cultivars and variety mixtures for disease resistance. Annu. Rev. Phytopathol. 23:251-273.

Wolfe, M.S. 1992. Maintaining the value of our varieties. Pages 1055-1067 in: Barley Genetics VI. Munksgaard International Publishers, Copenhagen.

Wolfe, M.S., and Barrett, J.A. 1980. Can we lead the pathogen astray? Plant Dis. 64:148-155.

Zhu, Y., Chen, H., Fan, J., Wang, Y., Li, Y., Chen, J., Fan, J.-X., Yang, S., Hu, L., Leung, H., Mew, T.W., Teng, P.S., Wang, Z., and Mundt, C.C. 2000. Genetic diversity and disease control in rice. Nature 406:718-722.

Transgenic Tomatoes Expressing the Pepper *Bs2* Resistance Gene Confer Resistance to *Xanthomonas campestris* pv. *vesicatoria* in the Field

Brian Staskawicz, Doug Dalhbeck, Walter Gassmann, Mary Beth Mudgett, Olga Chesnokova, Jeff Jones, and Robert Stall

Department of Plant and Microbial Biology, University of California, Berkeley, CA 94720 and Department of Plant Pathology, University of Florida, Gainsville, FL

Xanthomonas campestris pv. *vesicatoria (Xcv),* the causal agent of the bacterial spot disease of pepper and tomato, causes severe problems in warm and humid climates (Minsavage et al. 1990). The disease is controlled by copper sprays and genetic resistance. Several sources of genetic resistance have been introgressed into pepper by classical breeding. The *Bs2,* gene originally identified in *Capsicum chacoense,* confers resistance to the majority of *Xcv* strains that contain a wild type allele of the *avrBs2* gene (Minsavage et al. 1990). However, mutations in the *avrBs2* gene, give rise to strains that are no longer recognized by *Bs2* lines of pepper and are able to cause disease. Our studies in the past, have shown that at least four classes of mutations can occur in strains that have overcome *Bs2* resistance (Gassmann et al. 2000)

Interestingly, all the mutations seem to occur in the region of the gene that has high homology with phophodiesterase synthase activity. The significance this observation is still unknown. The *avrBs2* gene was one of the first avirulence genes that was shown to be involved with pathogen virulence (Kjemtrup et al. 2000). Mutations in the *avrBs2* gene often render the bacterium "less fit" as bacterial growth curves of mutants in isogenic susceptible pepper lines are lower than the wild type strains.

The cloning of disease resistance genes over the past eight years has been a great achievement for molecular plant pathology. Although there are several classes of disease resistance genes, the NBS/LRR class of genes in by far the most prevalent (Dangl and Jones 2001). The *Bs2* gene was recently cloned from pepper using a map-based approach. The gene encodes an approximately 100kD protein that contains a NBS/LRR domains

Mutations in AvrBs2 of 20 *Xcv* field isolates fall into four classes

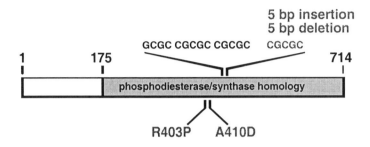

Fig. 1. Mutations in AvrBs2.

(Tai et al. 1999). However, the *Bs2* gene does not contain either a CC (coiled-coil) or TIR (Toll-interleukin receptor) domain at the N-terminus of the protein.

The ability to selectively introduce genes into plants by *Agrobacterium*-mediated transformation has allowed us to express the *Bs2* gene in tomato plants that normally do not contain resistance to *Xcv*. Transgenic tomato plants expressing the *Bs2* gene were resistance to strains of *Xcv* that contained the corresponding *avrBs2* avirulence gene as assayed by the production of the hypersensitive response or inhibition of bacterial growth. In collaboration, with Jeff Jones at the University of Florida, we have begun to evaluate transgenic tomatoes that contain *Bs2* for disease resistance to bacterial spot disease in the field. Tomato transplants of the wild-type genotype, VF36, and the transformed line, VF36(*Bs2*) were grown to transplant size in the greenhouse. The transplants were inoculated August 22, 2000 in the greenhouse by spraying the plants with a suspension of 10^8 CFU/ml of a tomato race 3 strain of *Xanthomonas campestris* pv. *vesicatoria*, The suspension also contained 0.025% (v/v) of Silwet L77 to increase infection by the bacterium. The plants were transplanted to the field on August 29, 2000 and were planted in a randomized complete block design and consisted of six replications. The plants received routine maintenance sprays of insecticides to reduce insect problems.

Disease ratings were made four times during the experiment. The ratings were made on September 14th, October 1st, October 17th, and November 3rd of 2000. Disease ratings were made by assessing the percent defoliation attributed to bacterial spot by using the Horsfall-Barratt scale where, 1=0%; 2=0-3%; 3=3-6%; 4=6-12%; 5=12-25%; 6=25-50%; 7=50-75%; 8=75-87%; 9=87-93%; 10=93-97%;11=97-100%; and 12=100% defoliation. The disease ratings for each date were used to determine the area under the disease progress curve (AUDPC). Disease severity was not observed on the transformed line, VF36(*Bs2*), and thus was significantly lower than in the wild-type line VF36 (Table 1). As a result of a severe freeze, fruit were harvested on November 21, 2000 before fruit matured. The transformed line had more fruit per plant than VF36.

Table 1. Comparison of VF36 and VF36(*Bs2*) on bacterial spot severity and yield in the field in the fall 2000 in Gainesville, FL

Genotype	AUDPC	Yield Per Plant	
		Fruit Number	Weight (lbs)
VF36	332.4	2.28	0.44
VF36(*Bs2*)	66.5	3.68	0.69

Our preliminary results have shown that transgenic tomato plants containing the *Bs2* resistance gene confer resistance to *Xcv* in the field. Obviously, we are interested to determine the durability of this resistance as there are strains with mutant *avrBs2* alleles. Future studies employing more and larger field trials will be necessary to answer this important question.

Literature Cited

Minsavage, G.V., et al. 1990. Gene-for-gene relationships specifying disease resistance in *Xanthomonas campestris pv. vesicatoria*-pepper interactions. Mol Plant Microbe Interact. 3:41-47.

Gassmann, W., et al. 2000. Molecular evolution of virulence in natural field strains of *Xanthomonas campestris pv. vesicatoria*. Journal of Bacteriology. 182(24):7053-9.

Kjemtrup, S., Z. Nimchuk, and Dangl, J.L. 2000. Effector proteins of phytopathogenic bacteria: Bifunctional signals in virulence and host recognition. Current Opinion in Microbiology 3(1):73-78.

Dangl, J. and Jones, J. 2001. Plant pathogens and integrated defence responses to infection. Nature 411:826-833.

Tai, T.H., et al. 1999. Expression of the Bs2 pepper gene confers resistance to bacterial spot disease in tomato. Proc Natl Acad Sci U S A 96(24):14153-14158.

The Use of a *proU-gfp* Transcriptional Fusion to Quantify Water Stress on the Leaf Surface

Gwyn A. Beattie and Catherine A. Axtell

Department of Microbiology, Iowa State University, Ames, IA 50011 USA.

The availability of water on plant surfaces is probably a critical factor influencing the physiology and ecology of plant-associated microorganisms. We report here recent progress in our efforts to quantify the extent to which leaf-associated bacterial cells and populations are exposed to limited water availability, i.e. *water stress*. This type of quantitative information is important to our understanding of the extent to which water deprivation has been a selective force during the adaptation of bacterial species to growth on leaves, as well as to our understanding of the role of water deprivation in driving bacterial population dynamics on plants.

Aerial plant leaves have topographically complex surfaces with niches that may favor water accumulation. In addition to spatial heterogeneity in water distribution, leaf-derived nutrients and their accompanying salts may serve as osmotically active solutes. Thus, leaf-associated microorganisms may experience water deprivation due not only to the absence of water, i.e. desiccation, but also to high osmolarity conditions.

To really understand the impact of water deprivation on the physiology and ecology of leaf-associated bacteria, it is important to have a tool that can measure water availability on a microscale. The instruments that have been used for measuring leaf water potential and leaf surface wetness include *in situ* leaf psychrometers (Campbell and McInnes 1999), electrical conductivity sensors (Giesler et al. 1996), hemp string (Brown and Sutton 1995), and magnetic resonance imaging (Veres et al. 1993). None of these instruments, however, are capable of functioning on the scale of a bacterium. Thus, we turned to another tool, a biological sensor.

Water Deprivation-Responsive Bacterial Biosensor

We constructed a biological sensor for measuring water availability by utilizing a transcriptional fusion between a water deprivation-responsive promoter and a reporter gene, *gfp*, which encodes a green fluorescent protein. The key component of this biosensor was the *proU* promoter, which controls the *proU* operon involved in proline and glycine betaine uptake in *Escherichia coli* and *Salmonella typhimurium* (Lucht and Bremer 1994, Overdier et al. 1992). The useful highlights of this promoter were that 1) it responds rapidly to a decrease in water potential, 2) it maintains a high level of expression as long as the cells remain under low water potential conditions, and 3) it functions without a regulatory protein.

We introduced the *proU-gfp* fusion into a broad-host-range plasmid, and introduced this plasmid into *Pantoea agglomerans* (formerly *Erwinia herbicola*). This bacterial species is a common inhabitant of leaves, is not a phytopathogen, and is found primarily, if not exclusively, on the leaf surface (Sabaratnam and Beattie, unpublished data). In *P. agglomerans*, the *proU-gfp* fusion was responsive to all forms of water stress, including osmotic stress caused by various permeating solutes (e.g. NaCl, KCl, and Na_2SO_4), and desiccation stress caused by the non-permeating solute polyethylene glycol 8000 (PEG 8000) (Halverson and Firestone 2000). The similarity in induction by each of these types of water stress at comparable water potentials (Figure 1) indicates that the signal for the *proU* promoter was water deprivation rather than the activity of any single osmolyte.

Quantification of Bacterial Water Stress Exposure on Bean Leaves

We applied the *P. agglomerans* cells containing the *proU-gfp* fusion onto bean (*Phaseolus vulgaris*) leaves, subjected the leaves to conditions that favored evaporation, recovered the bacteria, and measured their fluorescence using flow cytometry. We observed a steady increase in the mean fluorescence of the leaf populations over a 30 min drying period (Table 1). In fact this increase was significant after only 10 min. We

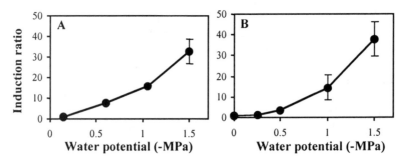

Fig. 1. The extent of *proU-gfp* induction by various levels of A) osmotic stress conferred by NaCl, and B) desiccation stress conferred by PEG 8000.

Table 1. Induction of the *proU-gfp* fusion in *P. agglomerans* on bean leaves at various times during exposure of leaves to drying conditions.

Drying time (min)	Mean Fluorescence[a]	Induction ratio	Estimated water potential (mM NaCl equivalent)[b]
0	10.4 ± 0.2 a	1.00	6.6
5	11.5 ± 0.2 ab	1.11	17.9
10	11.8 ± 0.6 b	1.13	20.5
15	12.8 ± 0.1 b	1.22	29.4
30	15.0 ± 0.7 c	1.44	47.7

[a] The mean of 3 replicate measurements ± SE is shown. Each measurement is the mean fluorescence of the population of cells recovered from a leaf.
[b] The values were derived from a standard curve relating *proU-gfp* induction levels (y) to mM NaCl (x) (y = 0.943 $e^{0.0089x}$).

related the mean fluorescence of a population on a leaf to the perceived water deprivation levels by using a standard curve of the *proU-gfp* induction ratio at various NaCl concentrations. For example, the average level of exposure of *P. agglomerans* cells that were recovered from bean leaves after 30 min was to a water potential that was equivalent to that imposed by 47.7 mM NaCl. In a replicate experiment, the average exposure level after 35 min was to a water potential equivalent to 57 mM NaCl. The increases in the fluorescence of the cells slowed dramatically between 30 and 60 min of exposure, and no significant increases occurred between 60 min and 4 h. The maximum average exposure level was to a water potential equivalent to 79 mM NaCl.

We predicted that some cells on a leaf are located in sites where water is abundant, while others are located in sites where water availability is limited. We found evidence for the presence of subpopulations of cells that were exposed to high levels of water stress based on the right-skewed histogram of the fluorescence of the *P. agglomerans* cells recovered from each leaf (data not shown). The percentage of cells in these subpopulations increased from 6% to 18% during a 4 h drying period, and these cells were exposed to water stress levels greater than those imposed by 300 mM NaCl.

To identify the potential consequences of *P. agglomerans* exposure to water stress, we grew cells on plates in the presence of 0 to 600 mM NaCl. *P. agglomerans* grew at a similar rate in the presence of NaCl concentrations from 0 to 300 mM, although it grew slower at higher concentrations. The time between the arrival of a cell on an agar surface and the presence of a visible colony increased linearly with increasing NaCl concentration from 0 to 600 mM. We observed a similar trend with increasing concentrations of PEG 8000. If extrapolated to the single cell level, these results suggest that the time required for the initiation of cell division was affected by the water potential to which the cell was exposed. Thus, although on bean leaves the exposure of many of the *P. agglomerans* cells to water deprivation was relatively low, the exposure was sufficiently high to affect the subsequent growth dynamics of the cells.

Quantification of Bacterial Water Stress Exposure on Maize Leaves

In other studies, we used mutants of maize (*Zea mays*) that varied in their production of cuticular waxes to demonstrate that specific leaf surface properties can influence bacterial colonization (L. M. Marcell and G. A. Beattie, submitted for publication). One of the major mechanisms by which these leaf surface properties likely affect colonization is via their influence on water availability. For example, whereas the wild type was sufficiently hydrophobic to promote the formation of large rounded water droplets, two of the mutants were reduced in their leaf surface hydrophobicity, and thus these mutants promoted greater adherence of the water to the leaf (Figure 2) (G. A. Beattie and L. M. Marcell, submitted for publication). When we applied the *P. agglomerans* biosensor cells to the wild-type maize and these two mutants, incubated the leaves under conditions that favored evaporation, and recovered the bacteria from the leaves, we found that the mean fluorescence of the populations was highest on those leaves from the mutant with the lowest leaf surface hydrophobicity, i.e. mutant *gl1* (Figure 2). This can be explained by the fact that water droplets on *gl1* should have the largest surface-to-volume ratio and thus should evaporate the fastest. In these studies, mutant *gl1* supported large populations ($>10^7$ cells/leaf) due to the greater adherence of bacteria-containing water droplets, whereas the

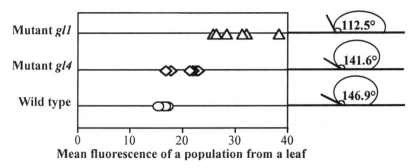

Fig. 2. The mean fluorescence of *proU-gfp* fusion-containing *P. agglomerans* cells recovered from maize leaves. Each point represents the mean fluorescence of a population recovered from a single leaf. For each the wild type and the two cuticular mutants, the leaf surface hydrophobicity is illustrated on the right by both a diagram of a water droplet on the leaf surface and the angle at which the water droplet contacts the leaf surface.

wild type supported small populations ($<10^6$ cells/leaf) due to the poor adherence of the bacteria-containing water droplets. The population sizes and water stress exposure levels of *P. agglomerans* on mutant *gl4* were intermediate between those of mutant *gl1* and the wild type. These studies illustrated the complex effects of leaf surface hydrophobicity on leaf-associated bacterial populations: a high leaf surface hydrophobicity can negatively impact population size, but the few cells present may be well protected from water stress. In contrast, a low leaf surface hydrophobicity can favor the presence of large populations, but these cells may be exposed to elevated levels of water stress.

In summary, we demonstrated that the *proU-gfp* fusion-based bacterial biosensor that we developed can serve as an effective tool for quantifying bacterial exposure to limited water availability on leaves. In the studies presented here, we demonstrated that for *P. agglomerans* cells on bean leaves, the average cell was exposed to relatively low levels of water stress under the conditions tested, but even these levels could potentially impact subsequent bacterial growth. Furthermore, we found evidence for the presence of subpopulations of cells that were exposed to particularly high levels of water stress. These subpopulations, which comprised as much 18% of the population at 30 min after inoculation, likely reflected the presence of cells in leaf sites where water availability was limited. Lastly, we demonstrated that under conditions that favor evaporation, maize leaf surface hydrophobicity was inversely related to the extent to which recently inoculated bacteria were exposed to water stress.

Acknowledgements

This work was supported in part by funds provided by NSF(IBN-9974059) and USDA-NRICRG (99-35303-8301).

Literature Cited

Brown, E. M., and Sutton, T. B. 1995. An empirical model for predicting the first symptoms of sooty blotch and flyspeck of apples. Plant Dis. 79:1165-1168.

Campbell, C. S., and McInnes, K. J. 1999. Response of in situ leaf psychrometer to cuticle removal by abrasion. Agron. J. 91:859-862.

Giesler, L. J., Yuen, G. Y., and Horst, G. L. 1996. The microclimate in tall fescue turf as affected by canopy density and its influence on brown patch disease. Plant Dis. 80:389-394.

Halverson, L. J., and Firestone, M. K. 2000. Differential effects of permeating and nonpermeating solutes on the fatty acid composition of *Pseudomonas putida*. Appl. Environ. Microbiol. 66:2414-2421.

Lucht, J. M., and Bremer, E. 1994. Adaptation of *Escherichia coli* to high osmolarity environments: osmoregulation of the high-affinity glycine betaine transport system *proU*. FEMS Microbiol. Rev. 14:3-20.

Overdier, D. G., Fletcher, S., and Csonka, L. N. 1992. Osmotic control of transcription of the *proU* operon of *Salmonella typhimurium*. Pages 61-69 in: G. N. Somero, C. B. Osmond, and L. Bolis, eds. Springer-Verlag, Berlin.

Veres, J. S., Cofer, G. P., and Johnson, G. A. 1993. Magnetic resonance imaging of leaves. New Phytol. 123:769-774.

Characterizing the Microhabitats of Bacteria on Leaves

Steven Lindow, Jean-Michel Monier, Johan H.J. Leveau

Department of Plant and Microbial Biology, University of California, 111 Koshland Hall, Berkeley, CA 94720-3102

Leaf surfaces can support the development of large population sizes of bacteria of different kinds. Bacteria that both grow and survive on plant surfaces are called epiphytes. Bacterial epiphytes are important to plant health in several different ways. Most plant pathogenic bacteria multiply on the surface of healthy plants before they initiate disease (Beattie and Lindow 1995; 1999; Hirano and Upper 1993; 2000; Hirano et al. 1995). Disease apparently is always preceded by large epiphytic bacterial populations on healthy leaves. The probability of foliar bacterial diseases is strongly correlated with the epiphytic population size of phytopathogenic bacteria on healthy plants; the incidence of diseases such as bacterial brown spot of bean can be accurately predicted with knowledge of the proportion of leaves with high population sizes of the pathogen (Hirano and Upper 2000; Rouse et al. 1985). Other deleterious bacteria such as ice nucleation active (Ice[+]) strains of *Pseudomonas syringae*, *Erwinia herbicola*, *Pseudomonas fluorescens*, and *Xanthomonas campestris* are also common on plants (Hirano and Upper 1993; 2000; Lindow et al. 1978; Lindow 1983; 1995). These bacteria can catalyze ice formation at temperatures as warm as -2 C, thus damaging frost-sensitive plant species such as many vegetable crops, flowers of fruit trees, and fruit of sub-tropical crops such as citrus which can not tolerate ice in their tissues (Lindow et al. 1978; Lindow 1983; 1995). Thus, factors which influence the population size of epiphytic bacteria can have a great influence on the health of the plant.

Aggregated Nature of Epiphytes

Bacteria are not randomly distributed across a leaf surface. Large differences in the number of bacteria that occur in adjacent regions of a given leaf have been reported. (Ercolani 1978; Leben et al. 1970; Roos and Hattingh 1983); the numbers of cells in different 4mm^2 leaf sections varied by over 100-fold (Leben 1969). While bacteria can be found on nearly all parts of a leaf, they are much more likely to occur in the crevices formed by the junction of epidermal cells and by the edge of veins than on more planar portions of the leaf (Ercolani 1978; Leben et al. 1970; Roos and Hattingh 1983). Epiphytic bacteria are also commonly found at the bases of trichomes (Leben et al. 1970; Beattie and Lindow 1995) and are occasionally associated with stomatal or hydathode openings (Ercolani 1978). While most published images of bacteria on leaves depict relatively scattered colonization, with only a few cells in close proximity to each other, a few have revealed the presence of aggregates (Dickinson 1986; Surico 1993; Timmer et al. 1987). Most of the aggregates depicted are relatively small (< 20 μm in length). Recently, however, Morris et al. (1997) demonstrated that aggregates as large as 20 μm deep and 1000 μm in length could be observed on plants, particularly field grown plants that were naturally contaminated with bacteria. We recently have undertaken a detailed and quantitative evaluation of the bacterial colonization of both inoculated leaves incubated in varying conditions in a greenhouse as well as on field-collected leaves. Our analyses have utilized primarily direct visualization of bacteria by epifluorescence microscopy following topical staining with acridine orange using a method similar to that of Morris et al. (1997; 1998). Large numbers of random fields of view from each of many different leaves were observed to define the typical pattern of colonization. Most images revealed relatively scattered patterns of colonization, while in some images relatively large bacterial aggregates are noted (unpublished data). Frequency histograms of the number of colonized sites having different numbers of cells/site reveals a strongly right hand-skewed description. Thus, many of the cells on leaves are apparently relatively solitary and isolated from one another, but some large aggregates occur. These aggregates are comprised of many cells that usually appear to be encased in a polymeric matrix, presumed to be bacterial extracellular polysaccharides (EPS). On many leaves, over 50% of the total bacterial population is present in aggregates of 200 or more cells (unpublished data). Thus, while the number of aggregates on a given leaf appears to be relatively small, aggregates often account for the majority of cells on a leaf. Cell aggregates are therefore an apparent, but unappreciated feature of epiphytic bacterial populations. The aggregated nature of bacterial colonists of plant surfaces is a conspicuous feature that presumably has important implications for the interactions of these microbes with themselves on leaves, as well as with the plant itself.

The presence of bacterial epiphytes in large, polymer-encased aggregates on leaves has many similarities to that of biofilms that have been described in other (mostly aquatic) habitats. Biofilms generally are comprised of a polysaccharide matrix in which one or more bacterial species are embedded (Beveridge et al. 1997; Costerton et al. 1995). The EPS matrix leads to the creation of physical barriers and the establishment of chemical gradients.

Biofilms can concentrate nutrients from dilute sources, provide protection from predators, and shield cells from lytic enzymes, antibiotics, and other inhibitory compounds (Allison and Gilbert 1995; Berveridge et al. 1997; Costerton et al. 1995; De Beer et al. 1994). The microenvironment of cells in biofilms and hence their physiology is markedly different from the same species in a planktonic condition due to the nature of the biofilm environment (Allison and Gilbert 1995; Berveridge et al. 1997; Costerton et al. 1995; De Beer et al. 1994). The cells within biofilms are apparently markedly different phenotypically from planktonic cells of the same species; as many as 30% of the genes of a given species are expressed selectively within a biofilm (Costerton et al. 1995). Extrapolating to the perspective of leaf aggregates, EPS may anchor cells to the leaf surface and prevent cells from desiccation (Leben 1981), as well as modify the environment around the cell to one more favorable for growth and survival. Thus bacterial production of such a matrix on leaves could be highly advantageous for growth and survival. It seems clear that epiphytic bacteria have modified their environment to one that does not resemble the exposed cuticular surface of plants.

Cell-Density Dependent Behavior of Bacteria

The apparent presence of a majority of cells of epiphytic bacteria residing in large aggregates has many implications for their behavior on leaves. There is substantial evidence that many microbial traits are expressed in a density-dependent fashion. Bacteria express a subset of their genes in response to their cell density by a process of quorum sensing (also called autoinduction)(Fuqua et al. 1996; de Kievit and Iglewski 2000). In this process, bacteria determine their local population size by sensing the concentration of small, diffusible, signal molecules that they themselves produce (Fuqua et al. 1996; de Kievit and Iglewski 2000). As these so-called autoinducers accumulate in the extracellular environment of the cell, a concentration is reached (if a sufficiently high number of cells is present) so that these molecules can act as co-inducers to regulate transcription of genes which are of benefit to the cell in a habitat under the condition that other cells of the same species are present. Several traits important in plant-microbe interactions have been shown to be regulated by a quorum sensing mechanism (de Kievit and Iglewski 2000). We have recently found that mutants of *P. syringae* altered in patterns of autoinducer production also exhibit a reduced ability to grow on plants and a reduced ability to survive desiccation stress after multiplying on plants (unpublished data). This strongly suggests that cells within aggregates on plants produce, and benefit from, autoinducers within aggregates on leaves, presumably by expression of traits important in epiphytic fitness in a density-dependent fashion. The apparent autoinducer-mediated fitness of epiphytes also suggests that relatively solitary cells on plants may not benefit from such density-dependent fitness traits.

Behavior of Aggregated Bacteria on Plants

Several aspects of the epiphytic behavior of bacteria on plants have also been seen to be density-dependent. For example, the survival of cells applied to plants under stressful conditions was found to be directly proportional to the concentration of cells that were applied; the proportion of cells applied at relatively high numbers that survived desiccation stress was up to 80-fold higher than that of cells applied at a low cell density (Wilson and Lindow 1994). Likewise, the survival of cells of a *P. syringae* strain varied greatly after application to different plant species in a "common garden" experiment in the field, and a strong correlation was seen between the population size of indigenous bacteria on a plant species and the population size of *P. syringae* that survived inoculation onto plants (Kinkel et al. 1996). A positive correlation was also found between the population sizes of a particular strain of *P. syringae* that had been inoculated onto plants in a field study and the subsequent total *P. syringae* populations (i.e. all *P. syringae* strains) on individual leaflets throughout the growing season (Hirano and Upper 1993). Such results suggest that leaves colonized by bacteria provide a habitat that is different from that of uncolonized leaves, and that leaf surface modifications made by bacterial epiphytes in aggregates to facilitate their colonization of the leaf also benefit immigrants to the same leaf.

Nutrients on Leaves

Many leaf-associated microbes are capable of growth, i.e. multiplying, by exploitation of the few resources that the leaf surface offers. Exogenous nutrients may be available fortuitously in the form of pollen, honeydew, dust, air pollution, or microbial debris (Stadler and Mueller 2000; Warren 1972). Occasionally, plant sap may ooze from wounds inflicted by insect feeding (Stadler and Mueller 2000) or frost damage (Hirano and Upper 2000). But even healthy plants passively leak small amounts of metabolites such as carbohydrates, amino acids and organic acids to the leaf surface (Tukey 1970). The amounts that are leaked depend on many factors, including the leachate itself, the plant species, leaf characteristics such as wettability, waxiness, and age, and duration and intensity of rain or dew (Tukey 1970).

It has been demonstrated that leached compounds are used for growth by the microbes residing on a leaf (Dik et al. 1991; Rodger and Blakeman 1984; Wilson et al. 1995). Photoassimilates like sucrose, fructose and glucose, which are found in abundances of 0.2 to 2.0 micrograms per leaf on uninhabited bean leaf surfaces, were readily consumed and converted into biomass by the bacterium *Pseudomonas fluorescens* A506 (Mercier and Lindow 2000). However, since bacterial and fungal colonization of the phyllosphere does not occur evenly across the leaf, these resources may not be evenly available or exploitable. The factors that influence the availability of nutrients within or beyond preferred sites remain elusive. Also, there is no information on leaf nutrient availability at the scale that is most relevant to microbial colonizers. It seems unlikely that nutrient abundance as averaged over an entire leaf surface is of any relevance to an individual bacterial colonizer. Instead, a bacterium probably perceives its local environment in multiples of its own dimensions, i.e. on a micrometer scale.

To quantify the availability of nutrients to individual microbial residents in the phyllosphere we targeted sugars as the model nutrient, as they are generally recognized as the most abundant carbon source available in the phyllosphere (Mercier and Lindow 2000). Our strategy involved the use of reporter gene technology in which the well-characterized bacterial epiphyte *Erwinia herbicola* 299R (*Eh*299R) harbored a sugar-responsive element that was fused to a gene for green fluorescent protein (GFP). The GFP content of single cells thus becomes a measure for local sugar availability. We opted for the promoter region of the *fruBKA* operon from *Escherichia coli* (Reizer et al. 1994) to drive expression of GFP. This gene cluster codes for the metabolism of fructose and its expression is controlled by the catabolite repressor/activator or Cra protein (FruR) (Saier and Ramseier 1996) in response to fructose 1-phosphate, the first intermediate in the fructose metabolic pathway (Ramseier 1996). Because *E. coli* and *E. herbicola* are closely related bacteria, we anticipated that the *fruB* promoter would function properly in *Eh*299R. It is important to note that *Eh*299R can metabolize sugars such as fructose, so that its ability to report the presence of fructose is a function not only of local fructose abundance but also of fructose consumption. Instead of the original GFP from *Aequorea victoria* (Tsien 1998), we used variant GFP[AAV] (Andersen et al. 1998) which matures faster and yields a brighter fluorescence and also has a reduced stability, which allows for real-time monitoring of gene expression (Ramos et al. 2000; Sternberg et al. 1999). Analysis of individual *Eh*299R fructose bioreporters that were exposed to leaf surfaces for different periods of time disclosed a substantial heterogeneity in the availability of this sugar, both spatially (i.e. at different sites along the leaf surface) and temporally (i.e. at different times during leaf colonization).

Based on our observations with the fructose bioreporter *Eh*299R (pP$_{fruB}$-*gfp*[AAV]) (Leveau and Lindow 2001), we propose the following model for the role of local sugar availability in the colonization of bean plant leaves. Upon arrival to a previously uncolonized leaf surface, an individual cell has a good chance of finding itself in a place where it is presented with an amount of sugar that is sufficient to allow for a short and transient adaptation to its new environment. There usually remains ample sugar, predominantly in the form of fructose and/or sucrose, to then multiply and start colonization of the local area. As this fate is shared by most immigrants in other places on the same leaf, the total leaf population rapidly increases during the initial stage of leaf colonization. However, due to heterogeneity in initial availability, sugar pools are depleted earlier in some localities than in others. The majority of these pools are relatively small in size: almost all initial colonizers were exposed to at least 0.15 pg fructose equivalents, but only few (roughly 11% or less) had access to abundances close to or exceeding 4.6 pg. As increasingly more cells run out of resources and cease to multiply, growth of the total population slows down and eventually halts. This suggests that sugar pools on previously uncolonized bean leaves are discontinuous, i.e. they are not replenished by the plant at rates that support continual fast growth of the bacteria.

Clearly the process by which sugars are released onto the leaf is complex, as is the process by which epiphytes come into contact with and consume such resources. The further application of bioreporters such as that developed for fructose should help clarify the spatial and temporal patterns of nutrient consumption on leaves. Hopefully such information will provide the information needed to predict the behavior of cells that immigrate to plants in different ways, as well as the interactions between different species on plants.

Literature Cited

Allison, D. G., and Gilbert, P. 1995. Modification by surface association of antimicrobial susceptibility of bacterial populations. J. Indust. Microbiol. 15:311-317.

Andersen, J. B., Sternberg, C., Kongsbak-Poulsen, L, Petersen-Bjorn, S., Givskov, M., and Molin, S. 1998. New unstable variants of green fluorescent protein for studies of transient gene expression in bacteria. Appl. Environ. Microbiol. 64:2240-2246.

Beattie, G.A. and S.E. Lindow. 1995. The secret life of bacterial colonists of leaf surfaces. Ann. Rev. Phytopathology 33:145-172.

Beattie, G.A., and S.E. Lindow. 1999. Bacterial colonization of leaves: A spectrum of strategies. Phytopathology 89:353-359.

Beer, S.V., Rundle, J.R., and Norelli, J.L. 1984. Recent progress in the development of biological control of fire blight - a review. Acta. Hortic. 151:195-201.

Beveridge, T. J., S. A. Makin, J. L. Kadurugamuwa, and Z. Li. 1997. Interactions between biofilms and the environment. FEMS Microbiol. Rev. 20:291-303.

Cha, C., Gao, P., Chen, Y, Shaw, P.D., and Farrand, S.K. 1998. Production of acyl-homoserine lactone quorum-sensing signals by gram-negative plant-associated bacteria. Molec. Plant-Microbe Interact. 11:1119-1129.

Costerton, J. W., Z. Lewandowski, D. E. Caldwell, D. R. Korber, and H. M. Lappin-Scott. 1995. Microbial biofilms. Annu. Rev. Microbiol. 49:711-745.

De Beer, D., P. Stoodley, F. Roe, and Z. Lewandowski. 1994. Effects of biofilm structures on oxygen distribution and mass transport. Biotechnol. Bioengin. 43:1131-1138.

de Kievit, T.R., and Iglewski, B.H. 2000. Bacterial quorum sensing in pathogenic relationships. Infect. Immun. 68:4839-4849.

Dickinson, C. H. 1986. Adaptations of micro-organisms to climatic conditions affecting aerial plant surfaces, Pages 77-100 in: Microbiology of the phyllosphere. N. J. Fokkema and J. van den Heuvel, eds. Cambridge University Press, New York.

Dik, A. J., N. J. Fokkema, and J. A. van Pelt. 1991. Consumption of aphid honeydew, a wheat yield reduction factor, by phyllosphere yeasts under field conditions. Neth. J. Plant Pathol. 97:209-232.

Ercolani, G. L. 1978. *Pseudomonas savastanoi* and other bacteria colonizing the surface of olive leaves in the field. J. Gen. Microbiol. 109:245-258.

Fuqua, W.C., Winans, S.C., and Greenberg, E.P. 1996. Census and consensus in bacterial ecosystems: The LuxR-LuxI family of quorum-sensing transcriptional regulators. Ann. Rev. Microbiol. 50:727-751.

Hirano, S. S., and Upper, C.D. 1993. Dynamics, spread, and persistence of a single genotype of *Pseudomonas syringae* relative to those of its conspecifics on populations of snap bean leaflets. Appl. Environ. Microbiol. 59:1082-1091.

Hirano, S.S., D.I. Rouse, M.K. Clayton, and C.D. Upper. 1995. *Pseudomonas syringae* pv. *syringae* and bacterial brown spot of bean: A study of epiphytic phytopathogenic bacteria and associated disease. Plant. Dis. 79:1085-1093.

Hirano, S. S. and C. D. Upper. 1990. Population biology and epidemiology of *Pseudomonas syringae*. Annu. Rev. Phytopathol. 28:155-177.

Hirano, S. S., and C. D. Upper. 2000. Bacteria in the leaf ecosystem with emphasis on *Pseudomonas syringae*: A pathogen, ice nucleus, and epiphyte. Microbiology and Molecular Biology Reviews. 64(3):624-653.

Kinkel, L. L., Wilson, M. and Lindow, S. E. 1996. Utility of microcosm studies for predicting phylloplane bacterium population sizes in the field. Appl. Environ. Microbiol. 62:3413-3423.

Leben, C. 1969. Colonization of soybean buds by bacteria: observations with the scanning electron microscope. Can. J. Microbiol. 15:319-320.

Leben, C. 1981. How plant-pathogenic bacteria survive. Plant Dis. 65:633-637.

Leben, C., Schroth, M. N., and Hildebrand, D. C. 1970. Colonization and movement of *Pseudomonas syringae* on healthy bean seedlings. Phytopathology 60:677-680.

Leveau, J.H.J., and S.E. Lindow. 2000. Appetite of an epiphyte: Quantitative monitoring of bacterial sugar consumption in the phyllosphere. Proc. Natl. Acad. Sci. 98:3446-3453.

Lindow, S.E. 1995. Control of epiphytic ice nucleation-active bacteria for management of plant frost injury. Pages 239-256 in: Biological Ice Nucleation And Its Applications. R.E. Lee, G.J. Warren, and L.V. Gusta, eds. American Phytopathological Society Press, St. Paul, MN.

Lindow, S.E. 1983. The role of bacterial ice nucleation in frost injury to plants. Ann. Rev. Phytopathology 21:363-384.

Lindow, S.E., Arny, D.C., and Upper, C.D. 1978. Distribution of ice nucleation active bacteria on plants in nature. Appl. Environ. Microbiol. 36:831-838.

Mercier, J., and S. E. Lindow. 2000. Role of leaf surface sugars in colonization of plants by bacterial epiphytes. Appl. Environ. Microbiol. 66:369-374.

Mew, T. W., Mew, I. C., and Huang, J. S. 1984. Scanning electron microscopy of virulent and avirulent strains of *Xanthomonas campestris* pv. *oryzae* on rice leaves. Phytopathology 74:635-641.

Morris, C. E., J. M. Monier, and M. A. Jacques. 1997. Methods for observing microbial biofilms directly on leaf surfaces and recovering them for isolation of culturable microorganisms. Appl. Environ. Microbiol. 63:1570-1576.

Morris, C.E., Monier, J-M., and Jacques, M-A. 1998. A technique to quantify the population size and composition of the biofilm component in communities of bacteria in the phyllosphere. Appl. Environ. Microbiol. 64:4789-4795.

Ramos, C., L. Molbak, and S. Molin. 2000. Bacterial activity in the rhizosphere analyzed at the single-cell level by monitoring ribosome contents and synthesis rates. Appl.Environ. Microbiol. 662:801-809.

Ramseier, T. M. 1996. Cra and the control of carbon flux via metabolic pathways. Res. Microbiol. 147:489-493.

Reizer, J., A. Reizer, H. L. Kornberg, and M. H. Saier. 1994. Sequence of the *fruB* gene of *Escherichia coli* encoding the diphosphoryl transfer protein (DTP) of the phosphoenolpyruvate:sugar phosphotransferase system. FEMS Microbiol. Let. 118:159-161.

Rodger, G., and J. P. Blakeman. 1984. Microbial colonization and uptake of ^{14}C label on leaves of sycamore. Trans Br Mycol Soc. 82:45-51.

Roos, I. M. M., and Hattingh, M. J. 1983. Scanning electron microscopy of *Pseudomonas syringae* pv. *morsprunorum* on sweet cherry leaves. Phytopathol. Z. 180:18-25.

Rouse, D. I., E. V. Nordheim, S. S. Hirano and C. D. Upper. 1985. A model relating the probability of foliar disease incidence to the population frequencies of bacterial plant pathogens. Phytopathology 75:505-509.

Saier, M. H., and T. M. Ramseier. 1996. The catabolite repressor/activator (Cra) protein of enteric bacteria. Journal of Bacteriology. 178:3411-3417.

Stadler, B., and T. Mueller. 2000. Effects of aphids and moth caterpillars on epiphytic microorganisms in canopies of forest trees. Can. J. For. Res. 30:631-638.

Sternberg, C., B. B. Christensen, T. Johansen, A. T. Nielsen, J. B. Andersen, M. Givskov, and S. Molin. 1999. Distribution of bacterial growth activity in flow-chamber biofilms. Applied and Environmental Microbiology. 65:4108-4117.

Surico, G. 1993. Scanning electron microscopy of olive and oleander leaves colonized by *Pseudomonas syringae* subsp. *savastanoi*. J. Phytopathology 138:31-40.

Timmer, L. W., J. J. Marois and D. Achor. 1987. Growth and survival of xanthomonads under conditions nonconducive to disease development. Phytopathology 77:1341-1345.

Tsien, R. Y. 1998. The green fluorescent protein, Ann. Rev. Biochem.. 67: 509-544.

Tukey, H. B., Jr. 1970. The leaching of substances from plants. Annu. Rev. Pl. Physiol. 21:305-324.

Warren, R. C. 1972. The effect of pollen on the fungal leaf microflora of *Beta vulgaris* L. and on infection of leaves by *Phoma betae*. Netherlands J. Pl. Pathol. 78:89-98.

Wilson, M., and Lindow, S. E. 1994. Inoculum density-dependent mortality and colonization of the phyllosphere by *Pseudomonas syringae*. Appl. Environ. Microbiol. 60:2232-2237.

Wilson, M., M. A. Savka, I. Hwang, S. K. Farrand, and S. E. Lindow. 1995. Altered epiphytic colonization of mannityl opine-producing transgenic tobacco plants by a mannityl opine-catabolizing strain of *Pseudomonas syringae*. Appl. Environ. Microbiol. 61:2151-2158.

Wolfaardt, G. M., J. R. Lawrence, J. V. Headley, R. D. Robarts, and D. E. Caldwell. 1994. Microbial exopolymers provide a mechanism for bioaccumulation of contaminants. Microbial Ecol. 27:279-291.

Integrating Findings from the Lab and Field: Toward Understanding the Biology of *Pseudomonas syringae* - Plant Interactions

Susan S. Hirano[1] and Christen D. Upper[1,2]

[1]University of Wisconsin-Madison and [1,2]USDA Agricultural Research Service, USA.

Diseases of plants that occur in the field are the central biological phenomena motivating research on pathogen-plant interactions regardless of whether the approach taken to study these diseases stems from molecular, ecological, and/or epidemiological perspectives. For nearly two decades, much energy has been focused on elucidating molecular mechanisms of pathogen-plant interactions. Large numbers of genes associated with disease or resistance reactions have been isolated and characterized from both pathogens and hosts. For the most part, the role(s) and functions of these genes have been examined in laboratory experiments. In this chapter, we discuss our efforts to bridge the gap between what is known about the molecular biology of pathogen-host interactions from laboratory studies and the real world biological phenomena that they would explicate. We use the *P. syringae* pv. syringae (Pss) - bacterial brown spot of snap bean (*Phaseolus vulgaris*) and *P. syringae* pv. tomato (Pst) - bacterial speck disease on tomato (*Lycopersicon esculentum*) systems to study the role(s) of pathogenicity-associated genes in natural interactions of *P. syringae* (Ps) with plants and the effects of these genes on field fitness of the bacterium.

Lifestyle of *Pseudomonas syringae,* or Why Go to the Field?

P. syringae causes disease. This is what the bacterium is most noted for. However, the bacterium often spends many generations in association with leaves without causing disease. In this sense, Ps behaves similarly to the numerous commensals that inhabit the surfaces of leaves. Unlike these commensals, however, Ps is able to exploit the intercellular spaces as well as the surfaces of leaves (cf. Hirano and Upper 2000).

Colonization of leaves in the field is initiated by the arrival of Ps on leaf surfaces but is only successful if the immigrants multiply there. In Wisconsin, intense rains provide the environmental conditions favorable for rapid multiplication of *P. syringae* on snap beans, tomato, and other annual crops. The increased pathogen population sizes resulting from intense rains frequently, but not always, result in the development of disease. In the absence of intense rains, population sizes of *P. syringae* remain small and little or no disease develops. Indeed, the quantitative dose-response relationships established for Pss population sizes and likelihood of disease development in the field (Lindemann et al. 1984; Rouse et al. 1985) demonstrate that any factor that limits multiplication of the bacterium will decrease the likelihood of disease occurrence.

Disease in the field may be viewed as the last stage in a series of processes many of which can affect the amount of disease that occurs. In the laboratory, pathogenicity/virulence is commonly assessed by infiltrating bacteria into leaves. Although such assays are an appropriate first step toward understanding the effects of genes in pathogen-plant interactions, they circumvent a large proportion of the natural interactions that occur between bacteria and plants in the field. Environmental conditions are held constant in laboratory assays. It is paradoxical that in the field intense rainfalls are crucial to increases in pathogen population sizes and hence, the likelihood of disease occurrence but such events are not necessary for multiplication of *P. syringae* in/on growth chamber grown plants.

In the experiments with the Pss-snap bean system described below, we introduced test bacterial strains onto the seeds at the time of planting. The bacteria grew for many generations in association with the germinating seeds and were presumably well adapted to field conditions by the time the plants emerged. The effects of genes on iterative cycles of immigration, emigration, growth, and death were determined by measuring bacterial population sizes on plant samples over time. All mutant strains tested were derived from the field-competent wild type strain Pss B728a.

Genes in the *hrp* and *gac* Regulons

Among the genes that are reported to be required for pathogenicity in *P. syringae* pathovars, none has received as much attention as genes in the *hrp* cluster. A subset of *hrp* genes encode components of a novel type III secretion system via which effector molecules are thought to be delivered directly into plant cells. In laboratory assays, *hrp* mutants are impaired in their abilities to cause disease and to grow to wild-type levels on susceptible plants. Thus, we expected that in the field, *hrp* secretion mutants of Pss B728a would not colonize plants well and would not cause brown spot lesions. Our predictions were not entirely correct.

Growth of the two *hrp* secretion mutants tested (Δ*hrcC::nptII* and *hrpJ*::ΩSpc) was similar to that of the wild-type strain on pre-emergent seedlings (Hirano et al. 1999). Thus, the type III secretion system appears not to be required for growth of B728a before plant emergence. In one field experiment, environmental conditions were unusually favorable and unusually large population sizes of the mutants and wild type occurred on seedlings just prior to their emergence. At 12 days after planting (DAP), some primary leaves taken from plots inoculated with the mutants harbored population sizes that were sufficiently large to be predictive of brown spot disease for strains capable of causing disease. At 14 DAP, brown spot lesions were detected in plots inoculated with the *hrp* secretion mutants. Amounts of disease found in the plots inoculated with mutants (~4% incidence) and wild type (~60% incidence) were consistent with the previously demonstrated dose-response relationship for brown spot disease in the field. Over time, population sizes of the secretion mutants associated with leaves decreased significantly relative to B728a. The mutants did not grow in response to rains that triggered growth of the wild type strain.

Findings from the field confirm laboratory findings that *hrp* genes are required for leaf-associated growth of Pss. *hrp* genes are fundamental growth-enabling genes that are critical for the successful colonization of leaves by Pss. However, the secretion mutants did cause disease under conditions that favored pathogen population growth on pre-emergent and very young emergent plants, indicating that *hrp* genes are not absolutely required for lesion formation, if at all.

The genetic determinants most directly responsible for brown spot lesion formation appear to be in the *gac* regulon. *gacS* and *gacA* encode a two-component regulatory system that function as the master regulator of a signal transduction pathway with branches leading to lesion formation and many other phenotypes (Hrabak and Willis 1992; Kitten et al. 1998). We tested *gacS*, *salA* and *syrB* mutants of B728a. GacS and GacA regulate expression of *salA*. SalA regulates expression of genes required for lesion formation and production of syringomycin. *syrB* is a structural gene required for syringomycin production.

Similar to *hrp* mutants, *gacS* and *salA* mutants of B728a are impaired in lesion formation in laboratory leaf infiltration assays. However, unlike *hrp* mutants, growth of *gacS* and *salA* mutants is indistinguishable from that of B728a in infiltration assays. B728a *syrB* mutants cause pathogenic reactions similar to the wild-type strain. Because the phenotypes of the mutants exhibit different levels of pleiotropy and the genes function at different tiers in the regulon, we want to determine the relative quantitative effects of these genes on fitness of Pss in the field.

In contrast to the laboratory findings, under field conditions population sizes of the *gacS*, *salA*, and *syrB* mutant were significantly different from B728a and from each other (Hirano and Upper, unpublished). In one experiment, population sizes of the mutants relative to B728a were decreased by ~150-fold for *gacS* (range ~10 to 1,000-fold), 5 to 6-fold for *salA* (range ~2 to 20-fold), and 2-3-fold for *syrB*. In a different experiment, a few brown spot lesions were detected in plots inoculated with the *salA* mutant. However, the amount of disease caused by the *salA* mutant (~2% incidence) was much less than expected based on the relatively large population sizes that the mutant established in association with bean leaves. Incidence of disease caused by the *syrB* mutant was ~40% and not statistically different from B728a (~50%).

Although the *hrp* and *gac* regulon mutants have not been compared in the same experiment, findings from multiple field experiments indicate that the relative fitness of these mutants and B728a may be ordered as: *hrcC* and *hrpJ* mutants < *gacS* mutant < *salA* mutant < *syrB* mutant < B728a. Thus, *hrcC* and genes in the *hrpJ* operon (and therefore, presumably the type III secretion system) have the greatest impact on growth of Pss. *hrp* genes may control the outcome of early interactions between bacterium and leaf soon after immigration. Genes in the *gacS* regulon but not regulated by *salA* also contribute significantly to overall fitness of Pss. The findings to date suggest that the genes regulated by *salA* other than those involved in syringomycin production may be the genetic determinants that are directly involved in brown spot lesion formation. Population sizes of the *salA* mutant relative to wild type indicate that lesion formation *per se* may not have as large an effect on fitness as we expected. Syringomycin production had a quantitative, albeit small, effect on population sizes of B728a.

The *avrpto - Pto* System

To study the role of avirulence (*avr*) genes in the ecology of Ps, we extended our field experiments to the Pst - bacterial speck disease system. *avrPto* (Ronald et al. 1992) and the corresponding resistance gene *Pto* (Martin et al., 1993) have emerged as a model system for studies on the genetic and biochemical basis for race-cultivar specificity. However, at least one important aspect of the biology of the *avrPto-Pto* system remains to be resolved. While plasmid-borne *avrPto* converted previously virulent strains of Pst (i.e. race 1) to avirulence on *Pto* plants, mutation of *avrPto* in race 0 strains (source of the *avrPto* gene) did not alter their race specificity (Ronald et al. 1992). Thus, *avrPto* alone does not explain the avirulence phenotype of race 0 strains on *Pto* plants.

The availability of the near-isogenic lines Rio Grande (susceptible; RG-S) and Rio Grande PtoR (resistant, RG-PtoR) rendered this an attractive system to explore in the field. Although DC3000 has been used extensively in laboratory studies, the strain performed poorly in the field. Hence, we chose a strain (streptomycin resistant derivative of SM78-1) that is field-competent and highly virulent under field conditions. Similar to the Pss-snap bean system, the dynamics of populations sizes of SM78-1Sm[r] on RG-

S plants could be largely explained by the occurrence of intense rainfalls. Mean pathogen population sizes were roughly 4 to 5 orders of magnitude larger on RG-S than RG-PtoR plants. Thus, RG-PtoR plants were remarkably effective in attenuating pathogen population development.

Although most leaflets from RG-PtoR plots had very small numbers of SM78-1Sm[r], a few leaflets bore 10^5 to 10^6 CFU/leaflet. Isolates recovered from these leaves caused typical speck lesions on RG-PtoR plants in growth chamber assays. The phenotype of the isolates on growth-chamber inoculated RG-PtoR and RG-S plants was characteristic of race 1 strains of Pst. Hence, the isolates appeared to be race-shift mutants of SM78-1Sm[r]. Similar race-shift mutants were found in growth chamber experiments with SM78-1 on RG-PtoR plants. When total genomic DNA from the race-shift mutants was probed with the *avrPto* gene in Southern analysis, no hybridizing bands were found as was the case for naturally occurring race 1 strains (Ronald et al. 1992). Thus, the SM78-1 race-shift mutants appear to carry a deletion that includes the *avrPto* gene. Whether the deleted region contains additional avirulence genes that govern race-specificity in race 0 strains is under investigation as is the effect of the mutation on fitness of SM78-1 on RG-S and RG-PtoR plants in the field.

Literature Cited

Hirano, S. S., A. O. Charkowski, A. Collmer, D. K. Willis, and C. D. Upper. 1999. Role of the Hrp type III protein secretion system in growth of *Pseudomonas syringae* pv. *syringae* B728a on host plants in the field. Proc. Natl. Acad. Sci. USA 96:9851-9856.

Hirano, S. S., and C. D. Upper. 2000. Bacteria in the leaf ecosystem with emphasis on *Pseudomonas syringae*--a pathogen, ice nucleus, and epiphyte. Microbiol. Mol. Biol. Rev. 64:624-653.

Hrabak, E. M., and D. K. Willis. 1992. The *lemA* gene required for pathogenicity of *Pseudomonas syringae* pv. syringae on bean is a member of a family of two-component regulators. J. Bacteriol. 174:3011-3020.

Kitten, T., T. G. Kinscherf, J. L. McEvoy, and D. K. Willis. 1998. A newly-identified regulator is required for virulence and toxin production in *Pseudomonas syringae*. Mol. Microbiol. 28:917-929.

Lindemann, J., D. C. Arny, and C. D. Upper. 1984. Use of an apparent infection threshold population of *Pseudomonas syringae* to predict incidence and severity of brown spot of bean. Phytopathology 74:1334-1339.

Martin, G. B., S. H. Brommonschenkel, J. Chunwongse, A. Frary, M. W. Ganal, R. Spivey, T. Wu, E. D. Earle, and S. D. Tanksley. 1993. Map-based cloning of a protein kinase gene conferring disease resistance in tomato. Science 262:1432-1436.

Ronald, P. C., J. M. Salmeron, F. M. Carland, and B. J. Staskawicz. 1992. The cloned avirulence gene *avrPto* induces disease resistance in tomato cultivars containing the *Pto* resistance gene. J. Bacteriol. 174:1604-1611.

Rouse, D. I., E. V. Nordheim, S. S. Hirano, and C. D. Upper. 1985. A model relating the probability of foliar disease incidence to the population frequencies of bacterial plant pathogens. Phytopathology 75:505-509.

Positive and Negative Cross-Communication Among Rhizobacteria

Leland S. Pierson, Elizabeth A. Pierson and Joanne E. Morello

Department of Plant Pathology, The University of Arizona, Tucson, AZ USA

The establishment of a stable rhizosphere community requires sophisticated interactions among the members of that community. A common view is that most rhizosphere interactions are aimed at removing competition and establishing a majority population. In reality, however, rhizosphere interactions may result in the establishment of mixed communities (biofilms) that optimize the rhizosphere environment. For example, some members of a community may convert plant exudates into forms available to other community members. Alternatively, some members may alter the redox environment, thus favoring others. In return, some community members may provide survival advantages, such as the inhibition of other species via antagonism, etc. This is not to imply that natural selection is occurring at the community level, only that natural selection occurring on individuals may result in the formation of organized communities. If we are going to try to manipulate this complex rhizosphere ecosystem for improved plant health, these complex interactions need to be better understood. One focus of our group is to study mechanisms responsible for the survival and persistence of beneficial bacterial species as members of a rhizosphere community.

The regulation of phenazine antibiotic production in the biological control bacterium *Pseudomonas aureofaciens* 30-84 is a model system to study the influence of the root microbial community on the expression of microbial genes involved in competition and pathogen inhibition. *P. aureofaciens*, isolated from wheat roots taken from a field in which the take-all pathogen *Gaeumannomyces graminis* var. *tritici* (Ggt) was naturally suppressed, produces three phenazine antibiotics (Pierson & Thomashow 1992). These orange phenazines are responsible for the strain's ability to inhibit fungal pathogens and survive in the rhizosphere in competition with the indigenous community (Mazzola et al. 1992). We are studying the influence of the microbial community on phenazine production by strain

30-84. We showed that phenazine gene (*phz*) expression is dependent on the PhzR/PhzI *N*-acyl-homoserine lactone (AHL)-mediated regulatory system (Pierson et al. 1994; Wood & Pierson 1996). PhzR is the transcriptional activator, and PhzI is the AHL synthase. Under *in vitro* conditions, *phz* expression only occurs when the level of endogenous AHL signal reaches a threshold concentration. We previously identified a subpopulation of the wheat rhizosphere community (*ca.* 8%) that stimulated *phz* gene expression via AHL production (Wood et al. 1997).

Here we re-screened this rhizosphere community to determine whether other subpopulations inhibited phenazine production in strain 30-84.

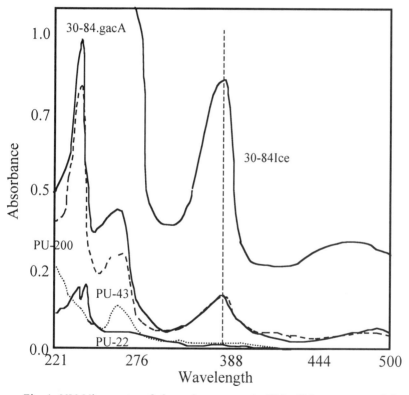

Fig. 1. UV-Vis spectra of phenazines grown in CM. CM was prepared from 30-84.gacA (Chancey et al. 1999) (produces no AHLs), two negative strains (PU-22, PU-43), a neutral strain (PU-200), and 30-84Ice (produces HHL but does not synthesize phenazines). Phenazines are quantified by absorbance at 367 nm. Note the loss of absorbance at 367 nm indicative of inhibition of phenazine production by CM from the negative strains.

Isolating and Screening Rhizobacteria for Cross-Communication

Wheat plants taken from 3 geographic areas were used to isolate a random library (*ca.* 800 strains) of wheat rhizobacteria. Individual isolates were grown and spotted onto strain 30-84I (PhzI⁻), an AHL-dependent indicator strain that appears white due to the loss of phenazine production, and onto strain 30-84. Positive cross-communication was indicated by an orange halo surrounding the strains spotted onto strain 30-84I indicative of the production of a signal that complemented 30-84I for phenazine production. Negative cross-communication was indicated by white halos surrounding the strains spotted onto strain 30-84 indicative of the inhibition of phenazine production.

Uv-Vis Spectra of Phenazines Produced by Strain 30-84 Grown in Different Conditioned Medium (Cm)

CM was comprised of filter-sterilized culture supernatant mixed with fresh medium. Strain 30-84 was inoculated and total phenazines extracted after 24 h (Fig. 1).

NEGATIVE STRAINS BLOCK *PHZ* GENE EXPRESSION

Table 1 indicates the results when the *phzB::lacZ* reporter 30-84Z is grown in CM prepared from several negative strains.

Table 1. Expression of *lacZ* in Conditioned Medium by Negative Strains

CM Source	β-Galactosidase Activity
30-84.gacA (Control)	117 ± 19
PU-5	29 ± 9
PU-15	28 ± 8
PU-22	21 ± 0
PU-31	31 ± 14
PU-43	34 ± 5
PU-200 (Neutral Control)	106 ± 19
PI-34 (Positive Control)	241 ± 0

CM was prepared from the indicated strains. Strain 30-84Z was washed, inoculated, and β-galactosidase activity was measured after 24 h.
Note: as compared to strain 30-84.gacA, the neutral strain (PU-200) and the positive cross-communicating strain PI-34, CM prepared from all negative strains resulted in lower β-galactosidase activity by strain 30-84Z.

ETHYL ACETATE EXTRACTS OF NEGATIVE STRAINS INDICATE TWO MECHANISMS OF NEGATIVE CROSS-COMMUNICATION

Ethyl acetate extractions were prepared from several negative strains. These dried extracts could contain, among other compounds, *N*-acyl-homoserine lactones (AHLs), furanones and diketopiperazines that have been shown to be involved in inhibition of AHL-mediated gene expression (Givskov et al. 1996; Holden et al. 1999; Tepliski et al. 2000). The effect of these extracts on *phzB::lacZ* expression in the AHL-reporter strain 30-84I/Z (a *phzI* mutant unable to produce its endogenous AHL signal) is shown in Table 2 while Table 3 indicates their effect on strain 30-84Z (*phzI⁺*).

EXTRA COPIES OF PHZI REDUCE INHIBITION OF PHZ EXPRESSION

The presence of *phzI* on a low copy number plasmid decreased the effect of the negative signals on *phz* expression (data not shown). This result is consistent with the hypothesis that these signals may compete for PhzR binding.

NEGATIVE STRAINS REDUCE GGT INHIBITION BY STRAIN 30-84 *IN VITRO*

Co-inoculation of strain 30-84 with negative strains reduced its ability to inhibit growth of the take-all pathogen *Gaeumannomyces graminis* var. *tritici* (Ggt) (Table 4).

Table 2. Effect of extracts on *phzB* expression in strain 30-84I/Z.

AHL Source	β-Galactosidase Activity
30-84.gacA (Control)	46 ± 8^A
30-84Ice	455 ± 8^B
PU-5	30 ± 11^A
PU-15	49 ± 9^A
PU-22	76 ± 11^C
PU-177	51 ± 3^A
PU-200 (Neutral strain)	36 ± 17^A
PU-295	53 ± 7^A

Cell-free supernatants of the indicated strains were extracted. Fresh medium was added to the dried extracts, the extracts were inoculated with washed 30-84IZ, and β-galactosidase activity was measured after 24 h. Note that none of the AHL extracts affected *phzB::lacZ* expression except for strain PU-22.

Table 3. Effect of extracts on *phzB* expression in strain 30-84Z.

AHL Source	β-Galactosidase Activity
30-84.gacA (Control)	415 ± 52^A
30-84Ice	636 ± 488^B
PU-5	197 ± 37^C
PU-7	392 ± 20^A
PU-15	186 ± 51^C
PU-22	475 ± 77^A
PU-43	776 ± 221^B
PU-86	530 ± 270^A
PU-200 (Neutral strain)	342 ± 185^A
PU-295	334 ± 177^A

Fresh medium was added to the extracts and strain 30-84Z, and β-galactosidase activity was measured (24 h). Note the AHL extracts had no effect, except for strains PU-5 & PU-15 that reduced *phzB::lacZ* expression while the strain PU-43 actually increased expression.

Table 4. *In vitro* Ggt plate inhibition assays.

Strain(s)	(FI) Fungal Inhibition (mm)
30-84	9 ± 1
PU-5	0 ± 0
PU-15	0 ± 0
30-85 & 5 (1:1)	2 ± 1.1
30-84 & 15 (1:1)	1 ± 2.3

Strain 30-84 alone, a negative strain alone, or a 1:1 mix were spotted onto KMPE plates. A fresh Ggt plug was placed in the center of the plate and fungal growth was followed. FI = zone of inhibition between the bacterial colony to the edge of the mycelium. Note the loss of inhibition in the mix.

Summary

We showed previously that a sub-population of the wheat rhizosphere community activated phz expression. We now show that:

(1) A 2nd sub-population of this community negatively affected the ability of strain 30-84 to produce phenazines.

(2) 'Conditioned medium' from these strains interfered with the *phz* gene expression. This inhibition could be overcome by introducing additional copies of *phzI*, consistent with the hypothesis that these signals may compete for PhzR binding.

(3) The nature of the signal(s) responsible for *phz* gene inhibition is currently unclear, but our results suggest at least two separate mechanisms of negative signaling may exist.

Current work is focused on studying the mechanisms involved in these negative interactions using both genetic and natural product approaches.

Conclusion: Inter-population signaling among the rhizosphere community may play a major role in determining the success or failure of introduced biological control strains by directly influencing colonization, persistence and expression of the mechanism(s) responsible for pathogen inhibition.

Literature Cited

Chancey, S.T., Wood, D.W., and Pierson, L.S. 1999. Two-component transcriptional regulation of *N*-acyl-homoserine lactone production in *Pseudomonas aureofaciens*. Appl. Environ. Microbiol. 65:2294-2299.

Givskov, M., de Nys, R., Manefield, M., Gram, L., Maximilien, R., Eberl, L., Molin, S., Steinberg, P.D., and Kjelleberg, S. 1996.Eukaryotic interference with with homoserine lactone-mediated prokaryotic signaling. J. Bacteriol. 178:6618-6622.

Holden, T.G., Chhabra, S.R., de Nys, R., Stead, P., Bainton, N.J., Hill, P.J., Manefield, M., Kumar, N., Labatte, M., England, D., Rice, S., Givskov, M., Salmond, G.P.C., Stewart, G.S.A.B., Bycroft, B.W., Kjelleberg, S., and Williams, P. 1999. Quorum-sensing cross talk: isolation and chemical characterization of cyclic dipeptides from *Pseudomonas aeruginosa* and other Gram-negative bacteria. Molec. Microbiol. 33:1254-1266.

Mazzola, M., Cook, R.J., Thomashow, L.S., Weller, D.M., and L.S. Pierson. 1992. Contribution of phenazine antibiotic biosynthesis to the ecological competence of fluorescent pseudomonads in soil habitats. Appl. Environ. Microbiol. 58:2616-2624.

Pierson, E.A., Wood, D.W., Cannon, J.A., Blachere, F.M., and Pierson, L.S. 1998. Interpopulation signaling via *N*-acyl-homoserine lactones among bacteria in the wheat rhizosphere. Molec. Plant-Microbe Interact. 11:1078-1084.

Pierson, L.S., Keppenne, V.D., and Wood, D.W. 1994. Phenazine antibiotic biosynthesis in *Pseudomonas aureofaciens* 30-84 is regulated by PhzR in response to cell density. J. Bacteriol. 176:3966-3974. Pierson, L.S., and L.S. Thomashow. 1992. Cloning and heterologous expression of the phenazine biosynthetic locus from *Pseudomonas aureofaciens* 30-84. Mol. Plant Microbe Interact. 5:330-339.

Teplitski, M., Robinson, J.B., and Bauer, W.D. 2000. Plants secrete substances that mimic bacterial *N*-acyl-homoserine lactone signal activities and affect population density-dependent behaviors in associated bacteria. Mol. Plant Microbe Interact. 13:637-648.

Thomashow, L.S., and Weller, D.M. 1988. Role of a phenazine antibiotic from *Pseudomonas fluorescens* in biological control of *Gaeumannomyces graminis* var. *tritici*. J. Bacteriol. 170:3499-3508.

Wood, D.W., and Pierson, L. S. 1996. The *phzI* gene of *Pseudomonas aureofaciens* 30-84 is responsible for the production of a diffusible signal required for phenazine antibiotic production. Gene 168:49-53.

Wood, D.W., Gong, F,. Daykin, M.M., Williams, P., and Pierson, L.S. III. 1997. *N*-acyl-homoserine lactone-mediated regulation of phenazine gene expression by *Pseudomonas aureofaciens* 30-84 in the wheat rhizosphere. J. Bacteriol. 179:7663-7670.

Life in Grasses: Interactions of Diazotrophic Endophytes and Rice

Sonja Wiese[1], Jörg Plessl[1], Thomas Hurek[2] and Barbara Reinhold-Hurek[1]

[1]University Bremen, [2]Max-Planck-Institute for Marine Microbiology, Bremen, Germany

Plant roots offer a variety of microhabitats for microbial colonization. In addition to the rhizosphere soil and the plant surface (rhizoplane), inner root tissues may be colonized, as well. Plant-bacteria systems which have recently gained attention are associations between endophytic, nitrogen-fixing bacteria and grasses or cereals (Reinhold-Hurek and Hurek 1998). Well-studied examples are members of the beta-subclass of the *Proteobacteria*, *Azoarcus* spp. and *Herbaspirillum seropedicae*, or a member of the alpha-subclass, *Gluconacetobacter diazotrophicus* (formerly *Acetobacter diazotrophicus*). They infect Kallar grass and rice (Hurek et al. 1994), a wide range of grasses and cereals (James and Olivares 1998; James et al. 1997) or sugar cane and coffee plants (James et al. 1994; Jiminez-Salgado et al. 1997), respectively. Surprisingly, also rhizobia have been found to be natural endophytes of non-legumes, e.g. in rice (Engelhard et al. 2000; Yanni et al. 1997); other endophytes were detected in maize (Palus et al., 1996).

Plant Colonization

These diazotrophic endophytes have several features in common. Unlike rhizobia, they do not survive well in soil. In most cases they cannot be isolated from soil but only from plant material and are thus ecologically dependent on plants (James and Olivares 1998; Reinhold-Hurek and Hurek 1998). In gnotobiotic culture, it was demonstrated that pure cultures of these bacteria are capable of invading plant roots. Points of invasion are the zone of elongation and differentiation close to the root tip and the emergence points of lateral roots (Hurek, et al. 1994; James et al. 1997; James et al. 1994). The colonization is mostly intercellular, only rarely intracellular plant cell colonization is observed. However, these plant cells are not viable (Hurek et al. 1994), and there is no evidence for an endosymbiosis in living plant cells (Reinhold-Hurek and Hurek 1998) in contrast to the rhizobium-legume symbiosis.

The major site of endophytic colonization appears to be the root cortex, especially in the aerenchyma of flood-tolerant plants such as Kallar grass (*Leptochloa fusca* L. (Kunth)) and rice, where large microcolonies of *Azoarcus* sp. BH72 can be found (Egener et al. 1999; Hurek et al. 1994). However, rarely these endophytes do also invade the stele and penetrate xylem vessels, which were previously thought to be sterile in healthy plants. Xylem colonization may facilitate the systemic infection of plants, the bacteria spreading from roots to shoots of young rice plants (Gyaneshwar et al. 2000; Hurek et al. 1994). For other diazotrophic endophytes (*Heraspirillum* spp., *Gluconacetobacter diazotrophicus*), xylem cells appear to be a more frequent colonization site (James and Olivares 1998; Olivares et al. 1997).

Despite the relatively dense colonization (up to almost 10^8 bacteria per g root dry weight for *Azoarcus* sp. BH72 in field-grown Kallar grass (Reinhold et al. 1986), the endophytes do not cause symptoms of plant disease in their host plants. In contrast, in several plants they have been shown to promote plant growth (Hurek et al. 1994; Sevilla et al. 2001). Whether these growth responses are due to bacterial phytohormone production, nitrogen fixation, or other mechanisms may vary with the system and is still under investigation.

Bacterial Gene Expression In Plants

Studies on endophytic bacterial gene expression may lead to a better understanding of the endophyte functions and of their interactions with host plants. Dissecting bacterial gene expression outside and inside roots requires visualization of the gene expression. We used transcriptional fusions of target genes such as *nifH*, one of the structural genes for the nitrogenase complex reducing N_2 to ammonia, with the reporter gene *gfp* (encoding the jellyfish green fluorescent protein) or *gus* (encoding ß-glucuronidase). Infection studies using *Azoarcus* sp. BH72 on rice seedlings in gnotobiotic culture revealed, that bacterial *nifH::gfp* is expressed at high levels inside the roots (Egener et al. 1998; Reinhold-Hurek and Hurek 1998). The sites of nitrogenase gene expression are the infection sites at emerging lateral roots and root tips as well as microcolonies inside the cortex in the aerenchymatic air spaces (Egener et al. 1999). It is remarkable that this endophytic gene expression occurs in the apoplast, apparently depending on apoplastic nutrient flow. Only small amounts of carbon sorce (5 mg of malate per l) were added to the plant medium, thus the endophytic *nifH* gene expression appears to be driven by carbon- and energy sources supplied by the plant. In contrast, in other systems studied such as *Gluconacetobacter diazotrophicus* in sugar cane (James and Olivares 1998) or *Serratia marcescens* in rice (Gyaneshwar, et al. 2000), significant *nif* gene expression was only detected in gnotobiotic systems when high amounts of carbon source were added to the plant medium.

Since *nifH* gene expression in *Azoarcus* sp. BH72 is similarly regulated in response to O_2 and ammonium as is nitrogenase activity (Egener et al. 1999), the reporter gene studies demonstrate that the rice root apoplast may provide a suitable microhabitat for endophytic nitrogen fixation of *Azoarcus* sp. BH72. This is also the case for the host plant from which this strain was originally isolated, Kallar grass (Reinhold et al. 1986). It was shown by *in situ* hybridization studies that field-grown plants harbor *Azoarcus* sp. *nifH* mRNA in the aerenchyma (Hurek et al. 1997).

Rice Cultivars Show Differences In Endophytic *Nif*-Gene Expression By *Azoarcus* Sp.

Recent findings suggest that the assumption that diazotrophic endophytes do not cause damage of plants cannot be generalized. Previously, a phytopathogenic species closely related to *Herbaspirillum seropedicae, H. rubrisubalbicans*, was detected to cause mild symptoms of disease in leaves of certain sugar cane cultivars, in others it grew as a non-pathogenic endophyte (Olivares et al. 1997). In our laboratory, a recent screening of rice cultivars with respect to endophytic *nifH::gus* expression revealed significant, cultivar-specific differences in response to *Azoarcus* sp. strain BH72. Some cultivars supported high levels of root-associated *nifH::gus* expression, while no significant expression could be detected in others. All of the latter cultivars showed browning of roots upon inoculation, probably due to lignification and accumulation of phenolic substances. This plant reaction, which resembled a plant defense response, required bacterial colonization: A mutant of *Azoarcus* sp. strain BH72 lacking type IV pili was previously shown to be deficient in effective colonization of rice roots (Dörr et al. 1998). Type IV pili are are also know in animal and human pathogens as virulence factors mediating attachment to the host tissue. This mutant did not cause the plant response upon inculation, indicating that physical contact of roots and bacteria is necessary to elicit that plant response. Further studies on plant defense genes which might be induced are on the way. Interestingly, the structural genes of the type IV pilin, *pilAB*, are transcriptionally upregulated in response to carbon source starvation and in a culture-density-dependent manner, probably by a novel type of autoinducer for quorum sensing.

Literature Cited

Dörr, J., Hurek, T. and Reinhold-Hurek, B. 1998. Type IV pili are involved in plant-microbe and fungus-microbe interactions. Molecular

Microbiology 30:7-17.

Egener, T., Hurek, T. and Reinhold-Hurek, B. 1998. Use of green fluorescent protein to detect expression of *nif* genes of *Azoarcus* sp. BH72, a grass-associated diazotroph, on rice roots. Mol. Plant Microbe Interact. 11:71-75.

Egener, T., Hurek, T. and Reinhold-Hurek, B. 1999. Endophytic expression of *nif* genes of *Azoarcus* sp. strain BH72 in rice roots. Mol. Plant Microbe Interact. 12:813-819.

Engelhard, M., Hurek, T. and Reinhold-Hurek, B. 2000. Preferential occurrence of diazotrophic endophytes, *Azoarcus* spp., in wild rice species and land races of *Oryza sativa* in comparison with modern races. Environmental Microbiology 2:131-141.

Gyaneshwar, P., James, E. K., Mathan, N., Reddy, P. M., Reinhold-Hurek, B. and Ladha, J. K. 2001. Endophytic colonization of rice by a diazotrophic strain of *Serratia marcescens*. J. Bacteriology 183:2634-2645.

Hurek, T., Egener, T. and Reinhold-Hurek, B. 1997. Divergence in nitrogenases of *Azoarcus* spp., *Proteobacteria* of the ß-subclass. J. Bacteriology 179:4172-4178.

Hurek, T., Reinhold-Hurek, B., Turner, G. L. and Bergersen, F. J. 1994. Augmented rates of respiration and efficient nitrogen fixation at nanomolar concentrations of dissolved O_2 in hyperinduced *Azoarcus* sp. strain BH72. J. Bacteriology 176:4726-4733.

Hurek, T., Reinhold-Hurek, B., Van Montagu, M. and Kellenberger, E. 1994. Root colonization and systemic spreading of *Azoarcus* sp. strain BH72 in grasses. J. Bacteriology 176:1913-1923.

James, E. K. and Olivares, F. L. 1998. Infection and colonization of sugar cane and other graminaceous plants by endophytic diazotrophs. Critical Reviews in Plant Sciences 17:77-119.

James, E. K., Olivares, F. L., Baldani, J. I. and Döbereiner, J. 1997. *Herbaspirillum*, an endophytic diazotroph colonizing vascular tissue in leaves of *Sorghum bicolor* L. Moench. J. Experimental Botany 48: 785-797.

James, E. K., Reis, V. M., Olivares, F. L., Baldandi, J. I. and Döbereiner, J. 1994. Infection of sugar cane by the nitrogen-fixing bacterium *Acetobacter diazotrophicus*. J. Experimental Botany 45:757-766.

Jiminez-Salgado, T., Fuentes-Ramirez, L. E., Tapia-Hernandez, A., Mascarua-Esparza, M. A., Martinez-Romero, E. and Caballero-Mellado, J. 1997. *Coffea arabica* L., a new host plant for *Acetobacter diazotrophicus*, and isolation of other nitrogen-fixing acetobacteria. Appl. Environ. Microbiology 63:3676-3683.

Olivares, F. L., James, E. K., Baldani, J. I. and Döbereiner, J. 1997. Infection of mottled stripe disease-susceptible and resistant sugar cane varieties by the endophytic diazotroph *Herbaspirillum*. New Phytologist 135:723-737.

Palus, J. A., Borneman, J., Ludden, P. W. and Triplett, E. W. 1996. A diazotrophic bacterial endophyte isolated from stems of *Zea mays* L and

266

Zea luxurians Iltis and Doebley. Plant and Soil 186:135-142.

Reinhold, B., Hurek, T., Niemann, E.-G. and Fendrik, I. 1986. Close association of *Azospirillum* and diazotrophic rods with different root zones of Kallar grass. Appl. Environ. Microbiology 52:520-526.

Reinhold-Hurek, B. and Hurek, T. 1998. Interactions of gramineous plants with *Azoarcus* spp. and other diazotrophs: Identification, localization and perspectives to study their function. Critical Reviews in Plant Sciences 17: 29-54.

Reinhold-Hurek, B. and Hurek, T. 1998. Life in grasses: diazotrophic endophytes. Trends in Microbiology 6:139-144.

Sevilla, M., Burris, R. H., Gunapala, N. and Kennedy, C. 2001. Comparison of benefit to sugarcane plant growth and $^{15}N_2$ incorporation following inoculation of sterile plants with *Acetobacter diazotrophicus* wild-type and *nif* mutant strains. Mol. Plant Microbe Interact. 14:358-366.

Yanni, Y. G., Rizk, R. Y., Corich, V., Squartini, A., Ninke, K., Philip-Hollingsworth, S., Orgambide, G., De Bruijn, F., Stoltzfus, J., Buckley, D., Schmidt, T. M., Mateos, P. F., Ladha, J. K. and Dazzo, F. B. 1997. Natural endophytic association between *Rhizobium leguminosarum* bv. *trifolii* and rice roots and assessment of its potential to promote rice growth. Plant and Soil 194:99-114.

Biochemical Bases of Marine Plant-Microbe Interactions : Novel Evidence on the Evolution of Plant Immunity

B. Kloareg, K. Bouarab, F. Adas, G. Pohnert[1], J.-P. Salaün and P. Potin

UMR 1931, CNRS and Laboratoires Goëmar, Station Biologique de Roscoff, France; [1] Max-Planck Institut für Chemische Ökologie, Jena, Germany

Marine red algae (Rhodophytes) have emerged as independent eukaryotic lineages as early as one billion years ago, and one may ask whether the principles that govern plant-pathogen interactions in terrestrial organisms also apply to the distant lineages found in the sea. Using a pathosystem consisting of the red alga *Chondrus crispus* (the host) and of the filamentous green alga *Acrochaete operculata* (the pathogen), we here report the first data on the biochemical bases of natural immunity in red algae. It appears that these marine plants are endowed with defense mechanisms similar to those found in other lineages, such as the oxidative burst response, the induction of oxylipins and of the phenylpropanoid metabolism, thus providing new insights as to the evolution of immunity in eukaryotes. In addition, and probably specific to their marine environment, *C. crispus* releases halogenated, toxic compounds and does not exhibit systemic responses.

In the Sea Also, Plant and Microbes Interact

MARINE ALGAE FACE A NUMBER OF ENEMIES

In the last decade, we have gained knowledge on the phenomenology of the diseases that can affect marine magroalgae, both in terms of causative agents and symptoms. Altogether, struggle for life in the sea appears as tough as on land, as marine algae have to fend off a number of foes, including viruses, bacteria, fungi, other algae, as well as grazers. These pests can cause problems in the mariculture of algal crops, such as kombu (*Laminaria japonica*) and nori (*Porphyra yezoensis*, *P. tenera*) in Eastern Asia. Yet, in the natural algal populations, outbreaks of diseases are rarely seen and grazers are kept in check. It obviously follows that marine algae are naturally immunised against these potential pathogens.

PATHOGENS ARE NO FOOLS, THEY RECOGNIZE THEIR HOST

In order to decipher the biochemistry of defenses in red algae, we are investigating a marine plant-pathogen model system in which the host is a parenchymatous red alga, *Chondrus crispus*, and the pathogen a filamentous green alga, *Acrochaete operculata* (Correa and MacLachlan 1991). *C. crispus* features an isomorphic life history, in which the gametophytic and sporophytic generations differ by minor traits only, such as the sulfate-ester group distribution of their matrix polysaccharides, kappa- and lambda-carrageenans, respectively. Interestingly, the sporophytic generation is highly susceptible to infection by the green algal pathogen, whereas the gametophytic phase is naturally resistant. Using unialgal cultures of *A. operculata* grown in the presence of carrageenan oligosaccharides, we demonstrated that oligosaccharide signals from the sensitive generation of the host enhanced the virulence of the pathogen. Reciprocally, those carrageenan oligosaccharides prepared from the host resistant generation inhibited the virulence of the pathogen zoospores, to the extent that they could no longer infect the naturally sensitive *C. crispus* sporophytes (Bouarab et al. 1999). Another example of host recognition through its matrix polysaccharides was reported recently in marine pathosystems. Porphyran, a sulfated agar, was shown to enhance appressorium formation in *Pythium porphyrae*, the agent of red rot disease in cultures of *Porphyra yezoensis* (Uppalapati and Fujita 2000).

The Biochemical Bases of Natural Immunity in Red Algae

PATHOGEN RECOGNITION AND EARLY DEFENSES RESPONSES

Irrespective of the pathogen behavior, however, the first line of defense of the red algal host is recognition of the attacker. Unlike the sensitive, sporophytic generation, *C. crispus* gametophytes reacted by a significant release of hydrogen peroxide in their culture medium when challenged by *A. operculata* cell-free extracts. That this oxidative burst reaction is an essential element in *C. crispus* immunity was demonstrated in loss-of-function experiments with diphenylene iodonium, which both completely inhibited the oxidative burst and abolished the natural resistance of the gametophytes (Bouarab et al. 1999). A further indication is the observation that *A. operculata* cells are killed by short (30 min) exposures to 0.5-1 mM hydrogen peroxide, a concentration which is consistent with the amount of H_2O_2 accumulated in the host apoplasm at the peak of the burst. Examples of attack recognition through the perception of endogenous elicitors were also reported recently in marine algae. Both the brown alga *Laminaria digitata* and the red alga *Gracilaria conferta* react by an oxidative burst to the presence of degradation products from their own cell walls (Küpper et al. 2001; Weinberger et al. 2001).

Perhaps more unique to marine algae is the release, concomitantly with the oxidative burst, of halogenated, toxic chemicals. Halocarbons are the reaction products of carbon skeletons with hypohalous acids, produced from halides (X^-) and oxygen radicals by haloperoxidases (Fig. 1). Compared to controls, *C. crispus* gametophytes challenged with *A. operculata* extracts produced ten times more of iodoethane, chloroform and bromoform, and these accumulated in the culture medium up to concentrations as high as 50-1000 ng$\,l^{-1}$. Since their IC50 values against *A. operculata* cells were as low as in the 0.5-5 nmolar range, these halocarbons are very likely to account in the natural immunity of *C. crispus* gametophytes against this pathogen.

TRANSDUCTION OF DEFENSE SIGNALS

The transduction pathways that are essential in the natural immunity of *C. crispus* (Fig. 1) were then dissected by monitoring or inhibiting the activity of likely candidates for these routes. Activation of the oxidase requires the opening of ion channels, the action of phospholipases, as well as the involvement of protein kinases. Inhibition of any of these steps by the appropriate drugs (Fig.1) suppressed the resistance. Various lipid hydroperoxides are produced with the oxidative burst, which were identified by GC-MS. They were not only derived from arachidonic acid, the "animal-type" eicosanoic fatty acid already well documented in red algae (Gerwick et al. 1993), but also from linolenic and linoleic acids, the octadecanoids common in higher plants. Two lipoxygenase isoforms were shown to be upregulated, specific for the metabolisation of linoleic acid, and lipoxygenase inhibitors again abolished the natural resistance of *C. crispus* gametophytes. Moreover, in gain-of-function experiments by which *C. crispus* sporophytes were treated with HPETE, HPODE or methyl-jasmonate, transient resistance to *A. operculata* was induced, confirming the dual nature of the oxylipin defense pathway in this alga.

ACTIVATION OF THE PHENYPROPANOID METABOLISM

Reminiscent of the deposition of phenolics in higher plants, *C. crispus* gametophytes synthesise UV-absorbing compounds around the settling sites of *A. operculata* zoospores, whereas this response is absent in the sensitive generation. Although the exact structure of these compounds remains to be identified, HPLC analysis confirmed that they are aromatic in nature, suggesting the involvement of phenylpropanoid metabolism. *A. operculata* extracts indeed activated two key enzymes of this pathway, shikimate dehydrogenase and phenylalanine-ammonia lyase. Consistently again, glyphosate and AOPP inhibited the activation of these enzymes, prevented

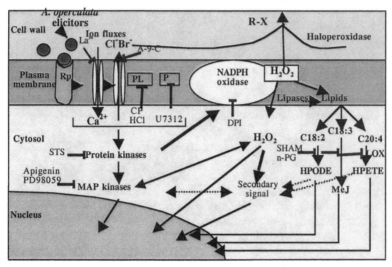

Fig. 1. Signaling events and early defense responses in the marine red alga
C. crispus following challenging by the green alga *A. operculata*.

the acumulation of UV-fluorescent compounds and abolished the resistance
of *C. crispus* gametophytes. Phenypropanoids could serve two functions
that would concur to contain the pathogen, a direct toxicity or an
involvement in cell wall cross-linking.

INDUCED IMMUNITY IS NOT SYSTEMIC

Both the gametophytes and the sporophytes of *C. crispus* exhibited a
strong oxidative response in the presence of alginate oligosaccharides, a
property which can be accounted for by the fact that this alga is naturally
challenged by filamentous brown algae. This observation opened the way
for another series of gain-of-function experiments, in which alginate
oligosaccharides were used to enhance the immunity of the sporophytes.
That induced resistance involved activation of the phenyl-propanoid
metabolism was established within one day of elicitation and lasted for
about one week. However, this induced resistance was not systemic. Only
those parts of the thallus which had been bathed by the elicitor were
protected against *A. operculata*.

271

Concluding Remarks

In conclusion, marine red algae feature natural immunity traits which are conserved in the other eukaryotic lineages as well as others that appear phylum- or environment-specific. The cellular bases of pathogen recognition and signaling are strikingly similar to those found in animals and land plants, suggesting that the underlying biochemical machinery has arisen early in Evolution. For example, since *C. crispus* is responsive to hydroperoxides from both eicosanoic and octadecanoic fatty acids, parsimony rules tend to suggest that the oxylipin pathway ancestrally featured these two categories of lipid signals. Regarding genuine defense reactions, the observation that the phenylpropanoid pathway is involved with the immunity of *C. crispus* may be linked to the fact that red algae are considered as a sister lineage to higher plants (Leblanc et al. 1997).

On the other hand *C. crispus* departs from terrestrial plants by the absence of systemy, a characteristic which is likely to be associated with the absence of vascularisation in this alga. Marine algae are thought to have evolved water-borne distance signals (Toth and Pavia 2000) which, in an aquatic environment, would alleviate the need for tissue-driven systemic responses. Another specificity of the marine environment is the abundance of halides, which are used by *C. crispus* to produce antimicrobial compounds. In the light of this latter behaviour one may ask whether the halogenating myeloperoxidases of human neutrophils are a paralogous trait or an ancestral characteristic.

Literature Cited

Bouarab K., Potin P., Correa J., and Kloareg B. 1999. Sulfated oligosaccharides mediate the interaction between a marine red alga and its green algal pathogenic endophyte. Plant Cell 11:1635-1650.

Correa J. A. and McLachlan J. L. 1991. Endophytic algae of *Chondrus crispus* (Rhodophyta). III. Host specificity. J. Phycol. 27:448-459.

Gerwick W. H., Proteau P. J., Nagle G. D., Wise M. L., Jiang Z. J., Bernart M. W., and Hamberg M. 1993. Biologically active oxylipins from seaweeds. Hydrobiologia 260/261:653-665.

Küpper F. C., Kloareg B., Guern J., and Potin P. 2001. Oligoguluronates elicit an oxidative burst in the brown algal kelp, *Laminaria digitata*. Plant Physiol. 125:278-291.

Leblanc C., Richard O., Kloareg B., Viehmann S., Zetsche K., Boyen C. 1997. Origin and evolution of mitochondria: what have we learnt from red algae? Curr Genet 31:193-207

Toth G. B. and Pavia H. 2000. Water-borne cues induce chemical defense in a marine alga (*Ascophyllum nodosum*). Proc. Natl. Acad. Sci. USA 97:14418-14420.

Uppalapati S. R. and Fujita Y. 2000. Carbohydrate regulation of attachment, encystment, and appressorium formation by *Pythium porphyrae* (Oomycota) zoospores on *Porphyra yezoensis* (Rhodophyta). J. Phycol. 36:359-366.

Weinberger F., Richard C., Kloareg B., Kashman Y., Hoppe H.-G., Friedlander M. 2001. Structure-activity relationships of oligoagar elicitors towards *Gracilaria conferta* (Rhodophyta). J. Phycol. 37:418-426.

Improving Root Colonization by *Pseudomonas* Inoculants

Ben Lugtenberg[a], Guido Bloemberg[a], Annouschka Bolwerk[a], Margarita Camacho[a], Thomas Chin-A-Woeng[a], Linda Dekkers[a], Lev Kravchenko[b], Irene Kuiper[a], Ellen Lagendijk[a], Anastasia Lagopodi[a], Ine Mulders[a], Monique Radjkoemar-Bansraj[a], Sietske Tuinman[a], Sandra de Weert[a] and André Wijfjes[a]

[a] Leiden University, IMP, Clusius Laboratory, Leiden, The Netherlands
[b] RIAM, Saint-Petersburg, Russian Federation

Importance of Root Colonization

It is generally agreed that root colonization by bacteria is important for the beneficial action of bacterial inoculants used for applications, such as biofertilization, phytostimulation, biocontrol, and bioremediation. Poor root colonization is considered the major factor responsible for failure of biocontrol in the field. For these reasons we initiated about a decade ago a study to elucidate the molecular basis of root colonization by bacteria. Our model bacteria are *P. fluorescens* WCS365 and *P. chlororaphis* PCL1391. Both strains control tomato foot and root rot caused by *Fusarium oxysporum* f. sp. r*adicis-lycopersici.*

Root Colonization Genes and Traits

We study root colonization in a controlled gnotobiotic sand system with tomato (*Lycopersicon esculentum* Mill. cv. Carmello) as the test plant. Tomato seeds or seedlings are inoculated with a 1:1 mixture of two bacterial strains, planted and the microbial composition of the root tip is investigated after plant growth for one week. After interesting results have been obtained, we check whether these also apply in potting soil and for other plants. Usually this is the case (Lugtenberg et al. 2001). Major colonization traits appeared to be motility, later refined to chemotaxis - presumably to root exudates, and the production of the O-antigen of lipopolysaccharide, amino acids, uracil, and vitamins. Type 4 pili also appear to play a role (Camacho 2001). Organic acids constitute the major group of tomato exudate compounds. A WCS365 mutant such as PCL1085, which grows poorly on organic acids, looses competitive root tip colonization from the parent WCS365. The mutation was found just upstream *mqo*, which encodes malate: quinone oxidoreductase (Wijfjes et al. 2001).

Interestingly, an enrichment procedure used to isolate enhanced grass root tip colonizers (see below) appeared to result in the selection of a strain which has its highest growth rate on the major grass exudate components, suggesting that selection for this trait is a major result of the procedure (Kuiper 2001a).

Using colonization mutants we discovered that the polyamine putrescine is an important exudate component. High levels of putrescine are bacteriostatic to *Pseudomonas*. Therefore this bacterium regulates its uptake carefully (Kuiper et al. 2001b).

One of the most severe WCS365 colonization mutants, PCL1210, is impaired in the *colR/colS* two-component system (Dekkers et al. 1998a). Downstream of this operon a putative *orf222 – wapQ* operon is located. Since *wapQ* encodes a putative heptose kinase, we tested the possibility that the mutant has an altered outer membrane function. Indeed, mutant PCL1210 is more resistant to various chemically unrelated antibiotics, grows slower on some nutrients (but normal in standard media) and is more sensitive than WCS365 towards the antibiotic polymixin B, which attacks at the outside of the outer membrane. These results can only be explained by an altered outer membrane structure. Direct proof for this notion was obtained by showing that the rate of permeation of the antibiotic ampicillin through the outer membrane was 3- to 5-fold higher in wild type than in mutant cells. Bacteria with a less permeable outer membrane will be less competitive in the rhizosphere than wild-type cells. The results provide a clear explanation for the mutant's defect in competitive rhizosphere colonization. (Dekkers et al. 2001).

The *xerC/sss* we have shown that a functional *xerC/sss* homologue is required for competitive root colonization of WCS365 gene belongs to the integrase family of site-specific recombinases which play a role in phase variation caused by DNA rearrangements (Dekkers et al. 1998b). Sss can lead to inversion or excision of DNA.

Use of Colonization Mutants to Test the Importance of Root Colonization for Biocontrol

P. chlororaphis strain PCL1391 controls tomato foot and root rot through production of phenazine-1-carboxamide (PCN) (Chin-A-Woeng et al. 1998). PCL1391 mutants defective in the competitive root tip colonization traits motility, prototrophy for the amino acid phenylalanine or production of the site-specific recombinase Sss have lost the ability to control the disease despite the fact that they produce normal amounts of PCN. These results show that root tip colonization is essential for suppression of tomato foot and root rot by strain PCL1391 (Chin-A-Woeng et al. 2000).

P. fluorescens WCS365 also controls tomato foot and root rot, most likely through Induced Systemic Resistance (ISR). All three tested WCS365 colonization mutants were not consistently decreased in biocontrol activity. As the most likely explanation for the different effects of competitive colonization mutations on biocontrol by PCL1391 and WCS365 we favour the hypothesis that, whereas PCN should be present near the whole root system, the presence of WCS365 bacteria on the root tip is sufficient to induce ISR (Dekkers et al. 2000).

Improvement of Root Colonization

Recently we have found three methods to improve competitive root tip colonization. Firstly, introduction of multiple copies of an *sss* containing DNA fragment from *P. fluorescens* WCS365 into the poor colonizer *P. fluorescens* WCS307 and into the good colonizer *P. fluorescens* F113 increased the competitive tomato root tip colonization abilities 16- to 40-fold and 8- to 16-fold, respectively. (Since these strains do not control tomato foot and root rot the effect on biocontrol was not tested). In contrast, introduction of multiple copies of the same DNA fragment into WCS365 improved neither colonization nor biocontrol (Dekkers et al. 2000).

Secondly, an enrichment procedure was used to isolate the best competitive root tip colonizers. Grass seeds were inoculated with a mixture of rhizosphere bacteria, and the bacteria which were able to reach the root tip were collected and used for a second enrichment cycle. After three cycles *P. putida* PCL1444 was isolated which is 10-fold better in competitive grass root tip colonization than WCS365, our best colonizer thus far (Kuiper et al. 2001b).

The same enrichment procedure was applied on a mutant bank of strain WCS365. Several mutants were found with 100- to 1000- fold improved competitive root tip colonization ability. Preliminary results on one mutant indicate that the mutation is located in a homologue of the ferri-siderophore receptor gene (de Weert et al. 2001b).

Visualization of Root Colonization

Pseudomonas biocontrol bacteria coated on seeds follow the growing root, multiply, and are found on the root surface as microcolonies and smaller units, usually as elongated stretches on indented areas, such as junctions between epidermal cells, the deeper parts of the epidermis and sites where lateral roots appear (Bloemberg et al. 1997; Chin-A-Woeng et al. 1997; Camacho 2001). Some strains, such as PCL1391 on tomato (Dekkers et al. 2000) and PCL1445 on grass (Kuiper 2001) can also be found on root hairs. Using different forms of *gfp* and the recent *rfp* we are able to visualize simultaneously and clearly distinguish from each other up to three different bacterial populations in the rhizosphere using confocal laser scanning microscopy (Bloemberg et al., 2000).

The observation that two different *Pseudomonas* strains can occupy different niches on one root system offers opportunities for the application of a mixture of two strains with complementary beneficial properties. Examples of such combinations are (i) PCL1444 and PCL1445 on the main root and root hairs, respectively, of grass (Kuiper et al. 2001c) and (ii) WCS365 and PCL1391 on the main root and root hairs, respectively, of tomato (Dekkers et al. 2000).

The use of Green Fluorescent Protein as a marker allowed us to study the processes of colonization and infection of tomato roots by the pathogenic fungus *Fusarium oxysporum* f.sp. *radicis-lycopersici* (F.o.r.l.) in detail. It appeared that the first contacts take place at the root hair zone by mingling and attachment of hyphae to root hairs. Like biocontrol pseudomonads, also the pathogen colonizes the grooves along the junctions of the epithelial cells (Lagopodi et al. 2001).

The use of *gfp*-containing mutants allowed the visualization of the interaction of a pathogenic fungus with a biocontrol bacterium on the root. When the seed was inoculated with the bacterium and the fungus was present in the sand, it appeared that both microbes colonized the same sites on the root. However, the bacterium reached those sites faster. Moreover, the presence of the bacterium prevented penetration of the root surface by the fungus. Finally, the bacterium not only colonized the root but also the surface of the hyphae.

The use of *gfp* mutants also allows, for the first time, to study the interactions between the biocontrol fungus *Fusarium oxysporum* strain 47 (Rouxel et al. 1979) and the pathogenic F.o.r.l. on the root surface.

Literature Cited

Bloemberg, G. V., O'Toole, G. A., Lugtenberg, B. J. J., and Kolter, R. 1997. Appl. Environ. Microbiol. 63:4543-4551.

Bloemberg, G. V., Wijfjes, A. H. M., Lamers, G. E. M., Stuurman, N., and Lugtenberg, B. J. J. 2000. Mol. Plant-Microbe Interact. 13:1170-1176.

Camacho, M. M. 2001. Molecular characterization of type 4 pili, NDHI and PyrR in rhizosphere colonization of *Pseudomonas fluorescens* WCS365. PhD Thesis, Leiden University.

Chin-A-Woeng, T. F. C., de Priester, W., van der Bij, A. J., and Lugtenberg, B. J. J. 1997. Mol. Plant-Microbe Interact. 10:79-86.

Chin-A-Woeng, T. F. C., Bloemberg, G. V., van der Bij, A. J., van der Drift, K. M. G. M., Schripsema, J., Kroon, B., Scheffer, R. J., Keel, C., Bakker, P. A. H. M., Tichy, H.-V.., de Bruijn, F. J., Thomas-Oates, J. E., and Lugtenberg, B. J. J. 1998. Mol. Plant-Microbe Interact. 11:1069-1077.

Chin-A-Woeng, T. F. C., Bloemberg, G. V., Mulders, I. H. M., Dekkers, L. C., and Lugtenberg, B. J. J. 2000. Mol. Plant-Microbe Interact. 13:1340-1345.

Dekkers, L. C., Bloemendaal, C. J. P., de Weger, L. A., Wijffelman, C. A., Spaink, H. P., and Lugtenberg, B. J. J. 1998a. Mol. Plant-Microbe Interact. 11:45-56.

Dekkers, L. C., Phoelich, C. C., van der Fits, L., and Lugtenberg, B. J. J. 1998b. Proc. Natl. Acad. Sci. USA 95:7051-7056.

Dekkers, L. C., Mulders, I. H. M., Phoelich, C. C., Chin-A-Woeng, T. F. C., Wijfjes, A. H. M., and Lugtenberg, B. J. J. 2000. Mol. Plant-Microbe Interact. 13:1177-1183.

Dekkers, L. C., Tuinman, S., Bitter, W., Wijfjes, A., and Lugtenberg, B. J. J. 2001. The two-component *colR/colS* system of *Pseudomonas fluorescens* WCS365 plays a role in rhizosphere competence through maintaining the structure and function of the outer membrane. *Submitted.*

de Weert, S., Dekkers, L. C., and Lugtenberg, B. 2001. *Unpublished results.*

Kuiper, I., Bloemberg, G. V., Noreen, S., Thomas-Oates, J. E., and Lugtenberg, B. J. J. 2001a. Increased uptake of putrescine inhibits competitive root colonization by *Pseudomonas fluorescens* strain WCS365. Mol. Plant-Microbe Interact. *In press.*

Kuiper, I., Bloemberg, G. V., and Lugtenberg, B. J. J. 2001b. Selection of a plant-bacterium pair of which the bacterium prevents xenobiotic phytotoxicity and of which the plant injects the xenobiotic-degrading bacterium into the soil. *Submitted.*

Kuiper, I., Lagendijk, E., Lamers, G. E. M., Bloemberg, G. V., and Lugtenberg, B. J. J. 2001c. *Unpublished results.*

Lagopodi, A. L., Ram, A. F. J., Lamers, G. E. M., Punt, P. J., van den Hondel, C. A. M. J. J., Lugtenberg, B. J. J., and Bloemberg, G. V. 2001. Confocal laser scanning microscopy analyses of tomato root colonization and infection by *Fusarium oxysporum* f.sp. *radicis-lycopersici* using the green fluorescent protein as a marker. *Submitted.*

Lugtenberg, B. J. J., Dekkers, L., and Bloemberg, G. V. 2001. Annu. Rev. Phytopathol. 39:461-490.

Rouxel, F., Alabouvette, C., and Louvet, J. 1979. Annls. Phytopathol. 11:199-207.

Wijfjes, A. H. M., Kravchenko, L. V., Tikhonovich, I., Radjkoemar-Bansraj, M. R. K. S., Phoelich, C., Simons, M., Bloemberg, G. V., and Lugtenberg, B. J. J. 2001. Utilization of exudate organic acids is the nutritional basis of tomato root colonization by *Pseudomonas fluorescens* WCS365. *Submitted.*

Macromolecular Trafficking Within and Between Plant Cells as Revealed by Virus Movement Proteins

Sondra G. Lazarowitz[1], Roisin C. McGarry[1] Janet E. Hill[2] Yoshimi D. Barron[1], Daniel Gold[1], Miguel F. Carvalho[1], Anton A. Sanderfoot[3], Brian M. Ward[4]

[1]Cornell University, Department of Plant Pathology, Ithaca, NY USA
[2]Plant Biotechnology Institute, Saskatoon, Saskatchwan, Canada
[3]DOE Plant Research Laboratory, Michigan State University, E. Lansing, MI USA
[4]Laboratory of Viral Diseases, National Institute of Allergy and Infectious Diseases, National Institutes of Health, Bethesda, MD USA

Plant viruses must move locally cell-to-cell within a leaf to enter the vascular system (the phloem for most viruses, although some move via the xylem), through which they will move long distance to systemically infect the host plant. To do this, viruses must overcome the primary physical defense of the plant – the cell wall – a feat they accomplish by encoding movement proteins (MPs). MPs were first defined in classic genetic studies of the tobacco mosaic virus (TMV) *Ls1* mutant: in the absence of MP function, the virus would still replicate and encapsidate progeny virus particles. However, these progeny could not move out of the inoculated cells (Nishiguchi et al. 1978). These classic studies indicated that MPs act to eliminate the cell wall barrier to plant virus movement, suggesting that they some how alter cell structure.

Recent molecular studies of MP function have confirmed and extended this conclusion. Our understanding of the how MPs act at the molecular and cellular level has increased enormously in the past decade and ushered in an exciting new era of plant virology as an approach to investigating plant cell structure and function. With the demonstration that the TMV MP (the 30 kD protein mutated in the *Ls1* mutant) could bind the viral RNA genome and increase the size exclusion limits of plasmodesmata when expressed in transgenic plants or microinjected into tobacco mesophyll cells, studies of MPs were understandably focused on how these proteins interacted with plasmodesmata. As more recent studies have focused on the interactions of these proteins with subcellular components during virus infection, it has become clear that MPs are important for coordinating the replication of viral genomes with their directed movement through the infected cell as well as into adjacent cells (Carrington et al. 1996; Lazarowitz and Beachy 1999). Thus, MPs are providing unique approaches to unravel the fundamental mechanisms by which macromolecular transport is directed and integrated within and between plant cells.

Movement Protein Function

CURRENT MODELS

Four well-developed models currently exist for the function of MPs encoded by diverse plant viruses. While at first glance these may appear to be distinct , they represent common themes that have been adapted to best suit the particular replication strategies and tissue specificities of different viruses.

TMV represents the simplest case of a single-stranded RNA (ssRNA) virus that replicates in the cytoplasm of mesophyll cells and requires only a single MP (30 kD protein) to move cell to cell. Coat protein (CP) is not required for local movement, although it is required for the virus to enter and move systemically via the phloem. Molecular genetic studies, *in vitro* binding assays and dye-coupling studies in transgenic and wild type tobacco plants led to the proposal that the 30 kD protein is a molecular chaperone that binds the viral RNA genome and targets it to plasmodesmata, where it then acts to increase the size exclusion limits and facilitate movement of the viral genome into adjacent uninfected cells (Carrington et al. 1996; Lazarowitz and Beachy 1999). Studies investigating the subcellular localization of functional GFP-30 kD fusion proteins during infection in expanding TMV lesions or in protoplasts have refined this model. The 30 kD protein appears to be important in establishing endoplasmic reticulum (ER) associated viral sites for protein synthesis and replication (viroplasms), and to amplify these during infection by directing the viral genome along microtubules to additional ER sites. For those sites at cortical ER, the MP is proposed to direct the genome along actin microfilaments to the plasmodesmata for movement into adjacent cells (Heinlein et al. 1998; McLean et al. 1995; Reichel and Beachy 1998).

A number of diverse plant viruses from very different families require CP in addition to a dedicated MP for cell-to-cell movement as well as systemic infection. The best studied of these include cauliflower mosaic virus (CaMV) (caulimo), tomato spotted wilt virus (TSWV) (tospo), cowpea mosaic virus (CPMV) (como) and tobacco ringspot virus (ToRSV) (nepo) (Lazarowitz 2001). Although using diverse replication strategies, each of these viruses replicate in the cytoplasm and have been reported to induce the formation of large tubular structures that extend from what appear to be highly modified plasmodesmata in mesophyll cells (Lazarowitz and Beachy 1999). The viral MP has been immune localized to these tubules, and electron microscopic studies have identified virus-like particles within and

associated with these tubules. Thus, CP is needed for cell-to-cell movement because the genome is transported as a subviral or virus particle.
Mutational and expression studies in protoplasts suggest that the viral MP is necessary and sufficient for tubule formation, and that CP is not required for tubule formation. However, the possible involvement of cellular components remains to be resolved. Based on these studies, TSWV, CPMV, CaMV and ToRSV are proposed to move the encapsidated genome through tubules that contain MP and extend from what appear to be modified plasmodesmata (no desmotubule is visible) (Lazarowitz and Beachy 1999). In a variation of this theme, the potyvirus tobacco etch virus (TEV) also requires both CP and a MP – the cylindrical inclusion (CI) protein – to move cell to cell . CI, as its name implies, forms cylindrical structures, rather than tubules, that have been reported to be associated with what may be modified plasmodesmata, and mutational studies suggest that TEV may move cell to cell as virus particles (Carrington et al. 1998; Dolja et al. 1995).

A number of diverse RNA viruses encode a cluster of 3 proteins (the 'triple gene block', TGB) that is required for cell-to-cell as well as systemic movement. Of these, the best characterized are potato virus X (PVX, potex) and barley stripe mosaic virus (BSMV, hordei). PVX also requires CP for local movement because it moves cell-to-cell as virions, but without the involvement of tubules (Santa p et al. 1998), however BSMV does not. Recent localization, dye-coupling and transient expression studies in plants have led to a model in which the smallest two TGB proteins act to localize and anchor complexes of the largest TGB protein and the viral genome at the plasma membrane at plasmodesmata (Lawrence and Jackson 1999; Yang et al. 2000). For PVX, one model proposes that CP is exchanged for the largest TGB protein to assemble virions that move cell to cell, the largest TGB protein affecting gating of plasmodesmata but being retained in the infected cell by the membrane anchor. For BSMV, the largest TGB protein is proposed to affect the plasmodesmal gating properties and move the viral genome into adjacent cells (Lazarowitz, 2001).

BIPARTITE GEMINIVIRUS MOVEMENT PROTEIN FUNCION

The bipartite geminiviruses require two MPs, a nuclear shuttle protein(NSP) and a cell-to-cell MP to move the viral single-stranded DNA (ssDNA). genome cell to cell and for systemic infection. CP is not required for local or systemic infection of natural hosts (Qin et al. 1998). These viruses replicate through dsDNA intermediates in the nucleus, and NSP and MP act cooperatively to move the viral genome from this nuclear site to and across the cell wall (Lazarowitz and Beachy 1999). NSP binds the viral ssDNA genome and moves it between the nucleus and cytoplasm; MP traps these NSP-genome complexes in the cytoplasm to move them through the cytoplasm and into uninfected cells. The functions and interaction of NSP and MP encoded by the phloem-limited squash leaf curl virus (SqLCV) SqLCV have been studied in detail in our lab and form the basis for the model shown in Fig. 1 (Pascal et al. 1994; Sanderfoot et al. 1996; Sanderfoot and Lazarowitz 1995; Ward and Lazarowitz 1999). More recently we have characterized the infectivity in *Arabidopsis* of cabbage leaf curl virus (CLCV), which is closely related to SqLCV, and used this bipartite geminivirus to begin to identify host proteins with which NSP and MP interact.

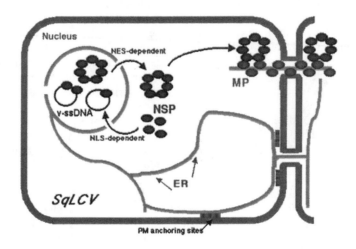

Fig. 1. Model for bipartite geminivirus movement.

In support of this model, SqLCV NSP in immune labeling studies is localized to nuclei of phloem parenchyma cells in infected plants and of tobacco protoplasts, and in vitro has the properties of a ssDNA binding protein (Pascal et al. 1994; Sanderfoot et al. 1996). SqLCV MP has been immune localized to unique tubules that extend from and cross the walls of developing phloem cells in infected pumpkin plants. MP targets to cortical ER, and several lines of evidence suggest that the MP-associated tubule may be derived from the ER. This has led to the suggestion that these may be the analog of the desmotubule (Lazarowitz and Beachy 1999; Ward et al. 1997). Using a transient expression assay in tobacco protoplasts, we have shown that NSP and MP interact, an interaction that redirects NSP to the cortical cytoplasm, and we have used this cell-based assay to identify functional domains within NSP and MP, including nuclear targeting signals and an essential nuclear export sequence (NES) in NSP (Sanderfoot et al. 1996; Sanderfoot and Lazarowitz 1995; Ward and Lazarowitz 1999). The NSP NES is typical of those found in rapidly shuttling nuclear proteins such as HIV Rev and TFIIIA, and similar to these other NESs, mutational studies show that the leucine residues are essential for its function in export. The NES from *Xenopus laevis* TFIIIA can be functionally substituted for the

NSP NES in terms of nuclear shuttling and for partial virus infectivity, thus suggesting that the mechanism of nuclear export is highly conserved in plant cells, as it is in animals and yeast (Ward and Lazarowitz 1999).

To better how shutting of the viral ssDNA genome by NSP is regulated during infection, as well as the mechanism of nuclear export in plant cells, we have begun to identify plant proteins that interact with NSP. Using the classic yeast two-hybrid screen, we have identify an *Arabidopsis* protein that interacts with CLCV NSP (McGarry et al., submitted). This protein, termed AtNSI (*A. thaliana* Nuclear Shuttle Protein Interactor) appears to be a novel nuclear protein that is highly conserved in plants and may act by modifying host and/or viral proteins to facilitate NSP export of the viral genome from the nucleus.

Acknowledgements

Studies from our lab have been supported by grants from the National Science Foundation to S.G.L

Literature Cited

Carrington, J. C., Jensen, P. E., and Schaad, M. C. 1998. Plant J 14:393-400.

Carrington, J. C., Kasschau, K. D., Mahajan, S. K., and Schaad, M. C. 1996. Plant Cell 8:1669-1681.

Dolja, V. V., Haldeman-Cahill, R., Montgomery, A. E., VandenBosch, K. A., and Carrington, J. C. 1995. Virology 207:1007-1016.

Heinlein, M., Padgett, H. S., Gens, J. S., Pickard, B. G., Casper, S. J., Epel, B. L., and Beachy, R. N. 1998. Plant Cell 10:1107-1120.

Lawrence, D. M., and Jackson, A. O. 1999. Hordeiviruses. Pages 749-753 in: Encyclopedia of Virology, A. Granoff, and R. G. Webster, eds. Academic Press, San Diego.

Lazarowitz, S. G. 2001. Pages *in press* in: Fields' Virology, P. M. Howley and D. M. Knipe, eds. Lippincott, Williams and Wilkins, Philadelphia.

Lazarowitz, S. G., and Beachy, R. N. 1999. Plant Cell 11:535-548.

McLean, B. G., Zupan, J., and Zambryski, P. C. 1995. Plant Cell 7:2101-2114.

Nishiguchi, M., Motoyoshi, F., and Oshima, N. 1978. J Gen Virol 39:53-61.

Pascal, E., Sanderfoot, A. A., Ward, B. M., Medville, R., Turgeon, R., and Lazarowitz, S. G. 1994. Plant Cell 6:995-1006.

Qin, S., Ward, B. M., and Lazarowitz, S. G. 1998. J Virol 72:9247-9256.

Reichel, C., and Beachy, R. N. 1998. Proc Natl Acad Sci USA 95:11169-11174.

Sanderfoot, A. A., Ingham, D. J., and Lazarowitz, S. G. 1996. Plant Physiol 110:23-33.

Sanderfoot, A. A., and Lazarowitz, S. G. 1995. Plant Cell 7:1185-1194.

Santa Cruz, S., Roberts, A. G., Prior, D. A. M., Chapman, S., and Oparka, K. J. 1998. Plant Cell 10(4):495-510.

Ward, B. M., and Lazarowitz, S. G. 1999. Plant Cell 11:1267-1276.

Ward, B. M., Medville, R., Lazarowitz, S. G., and Turgeon, R. 1997. J Virology 71:3726-3733.

Yang, Y., Ding, B., Baulcombe, D. C., and Verchot, J. 2000. MPMI 13: 599-605.

Multi-Color Confocal Imaging

Stephen W. Paddock

Howard Hughes Medical Institute, Department of Molecular Biology,
University of Wisconsin, Madison, WI 53706, USA.

Mapping the distribution of more than one macromolecule in plant tissues is now a relatively routine technique using multiple label fluorescence and one of several different digital imaging methods including wide field, confocal, deconvolution or multiple photon microscopy. Methods of specimen preparation continue to be refined especially as new fluorescent probes are developed and become generally available for immunofluorescence and for fluorescent in situ hybridization (FISH).

The confocal laser scanning microscope (CLSM) is essential for excluding the fluorescence from both labeled and autofluorescing cells that are positioned out of the focal plane of interest (White et al. 1987). Moreover, background can be higher in images of multiple labeled specimens where noise from the multiple wavelength excitation of several fluorescent probes is increased, especially when two or more images are combined into a single multi-color image (Paddock 2001).

Modern CLSMs have been designed to collect images from multiple-labeled specimens either simultaneously or sequentially (Brelje et al.1993). The krypton argon laser is an extremely convenient light source for multiple labeling experiments since it produces three major lines around 488nm (blue), 568nm (yellow) and 647nm (red). These wavelengths are matched to the excitation spectra of some of the more commonly-used fluorochromes including fluorescein, exc. max. 496nm, lissamine rhodamine, exc. max. 572nm and cyanine 5, exc. max. 649nm. In addition, the peak emission spectra of these dyes (fluorescein em. 518nm.; lissamine rhodamine em. 590nm.; CY5 em. 672nm.) are sufficiently separated to enable optical filtering for detection of the emission of the three fluorophores, and are within the range of detection of the photomultiplier tube detectors used in most CLSMs (Fig. 1). Many of the recently available CLSMs have multiple laser light sources that have longer lifetimes than a single krypton/argon laser. For example, a 25mW Argon (488/514nm), a 1.5mW Green Helium/Neon (543nm) and a 5mW red diode laser (638nm).

One of the major sources of error when imaging multiple labeled specimens with the CLSM is bleed through when part of the emission of one channel appears in that of another (Fig. 1). Assuming that the CLSM is working correctly, the best solution for bleed through is to titrate the concentration of fluorescently-labeled secondary antibody probes so that the specimen is "tuned" to the characteristics of the microscope. Bleed through is most often a problem when there is more of one antigen in the specimen relative to the second one. For example, if the fluorescein channel tends to bleed through into the rhodamine channel, then the most concentrated antigen should be placed on the rhodamine channel. For double label experiments, cyanine 3 and cyanine 5 secondaries are good alternatives to the traditional choices of fluorescein and rhodamine since bleed-through from the cyanine 3 channel to the cyanine 5 channel is much reduced (Sargent 1994).

Remedies for bleed through include sequential rather than simultaneous imaging, and some CLSMs can be configured to sequentially scan several channels on a line-by-line basis. Alternatively, the proportion of the image that is bleeding through from one image to the other can be digitally subtracted either during imaging or after imaging (Fig. 1). Recently, an acousto-optic tunable filter (AOTF) rather than conventional glass filters has been used in CLSMs (Smallcombe 2001). The AOTF matches more precisely the power and wavelength of the laser to maximally excite the fluorophore, which enables the amount of bleed through between channels to be eliminated.

Autofluorescence from cellular components such as the cell walls or the chloroplasts in plants may present background problems (Fig. 1). In some instances, however, autofluorescence can be used as a low level background signal to give an outline of the tissue (Wymer et al. 1998). This is achieved by adjusting the gain and black level to give contrast between the background, the tissue autofluorescence and the labeled cells. Background autofluorescence of most tissues is much reduced when imaging in red light as compared to imaging with blue or green light (Cullander 1994). It is always good practice to check an unstained and fixed preparation for the levels of autofluorescence. If necessary, the gain, black level, pinhole setting and laser power for imaging autofluorescence should be recorded, with the result that any signal detected above these settings in the experimental preparation will be from the fluorochromes of interest, rather from autofluorescence.

Fluorescently-labelled antibodies and probes are used in multiple label experiments to provide landmarks within cells and tissues onto which proteins with unknown localization's can be mapped. Many fluorescent probes can be utilized in multiple label protocols as landmarks for mapping experimental ones. The green fluorescent protein (GFP) is an extremely useful reporter for such localization studies, for example, an engrailed/GFP was used in double label experiments with the lineage tracer DiI to map neurogenesis in both living and fixed embryos (Schmid et al. 1999).

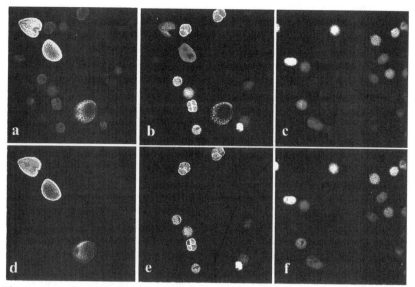

Fig. 1: Autofluorescence in mixed pollen grains imaged simultaneously using a BioRad MRC1024 CLSM and a Krypton Argon laser source; a) exc. 488nm; em. 518nm; b) exc. 568nm; em. 590nm; c) exc. 647nm; em. 672nm. Note the low level bleed through between channels can be reduced using the real time digital mixers (d,e,f).

Various probes that label specific cellular organelles are used in conjunction with antibodies in double or triple labeling strategies in order to confirm the cellular distribution of expression patterns of genes. For example, chromatin dyes that label nuclei are used in conjunction with antibody staining to determine whether a protein is located in the nucleus, the cytoplasm or to the extracellular matrix. Examples of useful nuclear probes for staining fixed tissues for analysis using the CLSM include propidium iodide, (exc. 536nm; em. 617nm) (Orsulic and Peiffer1994), acridine orange (exc. 502nm; em. 526nm) and the TOTO and TOPRO group of heterodimers (e.g. TOTO3 em. 642nm; em. 661nm) (Haugland, 1999). The excitation spectra of Hoechst (e.g. Hoechst 3342 exc. 346nm; em 460nm) and DAPI dyes (exc. 359nm.; em. 461nm) are too short to be excited by the Krypton/Argon laser, and require an additional UV excitation source attached to the LSCM, which itself would need to be fitted with UV-reflecting mirrors and UV-transmitting lenses for more efficient imaging of these dyes. Multiple photon imaging allows the excitation of these short wavelength dyes without specialized UV optics, and can also be used for multiple label imaging (White et al. 1997).

Fluorescent phalloidins are useful probes for imaging cell outlines in developing tissues, and that have been stained in this way appear as networks of bright rings in favorable optical sections of the tissues with the dividing cells appearing as slightly larger circles (Rothwell et al. 1998). In this case, phalloidin is directly-conjugated to a fluorophore such as fluorescein, rhodamine, Texas Red or Alexa, and in a relatively simple one step protocol, specifically stains the peripheral actin meshwork located directly beneath the cell membrane. When the distribution of two of the components are known, and do not overlap, they can be placed on the same channel in order to image four probes in a single sample. For example Alexa fluor phalloidin conjugate (exc. 647nm) for cell outlines and TO-PRO-3 iodide (exc. 647nm) for nuclei may be used in tandem in this way.

While immunofluorescence continues to be a major technique for mapping the distribution of specific macromolecules within cells and tissues using the CLSM, fluorescence *in situ* hybridization (FISH) has become a powerful and complementary technique for localizing DNA and RNA sequences in cells using non-radioactive fluorescent probes that can be detected with modern CLSMs. Protocols have been developed for FISH (Hughes and Krause 1998), and improved sensitivity can be achieved using the tyramide amplification system. Proteins and transcripts can be mapped in the same specimen using multiple labeling protocols that combine immunofluorescence and FISH (Goto and Hayashi 1997), and the CLSM for imaging. Triple label strategies have also been developed for imaging apoptosis, FISH and nuclear staining using ToPro (Davis et al. 1997). Cell death can also be imaged using the TUNEL method (Pazdera et al. 1998).

Multi-color confocal imaging of living tissues is now a practical option using spectral variants of GFP and DsRed (Hawley et al. 2001) together with vital fluorescent dyes or autofluorescence, and using sensitive CLSMs or multiple photon microscopes for imaging.

Literature Cited

Brelje, T.C., Wessendorf, M.W., and Sorenson R.L. 1993. Multicolor laser scanning confocal immunofluorescence microscopy: practical applications and limitations. Meth. Cell Biol. 38:98-177.

Cullander, C. 1994. Imaging in the far-red with electronic light microscopy: requirements and limitations. J. Microsc. 176:281-286.

Davis, W. P., Janssen, Y. M. W., Mossman, B. T., and Taatjes, D. J. 1997. Simultaneous triple fluorescence detection of mRNA localization, nuclear DNA, and apoptosis in cultured cells using confocal scanning laser microscopy. Histochem. Cell Biol. 108:307-311.

Goto, S., and Hayashi, S. 1997. Cell migration within the embryonic limb primordium of *Drosophila* as revealed by a novel fluorescence method to visualize mRNA and protein. Dev. Genes Evol. 207:194-198.

Haugland, R.P. 1999. Handbook of Fluorescent Probes and Research Chemicals. 7th ed. Molecular Probes Inc., Eugene, OR.

Hawley T.S., Telford W.G., Ramezani, A., and Hawley R.G. 2001. Four-color flow cytometric detection of retrovirally expressed red, yellow, green and cyan fluorescent proteins. BioTechniques 30:1028-1035

Hughes, S. C. and Krause, H. M. 1998. Double labeling with FISH in *Drosophila* whole mount embryos. BioTechniques 24:530-532.

Orsulic, S. and Peifer, M. 1994. A method to stain nuclei of *Drosophila* for confocal microscopy. BioTechniques 16:441-447.

Paddock, S.W. 2001. Channel surfing: creating different color combinations from multiple-labelled images. BioTechniques 30: 756-761.

Pazdera, T. M., Janardhan, P., and Minden, J. S. 1998. Patterned epidermal cell death in wild-type and segment polarity mutant *Drosophila* embryos. Development 125: 3427-3436.

Rothwell, W. F., Fogarty, P., Field, C. M., and Sullivan, W. 1998. Nuclear-fallout, a *Drosophila* protein that cycles from the cytoplasm to the centrosomes, regulates cortical microfilament organization. Development 125: 1295-1303.

Sargeant, P. B. 1994. Double-label immunofluorescence with the laser scanning confocal microscope using cyanine dyes. NeuroImage 1: 288-295.

Schmid, A., Chiba, A., and Doe, C.Q. 1999. Clonal analysis of *Drosophila* embryonic neuroblasts: neural cell types, axon projections and muscle targets. Development 126: 4653-4689.

Smallcombe, A. 2001. Multicolor imaging: the important question of co-localization. BioTechniques 30: 1240-1247.

White, J. G., Amos, W. B., and Fordham, M. 1987. An evaluation of confocal versus conventional imaging of biological structures by fluorescence light microscopy. J. Cell Biol. 105:41-48.

White, J., Centonze, V., Wokosin, D., and Mohler, W. 1997. Using multiphoton microscopy for the study of embryogenesis. Microscopy and Analysis 3: 307-308.

Wymer C.L., Beven A.F., Boudonck K., and Lloyd C.W. 1998. Confocal microscopy of plant cells. Meth. Mol. Biol. 122: 103-130.

FISH on Pachytene Chromosomes of *Medicago truncatula*

Olga Kulikova, René Geurts, J. Hans de Jong, and Ton Bisseling

Wageningen University, Department of Plant Sciences, the Netherlands

Introduction

Legumes have the unique ability to establish a symbiosis with rhizobia. This symbiotic interaction results in the formation of nitrogen fixing root nodules. Legume species have been selected as a model system for unraveling the molecular mechanisms that control the different steps of this symbiosis. *Medicago truncatula* Gaerth. (Barrel medic) has been selected for this purpose (Barker et al. 1990). This annual, autogamous diploid forage crop has 16 chromosomes and a relatively small genome (1.15 pg/2C, Blondon et al. 1994). In addition, molecular and genetic studies of *M. truncatula* became possible with the recently developed efficient transformation and regeneration procedures and the establishment of BAC libraries and genetic maps (Cook 1999).

We recently developed a cytogenetic map for *M. truncatula*. Cytogenetic maps can be highly informative to support the construction of physical maps, map-based cloning projects and to position genes in large heterochromatic regions where linkage distances are inaccurate by the low levels of meiotic recombination (Roberts 1965; Lambie and Roeder 1986; Zhong et al. 1999). In order to position BACs and other DNA sequences along the chromosomes fluorescence *in situ* hybridization (FISH) is mostly used (Jiang and Gill 1994; De Jong et al. 1999). Such studies can be performed with metaphase complements, but chromosomes at this stage are highly condensed, which limits the optical resolution of adjacent FISH targets to Mbs rather than kbs. Therefore we used pachytene chromosomes because their complements measure 10-40 x longer. Pachytene chromosomes display a differentiated pattern of heterochromatic and euchromatic regions (Shen et al. 1987; Albini and Schwarzacher 1992; Zhong et al. 1996; Fransz et al. 1998; Fransz et al. 2000) and this heterochromatin banding along with chromosome length and centromere position are used for the identification of individual chromosomes.

Results

Pachytene spreads were made of pollen mother cells at late pachytene. DAPI staining of pachytene chromosomes demonstrated striking differences in chromatin density (Fig. 1). Brightly fluorescing heterochromatic blocks were detected in the pericentromeric regions of all chromosomes, although their lengths varied. In contrast, distal regions of the chromosome arms contained weakly fluorescing euchromatin.

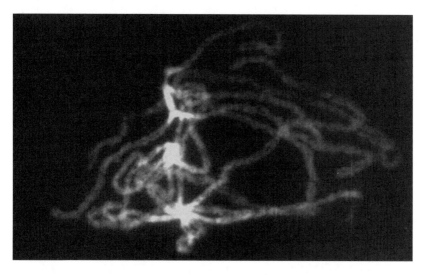

Fig. 1. DAPI stained pachytene chromosomes of *Medicago truncatula* Jemalong A17 revealing that heterochromatic blocks are located around the centromeres of the eight chromosomes, whereas the distal parts of the arms are euchromatic.

This relatively simple distribution of heterochromatic and euchromatic areas is reminiscent of that of *Arabidopsis thaliana* pachytene chromosomes (Ross et al. 1996; Fransz et al. 1998, De Jong et al. 1999), but strongly differs from other small genome species. For example, rice exhibits numerous smaller heterochromatic knobs distributed along all chromosome arms (Khan 1975). This simple organization of the *M. truncatula* chromosomes makes this legume species an attractive object for cytogenetic analyses.

THE PACHYTENE KARYOTYPE

To be able to use pachytene chromosomes for mapping studies a pachytene karyotype was made. A pachytene complement has eight fully

Table 1. Absolute and relative lengths of individual chromosomes and chromosome regions, positions of 5S rDNA, NOR and MtR1 on chromosomes. The chromosomes #3 and #4 can only be distinguished when FISH with MtR1 was used as diagnostic maker.

Chromosome[1]	1	2	3	4	5	6	7	8	total
Average Length[2]	60.3	49.3	68.1	66.0	49.5	29.28	50.4	33.4	406.2
Total Cell Complement[3]	14.9	12.1	16.8	16.2	12.2	7.2	12.4	8.2	100%
Centromere Index[4]	36.4	46.2	27.1	30.2	47.4	46.3	30.0	41.2	
% Heterochromatin[5]	15	14	8	8	215	25	15	22	14.6%
FISH signals[6]									
5S rDNA	-	L	-	-	S	S	-	-	
45S rDNA	-	-	-	-	L	-	-	-	
MtR1	L	L	-	S	-	-	L+S	L	

1)Chromosomes were ordered and numbered according to their corresponding linkage groups; 2) Chromosome length in μm; 3) Total cell complement is percentage chromosome length / total length of all chromosomes; 4) Centromere index is percentage of short arm / total chromosome length (Levan et al. 1964); 5) Value includes short arm heterochromatin + NOR; 6) Positions of the repeats on short arm (S) or long arm (L); 7) % heterochromatin in cell complement (from Kulikova et al. 2001).

paired bivalents with lengths varying from 29 to 68 µm and a total complement length of 406 µm, which is about 20x longer than that of the mitotic metaphase chromosomes. The morphological characteristics of the 8 chromosomes are summarized in Table 1.

Chromosome identification was based on their length, centromere position, and size of pericentromeric heterochromatin. These morphological characteristics of the DAPI stained pachytene complements proved to be sufficient to identify all chromosomes except #3 and #4. In general, chromosomes were hybridized with 45S and 5S rDNA and MtR1 to facilitate the recognition of the chromosomes. MtR1 is a 180 bp tandem repeat located in the pericentromeric region of some of the chromosomes (Kulikova et al. 2001) and with this repeat it became possible to distinguish chromosomes #3 and #4.

They were numbered according to their corresponding linkage maps as was decided during the 2nd *Medicago truncatula* Workshop (Amsterdam, The Netherlands, July 22-23, 1999), with their two arms denoted as S (short) and L (long), respectively. The numbering convention for the eight genetically identified linkage groups of *M. truncatula* was adopted from *M. sativa* (Kaló et al. 2000). For assigning individual linkage groups to the chromosomes we used BACs of which the position on the genetic map is known. Of each linkage group several BACs were used as probes for FISH mapping to the pachytene chromosomes.

DISTRIBUTION OF THE GENOME OVER EUCHROMATIC AND
HETEROCHROMATIC REGIONS

To calculate which part of the genome is located in the euchromatic arms the degree of chromatin condensation in a euchromatic part of chromosome 5 was determined (Kulikova et al. 2001). By FISH of BACs with a known physical distance it was shown that the condensation degree was about 300 kb per µm, similar to that of Arabidopsis euchromatin which varies between 150 - 300 kb/µm (Fransz et al. 1998; Fransz et al. 2000). This implies that the mapping resolution in euchromatic chromosome segments is about 60 kb Assuming that the average degree of condensation in the different euchromatic regions of *M. truncatula* is similar, one can estimate the fraction of the *M. truncatula* genome contained within euchromatic and heterochromatic regions, respectively. The total length of pachytene chromosomes is 406 µm, of which about 350 µm is euchromatic (Table 1). Thus, the total euchromatic regions of *M. truncatula* chromosomes is estimated to span 105 Mb (i.e. 300kb/µm x 350 µm). The genome size is about 500 Mb, 395 Mb, therefore almost 80% of the *M. truncatula* genome, is estimated to occupy heterochromatic regions. This shows that the majority of the genome is located in the heterochromatic parts

Heterochromatic regions are rich in repeated sequences and probably contain a low density of expressed genes (Dean and Schmidt 1995). The repetitive nature of heterochromatic regions is consistent with the location of MtR1 and the highly repeated ribosomal genes in heterochromatic pericentromeric regions. Whole BAC clone sequencing indicated a gene density of approximately 1 predicted gene/6 kb in gene-rich regions of *M. truncatula* (Kim and Cook, unpublished data) which is consistent with the idea that the euchromatic arms of *M. truncatula* are rich in transcribed genes and will contain only few repeats. This indicates that positional cloning strategies for genes located in the euchromatic regions will not be hampered by the occurrence of repeated sequences. The part of the genome that is located in the pericentromeric regions is predicted to contain few transcribed genes. Therefore it will be attractive to focus a future *M. truncatula* genome sequencing program on the euchromatic parts of the chromosome arms.

Acknowledgements

This work was financially supported by grants INTAS-96-1371, NWO 047-011-000, NSF IBN 9872664 and QLRT-2000-30676.

Literature Cited

Albini S.M. and Schwarzacher T. 1992. Genome 35:551-559.

Barker D., Bianchi S., Blondon F., Dattee Y., Duc G., Essad S., Flament P., Gallusci Ph., Genier G., Guy P., Muel X., Tourneur J., Denarie J. and Huguet T. 1990. Plant Mol. Biol. Rep. 8:40-49.

Blondon F., Marie D., Brown S. and Kondorosi A. 1994. Genome 37:264-275.

Cook D. 1999. Current Opinion in Plant Biology 2:301-304.

Dean C. and Schmidt R. 1995. Annu. Rev Plant Physiol Plant Mol. Biol. 46:395-418.

De Jong H., Fransz P. and Zabel P. 1999. Trends Plants Sci. 4:258-263.

Fransz P., Armstrong S., Alonso-Blanco C., Fischer T.C., Torrez-Ruiz R.A. and Jones G. 1998. Plant J. 13:867-876.

Fransz P., Armstrong S., De Jong J.H., Parnell L.D., van Drunen C., Dean C., Zabel P., Bisseling T., and Jones G.H. 2000. Cell 100:367-376.

Jiang J.M. and Gill B.S. 1994. Nonisotopic *in situ* hybridization and plant genome mapping: the first 10 years. Genome 37:717-725.

Kaló P., Endre G., Zimányi L., Csanádi G. and Kiss G.B. 2000. Theor. Appl. Genet. 100:641-657.

Khan S.H. 1975. Cytologia 40:595-598.

Kulikova O., Gualtieri G., Geurts R., Kim D.J., Cook D., Huguet T., De Jong J.H., Fransz P.F., and Bisseling T. 2001. Plant J. (in press).

Lambie E.I., Roeder G.S. 1986. Genetics 114:768-769.

Levan A., Fredga K. and Sandberg A. 1964. Hereditas 52, 201-220.

Roberts P.A. 1965. Nature 205:725-726.

Ross K., Fransz P.F., and Jones G.H. 1996. Chromosome Res. 4:507-516.

Shen D.L., Wang Z.F. and Wu M. 1987. Chromosoma 95:311-314.

Zhong X-B., Fransz P.F., Wennekes-van Eden J., Zabel P., van Kammen A., and de Jong J.H. 1996. Plant Mol. Biol. Rep. 14:232-242.

Zhong X-B., Bodeau J., Fransz P.F., Williamson V.M., van Kammen A., de Jong J.H. and Zabel P. 1999. Theor. Appl. Genet. 98:365-370.

Comparative Analyses of Enterobacterial Genomes

Nicole T. Perna, Guy Plunkett III, Valerie Burland, Bob Mau, Jeremy D. Glasner, Jihyun F. Kim* and Frederick R. Blattner

University of Wisconsin, Madison, Wisconsin, USA; *Microbial Genomics Laboratory, Korea Research Institute of Bioscience and Biotechnology (KRIBB), Yusong, Taejon 305-600, Republic of Korea

The family Enterobacteriaceae is phenotypically diverse, ranging from commensals to pathogens of mammals, birds, reptiles and plants. The species *Escherichia coli* alone includes harmless intestinal flora as well as strains associated with diarrheal disease, urinary tract infections, neonatal septicemia and meningitis. We are investigating genome-scale genetic variation among enterobacterial genomes in several ways, including complete genome sequencing, random sample (low coverage) sequencing, PCR, and microarray hybridization. Sample sequencing is used to establish the overall levels of similarity of several strains of *E. coli*, *Shigella*, *Salmonella*, *Yersinia*, and *Erwinia*. The utility of sample sequencing for identification of novel genes and functions is illustrated with data collected from *Erwinia chrysanthemi* 3937. A fine-scale comparison of complete genome sequences from the harmless *Escherichia coli* K-12 laboratory strain and a deadly enterohemorrhagic *E. coli* O157:H7 strain shows the mosaic structure of the chromosome. Together these data reveal an extraordinary level of horizontal transfer punctuating a conserved clonally diverging ancestral genomic framework.

Complete Genome Comparison

Whole genome sequences provide the greatest possible resolution for genome-scale comparisons. We have now sequenced two complete enterobacterial genomes- both representatives of the species *Escherichia coli*. Figure 1 illustrates the organization of the genome from a deadly enterohemorrhagic *E. coli* O157:H7 strain EDL933 (Perna et al. 2001) and a comparison with the chromosome of the K-12 laboratory strain MG1655 (Blattner et al. 1997). The two *E. coli* genomes revealed an unexpectedly complex segmented relationship. They share a common "backbone" sequence, which is co-linear except for one 422 Kb inversion spanning the replication terminus. Homology is punctuated by hundreds of islands of apparently introgressed DNA, designated "K-islands" (KI) or "O-islands" (OI), where K-islands are DNA segments present in MG1655 but not in EDL933, and O-islands are lineage-specific segments of EDL933.

Single nucleotide polymorphisms (75,168 differences) are distributed throughout the 4.1 Mb backbone. There are 3,574 protein-coding genes encoded within backbone with an average nucleotide identity of 98.4%. Many orthologous genes (3,181/3,574=89%) are equal length in the two genomes; however, only 25% (911) encode identical proteins.

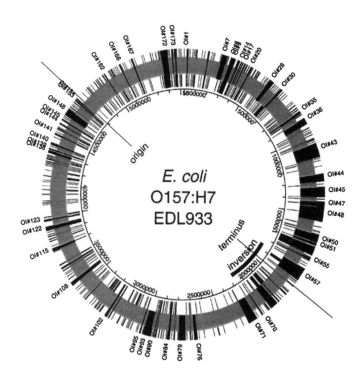

Fig. 1. Map of the *E. coli* O157:H7 strain EDL933 genome and comparison to *E. coli* K-12 strain MG1655 chromosome. Regions of the genome conserved between the two strains (backbone) are shown in gray. Black spokes radiating outward from the gray band mark the boundaries of lineage-specific regions of EDL933 (O-islands). The 47 O-islands greater than 5000 bp in length are labeled along the outside of the ring. Black

spokes pointing toward the center of the circle indicate comparable lineage-specific elements in MG1655 (K-islands). The origin and terminus of replication are indicated. Endpoints of an inversion spanning the terminus are shown as a black bar. A scale is shown in basepairs.

O-islands total 1.34 Mb of DNA and K-islands total 0.53 Mb. These lineage-specific segments are found throughout both genomes in clusters of up to 88 Kb. There are 177 O-islands and 234 K-islands greater than 50 bp in length. Roughly 26% of the EDL933 genes (1387/5416) lie completely within O-islands. In 189 cases, backbone-island junctions are within predicted genes. Of the O-island genes, 40% (561) can be assigned a function. Another 338 EDL933 genes marked as unknowns lie within phage-related clusters and are likely remnants of phage genomes. Approximately 33% (59/177) of the O-islands contain only genes of unknown function. Many classifiable proteins are related to known virulence-associated proteins from other *E. coli* strains or related enterobacteria. The MG1655 genome contains 528 genes (528/4,405 = 12%) not found in EDL933. Approximately 57% (303) of these were classified into known functional groups and include genes, such as a ferric citrate utilization system, that would suggest a role in virulence if identified in a pathogen. It is unclear whether these are remnants of a recent pathogenic ancestor, steps along a path to evolution of a novel pathogen, indicators that K-12 strains may be pathogenic for non-human hosts, or completely unrelated to pathogenicity.

Sample Sequencing Enterobacterial Genomes

We have also explored the relationships between genomes by sample sequencing random clones from shotgun M13 libraries for each of 7 enterobacterial pathogens. Results are shown in Figure 2 and Table 1. All genomes sampled yielded matches throughout the *E. coli* K-12 chromosome, suggesting that the core backbone identified in the genome comparison will be typical of the Enterobacteriaceae. However, we can not yet tell whether the co-linearity of this backbone will be conserved.

These data can also be used to estimate the amount of lineage-specific sequence in each genome. For example, given the 5.5 Mb O157:H7 chromosome, an estimate for the amount of lineage-specific sequence is 1.0 Mb (0.183 x 5.5 Mb). This is reasonably consistent with the 1.4 Mb of novel DNA identified in the complete genome comparison, with the difference accounted for by extensive similarity among distinct cryptic prophages. The proportion of the chromosome expected to differ from *E. coli* K-12 increases roughly with phylogenetic distance. Approximately 59% of the *E. chrysanthemi* queries have at least one match among the K-12 protein database with an average amino acid identity of 69.0%. At the DNA level, we detect matches for only 30.4% of the *E. chrysanthemi* queries. These results suggest that *E. chrysanthemi* 3937 has a genome with at least 1.5 Mb of sequence data not homologous to *E. coli* K-12. Given the density of coding regions in microbial genomes, this translates to over 1500 lineage-specific genes that we are expecting to find in *E. chrysanthemi*.

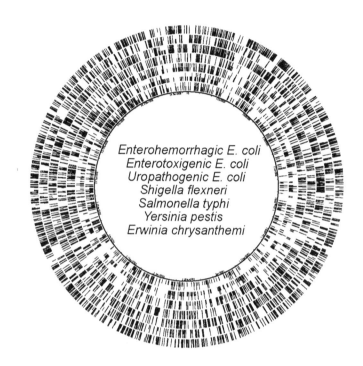

Fig. 2. Comparison of pathogenic enterobacteria to K-12 by sample sequencing. We analyzed 1076 random sequences from each genome, using BLASTX and BLASTN to query *E. coli* K-12 protein and DNA databases. Each match is plotted at the coordinates of the corresponding K-12 sequence (tickmarks indicate 0.25 Mb increments). The outer ring shows data from *E. coli* O157:H7 strain EDL933. Consecutive rings moving inward are analogous plots for enterotoxigenic *E. coli* (strain H10407), uropathogenic *E. coli* (CFT073), *Shigella flexneri* (2457T), *Salmonella typhi* (Ty2), *Yersinia pestis* (KIM5) and *E. chrysanthemi* (3937) sequences, respectively. For each species the protein matches are plotted on the inside of the ring, DNA matches on the outside.

Table 1. Percentage of 1076 sample sequence reads that match *E. coli* K-12.

Organism (Strain)	Protein (BLASTX)	DNA (BLASTN)	Genome (Mb)	Islands (Mb)
E. coli (EDL933)	81.7	80.0	5.5	1.0
E. coli (H10407)	77.0	79.1	~ 5	1.1
E. coli (CFT073)	81.1	78.4	~ 5	0.9
Shigella flexneri	68.9	69.1	~ 5	1.6
Salmonella typhi	72.4	62.1	~ 5	1.4
Yersinia pestis	62.1	24.8	~ 5	1.9
Erwinia chrysanthemi	59.3	30.4	3.7	1.5

Gene Discovery by Sample Sequencing

We conducted a more detailed analysis of 1777 sample sequences from *E. chrysanthemi* strain 3937 as a starting point for an *Erwinia* genome project. This amounts to 571,622 basepairs (bp) of sequence data or ~14% coverage of the *E. chrysanthemi* genome. Each random sequence was searched against the Genpept protein database using NCBI BLASTX 2.0. Approximately 69% (1230/1777) of the sequences have a least one match (E-value less than 1.0×10^{-05}). Most best matches (83%) are to other closely related Enterobacteriaceae. However, similarities to proteins available from *E. chrysanthemi* and other *Erwinia* species account for only 2.5% of the best hits.

Among the most interesting results thus far are sequence similarities to proteins implicated in pathogenicity of *E. chrysanthemi* and other pathogenic bacteria; 65 sequences (3.7% of total) are in this category. The list of potential pathogenicity determinants include those involved in Hrp (type III) protein secretion, pectinolysis, extracellular proteolysis, iron uptake, global regulation, quorum sensing, and exopolysaccharide production. In addition, the sequence data surprisingly suggest that genes for auxin biosynthesis, syringomycin biosynthesis, and opine utilization are present in the *E. chrysanthemi* genome. None of these functions have been linked to *E. chrysanthemi* pathogenesis before. Further, no phytotoxins have been reported from species of *Erwinia*, and no opine utilization systems outside plant-associated Rhizobiaceae. Other informative similarities to database entries are a set of elements associated with horizontal transfer of genes across bacterial species lines including phages, transposons and plasmid proteins (~2% of total).

Literature Cited

Blattner, F.R., Plunkett, G., III, Bloch, C.A., Perna, N.T., Burland, V., Riley, M., Collado-Vides, J., Glasner, J.D., Rode, C.K., Mayhew, G.F., Gregor, J., Davis, N.W., Kirkpatrick, H.A., Goeden, M.A., Rose, D.J., Mau, B. and Shao, Y. 1997. The complete genome sequence of *Escherichia coli* K-12. Science 277:1453-1474.

Perna, N.T., Plunkett, G., III, Burland, V., Mau, B., Glasner, J.D., Rose, D.J., Mayhew, G.F., Evans, P.S., Gregor, J., Kirkpatrick, H.A., Posfai, G., Hackett, J., Klink, S., Boutin, A., Shao, Y., Miller, L., Grotbeck, E.J., Davis, N.W., Lim, A., Dimalanta, E.T., Potamousis, K.D., Apodaca, J., Anantharaman, T.S., Lin, J., Yen, G., Schwartz, D.C., Welch, R.A. and Blattner, F.R. 2001. Genome sequence of enterohaemorrhagic *Escherichia coli* O157:H7. Nature 409:529-533.

The Complete Genome Sequence of *Ralstonia solanacearum* Reveals Over 200 Candidate Pathogenicity Genes

M. Salanoubat[*], S. Genin[†], F. Artiguenave[*], J. Gouzy[†], S. Mangenot[*], M. Arlat[†], A. Billault[‡], P. Brottier[*], J.C. Camus[†], L. Cattolico[*], M. Chandler[§], N. Choisne[||], C. Claudel-Renard[¶], S. Cunnac[†], N. Demange[*], C. Gaspin[¶], M. Lavie[†], A. Moisan[¶], C. Robert[*], P. Thébault[†], W. Saurin[*], T. Schiex[¶], P. Siguier[§], M. Whalen[†], P. Wincker[*], M. Levy[*], J. Weissenbach[*] & C.A. Boucher[†]

[*] Genoscope and CNRS UMR-8030 Evry, France; [†] Laboratoire de Biologie Moléculaire des Interactions Plantes-Microorganismes INRA-CNRS, Castanet-Tolosan, France; [‡] Fondation Jean Dausset-CEPH Paris, France; [§] LMGM CNRS Toulouse France; [||] Genoscope and INRA URGV Evry Cedex, France; [¶] Laboratoire de Biométrie et Intelligence Artificielle INRA, Castanet-Tolosan France

Ralstonia solanacearum is a widespread plant pathogenic bacterium that is used extensively as a model system to study the molecular mechanisms governing plant pathogenicity. These include production of extracellular hydrolytic enzymes, extracellular polysaccharide (EPS) biosynthesis, bacterial attachment to plant cells and delivery of effector proteins through the type III secretion machinery encoded by the *hrp* genes. As a tool to facilitate analysis of the functions governing pathogenicity, we have recently analysed in detail the complete genome sequence of *R. solanacearum* strain GMI1000, a race 1 strain isolated from tomato in French Guyana. In this article we present the general organisation of the genome of this bacterium and illustrate how this sequence has been used to identify candidate pathogenicity genes.

General Organization of the Genome

A BIPARTE GENOME

Following sequencing of randomly generated genomic DNA fragments, sequence data representing a 9X coverage of the genome were assembled in two circular contigs of 3,716,413 bp and 2,094,509 bp yielding a total genome size of 5,810,922 bp. This concurred with the estimated size of the two replicons as determined by relative mobility by pulsed field gel electrophoresis (Figures 1 and 2). With an average value close to 67%, the % G+C composition did not differ significantly between the two replicons.

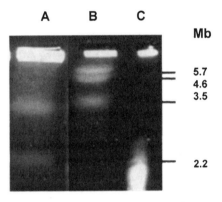

Fig. 1. Pulsed Field Gel Electrophoresis of genomic DNA from *R solanacearum* strain GMI1000 (A), *Schizosaccharomyces pombe* (B) and *Saccharomyces cerevisiae* (C).

Since the *hrp* gene cluster is located on the smaller replicon, this replicon corresponds to the megaplasmid previously identified in strain GMI1000 (Boucher et al. 1986). Analysis of gene distribution between the two replicons shows that the larger replicon probably encodes all of the genes absolutely essential to sustain life. These include all of the genes required for purine and pyrimidine biosynthesis, and all other absolutely essential genes encoding ribosomal proteins, 3 complete rDNA loci, and 55 identified tRNAs allowing recognition of all possible codons. In addition, the large replicon harbours all of the genes required for DNA replication and for cell division. This replicon is therefore most probably sufficient to support life of the bacterium and therefore is assumed to be the bacterial chromosome.

However genes governing amino acid and cofactor biosynthesis are distributed on both replicons. In addition, several chromosomal genes including a complete copy of a rDNA locus with 2 tRNA genes, a gene coding for the alpha subunit of DNA polymerase III, and a gene for the protein elongation factor G have been duplicated on the megaplasmid. This suggests that the two replicons might have co-evolved for a long time in this bacterium and that a process of redistribution of genetic information between the two replicons might be in progress.

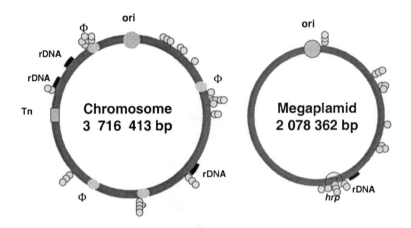

Fig. 2. Structural organization of the *R. solanacearum* genome : the two replicons are represented by circles. Localisation of the predicted origins of replication (ori), of the major prophage loci (Φ), of a conjugative transposon (Tn) and of the *hrp* gene locus (*hrp*) are represented on the maps. The 4 rDNA loci are represented by rectangles adjacent to the maps, and dots outside of the map localise structural genes for candidate type III secreted effector proteins.

Another example of a bacterium having a bipartite genome is *Vibrio cholerae* (Heildelberg et al. 2000)). However, in *V. cholerae* the smaller replicon (chromosome 2) carries essential genes which are not present on the large replicon (chromosome 1). This replicon has therefore been proposed to be a second chromosome and may have evolved from an original plasmid, captured by an ancestral *Vibrio* strain and that has acquired new functions through translocation of essential genes from the native chromosome. This model might be applicable to *R. solanacearum* and would explain the distribution of genes governing amino acids and cofactor biosynthesis on the two replicons. However, in *R. solanacearum* the evolution process might be less advanced that in *V. cholerae* since essential housekeeping genes such as *dnaE,* tDNA and rDNA genes are duplicated on the megaplasmid, although the corresponding genes have not yet been eliminated from the chromosome.

During the process of genome annotation we found that the codon usage for 7% of the *R. solanacearum* genes differs significantly from the standard codon usage established for the rest of the genome. Such regions, designated ACURs (Alternative Codon Usage Regions), were found in 91 distinct loci extending from 3 to over 20 kb. With a base composition ranging from 50% to 70% GC, ACURs differ significantly from the average 67% GC value calculated for the entire genome. Furthermore, ACURs have a tendency to form clusters and are most often found in close vicinity of phages, insertion sequences or other genetic elements such as Rhs and Vgr proteins generally associated with genetically unstable loci (Wang et al. 1998). This is an indication that ACURs might have been acquired relatively recently through horizontal gene transfers. It could also explain the reported genetic instability of the *R. solanacearum* genome.

New Candidate Pathogenicity Genes

Three criteria have been used to identify new candidate pathogenicity genes in *R. solanacearum* : (i) homology with known proteins governing traits potentially involved in plant-bacterial interactions, (ii) the predicted presence of structural features characteristic of eukaryotic proteins and (iii) the presence of upstream regulatory elements potentially relevant to pathogenicity ; such proteins are most likely translocated via the *hrp*-gene encoded type III secretion pathway.

ATTACHMENT DETERMINANTS

An unusual characteristic of the *R. solanacearum* genome is that it contains a large number of genes encoding outer-membrane proteins or components of bacterial appendages (pili, fimbriae) implicated in the attachment of the bacterium to external surfaces. These include genes for type IV pili and for a new type of pilus similar to the Tad pilus of *Actinobacillus actinomycetemcomitans* which is involved in tight adherence to surfaces (Kachlany et al. 2001). Interestingly, for these two types of pili/fimbriae, multiple copies of the pilin structural genes were found (5 and 8 respectively). In addition, strain GMI1000 caries 28 genes encoding proteins related to various adhesins and hemagglutinins such as the filamentous haemagglutinin (FhaB) of *Bordetella pertussis*, and the HMW1A/HMW2A adhesins of *Haemophilus influenzae* (see Jacob-Dubuisson et al. 2001). Accordingly, among the bacteria which have been entirely sequenced, *R. solanacearum* is the organism presenting the highest number of hemagglutinin-related proteins, a characteristic which may be correlated with its ability to colonise a wide range of host plants as well as other environments including soil.

Twenty nine proteins having either partial or global homology with Avr proteins found in other plant pathogenic bacteria have been identified in strain GMI1000. These include 2 homologs of the YopJ/AvrRxv proteins, one AvrBs3-related protein (so far exclusively found in *Xanthomonas* strains) and several avirulence proteins from *P. syringae* [AvrE, AvrPpiA1, AvrPpiC2, AvrPphD, AvrPphE, AvrPphF (orf2)]. *R. solanacearum* also harbors several proteins homologous to proteins encoded in the vicinity of the *hrp* gene clusters of *P. syringae* and *Erwinia amylovora*. Moreover, based on structural features, we have identified several ORFs (open reading frames) predicted to encode different repetitive motifs (Leucine Rich Repeats, Ankyrin repeats, and Pirin-like proteins) which are likely to be translocated into plant cells. Additional candidates with features characteristic of proteins from eukaryotes include : an EF-hand Ca^{++} binding protein, serine/threonine protein kinases, and a tyrosine phosphatase.

Figure 2 shows that genes for such candidate effectors are distributed on the two replicons where they have a tendency to form clusters, certain of which have the characteristics of pathogenicity islands.

Apart from attachment factors and type III effectors, over 30 additional candidate pathogenicity factors have been identified, including genes governing production of plant hormones and plant signaling molecules (salicylic acid degradation, ethylene synthesis and degradation, auxin synthesis), resistance to oxidative stress (SOD and hydrogen peroxide reductase), plant cell wall degrading enzymes and synthesis of hemolysins or other RTX toxins.

Conclusions

It is already clear that the knowledge of a complete pathogen genome sequence has tremendous potential for advancing our understanding of plant-pathogen interactions. Based on the criteria that are presented in this paper, we have identified about 200 candidate pathogenicity genes in the *R. solanacearum* genome, including about 50 type III secreted effectors have been defined. This list will most likely be expanded in the near future by complementary approaches such as comparative transcriptome analysis using the numerous regulatory mutants affected in pathogenicity that have been described in this bacterium. The complete sequence of the genome also offers new means for analysis of genetic diversity in this species and will lead to the identification of new genes governing host range and specificity. It will also contribute to the identification of functions encoded in ACURs and in the role of these loci in evolution.

Because *R. solanacearum* is a bacterium which survives for long time in the soil, the complete sequence of strain GMI1000 also offers new tools to investigate the mechanisms governing bacterial adaptation to such environments.

Acknowledgements

We thank Nigel Grimsley for editing of the manuscript.

Literature Cited

Boucher, C., Martinel, A., Barberis, P., Alloing, G., and Zischek C. 1986. Virulence genes are carried by a megaplasmid of the plant pathogen *Pseudomonas solanacearum*. Mol. Gen. Genet. 205:270-275.

Heidelberg, J.F. *et al*. 2000. DNA sequence of both chromosomes of the cholera pathogen *Vibrio cholerae*. Nature 406, 477-483.

Jacob-Dubuisson, F., Locht, C. & Antoine, R. 2001. Two-partner secretion in Gram-negative bacteria : a thrifty, specific pathway for large virulence proteins. Mol. Microbiol. 40:306-313.

Kachlany, S.C. *et al*. 2001. *flp-1*, the first representative of a new pilin gene subfamily, is required for non-specific adherence of *Actinobacillus actinomycetemcomitans*. Mol. Microbiol. 40:542-554.

Wang, Y.D., Zhao, S. & Hill, C.W. 1998. Rhs elements comprise three subfamilies which diverged prior to acquisition by *Escherichia coli*. J. Bacteriol. 180:4102-4110.

The Sequencing of Bacterial Plant Pathogen Genomes by the Organization for Nucleotide Sequencing and Analysis (ONSA) in São Paulo, Brazil

Claudia B. Monteiro-Vitorello and the Organization for Nucleotide Sequencing and Analysis (ONSA/FAPESP)

University of São Paulo, Escola Superior de Agricultura "Luiz de Queiroz", São Paulo, Brazil

We are currently working on the complete genome sequencing of four bacterial plant pathogens, *Xanthomonas axonopodis* pv. *citri, Xanthomonas campestris* pv. *campestris, Xylella fastidiosa*, Temecula 1 strain and *Leifsonia xyli* subsp. *xyli*. The project to sequence the grapevine *Xylella fastidiosa* strain is the result of an agreement between FAPESP and the United States Department of Agriculture (USDA-ARS), American Vineyard Foundation (AVF) and California Department of Food and Agriculture (CDFA). Our overall aim is to provide complete, very high quality sequences that allow the pursuit of comparative genomics in the context of very closely related organisms. Reduced coverage sequencing of genomes is not appropriate for such analyses since genomic differences can be extremely subtle. On the other hand, by using high quality, finished sequences, such comparative genomics can be highly instructive in identifying genomic regions associated with host specificity and pathogenicity.

Following our successful sequencing of the first plant pathogen, *Xylella fastidiosa* CVC(Simpson et al. 2000), we have extended the scope of bacterial genome sequencing in São Paulo. Given the many ONSA laboratories specialized in the study of organisms related to agronomy and the environment, we have launched a coordinated multi-genome sequencing effort in this area. The general objective of this project is to undertake massive genome sequencing and annotation of organisms selected based on their scientific relevance and economic impact in Brazil. So far, we have chosen plant pathogens important to Brazilian agriculture such as those of citrus and sugarcane crops. Organisms that may contribute to a general understanding of bacterial diseases and comparative genomics have also been selected; these include *X. campestris* pv. *campestris* and *X. fastidiosa* of Pierce's Disease.

Sequencing Strategy

All the sequencing projects rely on massive shotgun sequencing. The shotgun sequences are clustered into contigs and the end sequences of clones from a cosmid library are used to build a scaffold of the physical map. Direct sequencing methods are used to close gaps and resolve recalcitrant regions. Open reading frames are determined using Glimmer 2.0 (Delcher et al. 1999). A few ORFs are found by hand, guided by BLAST results. Annotation is carried out in a cooperative way mostly by comparison with sequences in public databases using BLAST (Altschul et al. 1997), COG (Tatusov et al. 2000) and PFAM (Bateman et al. 2000) and tRNAscan-SE (Lowe and Eddy 1997). The bioinfomatics system was developed by the Bioinformatics Laboratory of the University of Campinas, São Paulo.

General Features of the Organisms and their Genomes

XANTHOMONAS AXONOPODIS PV. *CITRI (XAC)*

Citrus-based agriculture is of fundamental importance to the Brazilian economy and ranks second in terms of economically important rural activities in the state of São Paulo. There are over 100,000 properties with more than 200 trees in the state of São Paulo. The number of citrus trees with citrus canker has grown exponentially over the past decade from less than a thousand before 1992 to 80,000 in 1998.

General features. The genome of *Xanthomonas axonopodis* pv. *citri* contains 5,175,554 bp with a GC content of 64.7 % and two plasmids, pXac33 and pXac65, of 33,699 and 65,124 bp, respectively. The genome sequence harbors 105 insertion sequences corresponding to 1.36 % of the main chromosome and plasmids. There are 35 ORFs related to bacteriophage sequences. Fifteen of them are grouped and resemble a defective prophage, most likely a P2-type phage. This region is 12 kbp long and contains ORFs similar to and with the same organization as the proteins for head assembly and part of tail formation of the φCTX phage particle of *Pseudomonas aeruginosa* (Nakayama et al. 1999).

XANTHOMONAS CAMPESTRIS PV. *CAMPESTRIS (XCC)*

The major disease that affects cruciferous crops in the state of São Paulo is black rot caused by Xcc. During hot and humid seasons, economic losses are significant.

General features. The genome scaffold is 4,938,212 bp long with a GC content of 64.7% and no plasmids were found. Sequencing of this genome has not been completed. Preliminary comparative genomic analyses show that the overall organization and gene order within the two *Xanthomonas* species are similar. So far, we have found 582 ORFs (13.8 % of the genome), which are present in *citri* and absent in *campestris,* while 350 ORFs (9.5 % of the genome) present in *campestris* and absent in *citri.* These ORFs are distributed unevenly throughout the conserved backbone. Although some of the specific ORFs are isolated, most of them are clustered into islands of up to 100 Kbp in size. So far, the total length of these regions is 375,344 bp, corresponding to 7.3% of the chromosome. An interesting feature is that most of the regions larger than 10 Kbp are located close to insertion sequence-like elements. There are two large-scale rearrangements, a deletion of 133 Kbp associated with an inversion of 75,572bp spanning the replication terminus and one translocation of approximately 190 Kbp.

XYLELLA FASTIDIOSA (PIERCE'S DISEASE) (*XF*-PD)

Brazil and the USA are undertaking a jointly funded project to sequence the genome of a grapevine-derived *X. fastidiosa* clone (Temecula1 strain) that is responsible for the potentially devastating outbreak of Pierce's disease in Californian vineyards. In addition to citrus variegated chlorosis (CVC) and Pierce's disease, *X. fastidiosa* is responsible for a number of other economically important plant diseases including alfalfa dwarf, phony peach disease, periwinkle wilt, and leaf scorch of plums, and is also associated with diseases in mulberry, pear, almond, elm, sycamore, oak, maple, pecan and coffee. The relationship between the isolates of this organism remains poorly understood, as does the basis of the varying host specificities of different *X. fastidiosa* pathovars or subspecies. The determination of these factors is likely to play a crucial role in understanding the pathogenicity of *X. fastidiosa* and directly contribute to the exploitation of the data in terms of practical measures for the improved control of diseases caused by *X. fastidiosa.*

General features. The genome is 2,507,178 bp long with a GC content of 51.7%. There is no large plasmid such as pXf51found in the *Xylella* of CVC (*Xf*-CVC) but the small plasmid, pXf1.3 (1345 bp), is present. The genome is 6.4% smaller than that of the CVC strain. There are large-scale genomic rearrangements due to the presence of prophages or prophage-like elements in comparison to genomic DNA of *Xylella* of CVC. The presence of the plasmid insertion region in the genome (15 Kbp) and a genomic island of 76 Kbp were not detected.

LEIFSONIA XYLI SUBSP. *XYLI* (*LXX*)

Lxx is an airborne, xylem-infecting bacterial pathogen, recently removed from the genus *Clavibacter* (Evtushenko et al. 2000). It is a small, fastidious, gram-positive, coryneform bacterium that causes ratoon stunting

310

disease (RSD) in sugarcane. The disease has been found in most sugarcane growing areas of the world and can cause yield losses of up to 50% in susceptible and intolerant varieties. Additionally, increasing incidence of the infection may contribute to a decline in yield during successive ratoon crops. Cumulative losses of sugarcane due to RSD have probably been greater than the losses caused by any other sugarcane disease over the last 40 years. Brazilian production of sugar is about 14 million tons. In Brazil, the total income loss by sugarcane producers of the State of São Paulo, due to RSD incidence, corresponds to approximately US$ 2 billion.

General features. Massive shotgun sequencing of the genome is completed. The assembly of shotgun and cosmid end sequences generated a scaffold of 2.8 Mb, with a GC content of 67 %. So far, six major classes of repeated regions were found to occur in variable frequencies. One of these, named ISLxx1, is present in at least 30 copies. It is a 1.2 Kbp fragment flanked by two perfect inverted repeats at its termini similar to the transposase of the *Corynebacterium striatum* Tn5664 transposon. This element is also present in the genome of *Leifsonia xyli* subsp. *cynodontis* (*Lxc*), the causal agent of retarded shoot growth in grasses from the genus *Cynodon* (Bermuda grass) (Davis et al. 1980). We are interested in performing comparative genome studies between the two subspecies. While Lxx also infects bermuda grass and causes symptoms identical to that caused by Lxc, the reciprocal is not true: Lxc infects and multiplies in sugarcane but does not incite any symptom (Davis et al. 1980). We also want to investigate the relatedness among several members of *Clavibacter* and *Leifsonia* genera. The repeated region, ISLxx1, is not present in *Clavibacter michiganensis* subsp. *michiganensis* nor in *C. michiganensis* subsp. *sepedonicus.*

Conclusions and Future Perspectives

Although most of the data is still preliminary regarding annotation, there is considerable potential for the identification of regions within the sequences of these plant pathogens that are homologous to genes known to be involved in pathogenesis. Comparison of these genomes might reveal genes present in *Xf* and *Lxx*, but absent from *Xac*, related to the colonization of the xylem as well as genes present in *Xf*, but absent from Xac and Lxx, related to insect transmission. We expect to gain interesting insight by comparing two organisms that live in the same host (*Xac* and *Xf*-CVC) but cause different diseases. We also intend to analyze these genomes under the scope of genome organization. Furthermore, interaction with the SUCEST project, the Brazilian sugarcane EST project, will permit the identification of plant vs. pathogen interaction mechanisms at the molecular level in the case of *Lxx*.

311

Literature Cited

Altschul, S.F., Madden, T.L., Schaffer, A.A., *et al.* 1997. Gapped BLAST and PSI-BLAST: a new generation of protein database search programs. Nucleic.Acids.Res. 25: 3389-3402.

Bateman, A., Birney, E., Durbin, R., Eddy, S.R., Howe, K.L., Sonnhammer, E.L. 2000. The Pfam protein families database. Nucleic Acids Res. 28(1):263-6.

Davis, M.J., Gillaspie, A.G., Vidaver, A.K., Harris, R.W. 1980. *Clavibacter -* a new genus containing some phytopathogenic coryneform bacteria, including *Clavibacter-xyli* subsp xyli sp-nov, subsp-nov and *Clavibacter-xyli* subsp cynodontis subsp-nov, pathogens that cause ratoon stunting disease of sugarcane and bermudagrass stunting disease. International Journal of Systematic Bacteriology 34: (2) 107-117.

Delcher, A.L., Harmon, D., Kasif, S., White, O. & Salzberg, S.L. 1999. Improved microbial gene identification with GLIMMER. Nucleic. Acids.Res. 27: 4636-4641.

Evtushenko, L.I., Dorofeeva, L.V., Subbotin, S.A., et al. 2000. *Leifsonia poae* gen. nov., sp nov., isolated from nematode galls on poa annua, and classification of *'Corynebacterium aquaticum'* leifson 1962 as *Leifsonia aquatica (*ex leifson 1962) gen.nov., nom.rev., comb.nov and *Clavibacter xyli* davis et al. 1984 with two subspecies as *Leifsonia xyli* (davis et al. 1984) gen.nov., comb.nov. Int. J. Syst. Evol. Micr. 50: 371-380.

Lowe, T.M. & Eddy, S.R. 1997. tRNAscan-SE: a program for improved detection of transfer RNA genes in genomic sequence. Nucleic.Acids.Res. 25: 955-964

Nakayama, K., Kanaya, S., Ohnishi, M., Terawaki, Y., Hayashi, T. 1999 The complete nucleotide sequence of ϕCTX, a cytotoxin-converting phage of *Pseudomonas aeruginosa*: implications for phage evolution and horizontal gene transfer via bacteriophages. Molecular Microbiology 31 (2): 399-419.

Simpson, A.G.J. et al. 2000. The genome sequence of the plant pathogen *Xylella fastidiosa*. Nature 406: 151-159

Tatusov, R.L., Galperin, M.Y., Natale, D.A., Koonin, E.V. 2000. The COG database: a tool for genome-scale analysis of protein functions and evolution. Nucleic Acids Res. 28(1):33-6.

Genome Wide Analysis of Fungal Pathogenicity to Plants

B. Gillian Turgeon[1,2] and O. C. Yoder[1]

[1]Torrey Mesa Research Institute, La Jolla CA 92121;
[2]Dept. of Plant Pathology, Cornell Univ., Ithaca NY 14853

In the last year and a half the process of fungal pathogenicity gene discovery has moved from a gene-by-gene to a genome-wide approach (Yoder and Turgeon 2001). This effort has been facilitated by the integration of biological endeavors and leading edge technologies. The goal is to apply genomics methodologies to aid discovery of the pathogenicity gene set and then experimentally validate candidate genes. The end result is expected to be a set of fungal genes that function in concert to effect plant parasitism; a different, but overlapping, set is likely to be found for fungal parasitism of humans.

When fungi interact with plants, there are at least three outcomes: 1) nothing happens, 2) resistance occurs, 3) disease develops. These are not discrete categories, of course, but rather form a continuum. Communication between microbe and plant (e.g., "I'm a pathogen, you're a host") is mediated by components of communication circuits (signal transduction pathways) that start with, or lead to, production of signaling effectors, some of which are small molecules elaborated *via* the enzymes of secondary metabolism.

Our approach to the identification of the fungal pathogenicity gene set includes a two-pronged functional strategy: directed gene deletion and random, saturation, deletion scanning, both underpinned by knowledge of genome sequence. In the first case, candidate genes are chosen based on existing information. Each candidate gene is deleted from the genome and the resulting mutant is tested for virulence on the host (forward genetics). In the second case, no assumptions are made. The fungus itself reveals genes required for pathogenesis. Mutations are made randomly in the genome, followed by functional tests on plants (reverse genetics). With either approach, coordinates of genes being tested can be determined by reference to the genomic sequence.

The focus of our program is on three filamentous ascomycete pathogens, representing wide phylogenetic distribution (Fig. 1). The genome of each is

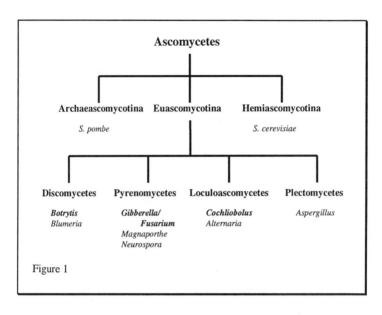

Ascomycetes

- **Archaeascomycotina**
  - *S. pombe*
- **Euascomycotina**
- **Hemiascomycotina**
  - *S. cerevisiae*

Euascomycotina:
- **Discomycetes**
  - *Botrytis*
  - *Blumeria*
- **Pyrenomycetes**
  - *Gibberella/*
  - *Fusarium*
  - *Magnaporthe*
  - *Neurospora*
- **Loculoascomycetes**
  - *Cochliobolus*
  - *Alternaria*
- **Plectomycetes**
  - *Aspergillus*

Figure 1

being sequenced using the shotgun strategy. Each genome is about 35 Mb in size, i.e., about a third the size of the *Arabidopsis* genome and an order of magnitude smaller than the rice genome. Our main interest is the corn pathogen *Cochliobolus heterostrophus* (Fig. 1), chosen for this project because it is readily manipulated by both conventional and molecular genetic procedures. Any gene can be efficiently deleted or disrupted if as little as 200 bp of homologous sequence is provided on the transforming DNA. We are also interested in *Gibberella zeae* (*Fusarium graminearum*), causal agent of wheat head scab disease, currently of great economic concern (O'Donnell et al. 2000). This fungus is also a pathogen of corn and rice. Completing the trio is *Botrytis cinerea*, a cosmopolitan pathogen of dicots. The latter two fungi are also genetically tractable. In addition to providing phylogenetic diversity (Fig. 1), these three fungi employ different modes of infection. When sequencing is complete, it will be possible to compare these three pathogen genomes to those of other fungi, such as the cotton pathogen, *Ashbya gossypii* smallest genome known among the filamentous fungi (and high similarity to the *Saccharomyces cerevisiae* genome, without the problem of gene duplication), and the saprophyte *Neurospora crassa* (Braun et al. 2000; http://www-genome.wi.mit.edu/annotation/fungi/neurospora/). Of major significance is the fact that the *Cochliobolus* spp. and members of a sister genus, the *Alternaria* spp., as well as the *Gibberella* spp., are notorious for their abilities to produce vast numbers of secondary metabolites, some of which are already known to have roles in pathogenesis (Desjardins and Hohn 1997; Yoder et al. 1997; Kohmoto and Yoder 1998). How many of these uncharacterized metabolites are effectors, belonging to the pathogenicity gene suite?

Fungal pathogenicity is a problem of basic biological concern. Fungi are the second largest group of organisms on the planet, next to the insects. They display a diverse set of complex behaviors, one of which is the ability to cause disease. Pathogenicity is rare, however, and the majority of fungi are not pathogens. Important questions regarding fungal pathogenicity to plants are: What is the molecular nature of pathogenicity? How do pathogens differ from non-pathogens? How do highly virulent races arise? Does pathogenicity evolve by simple point mutations, by genome rearrangements, by horizontal gene transfer, or are multiple evolutionary strategies employed? It is likely that sets of genes for pathogenicity will be found to include those controlling production of common factors, possibly co-opted from normal cellular metabolism. Others will be involved in production of factors unique to a particular fungus-host combination.

Among fungi that have acquired pathogenic capability, is there a common strategy for causing disease or are there multiple routes to this goal? Preliminary evidence suggests that different fungi have evolved different mechanisms for first entering their hosts and then colonizing host tissues. In this article we illustrate the foregoing point by comparing parasitism of the maize pathogen, *C. heterostrophus,* with that of the rice pathogen, *Magnaporthe grisea.* If corn leaves infected by *C. heterostrophus* are compared with rice leaves infected by *M. grisea,* the disease phenotypes are essentially the same- both fungi make spots on leaves. However, data available to date, scanty though they are, suggest that these two fungi achieve their pathogenic ends by substantially different routes. The existing knowledge base differs for the two fungi. Much is known about factors required for penetration by *M. grisea* (Howard and Valent 1996; Tucker and Talbot 2001) but little about those involved in colonization. The reverse is true for *Cochliobolus* spp. (Yoder et al. 1997). Let's first consider penetration processes by these two fungi.

For successful infection, *M. grisea* spores must land on hydrophobic leaf surfaces, germinate and elaborate melanized appressoria that then form infection pegs, each of which can penetrate the leaf epidermis (Howard and Valent 1996). Appressoria are large, about the same size as the spores. It is known that a G alpha protein, encoded by the *MAGB* gene, must be functional for the appressoria to form (Liu and Dean 1997), and that melanin must be produced in order for appressoria to effect penetration (Chumley and Valent 1990). In contrast, *C. heterostrophus* spores are not fussy about hydrophobicity of leaves; they germinate and elaborate appressoria that are considerably smaller than the spores and these appressoria do not require melanization for penetration to occur (Guillen et al. 1994). Furthermore, when the *C. heterostrophus* homolog of *MAGB* is deleted, appressorium production is almost eliminated, yet the fungus is as infectious as wild type (Horwitz et al. 1999). Clearly, genetic requirements are different for the two fungi during the penetration phase of infection.

What about colonization effectors? As stated above, *Cochliobolus* spp. are well known for production of secondary metabolite virulence factors, in particular toxins, such as the polyketide T-toxin produced by Race T of *C. heterostrophus* which is required for high virulence on T cytoplasm corn, the cyclic peptide HC-toxin produced by Race 1 of *C. carbonum,* which renders Race 1 pathogenic on *hm1hm1* corn, or the chlorinated cyclic peptide victorin produced by *C. victoriae* and required for pathogenicity on *Vb* oats (Yoder et al. 1997). Preliminary data (see below) suggest that additional small molecules are required for successful infection. To date, products of secondary metabolism have not been demonstrated to play a large role in the *M. grisea* infection. An exception to this statement is the recent report (Bohnert et al. 2001) of a polyketide synthase/nonribosomal peptide synthetase hybrid gene, thought to synthesize a small molecule that appears to play the role of an elicitor.

On the premise that small molecule production is an important element in pathogenicity, we have undertaken to identify and assay functionally, by gene deletion, all non-ribosomal peptide synthetase (NRPS) genes in the *C. heterostrophus* genome (Yoder and Turgeon 2001). At least one of these has a distinct reduced virulence phenotype when the gene encoding it is deleted. It is not yet known whether deletion of homologues of this gene in other fungi would also impact virulence. All of the *C. heterostrophus* NRPS genes have been aligned with known NRPS genes from fungi and bacteria; this analysis, combined with structural and phylogenetic treatments, offers powerful insight into function.

In addition to genes encoding NRPSs, we previously identified a NRPS-like gene, present in fungi and animals, but not plants and bacteria, that controls production of a factor involved in virulence of several fungi (Lu et al. 2001). This gene was identified in a REMI mutagenesis screen and has been shown to reduce virulence of *C. heterostrophus* on corn, *C. victoriae* on oats, and *G. zeae* on wheat, when deleted from the genome of each of these fungi. This gene appears to be a member of the AMP-binding superfamily and is most closely related to acyl CoA ligases associated with peptide synthetases and polyketide synthases (Huang et al. 2001). This is the type of general virulence factor that may offer a global solution to control of plant disease.

Another approach to teasing out the pathogenicity gene set is cross comparison of complete or nearly complete genomes. At this point, the fungal genomes available are those from the saprophytes *S. cerevisiae, S. pombe* and *N. crassa,* the plant pathogens *C. heterostrophus, G. zeae, B. cinerea* and *A. gossypii,* and the human pathogen *Candida albicans.* Ideally, one would want to make several types of comparison: 1) saprophytes *vs.* pathogens, 2) pathogen 1 *vs.* pathogen 2, etc., 3) tissue 1-specific pathogen *vs.* tissue 2-specific pathogen etc. (Yoder and Turgeon

2001). Preliminary data are available using *C. heterostrophus* sequence to query these genomes. Although existing gene prediction programs are inadequate for the fungi at this point in time, some measure of confidence that these predicted ORFs represent real genes is gained when ORFs with no match in the database, and thus no predicted function, are found in other fungi. When this was done for 2,417 predicted *C. heterostrophus* ORFs, without functional assignment, ~770 were common to *Cochliobolus, Fusarium, Botrytis, Neurospora* and also found in the GenBank NR (Table 1). These are obvious candidates for essential genes. Similarly, 75 were found only in the pathogens, *Cochliobolus, Fusarium,* and *Botrytis,* and not in the saprophyte, *Neurospora* or elsewhere. These become candidates for pathogenicity-specific genes.

Table 1. An example of identification of gene sets by cross genome comparison

773 common to *Cochliobolus, Fusarium, Botrytis, Neurospora* and NR	Candidates for essential genes
292 common to *Cochliobolus, Fusarium, Botrytis, Neurospora*	Candidates for fungal-specific genes
75 common to *Cochliobolus, Fusarium, Botrytis*	Candidates for pathogenicity genes

A final comment: the use of model systems to understand pathogenicity cannot be overemphasized. This point is illustrated by the current situation in plant genomics. The sequences of two plant genomes are available, one a monocot (rice, 430 Mb), the other a dicot (*Arabidopsis,* 130 Mb). Both can be transformed, and tagged insertional mutant lines are available for each. It has been clearly demonstrated that the degree of homology among the cereals is high; genes in rice have a >90% chance of a match in corn, and thus sequencing the smallest cereal genome (rice) reveals much about the larger genomes of the other cereals. On the fungal side, a sister taxon to *Cochliobolus, Alternaria brassicicola,* has been demonstrated as a pathogen of *Arabidopsis.* It can be predicted that > 95 % of genes in *Cochliobolus* would have a match in *Alternaria,* thus the *Cochliobolus* pathogenicity gene set data should be largely applicable to *A. brassicicola,* genes for host specificity notwithstanding. In addition, *C. heterostrophus* is closely related to *C. miyabeanus,* a rice pathogen responsible for the Bengal rice famine of 1942. Recall the similarity of disease lesion phenotypes of *C. heterostrophus* on corn and *M. grisea* on rice. Extension of the *C. heterostrophus* pathogenicity gene set to homologues in *C. miyabeanus* will reduce the dual host problem to one host and will allow comparisons of the two distantly related fungal pathogens (*Cochliobolus* and *Magnaporthe*) on a single host (rice).

Literature Cited

Bohnert, H. U., Fudal, I., Dioh, W., Tharreau, D., Notteghem, J. L., and Lebrun, M. H. 2001. The avirulence gene *ACE1* (AVR1-IRAT7) of the rice blast fungus *Magnaporthe grisea* encodes a polyketide synthase. *XXI* Fungal Genet. Newsl. 48 suppl.:100.

Braun, E. L., Halpern, A. L., Nelson, M. A., and Natvig, D. O. 2000. Large-scale comparison of fungal sequence information: mechanisms of innovation in *Neurospora crassa* and gene loss in *Saccharomyces cerevisiae*. Genome Res. 10:416-430.

Chumley, F. G., and Valent, B. 1990. Genetic analysis of melanin-deficient, nonpathogenic mutants of *Magnaporthe grisea*. Mol. Plant-Microbe Interact. 3:135-143.

Desjardins, A. E., and Hohn, T. M. 1997. Mycotoxins in plant pathogenesis. Mol. Plant Microbe Interact. 10:147-152.

Guillen, A., Turgeon, B. G., Thorson, P. R., Bronson, C. R., and Yoder, O. C. 1994. Linkage among melanin biosynthetic mutations in *Cochliobolus heterostrophus*. Fungal Genet. Newsl. 41: 41-42.

Horwitz, B. A., Sharon, A., Lu, S. W., Ritter, V., Sandrock, T. M., Yoder, O. C., and Turgeon, B. G. 1999. A G protein alpha subunit from *Cochliobolus heterostrophus* involved in mating and appressorium formation. Fungal Genet. Biol. 26:19-32.

Howard, R. J., and Valent, B. 1996. Breaking and entering: Host penetration by the fungal rice blast pathogen *Magnaporthe grisea*. Annu. Rev. Microbiol. 50:491-512.

Huang, G., Zhang, L., and Birch, R. G. 2001. A multifunctional polyketide-peptide synthetase essential for albicidin biosynthesis in *Xanthomonas albilineans*. Microbiology 147:631-642.

Kohmoto, K., and Yoder, O. C. 1998. Molecular Genetics of Host-Specific Toxins in Plant Disease. Dordrecht: Kluwer.

Liu, S., and Dean, R. A. 1997. G protein α subunit genes control growth, development, and pathogenicity of *Magnaporthe grisea*. *Mol. Plant-Microbe Interact.* 10:1075-1086.

Lu, S. W., Turgeon, B. G., and Yoder, O. C. 2001. Highly conserved virulence-related *CPS1* homologs from plant and human pathogenic fungi. Fungal Genetics Newsl. 48 suppl: 102.

O'Donnell, K., Kistler, H. C., Tacke, B. K., and Casper, H. H. 2000. Gene genealogies reveal global phylogeographic structure and reproductive isolation among lineages of *Fusarium graminearum*, the fungus causing wheat scab. Proc. Natl. Acad. Sci. U S A 97:7905-7910.

Tucker, S. L., and Talbot, N. J. 2001. Surface attachment and pre-penetration stage development by plant pathogenic fungi. Annu. Rev. Phytopathol. 39:385-417.

Wendland, J., Ayad-Durieux, Y., Knechtle, P., Rebischung, C., and Philippsen, P. 2000. PCR-based gene targeting in the filamentous fungus *Ashbya gossypii.* Gene 242:381-391.

Yoder, O. C., Macko, V., Wolpert, T. J., and Turgeon, B. G. 1997. *Cochliobolus* spp. and their host-specific toxins. Pages 145-166 in: The Mycota Vol. 5: Plant Relationships, Part A. G. Carroll and P. Tudzynski, eds. Springer-Verlag, Berlin.

Yoder, O. C., and Turgeon, B. G. 2001. Fungal genomics and pathogenicity. Curr. Opinion Plant Biol. 4:315-321.

Bioinformatic Tools for Functional Genomics

Michael Gribskov

San Diego Supercomputer Center & Department of Biology
University of California, San Diego
9500 Gilman Dr.
La Jolla CA 92093-0537

The sequencing of the complete genome of an organism opens the door to the eventual complete understanding of its physiology and development. However, the raw nucleotide sequence is not very useful in and of itself; each gene must be identified, and its function determined before we can understand the complex interactions that make up a living system. This larger task of understanding the funtion of each gene in the genome is what we call functional genomics.

Introduction

Functional genomics has two distinct phases: in the initial phase, the genes in a genome are largely unknown and the problem is to identify and assign tentative functions to each one; in the second phase, detailed experimental information must be associated with each gene and this information brought together into a picture of the physiology of the organism. With *Arabidopsis*, we are still in the first phase, although the NSF *2010* project (NSF 1999) is targeted on rapidly bringing us into the second.

In the initial phase of functional genomics, great emphasis is placed on phylogenetic inference. Genes are assigned tentative functions based on the similarity of their sequences to those of other known proteins. While this is a powerful approach, it should be thought of as generating testable hypotheses of gene function rather than conclusively making functional assignments.

Phylogenetic Inference

Phylogenetic inference is technically a misnomer since what we are discussing are trees of genes, not of species. Nevertheless, the approaches and tools used for assigning proteins and genes to families derive from phylogenetics, so the term seems appropriate. While commonly available tools such as BLAST (Altschul et al. 1990) make the classification of small groups of proteins and their close relatives relatively, it is quite difficult to deal with large families. This is both because it is difficult to identify all members of a homologous family using BLAST, as well as because BLAST does not give any insight into the hierarchical structure that relates groups of proteins to each other.

IDENTIFICATION OF MEMBERS OF LARGE GENE FAMILIES

Identification of large gene families is complicated by several factors. Among these are the presence of heterologous domains that may be present in other gene families, extreme diversity at the sequence level, and the presence of common features such as transmembrane domains. Protein kinases are a case in point; calcium-dependent protein kinases, for example, contain a calmodulin-like domain similar to domains found in many non-kinase protein families. Protein kinases are also extremely diverse: There are no kinase sequences that can detect all protein kinases in a BLAST search, even with an expectation-value cutoff as high as 100. Proteins containing transmembrane regions pose additional problems as they will often appear similar to proteins from completely different families whose only commonality is the presence of a transmembrane sequence.

A practical solution to these problems is to use a diverse panel of query sequences and to search for sequences that match to most of them, albeit at relatively large E-values. This approach is similar to the Family Pairwise search method (Grundy & Bailey 1999) in which the significance of matches between individual sequences and a query panel are combined to calculate the significance of the match to the entire group. The principle is the same: multiple matches to relatively independent queries increase one's confidence in the significance of the match; unrelated sequences will match to only a few of the query panel at most. Using this approach with the *Arabidopsis* genome, we were able to identify 1085 protein kinases (Gribskov et al. 2001) in comparison to the 860 identified in the initial annotation of the genomic sequence (AGI 2000).

LARGE – SCALE CLUSTER ANALYSIS

Analysis of the relationships between lineages of proteins is commonly done using programs such as ClustalW (Thompson et al. 1994), or other distance-based tree-building methods which build hierarchical cluster based on distances derived from sequence alignments. These methods are difficult to use with large and diverse protein families due both to the large number of proteins as well as the difficulty of determining correct multiple sequence alignments. What one needs is a method that determines pairwise distances between sequences without requiring a multiple sequence alignment. BLAST is such a method and we use it as the basis of our large–scale clustering.

Clustering of families of diverse multifunctional proteins such as protein kinases suffers from a second problem; commonly used methods such as UPGMA (Sokal & Michener 1958) or neighbor-joining (Saitou & Nei 1987) will often join sequences into a group when the new sequence is similar to only one or two of the members of the group. This results in clusters that contain many distinctly different and only distantly related proteins. Maximum linkage clustering (Lance & Williams 1967) is a more conservative method that joins sequences into groups only when they are close to all existing members in the group. While not widely used for phylogenetic trees, we find it works very well for hierarchical clustering of protein families. On the other hand, because of its conservative nature and the presence of artifacts such as fragmentary sequences in the data, maximum linkage clustering is unable to completely join the sequences of a superfamily into a single cluster. Our approach is to combine rounds of maximum linkage clustering, with a specific distance cutoff, with recalculation of average distances between the clusters. This is, in effect, a hybrid maximum-average linkage method that has advantages of both approaches.

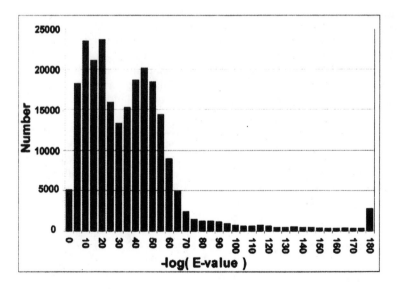

Fig. 1. Distribution of BLAST E-values in an all-against-all comparison of 1286 Plant protein kinases

A key question is how to determine the distance thresholds for the maximum linkage clustering. A set of distances with no internal clusters would produce a distribution of distances with a single peak. However, as shown in Fig. 1, the situation is very different for the protein kinases. The peaks in Fig. 1 correspond to distances characteristic of those within subfamilies (E-value about 10^{-120}), within families (E-value about 10^{-50}), and

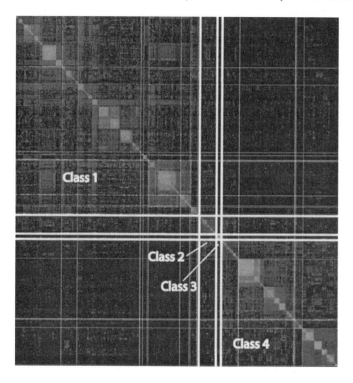

Fig. 2. BLAST E-values between sequences arranged in cluster order. Broad white lines separate classes: class 1 are receptor-like protein kinases, class 2 are ATN/CTR-like protein kinases, class 3 are type I casein kinases, and class 4 are cytoplasmic non-receptor-like protein kinases. Narrow white lines show the breakdown into 20 groups.

between families (E-value about 10^{-15}). Logical choices for the threshold distances for maximum linkage clustering would be the valleys between these peaks: We therefore use E-value thresholds of 10^{-110} (subfamily), 10^{-35} (family), and 10^{-5} (group). Groups were merged into classes by a final round of average linkage clustering.

The hybrid maximum-average linkage clustering method described above clusters *Arabidopsis* protein kinases into 4 general classes, 20 groups, and

77 families. This has allowed us to create a systematic classification system (PPC) for all plant protein kinases. At the family level, the clusters are similar to conventionally identified families: e.g., CDPKs, PEPCKs, SNRKs, and many other families can be identified. Complete details on classification of protein kinases can be viewed at the PlantsP web site (http://plantsp.sdsc.edu). One can get an overall picture of the quality of the clustering by making a plot of the BLAST E-values for each pair of sequences arranged in cluster order. A good clustering will place all of the small E-values near the diagonal, indicating that similar sequences are adjacent or nearby when arranged in cluster order. Fig. 2 shows such an analysis for the PPC. Note the clustering of the light regions (small E-values) along the diagonal, and the nearly solid black in the inter-class regions. This indicates that the clustering has been highly successful in placing similar proteins together. Simple average linkage (UPGMA) or neighbor joining cannot do this (not shown). These methods allow us to efficiently create a sequence-based classification to aid in understanding the function of "unknown" genes in genomic sequences.

Literature Cited

Altschul, S.F., Gish, W., Miller, W., Myers, E.W., and Lipman, D.J. 1990. Basic local alignment search tool. J. Molec. Biol., 215, 403-10.

The Arabidopsis Genome Initiative. 2000. Analysis of the genome sequence of the flowering plant *Arabidopsis thaliana*. Nature 408:796-815.

Gribskov, M., Fana, F., Harper, J., Hope, D.A., Harmon, A.C., Smith, D.W., Tax, F.E., and Zhang, G. 2001. PlantsP: a functional genomics database for plant phosphorylation. Nucleic Acids Research, 29:111-113.

Grundy, W.N., and Bailey, T.L. 1999. Family pairwise search with embedded motif models. Bioinformatics, 15:463-470.

Lance, G.N., and Williams, W.T. 1967 A general theory of classificatory sorting strategies. I hierarchical systems. Computer J. 9, 373-380.

National Science Foundation. 1999. Realizing the potential of plant genomics: from model systems to understanding diversity. NSF/bio011.

Saitou, N., and Nei, M. 1987. The neighbor-joining method: a new method for reconstructing phylogenetic trees. Mol. Biol. Evol. 4:406-425.

Sokal, R.R., and Michener, C.D. 1958. A statistical method for evaluating systematic relationships. Univ. Kansas Sci. Bull 28:1409-1438.

Thompson, J.D., Higgins, D.G., and Gibson, T.J. 1994. CLUSTAL W: improving the sensitivity of progressive multiple sequence alignment through sequence weighting, position-specific gap penalties and weight matrix choice. Nucleic Acids Research, 22:4673-4680.

Comparative Genomics of the
Symbiosis Island of *Mesorhizobium loti*

Clive W. Ronson[1], John T. Sullivan[1], Jodi R. Trzebiatowski[2], Jerome Gouzy[3], and Frans J. de Bruijn[2,3]

[1]Dept. of Microbiology, University of Otago, Dunedin, New Zealand; [2]Michigan State University, E. Lansing, MI 48824 USA; [3]LBMRPM, CNRS-INRA, Castanet-Tolosan, France

The *Mesorhizobium loti* strain R7A symbiosis island is a chromosomally-integrated element which transfers to nonsymbiotic mesorhizobia in the environment, bestowing on them the ability to nodulate and fix nitrogen with *Lotus* species (Sullivan et al. 1995). Four genomic species of nonsymbiotic mesorhizobia have been isolated from rhizosphere samples of field-grown *L. corniculatus* (Sullivan et al. 1996) and transfer of the island to three of these species has been demonstrated in the laboratory (Sullivan and Ronson 1998). The element integrates into a phenylalanine tRNA gene, reconstructing the gene at one end (arbitrarily defined as the left end), and producing a 17-bp direct repeat of the 3' end of the tRNA gene at the right end. Within the left end of the island, a gene *intS* that encodes a product with similarity to members of the phage P4 integrase subfamily is located 198 bp downstream of the tRNA gene (Sullivan and Ronson 1998). This gene is required for excision of the island as a circle as well as its integration (Sullivan et al. 2000). The island is representative of a class of chromosomal elements termed "fitness islands" (Preston et al. 1998) which are acquired by lateral transfer and confer a selective advantage on the host under specific environmental conditions. Such islands clearly play a key role in microbial evolution.

The element was termed a symbiosis island on the basis of its similarities to pathogenicity islands of gram-negative bacteria. Pathogenicity islands (PAIs) are defined regions of chromosomal DNA containing clusters of genes required for virulence, which are absent from benign isolates of the same or related species. PAIs are responsible for traits such as cell invasion, iron uptake, and production of fimbriae and hemolysin (Hacker and Kaper 2000). Most are integrated adjacent to stable RNA genes and several contain an integrase of the P4 family. Like pathogenicity islands, the symbiosis island converts an environmental strain (a soil saprophyte) into a strain capable of forming a close association with a eukaryotic host. The available evidence suggests that PAIs were acquired by lateral transfer but it has proved difficult to demonstrate their transfer under laboratory conditions; in contrast the symbiosis island is readily transferable. Examples of other fitness islands for which transfer has been demonstrated include the *Pseudomonas clc* element (Ravatn et al. 1998) and the *Salmonella* conjugative transposon CTnscr94 (Hochhut et al. 1997). The *clc* element is a 105-kb transferable element that contains chlorocatechol-degradative enzymes and integrates into a glycine tRNA gene using a P4-like integrase. CTnscr94 integrates into a phe-tRNA gene and contains genes for sucrose utilization.

Several considerations led us to determine the nucleotide sequence of the *M. loti* strain R7A symbiosis island. As it is transferable, the island provides a model system for studying the mechanisms involved in the acquisition and evolution of fitness islands. *Mesorhizobium loti* is the natural microsymbiont of *L. japonicus* which is one of two model legumes currently subject to intensive study to understand the biology of the plant contribution to the symbiosis (Cook et al. 1997). DNA sequence analysis rapidly provides information on the bacterial input to the symbiosis that is crucial to complement and advance genetic studies of the plant. The ability of the island to convert a soil saprophyte to a symbiont suggests that the island contains a large proportion of the microsymbiont genes required for the symbiosis. Comparison of the island sequence with those of the symbiotic regions of other rhizobia provides insight into the evolution of both the island and the symbiosis. Available sequences include those of the 536-kb symbiotic plasmid pNGR234a of *Rhizobium* sp. NGR234 (Freiberg et al. 1997), a 400-kb symbiotic region of *Bradyrhizobium japonicum* USDA110 (Gottfert et al. 2001), and the entire genomes of *M. loti* strain MAFF303099 (Kaneko et al. 2000) and *Sinorhizobium meliloti* strain 1021 (http://sequence.toulouse.inra.fr/meliloti.html). The 7.6 Mb MAFF303099 genome consists of a chromosome and 2 plasmids, pMla and pMlb. Comparison with R7A indicates that the chromosome contains a 610,975-bp symbiosis island integrated adjacent to the phe-tRNA gene. Here we highlight features of the R7A island uncovered by the sequence analysis and discuss comparative analysis of the R7A symbiosis island with that of *M. loti* strain MAFF303099.

Comparative Analysis the R7A and MAFF303099 Symbiosis Islands

The R7A island at 501,801 bp in size is 109 kb smaller than the *M. loti* MAFF303099 island and encodes 416 potential genes. The genes were grouped into 11 classes based on their predicted biological function (Table 1). Comparisons of the two *M. loti* symbiosis islands indicates that they have largely similar metabolic and symbiotic potential. The two islands share a conserved backbone sequence of 248 kb with about 98% DNA sequence identity, indicating that the two islands evolved from a common ancestral source. The backbone contains the key symbiotic gene complement including all the genes required for Nod factor synthesis. The backbone is interrupted by a series of strain-specific "islets" that represent DNA either lost or gained by each strain and range in size from a few base pairs up to 168 kb. The few non-syntenous regions that encode similar proteins are less conserved (less than 90% nucleotide identity), suggesting most were separately acquired by each island rather than arising through translocation. About 8% of the R7A island consists of insertion sequences (6 identifiable intact genes) or fragments thereof, compared to 19% for MAFF303099, which accounts for a significant portion of the size difference between the two islands. Analysis of the strain-specific segments of both islands reveals that in addition to IS genes, they contain largely hypothetical genes, metabolic genes and ABC transporters. Interestingly, 102 of the 114 hypothetical genes detected in R7A that have no database matches in other bacteria are not present in *M. loti* MAFF303099 indicating that they are strain- rather than species-specific.

Table 1. R7A symbiosis island genes by functional class and comparison to MAFF303099 Symbiosis Island, pNGR234a and *S. meliloti*

R7A Sym Isl Genes	No	Number Also in		
		MAFF303099 Sym. Island	*S. meliloti* 1021	pNGR234a
Nodulation	16	16	8a, 1b	15
N fixation	27	27	23a, 1c	18
Regulatory function	28	18	3a, 8b, 8c	7
Small molecule metabolism	90	70	7a, 16b, 25c	26
Macromolecule metabolism	6	2	1a, 1c	0
Cell processes	55	19	10a, 8b, 14c	16
Elements of external origin	14	2	4a	4
Structural elements	4	3	2c	2
Hypothetical global similarity	35	25	1a , 5b, 5c	19
Hypothetical partial similarity	27	7	2b	4
Hypothetical	114	12		
TOTAL	416	201	153 (57a, 40b, 56c)	111

Several features of the islands indicate that they are dynamic mosaics shaped by multiple recombination events. As well as the strain-specific regions, variable G+C content and insertion sequences, there are several gene fragments or pseudogenes, some of which are in differing stages of decay in the two islands. Some have intact orthologs on the R7A island whereas others do not. In addition, a number of gene clusters found on the R7A island are also present on pMLa in MAFF303099 and some of these are absent from the MAFF303099 island.

The R7A Island Contains a Type IV Secretion System

A common theme of microbe-host interactions is the secretion by the microbe of effector proteins directly into the cytoplasm of host cells via a Type III or IV secretion system (Burns 1999; Hueck 1998). Sequence of pNGR234a revealed a Type III system that has since been implicated in interactions with specific hosts (Viprey et al. 1998). The symbiosis island encodes two type IV systems, one is likely to be involved in island transfer and the other is similar to that required for the formation of the pilus used to transfer the T-DNA component of the *Agrobacterium* Ti plasmid to plant cells (Burns 1999). These include *virB1-B11* and *virD4*. Homologues of *virA* and *virG,* a two-component regulatory system required for expression of this system (Zupan and Zambryski 1997), are also present. No T-DNA processing genes were present, suggesting that the symbiosis island system may secrete proteins rather than a DNA/protein complex into plant cells. The *virA* gene is preceded by a *nod*-box, the promoter sequence responsible for nodulation gene induction, suggesting that the system has a symbiotic role.

A striking example of the complex recombination events that have occurred since the R7A and MAFF303099 islands diverged is the loss of the *vir* system from MAFF303099. MAFF303099 has undergone a deletion that removed almost the entire *vir* region, leaving the 5' end of *virD4* fused in an inverted orientation to a transposase gene. MAFF303099 has also gained a 168-kb islet that contains a type III secretion system similar to that found on pNGR234a. In addition a large ORF downstream of *virD4* in R7A has been translocated together with the 3' end of *virD4* close to the Type III gene cluster in MAFF303099.

Island Transfer

Analysis of the putative transfer genes of the symbiosis island suggests it is a site-specific conjugative transposon that utilises a type IV pilus to form a mating pore. It is unlikely to replicate as a plasmid as it lacks the highly-conserved *repABC* genes. However analysis of the sequence has not revealed a clear picture of the mechanism of DNA processing that must precede transfer.

We have shown by PCR that *intS* is required for excision of the island as a circle. The island also contains a *trb* operon and a *traG* gene that show similarity to those required for conjugative transfer of the *Agrobacterium* Ti plasmid, pNGR234a and RP4, except that two genes *trbK* and *trbH* found on these plasmids are missing. Interestingly the island *trb* operon is very similar to the *trb* operon on *M. loti* MAFF303099 pMLb. The island *trbG* and *I* gene products are also very similar to those from the partially sequenced *trb* operon of Tn4371, a composite transposon containing a *bph* gene cluster required for degradation of biphenyl. The Tn4371 trb operon also lacks a *trbH* gene between *trbG* and *I* (Merlin et al. 1999).

An orthologue of *traF* that encodes a protease which acts on the *trbC*, the precursor of the major pilin subunit is also found on the island. A gene encoding an orthologue of the incW plasmid pSa antirestriction protein ArdC (Belogurov et al. 2000) is found on the island. Homologues of this protein are also located on the *Agrobacterium* plasmid pTiSakura , pNGR234a (Freiberg et al. 1997; Suzuki et al. 2000) and pMLa and pMLb) (Kaneko et al. 2000).

A Family of Transferable Elements

A wide variety of genetic elements are known to use tRNA genes as their target sites including phages, integrative plasmids and several pathogenicity islands (Ochman et al. 2000). The regeneration of the tRNA gene following integration of the symbiosis island provides the opportunity for multiple insertion events at a single tRNA locus. It is interesting to note that the sequence immediately upstream from the tRNA gene was highly conserved in the six strains containing island that were examined, whereas the homology was much less pronounced downstream of the tRNA gene (Sullivan and Ronson 1998). Preliminary analysis of the DNA downstream of the phe-tRNA gene in three strains has revealed that the strains contain additional acquired elements that encode proteins involved in iron acquisition and adhesion. Such traits are commonly found on pathogenicity islands. Thus the island is one of several acquired fitness islands in mesorhizobia that may contribute to the diversity and adaptation of the bacteria.

Acknowledgments

This work was supported by grants from the Marsden Fund administered by the Royal Society of New Zealand, the US DOE (DE FG02-91ER200021) and by Otago and Michigan State Universities.

Literature Cited

Burns, D. L. 1999. Curr. Opin. Microbiol. 2:25-29.

Cook, D. R, K VandenBosch, F. J de Bruijn, and T. Huget. 1997. Plant Cell 9:275-281.

Freiberg, C., R. Fellay, A. Bairoch, W. J. Broughton, A. Rosenthal, and X. Perret. 1997. Nature 387:394-401.

Gottfert, M., S. Rothlisberger, C. Kundig, C. Beck, R. Marty, and H. Hennecke. 2001. J. Bacteriol. 183:1405-1412.

Hacker, J., and J. B. Kaper. 2000. Annu. Rev. Microbiol. 54:641-679.

Hochhut, B., K. Jahreis, J. W. Lengeler, and K. Schmid. 1997. J. Bacteriol. 179:2097-2102.

Hueck, C. J. 1998. Microbiol. Mol. Biol. Rev. 62:379-433.

Kaneko, T., et al. 2000. *DNA Res.* 7:331-338.

Merlin, C., D. Springael, and A. Toussaint. 1999. Plasmid 41:40-54.

Ochman, H., J. G. Lawrence, and E. A. Groisman. 2000. Nature 405:299-304.

Preston, G. M., B. Haubold, and P. B. Rainey. 1998. Curr. Opin. Microbiol. 1:589-597.

Ravatn, R., S. Studer, J. B. Zehnder, and R. J. van der Meer. 1998. J. Bacteriol. 180:5505-5514.

Sullivan, J. T, J. R. Trzebiatowski, F. J. de Bruijn, and C. W. Ronson. 2000. Pages 693-704 in: Prokaryotic Nitrogen Fixation: a Model System for Analysis of a Biological Process, E. Triplett, ed. Wymondham. Horizon Scientific Press.

Sullivan, J. T., and C.W Ronson. 1998. Proc. Natl. Acad. Sci. USA 95:5145-5149.

Sullivan, J. T., B. D. Eardly, P. van Berkum, and C. W. Ronson. 1996. Appl. Environ. Microbiol. 62:2818-2825.

Sullivan, J. T., H. N. Patrick, W. L. Lowther, D. B. Scott, and C. W. Ronson. 1995. Proc. Natl. Acad. Sci. USA 92:8985-8989.

Suzuki, K., Y. Hattori, M. Uraji, N. Ohta, K. Iwata, K. Murata, A. Kato, and K. Yoshida. 2000. Gene 242:331-336.

Viprey, V., A. Del Greco, W. Golinowski, W. J. Broughton, and X. Perret. 1998. Mol. Microbiol. 28:1381-1389.

Zupan, J., and P. Zambryski. 1997. Crit. Rev. Plant Sci. 16:279-295.

Applying the Sequence-to-Phenotype
Functional Genomics Paradigm to *Phytophthora*

Trudy A. Torto[1], Antonino Testa[1], Allison Styer[1], William R. Morgan[2], Diane Kinney[1], Edgar Huitema[1], Walid Hamada[1], Shujing Dong[1], and Sophien Kamoun[1]

[1]Department of Plant Pathology, The Ohio State University, Ohio Agricultural Research and Development Center, Wooster, Ohio, USA
[2]Department of Biology, The College of Wooster, Wooster, Ohio, USA

Oomycetes, such as *Phytophthora*, downy-mildews and *Pythium*, form a unique branch of eukaryotic plant pathogens with an independent evolutionary history (Kamoun et al. 1999c; 2000). Among the oomycetes, *Phytophthora* species cause some of the most destructive plant diseases in the world, and are arguably the most devastating pathogens of dicot plants (Erwin and Ribeiro 1996, Kamoun 2000). For example, *Phytophthora infestans*, known as the cause of the Irish potato famine, remains a destructive pathogen resulting in multibillion-dollar losses in potato and tomato production (Fry and Goodwin 1997a; 1997b). Other economically important diseases include root and stem rot caused by *Phytophthora sojae*, which hampers soybean production in several continents, black pod of cocoa caused by *Phytophthora palmivora* and *Phytophthora megakarya*, a recurring threat to chocolate production, and sudden oak death caused by a recently discovered *Phytophthora* species that is decimating oak trees along the Pacific coast of the United States. Typically, these destructive diseases are difficult to manage and sources of sustainable genetic resistance are limited.

Large scale DNA sequencing (genomics) approaches promise to impact our understanding of the molecular basis of pathogenicity and host-specificity in *Phytophthora* by facilitating the isolation of novel virulence and avirulence genes, as well as by helping to identify targets for chemical control (Kamoun et al. 1999b; Qutob et al. 2000). Based on these premises, we and others in the *Phytophthora* research community embarked onâ cDNA and genomic sequencing projects that provided a first insight into gene diversity in *Phytophthora* (Kamoun et al. 1999b; Qutob et al. 2000; Waugh et al. 2000). However, once large sets of sequence data are available, the research focus shifts to functional analyses of the newly discovered genes. The challenge in the post-genome era is to link a sequence to a

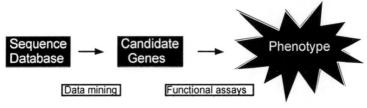

Fig. 1. Flowchart illustrating the sequence-to-phenotype paradigm. The two-step process consists first of mining for candidate genes from sequence databases using informatics, gene expression, proteomics, or a combination of these technologies. Then, functional assays are applied to the candidate genes to identify those that confer a desirable phenotype. Adapted from Kamoun et al. Can. J. Plant Pathol. (in press).

phenotype with as little experimental efforts as possible using computational tools for data mining and robust high throughput functional assays. To achieve this, we developed a sequence-to-phenotype (or functional genomics) paradigm for the discovery of novel virulence and avirulence genes, as well as the identification of novel fungicide targets in *Phytophthora* (Fig. 1). In this article, we review our progress in applying this paradigm to plant pathogenic *Phytophthora* spp.

Genomic Databases for *Phytophthora*

Structural genomic studies of *Phytophthora* are well under way within the framework of the *Phytophthora* Genome Initiative (PGI) (Waugh et al. 2000). These studies include expressed sequence tag (EST) projects from a variety of developmental and infection stages as well as targeted sequencing of BAC contigs. Completed pilot cDNA sequencing projects resulted in calculated, 2,500 ESTs for *P. infestans* and 3,000 ESTs for *P. sojae* (Kamoun et al. 1999b; Qutob et al. 2000), and were compiled in searchable databases available at the PGI website (Waugh et al. 2000). Recently, funding for an additional 50,000 ESTs from a series of *in vitro* and potato infection stages has been secured (B. Tyler, personal comm.). These sequences will be compiled in an expanded and improved version of the PGI database (named *Phytophthora* Genome Consortium or PGC, www.ncgr.org/pgc). In addition, industry funded projects have been initiated with academic collaborators and will complement public-sector efforts.

Mining for Candidate Genes

We developed a series of specific criteria to select candidate genes for functional assays (Table 1). The rationale behind these criteria is that genes exhibiting the listed features are more likely to be involved in virulence or avirulence and could serve as optimal targets for fungicides. We designed

Table 1. Example of features used for selecting candidate genes from sequence databases of *Phytophthora*. Adapted from Kamoun et al. Can. J. Plant Pathol. (in press).

Selection criteria	Rationale
Degradative enzymes	Putative virulence factors involved in host tissue penetration and degradation
Extracellular proteins	More likely to be involved in cross-talk with plants
Up-regulated during pre-infection and infection stages	More likely to be involved in pathogenicity/virulence; putative fungicide targets
Conserved among pathogenic oomycetes	Putative fungicide targets

specific algorithms and various data mining strategies to identify *Phytophthora* genes encoding degradative enzymes and extracellular proteins, as well as genes that are up-regulated during pre-infection and infection stages, and that are conserved among several pathogenic oomycetes. Such in silico approaches yield lists of candidate genes that can be tested experimentally to confirm the predicted features. In addition, the selected candidate genes can then be functionally assayed using one or several assays as described below.

Functional Assays of *Phytophthora* Genes in Plants

Plant pathogenic microbes produce an extraordinary diversity of signal molecules, encoded by virulence genes, that can manipulate molecular and cellular processes in plants by inducing symptom-like responses and altering defense responses. Ectopic expression of single pathogen genes in plant cells often leads to phenotypic effects. Typically, expression of bacterial, fungal, or oomycete avirulence genes in plant cells that contain the matching resistance gene results in cell death diagnostic of the hypersensitive response (Kamoun et al. 1999a; Kjemtrup et al. 2000; Lauge and De Wit 1998). Therefore, plant gene expression systems can be adapted to systematically screen large numbers of *Phytophthora* genes for functional response in plants. In our laboratory, we routinely perform high throughput functional expression screens of *P. infestans* cDNAs in tomato and tobacco using potato virus X (PVX) and *Agrobacterium tumefaciens*-based vectors (Kamoun et al. 1999a; Van der Hoorn et al. 2000). This approach allowed us to identify *P. infestans* cDNAs that induce resistance responses and disease-like symptoms (T. Torto, A. Testa, and S. Kamoun, unpublished).

Future Directions

With the advent of genomic technology, the pace of discovery and functional analyses of *Phytophthora* genes has greatly accelerated. Here, we outlined our strategy for systematic mining of the genome sequence data, selection of candidate genes, and high throughput functional screening of selected genes. In the future, this approach will be enhanced by additional improvements in computational methods and algorithms for data mining and increased sequence data for oomycetes and other organisms. In addition, even though ectopic expression of pathogen genes in plant cells can now be performed at a remarkable high throughput rate, there is still a need for improvement and adaptation to large scale analyses of the gene knockout and complementation assays currently available for *Phytophthora*.

For regular updates on this area of research, visit our laboratory web site at www.oardc.ohio-state.edu/phytophthora.

Acknowledgements

We thank Melissa Barty and Alessandra Borello for technical assistance. We thank our collaborators in the oomycete research community for their help and assistance. In particular, we thank Pieter van West and Neil Gow (University of Aberdeen, Scotland), Steve Whisson and Paul Birch (Scottish Crop Research Institute, Dundee), Dinah Qutob and Mark Gijzen (Agriculture Agri-food Canada, London, Ontario), Vivianne Vleeshouwers and Francine Govers (Wageningen Agricultural University, The Netherlands), Elodie Gaulin, Martina Rickauer and Marie-Therese Esquerre-Tugaye (Universite Paul Sabatier, France), Brett Tyler (University of California, Davis), Venkat Gopalan (The Ohio State University), and Isabelle Malcuit and David Baulcombe (Sainsbury Laboratory, Norwich, UK). Salaries and research support were provided by State and Federal Funds appropriated to the Ohio Agricultural Research and Development Center, the Ohio State University, by the Ohio Soybean Council, and by Syngenta.

Literature Cited

Erwin, D. C., and Ribeiro, O. K. 1996. *Phytophthora* Diseases Worldwide. APS Press, St. Paul, Minnesota.

Fry, W. E., and Goodwin, S. B. 1997a. Re-emergence of potato and tomato late blight in the United States. Plant Dis. 81:1349-1357.

Fry, W. E., and Goodwin, S. B. 1997b. Resurgence of the Irish potato famine fungus. Bioscience 47:363-371.

Kamoun, S. 2000. *Phytophthora*. Page 237-265 in: Fungal Pathology. J.Kronstad, ed. Kluwer Academic Publishers, Dordrecht.

Kamoun, S., Honee, G., Weide, R., Lauge, R., Kooman-Gersmann, M., de Groot, K., Govers, F., and de Wit, P. J. G. M. 1999a. The fungal gene *Avr9* and the oomycete gene *inf1* confer avirulence to potato virus X on tobacco. Mol. Plant-Microbe Interact. 12:459-462.

Kamoun, S., Hraber, P., Sobral, B., Nuss, D., and Govers, F. 1999b. Initial assessement of gene diversity for the oomycete pathogen *Phytophthora infestans* based on expressed sequences. Fun. Genet. Biol. 28:94-106.

Kamoun, S., Huitema, E., and Vleeshouwers, V. G. A. A. 1999c. Resistance to oomycetes: A general role for the hypersensitive response? Trends Plant Sci. 4:196-200.

Kjemtrup, S., Nimchuk, Z., and Dangl, J. L. 2000. Effector proteins of phytopathogenic bacteria: bifunctional signals in virulence and host recognition. Curr. Opin. Microbiol. 3:73-78.

Lauge, R., and De Wit, P. J. 1998. Fungal avirulence genes: structure and possible functions. Fungal Genet Biol 24:285-97.

Qutob, D., Hraber, P. T., Sobral, B. W., and Gijzen, M. 2000. Comparative analysis of expressed sequences in *Phytophthora sojae*. Plant Physiol 123:243-54.

Van der Hoorn, R. A., Laurent, F., Roth, R., and De Wit, P. J. 2000. Agroinfiltration is a versatile tool that facilitates comparative analyses of *Avr9/Cf-9*-induced and *Avr4/Cf-4*-induced necrosis. Mol. Plant-Microbe Interact. 13:439-46.

Waugh, M., Hraber, P., Weller, J., Wu, Y., Chen, G., Inman, J., Kiphart, D., and Sobral, B. 2000. The *Phytophthora* genome initiative database: informatics and analysis for distributed pathogenomic research. Nucleic Acids Res. 28:87-90.

Transgenic Rice in the Field and Beyond

S. K. Datta, N. Baisakh, J. Tu, N. N. Narayanan, S. Balachandran, L. Torrizo, E. Abrigo, N. Oliva, M. Arboleda, K. Datta

International Rice Research Institute, Metro Manila, Philippines

Although there was a quantum increase in rice productivity during the green revolution era because of the introduction of high yielding and semidwarf cultivars, yield per se has attained a plateau in recent years because of annual yield losses from biotic stress. Among several factors, severe diseases such as bacterial blight, blast, sheath blight, and tungro contribute to about 20% of the total yield loss in rice. Control with agrochemicals such as fungicides/pesticides and biological control including crop rotation are among the most common methods used to control diseases. However, research has revealed that such methods involve high cost, environmental and health hazard, and some inefficiency. This requires us to develop varieties with built-in disease resistance by genetic engineering as the best solution for disease control. This approach is inexpensive and environment-friendly and management would be easier than before as disease-resistant donors are not available in the rice gene pool.

Significant and new advances in cloning of disease resistance (R) genes and the activation of defense response genes (PR genes) in the signal transduction pathway, have greatly increased the options available for transgenic disease resistance. The combinatorial deployment of these strategies could also be exploited for engineering effective and durable resistance to pathogens in the field.

In this report, we summarize the progress of transgenic research in our laboratory with R and PR genes in rice leading to strategic management of fungal and bacterial diseases.

Developing and Field-Testing Transgenic Rice with *Xa21* for Bacterial Blight Resistance

Bacterial blight (BB) caused by *Xanthomonas* pv. *oryzae* (*Xoo*) is one of the most destructive diseases of rice worldwide, causing yield loss of up to 50% in some areas of Asia. The use of resistant cultivars is the most economical and effective method for controlling this disease.

Several R genes have been isolated and cloned from different crop plants. A dominant R gene, $Xa21$, was cloned (Song et al. 1995) from the wild rice *Oryza longistaminata* and confers resistance to all the known races of *Xoo* in India and the Philippines. In our laboratory, many transgenic lines have been developed in the background of several indica rice cultivars (Table 1), and have been advanced to fix the transgene locus (Fig. 1a). Transgenic plants when challenged with four prevalent races (2, 4, 6, and 10) of *Xoo* in the transgenic greenhouse and PXO79, PXO99, and PXO112 in field conditions in Wuhan, China (1998-2000), showed resistance compared with control plants (Fig. 1 b&c).

Table 1. Transgenic rice developed with *Xa21* gene

Cultivar	No. of transgenic lines*	Status
IR72	60	Homozygous
IR64	40	
IR50	3	T_2
CO39	8	T_1
Pusa Basmati	3	T_1
BPT 5204	7	T_1
Dinorado	5	T_1
Milagrosa	7	T_2

*Based on Southern and bioassay data

In addition, the higher level of resistance to race 4 of *Xoo* in IR72 was predicted to be due to the synergistic effect of *Xa21* with the endogenous *Xa4* gene. Also, IR50 transgenics with *Xa21* showed greater level of resistance, even in some cases more than the donor IRBB21 when bioassayed against race 1 (Narayanan et al. Unpublished findings).

The negative control variety IR24 was susceptible to all isolates under field conditions. The results demonstrated clearly the efficiency of *Xa21* transgene under natural field conditions without any phenotypic trade-off as the yield performance of the transgenic homozygous line was comparable with that of the control (Tu et al. 2000). The heritability of the resistance trait over generations showed the stability of *Xa21* in the rice genome.

Assuming a minimum yield loss of 1% from BB disease only, around $330 million could be saved over 30 million ha with an average yield of 5.5 t/ha in China, whereas a yield loss of 0.75% covering 132.5 million ha with an average yield of 3.6 t/ha in Asia translates into $715.5 million of savings.

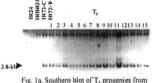

Fig. 1a. Southern blot of T₃ progenies from IR72 showing homozygosity for Xa21 gene integrated in the genome (arrow marked 3.8-kb fragment)

Fig. 1b. Green house bioassay of IR50 transgenic (T) showing resistance against 3 races of *Xoo* compared to control (C)

Fig. 1c. Field evaluation of transgenic IR72 for BB resistance in China showing resistance of transgenic (T) compared to control (C)

Transgenic Rice with *PR* genes for Sheath Blight Resistance

Since the pathogenesis-related proteins were first reported 30 years ago, several studies have concluded that overexpression of PR proteins in transgenic crops can delay the progression of diseases caused by several pathogens belonging to diverse genera. There is always some selectivity in the interaction between a PR protein and its intended target pathogens because PR proteins represent generalized plant defense responses for broad, albeit incomplete, protection against diverse pathogens (Datta and Muthukrishnan 1999). Many transgenic plants have now been developed with constitutive and inducible PR proteins at effective levels and could be used as a tool to enhance or stabilize yield in areas where pathogens and pests are endemic.

Sheath blight disease is the most widespread disease of rice, causing significant yield losses every year in all rice-growing countries. Resistance breeding for this disease is not feasible because of the unavailability of resistant donors in the rice gene pool. Genetic engineering is an attractive and powerful tool for introducing *PR* genes and optimizing the overexpression of PR proteins to manage sheath blight transgenic plants. Two different types of PR genes, PR3-chitinases (*Chi11* and *RC7*) and PR-5 thaumatin-like protein genes (*TLPD-34*) have been introduced into rice in our laboratory. The integration and inheritance of the PR genes were confirmed by molecular analyses (Fig. 2 a&b), along with the functional overexpression by enhanced resistance of the transgenics when challenged with the sheath blight pathogen (*Rhizoctonia solani*), (Fig. 2c). At least 12 rice cultivars have been transformed with several *PR* genes and the plants with normal phenotypes with enhanced levels of antifungal activity are at different stages of development and are being selected for future field testing and breeding (Table 2).

338

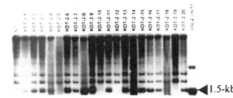 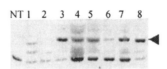

◀ 1.5-kb

Fig. 2a. Southern blot of T$_1$ progenies from *Agrobacterium*-transformed Tulasi exhibiting 3:1 segregation for *Chi11* gene demonstrating its single-locus integration

Fig. 2b. Western blot of dihaploid transgenics of Swarna showing expression of 35-kDa protein (arrow marked) corresponding to *Chi11* transgene

Table 2. Transgenic rice cultivars with chitinase (*PR*) genes

Cultivar	Gene of interest	Method used#	No. of transgenic lines*	Status	Reference
IR72	*Chi11*		60		Unpublished
	RC7	B	15		Datta et al. (2000b)
IR64	*RC7*		3		
CBII	*RC7*	P	42	H O M O Z Y G O U S	
	Chi11		30		Lin et al. (1995)
	D34		30		Datta et al. (1999)
ML7	*Chi11*	B	14		Unpublished
IRRI-NPT	*Chi11*	B	48		
Swarna	*Chi11*	B	7		Baisakh et al. (2000)
Basmati12 2	*Chi11*	A	15		Datta et al. (2000a)
Vaidehi	*Chi11*	A/B	64/48		
Tulasi	*Chi11*	A/B	115/75		
Dinorado	*D34*	B	40		Unpublished
Milagrosa	*D34*	B	7		
	Chi11	B	10		
C4-63g	*Chi11*	B	20		

#A: Agrobacterium; B: Bolistic transformation
*Based on Southern and Western blot analysis and bioassay

339

Combination of *R* and *PR* genes

The pyramiding of different *PR* genes with *R* genes such as *Xa21* and possibly *NPR1* will delay disease symptoms and protect plants in a sustainable manner, thus providing multiple and durable resistance against different pathogens. This could be achieved by either transgene pyramiding through conventional crossing or cotransformation of multiple genes. We combined the conventional breeding with transgenesis breeding, to pyramid *Xa21* with *RC7* and the resulting inbreds showed resistance against both *Xoo* and *R. solani* (Datta et al. unpublished data). These homozygous lines are awaiting field evaluation.

Similarly, *Pi* genes such as *Pi-1*, *Piz-5*, and *Pi-ta* (Jia et al. 2000) are known to confer resistance to rice blast. So, homozygous IR50 and CO39 breeding lines carrying the blast resistance genes (*Pi-1 and Piz-5*) developed through marker-assisted selection were used to introduce the *Xa21* gene through transformation. The pyramided transgenics showed resistance against blast fungus and BB (Fig. 3., Narayanan et al. unpublished data).

These results show that conventional and molecular breeding techniques could be a powerful combination in rice breeding. This can only be done if extensive field-testing of these engineered cultivars in different environments is carried out.

Fig. 2c. Transgenic (T) plant showing resistance to sheath blight compared with control (C) in greenhouse condition.

P   C   C   P

Fig. 3. Transgenic IR50 pyramided line (P) showing resistance to BB and blast compared with control (C) in greenhouse condition.

Acknowledgements

Financial support from BMZ/GTZ, Germany and the Rockefeller Foundation, USA is acknowledged. Thanks are due to Drs P. C. Ronald and S. Muthukrishnan for providing the plasmid constructs, and Dr. Bill Hardy for editorial assistance.

Literature Cited

Baisakh, N., Datta, K., Oliva, N., Ona, I., Rao, G.J.N., Mew, T.W., and Datta, S.K. 2001. Rapid development of homozygous transgenic rice using anther culture harboring rice *chitinase* gene for enhanced sheath blight resistance. Plant Biotechnology 18:101-108.

340

Datta, K., Koukolíková-Nicola, Z., Baisakh, N., Oliva, N., and Datta, S.K. 2000a. *Agrobacterium*-mediated engineering for sheath blight resistance of indica rice cultivars from different ecosystems. Theor. Appl. Genet. 100: 832-839.

Datta, K., Tu, J.,Oliva, N., Ona, I., Velazhahan, R., Mew, T. W., Muthukrishnan, S., and Datta, S. K. 2000b. Enhanced resistance to sheath blight by constitutive expression of infection-related rice chitinase in transgenic elite indica rice cultivars. Plant Sci. 160: 406-414.

Datta, K., Velazhahan, R., Oliva, N., Mew, T., Khush G.S., Muthukrishnan, S., and Datta, S.K. 1999. Over expression of cloned rice thaumatin-like protein (PR-5) gene in transgenic rice plants enhances environmental friendly resistance to *Rhizoctonia solani* causing sheath blight disease Theor. Appl. Genet. 98: 1138-1145.

Datta, S. K., and Muthukrishnan, S. eds, 1999. Pathogenesis-related proteins in plants. CRC Press, USA.

Jia, Y., McAdams, S. A., Bryan, G. T., Hershey, P., and Valent, B. 2000. Direct interaction of resistance gene and avirulence gene products confers rice blast resistance. EMBO J. 19(15): 4004-4014.

Lin, W., Anuratha, C. S., Datta, K., Potrykus, I., Muthukrishnan, S., and Datta, S. K. 1995. Genetic engineering of rice for resistance to sheath blight. Bio/technology 13: 686-691.

Song, W.Y., Wang, G.L., Chen, L.L., Kim, H.S., Pi, L.Y., Holsten, T., Gardner, J., Wang, B., Zhai, W.X., Zhu, L.H., Fauquet, C., and Ronald, P. 1995. A receptor kinase –like protein encoded by the rice disease resistance gene, *Xa21*. Science 270: 1804-1806.

Tu, J., Datta, K., Khush, G. S., Zhang, Q., Datta, S. K. 2000. Field performance of *Xa21* transgenic indica rice. Theor. Appl. Genet. 101: 15-20.

Teaching Courses in Molecular
Plant-Microbe Interactions

Caitilyn Allen

University of Wisconsin-Madison, Madison, Wisconsin USA

The 10th International Congress on MPMI in Madison included a half-day workshop on teaching courses in molecular plant-microbe interactions, adding a new dimension of professional development to the meetings as for the first time pedagogy became an explicit topic of discussion. Certainly teaching faculty have long taken advantage of the breadth and depth of the MPMI congresses to keep their teaching as current and authoritative as possible. Many congress participants are professors or instructors responsible for teaching a graduate or advanced undergraduate course in the area of molecular plant-microbe interactions. Moreover, many of the young postdoctoral scientists who attend these meetings will be teaching in this area in the next few years.

Courses in the area of molecular plant-microbe interactions serve several important functions. These courses create a gateway to attract sophisticated biochemistry, cell biology, and genetics students to our discipline. They demonstrate that host-pathogen interactions can be explored effectively without expensive and controversial animal experimentation. This advantage is particularly relevant as it becomes clear that mechanisms of pathogenesis and of disease resistance are often well conserved between plants and animals, resulting in dramatically increased communication between the formerly segregated disciplines studying plant and animal pathogenesis. Finally, the library of completed host and pathogen genomes is expanding rapidly, increasing the field's potential experimental power and breadth.

However, a number of special challenges are inherent to teaching a course in this area. These include:

- The course audience is often mixed in terms of background. Instructors must effectively serve a new audience of biochemistry, cell biology, and genetics students, while continuing to teach the traditional plant pathology majors. These two student groups often bring strikingly different background knowledge to the classroom, with complementary deficiencies and strengths.

- MPMI course instructors often have few or no colleagues who share their interests in their home departments, leaving them isolated and without opportunities to discuss their teaching ideas.

- Because MPMI comprises a broad area of biology characterized by rapidfire research breakthroughs, much of the course material must be revised and updated each time the course is taught.

- Overlap between plant and animal pathogenesis is a great teaching lure, but it also requires instructors to keep up with an enormous primary scientific research literature.

In addition, MPMI course instructors face the common challenge of graduate teaching: to move beyond memorization and regurgitation of facts. How can we teach our students the conceptual understanding and experimental creativity typical of effective research scientists?

Most graduate biology teachers are eager to teach well, but lack the opportunity to discuss teaching or learn about alternative approaches to traditional methods. Because biology faculty often receive no formal instruction in teaching beyond acting as laboratory teaching assistants, we can benefit from exchanging ideas with colleagues and experts in pedagogy about such issues as assessment, collaborative learning, writing across the curriculum, distance learning, etc. Unlike research, teaching is usually done alone, and can even be a lonely experience (albeit a very public kind of solitude). Traditionally there is little opportunity for the interaction with peers, and the exchange of ideas that enrich and stimulate research.

It was with these challenges and needs in mind that we organized a teaching workshop focussed on molecular plant-microbe interactions courses. There was a surprisingly strong interest in this workshop: over 70 people from 14 countries registered, and many participants contributed teaching materials or ideas to share with others.

Course Syllabi

Organizing the structure of a course and determining the assigned readings is often the single most difficult task facing an instructor, and arguably the single most important one as well. Workshop participants received complete syllabi from eight different MPMI courses, serving diverse audiences in France, Brazil, and Canada as well as various US graduate and undergraduate institutions. Many additional ideas and suggestions were developed during workshop discussions.

Although the assorted contributed syllabi were highly variable in some respects, there were significant common elements. Most notably, nearly all instructors use a course format that combines lectures with in-depth discussion of current research papers. Lectures deliver factual material, usually set in a historical context that allows students to understand how scientific understanding develops over time as new facts and techniques become available. In contrast, the discussion of current papers, often lead by one or two students rather than by the instructor, teaches critical reading of the literature, develops library and internet research skills, and plunges students into the specifics and details of particular research topics. Moreover, when students lead discussions, they develop teaching and presentation skills; this approach puts the emphasis on student perspectives and analysis rather than on a performance by the instructor.

Certain "hot" papers appeared in multiple instructors' syllabi, indicating a reassuring confluence of opinion regarding what is important and interesting in our field. These commonly assigned papers were sometimes short current reviews (e.g. D.C. Baulcombe 1999. Fast forward genetics based on virus-induced gene silencing. Current Opinion in Plant Biology 2:109-113). Others were regarded as great teaching opportunities because they described recent breakthroughs, thereby illustrating the emergence of a fresh new idea or a significant discovery (e.g. Schenk et al. 2000 Coordinated plant defense responses in Arabidopsis revealed by microarray analysis. PNAS 97:11655-60, or VerGunst et al 2000. VirB4/D4-dependent protein translocation from *Agrobacterium* into plant cells. Science 290:979-82).

Written Assignments

GRANT PROPOSAL

A discussion of written assignments in MPMI courses was lead by Tim Denny (University of Georgia). In this area as well, a single common element emerged from considerable background diversity in assignments. Nearly all instructors surveyed required their students to write a research grant proposal. These ranged in scale from a 5-page preproposal to a full-blown USDA-NRI format proposal, complete with budget.

The object of these assignments is to give students the opportunity to practice the form of writing that will be most important for their future professional life. Clearly, writing a proposal requires the literature review and summary associated with the traditional undergraduate term paper. However, it also demands logical assembly of arguments and a more persuasive, even emotional form of expression. Most importantly, a successful proposal has at its core a new and important hypothesis and a plausible means of testing it. The workshop discussion made it clear that writing in such a new form poses a substantial challenge to most of our students. To improve writing quality, many instructors chose to incorporate elements of peer review, revision, or both into this assignment.

For example, students may be asked to first submit a polished draft (their best effort at a proposal). This polished draft is simultaneously reviewed by a fellow student and by the instructor, but is not graded. The author then has the chance to revise and rewrite in response to the reviewer's comments. Only this revised version is graded. (It was noted that the experience of reviewing another student's proposal often had an extremely beneficial effect on a student's ability to effectively revise his/her own proposal!).

Alternatively, several instructors assembled all students into a grant review panel and asked them to review and rank all the proposals written by the class (anonymously). This process was also seen as very useful, since students realized the importance of clarity and originality in a proposal, as well as the interesting and sometimes unpredictable dynamic of a grant panel.

SUMMARIES AND SHORT PAPERS

Several instructors required students to submit short papers summarizing and critiquing a paper from the current research literature. This assignment resembles the in-class discussion of a current paper (and instructors found that a short written assignment effectively forced students to prepare thoughtfully for an in-class oral discussion). These papers ranged in size from an informal single page to a more in-depth 5 page analysis. One variation on this assignment required students to imagine that the data in the assigned paper were their own, and to describe the next hypothesis that should be tested, and what experimental approaches might effectively test their new hypothesis.

It was widely agreed that while student writing is difficult and time-consuming to read and grade, written assignments serve a vital purpose. In our collective experience, biology students are often not at all well-prepared for the immense amount of writing that awaits them in their professional future.

Testing and Grading

TO TEST OR NOT TO TEST?

A discussion of testing and grading in MPMI courses was lead by Caitilyn Allen and Tom German (University of Wisconsin). The first issue to arise was whether we should be testing at all in advanced biology courses. Those opposed to testing argued that graduate students have already amply demonstrated their ability to take tests, so it's not productive to subject them to additional tests. Moreover, they pointed out that extensive pedagogical research documents that students tend to study towards the tests, so if we don't test well (and constructing a good test is not easy), then students tend to learn the wrong things. Others countered that periodic testing supplies students with necessary motivation and focus to study and learn, that test results help us as instructors to assess how effectively we are teaching, and that good tests can be learning experiences in themselves.

Embedded in the question of whether to test at all is the issue of how frequently to test. A brief survey was administered to workshop participants to explore their approaches to testing. Workshop participants ran the gamut from a single final exam through weekly short quizzes, with most (67%) using a midterm-plus final formula.

ORAL EXAMINATIONS

A few MPMI course instructors (13%) at the workshop use oral examinations instead of written exams. In favor of this approach, they argued that oral exams allow instructors to explore the depth and limits of a student's understanding of the material; that students get feedback and correction in real time; that orals develop the ability to engage in scientific discourse, a significant professional skill; that they require less time for administration and grading as long as the class is not too large; and that at their best, orals are a creative and collegial experience. However, it was acknowledged that some students find oral exams very intimidating; that if neither students nor instructors are used to orals, they may not do well; and finally that every oral exam flows differently, so objective grading can be a challenge. One course deals with this last issue by having two instructors present during oral exams.

TAKE-HOME VS. IN-CLASS EXAMINATIONS

Among those instructors who used written exams in their courses, 23% gave open-book take-home exams. This type of exam is less stressful for students; allows contemplation and in-depth responses; more closely mimics the writing tasks of eventual professional life; and (not insignificantly) is typewritten and therefore easier to read during grading. On the other hand, take-home exams can absorb an enormous amount of student time, rely entirely on the honor system, and if they are not strictly limited as to length they can be time-consuming to grade. Practitioners of take-home exams recommended strict length limits and short turn-around times to mitigate these disadvantages.

In-class examinations normally do not raise concerns about excessive length or academic dishonesty, but if not carefully designed, they can emphasize memorization and factual knowledge at the expense of creative or in-depth analysis. They are also stressful for students, although the availability of open books during the test can reduce this stress. Open-book exams explicitly value concepts and analysis over facts. Some instructors distribute some or all questions in advance of the exam, although they acknowledge that this regrettably narrows the focus of student studies and

346

thereby reduces the scope of potential learning during preparation for the test.

The ability to assess and ensure students' fundamental knowledge base was perceived as the primary advantage of closed-book exams. Enthusiasts argued that such exams force students to prepare broadly and learn all the assigned material. However, others pointed out that extensive studies have shown that the consequent cramming and memorization does not result in good long-term retention of material. With respect to type of question posed during testing, 40% of instructors used "synthetic/creative long essay" questions, while another 40% used short answer questions. Less popular were multiple choice/fill-in questions (6%) and factual long essay questions (14%).

It was widely agreed that a good synthetic essay question that asks students to think like a researcher is preferable to testing for factual knowledge. But devising these good questions is very difficult. An example of the difference between such questions might be:

Factual: a) Define *avr* genes. b) Explain the function of *avr* genes.

Synthetic/creative: a) Several lines of evidence suggest that *avr* genes in plant pathogenic bacteria function as virulence effector proteins. Summarize this evidence. b) Propose two possible mechanisms of action for these effector proteins. Describe a set of experiments to test each of your two hypotheses.

However, the answers to synthetic questions are rarely strictly comparable and thus can be difficult to grade. Moreover, students regularly come up with unexpected (though not incorrect) answers, which pose a different kind of grading challenge. Workshop participants proposed that before grading, instructors should develop a common set of criteria for such answers (e.g.: Was the hypothesis reasonable? Did the proposed experiments test the hypothesis? Are the right controls present?).

During the ensuing discussion, workshop participants suggested that using several different sorts of examinations in the course of a semester might be optimal, since this approach is fairest to all students, who collectively bring a wide assortment of learning styles and strengths to the classroom; this mixed approach moreover avoids predictability.

Using Distance Learning Technology for Team Teaching

Jan Leach (Kansas State University) presented her experience with collaborative long-distance team teaching of an MPMI course. She and her colleagues Marty Dickman (Nebraska State University) and Tom Wolpert (Oregon State University) successfully overcame the challenges of new technology, different time zones, and even a quarter-semester system conflict to successfully co-teach a course at three different institutions.

Essentially, they were able to unite three classrooms using video sent over Internet 2, which is reserved for academic and scientific uses and is thus both faster and more reliable than the widely used Internet. The three instructors developed the course together, dividing the teaching responsibilities according to their expertise. Students in all three classrooms were able to see and hear the instructor, their counterparts at the other institutions, and the instructor's audiovisual materials. Long-distance team teaching of this kind required strong support and substantial investment on the part of all the institutions involved, notably a video technician, and a high-tech classroom. As this course represented the first such effort, it was especially demanding; computer technicians at Kansas State were writing software as the course took place to support the distance learning project as it was needed. In spite of the project's novelty, it worked surprisingly smoothly. A video shown at the workshop demonstrated that a lively and open discussion among students and faculty flowed naturally across the ether. Jan's detailed description of this pathbreaking approach has already been published in the MPMI Reporter (Spring 2000), so it will not be discussed further here.

A lower-tech approach to distance learning was also described. A program called PlaceWare uses no video but allows 2-way communication by audio and static computer images (e.g., PowerPoint slides) over the Internet. This program could be used for a low-cost "visiting lecturer" with open audio discussion during and after a presentation. This or similar software could allow instructors at remote institutions or those with modest budgets to expose their students to exciting research presentations and high-profile scientists.

Are We Serving Our Graduate Students?

The workshop also featured a keynote address by Dr. Chris Golde (Senior Scholar, Carnegie Foundation, Palo Alto) entitled "At Cross Purposes: What the experiences of students tell us about doctoral education". The full report describing this work is available at: http://www.phd-survey.org. Dr. Golde and colleagues conducted an extensive survey of US institutions granting doctoral degrees to examine their effectiveness. Dr. Golde's presentation discussed in detail the results from a subset of surveyed departments, those granting degrees in Ecology/Evolution and Biochemistry/Genetics. Disturbingly, her data indicate that there is often a three-way mis-match among the career expectations of students, the doctoral training they received, and the positions that awaited them in the scientific workplace. Briefly, most doctoral students expected to end up as tenured faculty in primarily research universities. Their doctoral training prepared them well for research, but not at all well for teaching or service. However, most doctoral students actually ended up working in four- or two-year undergraduate institutions, jobs they did not feel well prepared for by their doctoral training. In particular, doctorate recipients did not feel their degree work had prepared them well for careers in teaching.

This finding suggests that the way that we teach our graduate courses is particularly important. Most of us are in the habit of viewing our graduate courses primarily in terms of their content, and as a means of teaching how to conduct research. However, many of our students may end up remembering and using our courses when they design their own as they pursue primarily teaching careers. Thus, the most important function of our graduate classes may be indirect, as we teach, by our example, how to teach.

Acknowledgements

The ideas presented here reflect the generosity of the many workshop participants who shared their teaching materials, their experiences, and their perspectives. Thir contributions are gratefully acknowledged. In particular, I would like to thank Tim Denny, Tom German, Chris Golde, and Jan Leach for leading various workshop sessions.

Author Index

351

Subject Index

354

linolenic acid, 186, 187, 270
lipid, 186, 190
lipo-chitin oligosaccharides, 164, 165, 167
lipoxygenase, 186, 188, 189, 190
Listeria monocytogenes, 41
LjNin, 173
LjSym1, 172, 173
LjSym2, 172, 173
LjSym3, 172, 173
LjSym4, 172, 173
LjSym5, 172, 173
LjSym15, 172
LjSym23, 172
LjSym30, 172
Lm1, 181, 182, 183, 184
localization, 130
lsp, 149
Lotus
 corniculatus, 325
 japonicus, 172, 182, 326
lox, 187, 189
LOX2, 110, 111
LRR. *See* leucine-rich repeat
Ls1, 279
lsd1, 90, 91
Lycopersicon
 esculentum, 13, 250, 274
 pennellii, 12, 13, 210
 peruvianum, 210

mac1, 199
Macrosiphum euphorbiae, 208
magB, MAGB, 199, 315
Magnaporthe grisea, 197, 198, 199, 200,
 201, 229, 315, 316, 317
marine red algae, 268, 271, 272
matrix polysaccharide, 269
maximum linkage clustering, 322, 323
Medicago
 sativa, 158, 293
 truncatula, 158, 159, 160, 161, 162, 167,
 168, 169, 170, 192, 193, 194, 195, 196,
 290, 291, 293, 294
megaplasmid, 303, 304
melanin, 198
Meloidogyne, 118, 217
 arenaria, 208, 209
 incognita, 208, 209, 210, 213
 javanica, 208, 209, 210
Mesorhizobium loti, 325, 326, 327, 328
 strain MAFF303099, 326, 327, 328
 strain R7A, 325, 326, 327, 328
Mi-1, 208, 209, 210, 217, 218, 219, 220
microarray, 62, 152, 153
microbial community, 256
microhabitat, 241
Mi-DS1, 218, 219
Mi-DS2, 218, 219

Mi-DS3, 218, 219, 220
Mi-DS4, 218, 219
Mla, 17, 18, 19, 20
momilactone A, 85
monoclonal antibodies, 119
monoculture, 228, 229
movement protein, 279, 280, 281, 282
mpg1, 198
MtENOD11, 168, 169
Mtenod40, MtENOD40, 159, 168, 169
MtR1, 292, 293, 294
Mtzpt2-1, 162
multi-color imaging, 285, 288
multiline, 227
mycorrhization, 169, 172, 173
mycotoxin, 186, 187, 188, 189
myristylation, 59

N genes, 4, 6
NADPH oxidase, 83, 84, 113, 114, 115, 271
nahG, NahG, 30, 31, 64, 65, 66, 68, 69, 80,
 99, 103, 104, 108, 110, 184
NB, 217
NB-LRR, 218
NBS, 52, 53, 54
NBS-LRR, 23, 24, 25, 28, 36, 37, 52, 53, 54,
 232
ndr1, 30, 31, 65, 68
Neurospora crassa, 314, 316
Nicotiana
 benthamiana, 4, 59
 clevelandii, 4
nifH, 264, 265
nim1, NIM1, 89, 94, 99, 100, 101, 102, 103,
 104
nin, Nin, 173, 182
nitric oxide, 78, 80, 81, 89, 90
nitrogen fixation, 264, 265
Nod factor, 164, 165, 167, 168, 169, 170, 327
NodH, 125
NodIJ, 165
NodP, 124, 125
NodQ, 125
nodulation, 172,
NoeE, 125
nonparasitic SCN line, 204
nonribosomal peptide synthetase, 316
npr1, NPR1, 30, 31, 89, 94, 95, 96, 97, 99,
 100, 102, 103, 104, 108, 110, 111, 340
nsp, 168, 169
nuclear export signal, 282
nuclear localization signal, 136, 137
nuclear shuttle protein, 281, 282, 283
nutrient, 243, 244, 245, 246

O_2^-, 113, 114, 115, 116
ode, 187, 189
Oilseed rape mosaic virus, 153

357

358